Social contexts of health, illness, and patient care

Social contexts of health, illness, and patient care

ELLIOT G. MISHLER
Department of Psychiatry, Harvard Medical School

LORNA R. AMARASINGHAM   SAMUEL D. OSHERSON
STUART T. HAUSER   NANCY E. WAXLER
Department of Psychiatry, Harvard Medical School

RAMSAY LIEM
Department of Psychology, Boston College

CAMBRIDGE UNIVERSITY PRESS

Cambridge
London New York New Rochelle
Melbourne Sydney

Published by the Press Syndicate of the University of Cambridge
The Pitt Building, Trumpington Street, Cambridge CB2 1RP
32 East 57th Street, New York, NY 10022, USA
296 Beaconsfield Parade, Middle Park, Melbourne 3206, Australia

First published 1981

Printed in Canada
Typeset by David E. Seham Associates, Inc., Metuchen, New Jersey
Printed and bound by The Hunter Rose Company Ltd., Toronto, Canada

Library of Congress Cataloging in Publication Data
Main entry under title:
Social contexts of health, illness, and patient care.
Includes index.
1. Social medicine. 2. Social psychiatry.
I. Mishler, Elliot George, 1924–
[DNLM: 1. Sociology, Medical. 2. Community
psychiatry. WA31 S677]
RA418.S642   306'.4   80–22604
ISBN 0 521 23559 6 hard covers
ISBN 0 521 28034 6 paperback

Contents

Editorial preface

The term "context" figures prominently in the title and serves as the motif of this book. It seems appropriate to begin with a brief description of the contexts that shaped it – our backgrounds and the settings within which we have worked, our aims in writing the text, and how we approached the task as a collaborative effort.

Collectively, we are social–behavioral scientists with extensive experience as teachers and researchers in medical–psychiatric settings. Our backgrounds include training in a variety of disciplines: anthropology, clinical and community psychology, personality and human development, medicine and psychiatry, social psychology, and sociology. When the book began, we were all members of the laboratory in Social Psychiatry, a research and training unit in the social and behavioral sciences in the Harvard Department of Psychiatry at the Massachusetts Mental Health Center.

In teaching medical students, psychiatric residents, and other health professionals, we have been concerned primarily with the central task of this text, namely, an explication of the relevance to clinical theory and practice of the perspectives of the social–behavioral sciences. Our work on these problems and our experience in these settings have also informed our teaching of students in the latter academic disciplines. In addition, much though not all of our empirical research has focused on problems that bear on clinical issues. Thus, within the past decade, as individual investigators we have studied such topics as family interaction processes and schizophrenia, personality crises of midlife, adolescent development and adaptation to medical and psychiatric illnesses, posthospital adjustment of released mental patients, cross-cultural and interhospital variations in treatment practices, patient conceptions of illness and treatment, the language of clinical interviews, and the mental health consequences of unemployment.

We have tried to draw on our particular strengths as researchers and on our experiences as teachers. This has resulted in a text with several distinctive features. For example, it is selective rather than comprehensive in coverage. This applies both to the general topics reviewed as well as to specific materials used in our discussions. This selective approach reflects, as well, our view that the book should serve as a guide to further reading rather than as an encyclopedic reference. We neither intend nor assume that this is the "last" book that professionals and students in the health-care field may read on these topics. Rather, we hope it will serve as a beginning for the development of their own thought, as a stimulus to further reading and exploration, and as a basis for reflection on their practice. In accord with this aim, we have emphasized how social and behavioral scientists think about and approach the study of clinical problems. What are the main lines of theory and conceptualization? How are questions framed from research, and what methods are used? How are findings analyzed and interpreted? Finally, how might this perspective lead to a reformulation of problems in the health-care field? Our discussions of concepts, theories, and findings are intended as a framework for analysis and interpretation of studies other than those included here.

Through our work in clinical settings, we have become particularly sensitized to the particular ways of thinking that pervade medical work; we refer to this as the biomedical model. Our experience has made us acutely aware of differences between that model and alternative approaches used in the social and behavioral sciences. This difference is a key issue in the often-reported lack of effective communication between health professionals and social–behavioral scientists and the limited use in clinical medicine and in medical education of work in the social and behavioral sciences.

We believe that the social and behavioral sciences have an important contribution to make to the understanding of illness and the care of patients. However, effective integration of this work into the health-care field depends on the clarification of differences between it and the biomedical model. This text is organized so as to contribute to such a clarification; it begins with an exposition and critique of the biomedical model and then, in successive chapters, describes various approaches within the social–behavioral sciences that differ in significant and specific ways from that model.

Our primary intended audiences are members of the health professions–students, clinical practitioners, research scientists in medicine, nursing, and other disciplines whose work is centered on patients, illnesses, and clinical practices; and, students, teachers, and investigators in the various social and behavioral sciences who have applied themselves to the study of health issues.

Finally, we viewed the book as a collective task, and it developed and was shaped through the ways we came to work together. Although our views overlap on many topics covered in the text, they are far from identical. We wanted the book to express this diversity within a shared perspective. A suitable analogue might be a family whose members differ in interests and display their separate identities yet have a family resemblance that comes from their common life. Thus, the book presents a general framework within which each of us develops a particular topic. Chapters are individually authored, and authorship marks final responsibility, but each chapter benefited from and reflects an extensive exchange of views and mutual criticism.

Several colleagues read and commented on earlier drafts of various chapters. We would like particularly to acknowledge the suggestions and comments of Leslie Howard, Joan H. Liem, Anita L. Mishler, and Marianne Paget. We also benefited from the critical response of medical students who attended our lectures and seminars, which is where the book began. More generally, the text reflects our experiences and our aims as teachers. Partial support for our participation in teaching programs for medical students, psychiatric residents, and postdoctoral research fellows in the social and behavioral sciences came from the following NIMH training grants to the department of psychiatry at the Harvard Medical School: Psychiatry-Undergraduate Human Behavior (5 T02 MH11558) and Research Training-Social Sciences (5 T32 MH14246). The burdens of repeated revisions were eased considerably by the skills, care, and boundless good nature of Darlene Kaye, who typed the manuscripts through various drafts.

1   Viewpoint: critical perspectives on the biomedical model

Elliot G. Mishler

There is an urgent need to make medicine an examined profession, to subject all its presuppositions and axioms to rigorous re-examination . . . [by] the questioning of accepted opinion and belief, the rejection of unsupported dogmas, the demand for justification of beliefs however sacred. Medicine badly needs this illumination.[1]

Health, illness, and medical care are the central topics in this text. It is addressed to students, practitioners, and scientists in the various health professions whose work is organized around the traditional tasks of medicine: the prevention, diagnosis, care, and treatment of illness. Our perspective emphasizes the significance of social, cultural, and institutional contexts for understanding patient experiences and medical practices. The separate chapters are variations on one general theme, a premise that guides our work. This premise is that health and illness are social facts as well as biological facts.

We begin, in this chapter, with a reexamination of four key presuppositions that have shaped modern scientific medicine. These "silent assumptions" are the essential features of the biomedical model. The dominance of this model in medical theory and practice is universally recognized. Its assumptions are so deeply interwoven with ways of thinking and working in medicine that health professionals tend to forget that it is a conceptual model, a way of thinking about the world. That is, the biomedical model is treated as *the* representation or picture of reality rather than understood as *a* representation. Like other conceptual models, the biomedical model defines, classifies, and specifies relationships among events in particular ways. For example, the presupposition that there are specific disease entities, each associated with a specific biological process, is related to the further idea that etiology is biologically specific. An alternative model defines illness as a disturbance in social relationships; questions of etiology are then framed with reference to social rather than biological processes.

This different view of illness within an alternative social perspective

1

may seem strange to readers who usually think about these problems in biomedical terms. We hope it will be less strange after they have read the book.

The question might be raised as to why an alternative perspective is useful. Although the full answer is the text itself, the question deserves a brief introductory response. Essentially, we shall argue that the biomedical model strips away social contexts of meaning. Illness is then viewed as an autonomous entity, defined by standard universal criteria, isolated from the lives and experiences of patients and physicians.[2] Exclusive use of the biomedical model results in an approach to problems of illness and health care that abstracts them from the social, cultural, and institutional contexts within which they occur.

Thus, although symptoms and illnesses occur in people who live within sociocultural frameworks of belief and action, these contexts tend to be ignored in the biomedical approach. Problems are defined, diagnosed, and treated by physicians and other health professionals from a specialized point of view grounded in the biosciences. Further, the aims and standards of medical practice are guided by social norms and cultural values; they are shaped by political and economic interests. Health care is provided in specific settings and institutions with complex relations to other institutions in the society. These various contexts of medicine are also excluded from consideration in the biomedical model.

Health, illness, and medical care can be understood in different ways when they are placed in their sociocultural and institutional contexts. To do this, we shall rely on theory and research in the social and behavioral sciences. Several alternative approaches will be described in our analyses of problems in the four main sections of the text. These focus, respectively, on patients in social contexts, physicians in social contexts, the social construction of illness, and the functions of the medical system in the larger society.

A critical analysis of the biomedical model is a natural and necessary point of departure. Modern medicine is based on and dominated by concepts, methods, and principles of the biological sciences. As Engel notes, "The dominant model of disease today is biomedical, with molecular biology its basic scientific discipline. It assumes disease to be fully accounted for by deviations from the norm of measurable biological (somatic) variables."[3] We shall examine several critical assumptions and focus particularly on limitations of the biomedical model as the comprehensive and exclusive basis for either the science or practice of medicine.

The inherent limitations of the biomedical model are implicit in our general premise that health and illness are social as well as biological facts.

The social meanings of illness fall outside the province of the biological sciences. Therefore, these sciences cannot provide either a full understanding of illness or adequate principles and criteria for treatment. This is a limitation in principle and not a function of the current state of knowledge. A fuller and more adequate approach requires an alternative perspective in which the primary focus of inquiry is the social meaning of illness.

In the following sections of this chapter, we examine four assumptions of the biomedical model: (1) the definition of disease as deviation from normal biological functioning; (2) the doctrine of specific etiology; (3) the conception of generic diseases, that is, the universality of a disease taxonomy; and (4) the scientific neutrality of medicine.

Other assumptions might be added to this list, but together these four seem to characterize the framework of modern medicine. It is evident that a critique of these assumptions is necessary to our own task of developing an alternative perspective. Questions raised through our analyses of each of these assumptions will also serve as central topics in our presentation of alternative approaches.

The definition of disease

We begin with a central and basic assumption of the biomedical model, noted in the previous quotation from Engel, that disease is "to be fully accounted for by deviations from the norm of measurable biological (somatic) variables." In his essay on the evolution of the concept of disease, Cohen offers a similar definition: ". . . disease indicates deviations from the normal – these are its symptoms and signs."[4] For modern adherents of the biomedical model, these definitions are unlikely to stir dispute. However, there have been other conceptions, for example, the classical Platonic model of health as harmony among the body's structures or processes and disease as a state of discord and dissolution of harmony, or the Galenian conception of disease as a disturbance of function.[5]

That such broader definitions are neither obsolete, nor of historical and esoteric interest only, is indicated by the definition of health proposed by the World Health Organization as a ". . . state of complete physical, mental, and social well-being and not merely the absence of disease or infirmity."[6] Engel quotes Romano's slightly more restricted definition of health as a useful starting point for a "unified" theory of disease: "Health, in a positive sense, consists in the capacity of the organism to maintain a balance in which it may be reasonably free of undue pain, discomfort, disability or limitation of action." Engel defines disease in contrast to health as ". . . failures or disturbances in the growth, development, functions, and adjustments of the organism as a whole or of any of its systems."[7]

A reading of the literature on this issue shows clearly that whether a broad or narrow view is proposed, all commentators agree that the narrow concept of disease as deviation from a biological norm dominates medical thinking and practice at the present time. Those who espouse a broader view see themselves as critics of established doctrine. It is also evident that the broader the view of disease, the easier it is to recognize the significance of cultural, psychological, and social factors which are the substance of the social and behavioral sciences. Such terms as "harmony," "well-being," "balance," "reasonably free of undue pain," and "adjustment" not only leave room for nonbiological variables but require for their specification a description of the social and cultural contexts within which individuals live and function. In the absence of such a description, a broad conception of health can have no coherent theoretical or empirical meaning.

Although it may be less immediately evident, sociocultural variables are equally relevant to the narrow conception of disease. Briefly put, there is no way to define a biological "norm" or "deviations" without reference to specific populations and their sociocultural characteristics. Redlich poses the issue succinctly: "normal for what?" and "normal for whom?"[8] That is, assertions about the normality of levels of biological functioning, or about the normal structure of an organ, must be based on the relationship between the observed instance and the distribution in a specified population of these structures and functions. Further, implicit to any specified norm is a set of presupposed standard conditions with regard to when, how, and on whom measurements are taken.

Another problem is that the meaning of normality is ambiguous in both ordinary language and medical usage. Does normal refer to an ideal standard or to the average value of a population characteristic? The dictionary includes both meanings. The adjective is defined as an "established norm, rule, principle; type, standard, regular form; performing proper functions; regular; natural; analogical," and its noun form as an "archetypal state to which individuals may conform; ordinary or usual condition, degree, quantity, or the like, average, mean."[9]

It is obvious that the average value of a variable for some specified population may not correspond to an ideal standard. Specific characteristics of populations and their life situations are critical to understanding and interpreting the significance of average values and of "deviations" from universal or ideal standards of health. For example, personality crises of adolescents in Western societies are generally viewed as "normal" to this developmental stage. Similarly, the various bodily and mental changes that accompany aging are seen as "normal."

Ryle provides an instructive example that underscores the significance of this distinction between ideal standards and average population values as indicators of "normality." In a detailed clinical and epidemiological study of the size of thyroid glands among adolescents in populations living on different diets, he found considerable variability among the groups. He argues that the presence of "visible glands" in a population where they are common cannot be interpreted as a true clinical sign or precursor of goiter in later life, as it usually would be in Western clinical practice. He suggests that this "symptom" may represent normal adaptation rather than deviation from a universal standard of healthy thyroid function. "It might therefore be argued that clinical hyperplasia more usually represents a pronounced degree of adaptation – or physiological enlargement – rather than an early state of disease or that it is a true example of a borderline condition which may either revert to "normality" or advance to "disease.""[10]

Ryle recommends greater attention to and emphasis on the range of "normal variability." He points out ". . . that the normal, in biological usage, is something other than a mean or fixed standard can scarcely be disputed. In man, as in all animals, variation is so constantly at work that no rigid pattern – whether anatomical, physiological, psychological, or immunological – is possible."[11] He concludes that, given the natural range of variability of structure and function of "every organ and tissue" in the species as a whole and any population studied, the "normal" in biology and medicine might better be expressed in terms of variability than as a hypothetical mean or standard value.

On the way to this conclusion, Ryle makes an argument that resonates with our point of view. "The development of aetiological science must now be based more and more upon sociomedical investigation – upon the examination, that is to say, of societies or populations in relation to their own environments, their work and upbringing, their food and special hazards. The examination of individuals in the later stages of illness and in the remote and unnatural surroundings of the hospital ward can illuminate pathology and advance treatment, but they can make little contribution to studies in causation and prevention."[12]

Our examination of the concept of normality, which is an essential element in the biomedical model of disease, is a first step in our critique of this model as a guide to theory and practice in medicine. It is obvious that broad notions of health as "harmony" or "adjustment" cannot be specified without reference to sociocultural contexts. It is important to underline the general point that, even within a more limited definition of disease as "deviations from the norm of measurable biological (somatic) variables," the biomedical model is insufficient by itself to the critical task of defining normality and deviations therefrom. Normality is a standard of judgement, whether defined as an ideal or as a computed average. The development and application of this standard requires knowledge of the distribution of relevant signs and behaviors within and between populations that are specified by their particular patterns of sociocultural characteristics and life circumstances. The latter are core topics of the social and behavioral sciences, and for these reasons are as integral to the study of health and illness as the biological sciences.

Issues of normality and deviance will reappear in various sections of the text. For example, in later chapters on the social construction of illness and the social functions of medicine, we shall discuss how "deviance" is recognized and assessed as illness and how this process is influenced by sociocultural and institutional factors. As Ryle suggests, an understanding of normality requires sociomedical investigations. We shall begin our examination of relevant social research, after this first chapter on assumptions of the biomedical model, with a review of studies of the social contexts of patients. This will include epidemiological, community, and family studies.

The doctrine of specific etiology

There is a more specific assumption within the biomedical model which Dubos refers to as the "doctrine of specific etiology."[13]

Although this doctrine does not follow as a logically necessary consequence of the general assumption of illness as deviation from normal functioning, the doctrine has been the way in which this assumption has been specified and applied in modern medical theory and practice. Engel describes the general view in medicine that explanation of an illness is more complete and more adequate to the degree that description has moved through several stages, from an initial taxonomy based on distinct symptoms through a clustering of symptoms into syndromes, and ". . . finally to disease with specific pathogenesis and pathology."[14] The extent and adequacy with which this movement is carried through to its end, in research on a specific disease, is taken as the index of how "advanced" is our understanding of the disease. Thus, Engel points out, the scientific characterization of diabetes mellitus is considered more advanced than that of schizophrenia, because the former has ". . . progressed from the behavioral framework of symptoms to that of biochemical abnormalities."[15]

This approach is the signature of modern Western medicine. It developed out of the pioneering work of Pasteur and Koch in the nineteenth century, which demonstrated conclusively that specific diseases could be produced by introduction into the body of specific virulent microorganisms. The impact of this work was pervasive and powerful, both on the profession and on the general public. So much so, that Dubos comments, "Because the decrease in death rates appeared obvious to everyone after 1900, scientific medicine and the germ theory in particular have been given all the credit for the improvement of the general health of the people . . .," despite the fact that "In truth the mortality of many other infections had begun to recede in Western Europe and North America long before the introduction of specific methods of therapy, indeed before the demonstration of the germ theory of disease."[16]

The doctrine of specific etiology spread rapidly from infectious diseases to other diseases that could be produced by physiological lesions or reflected deficiencies in growth or metabolic processes. Yet, as Dubos again comments, although the doctrine of specific etiology ". . . and the theoretical and practical achievements to which it has led constitute the bulk of modern medicine . . . few are the cases in which it has provided a complete account of the causation of disease."[17]

Although it represents the dominant perspective within medicine, the doctrine has not been without its critics. Engel, for example, proposes an alternative model, which he calls a "unified concept of health and disease."[18] He argues that explanation of illness should be approached from a "naturalistic" rather than an "institutional" perspective. The former would direct attention to necessary and sufficient conditions rather than to isolable and singular etiological factors, would recognize multiple and interactive processes, and would take into account the possible adaptive functions of bodily responses. Within such an approach, there would be a legitimate and important place for the influence of psychological and sociocultural factors on the origin and course of illness, factors that are excluded in the search for a specific etiological agent.

In a penetrating essay on the problem of etiology, Dubos poses a critical question: Why is disease rare, although infectious agents are omnipresent? He points to ". . . one of the most neglected aspects of the germ theory of disease, namely the fact that infection rarely produces fatal disease under natural circumstances. . . . Much infection in the Western world at the present time is from parasites ubiquitous in the environment and occurring normally in a very large percentage of healthy individuals, which cause pathological disorders only when natural resistance to them has been undermined by the stresses and strains of life."[19] Whether or not such pathogens remain dormant or initiate an infective process is a function of many factors, which also play a significant role in the course of the infection; these include metabolic states, nutrition, and the susceptibility of tissues to infection. Dubos concludes: "Infection is the rule, and disease the exception."[20]

Dubos' analysis of the doctrine of specific etiology, and the simple cause – effect model with which it is associated, reveals serious inadequacies in this key assumption of the biomedical model. In addition to its limitations for the explanation or control of disease, there are problems with this assumption as a guide to clinical practice. These become apparent when we examine clinical situations where physicians are engaged in the tasks of diagnosing and treating patients.

From his analyses of psychological and psychiatric problems in general medical practice, Balint[21] observed that patients initially report a variety of vague and unfocused complaints and problems. Balint calls this the "unorganized" phase of an illness. The physician and patient together proceed to "negotiate" an illness. That is, they try to reach agreement on a specific illness that the patient "has" which may then be treated. This conception of medical work suggests that only one specific subset of symptoms may be selected as significant out of the variety of presenting complaints and signs. The physician attends to and selects a subset of symptoms that will allow him or her to match the patient's problem to a particular symptom cluster or syndrome representing a specific disease. Thus, the patient's illness is "diagnosed." Balint is proposing that the diagnosed disease is not simply "out there" in the patient, but is the result of negotiation between physician and patient. This is a view of clinical history taking and diagnosis as active processes through which a disease is constructed, rather than found.

Balint's observation has been documented in a number of recent studies in which medical interviews have been tape recorded. In these interviews, patients' initial complaints are often vague and diffuse; their illness is "unorganized." For example, in the interview transcripts presented by Byrne and Long,[22] from their extensive study of British physicians in general practice, we find patients stating their problems in such ways as the following: "I just keep feeling sick all the time," "I haven't been sleeping well for some months, I get very tired during the day and yet when I go to bed I don't sleep," "I just feel awful." A similar lack of specificity and coherence is apparent when patients report many specific but unrelated symptoms. For example, in a routine medical checkup, an elderly man responded positively to each of a series of successive questions about whether he had the following symptoms: loss of appetite, difficulty breathing, coughing up phlegm, legs swelling, blood pressure problems, headaches, dizziness, heart beating fast.

Our aim in this section has been twofold. We wished to raise some questions about the adequacy of the doctrine of specific etiology and, at the same time, suggest how an alternative perspective might be useful and relevant. Dubos and Engel argue that the doctrine, and the underlying model of disease and disease causation that it reflects, is an oversimplification of complex biological processes. Nonetheless, physicians search for specific diseases and specific pathogenic agents. From Balint's analysis and supporting clinical observations, we have drawn the implication that how these clinical tasks are accomplished depends on a process of negotiation between physician and patient. In our perspective, diseases are found, diagnosed, and treated within the interactive context of medical practice. Together, theoretical critique and empirical observations suggest the importance of studying clinical practice and factors that influence it.

Particular forms, styles, and modes of practice reflect general sociocultural values and norms. Additional influences may be found in the specific features of health-care institutions as forms of social organization, in patients' and physicians' attitudes to illness and health care, and in the social rules that define appropriate behavior in medical settings and regulate interaction between physicians and patients. These relationships will be explored at a number of points in the text, but they are the principal focus of Chapter 4, "Social Contexts of Health Care." There we shall examine the effects of specific social and institutional factors on the work of diagnosis, management, and treatment of illness. In Chapter 5, "Physician – Patient Relationships," studies of communication between physicians and patients will be discussed in detail.

The assumption of generic diseases

A third assumption of the biomedical model is that each disease has specific and distinguishing features that are universal to the human species. That is, disease symptoms and processes are expected to be the same in different historical periods and in different cultures and societies. This assumption usually takes a more specific form, namely, that diseases found in modern Western society provide a standard taxonomy much as the natural elements are represented by the standard table of atomic weights. This assumption of generic diseases is clearly a corollary of the assumptions discussed previously, that diseases may be defined as deviations from normal biological functioning and that each has a specific etiology. Nonetheless, there are specific properties and implications of this third assumption that merit separate attention.

A good vantage point for critical analysis is provided through work in cultural anthropology, particularly research in ethnomedicine. Students of ethnomedicine are interested in cultural variations in both formal and informal, or "folk," medical theories and practices. In the past, such cross-cultural studies tended to include invidious comparisons between the "scientific" medicine of advanced Western societies and the "primitive" folk medicine of less advanced societies; recent work is more descriptive and less evaluative in tone. One mark of this change is that modern Western medicine is now viewed as one alternative approach among others and, in this way, is placed more firmly in historical and cross-cultural perspective. One commentator states this view directly: "As a physician, one is trained to identify and treat disease, and as a consequence of assimilating much technical information, one often comes to view disease as an abstracted 'object' or condition. This is to say that disease is given a biomedical reality insofar as its chemical and physiological attributes are emphasized. . . . it is easy to lose sight of the fact that biomedicine and science in general are relatively recent developments in the evolution of man. Disease is and has been ubiquitous in human groups. The antiquity and universality of disease means that human groups have always had to develop theories about and treatment rationales for disease. . . . From this general frame of reference, biomedicine, the prevailing orientation of the contemporary physician, is but another view of disease."[23]

The "but" in the last sentence is an instructive qualifier. In a related essay on the need for an ethnomedical science, the same author expands the point: "Biomedicine thus constitutes our own culturally specific perspective about what disease is, and how medical treatment should be pursued; and like other medical systems, biomedicine is an interpretation which 'makes sense' in light of cultural traditions and assumptions about reality."[24]

At this juncture, it is important to clarify and emphasize the point that we are not questioning the validity of observations made by bioscientists of biological processes, functions, and structures. Biological events at various levels of complexity and organization are observable, measurable, and orderly. Modern theories in the biosciences are powerful explanatory systems. However, there is a critical difference between a description of a biological process and clinical definitions of signs and symptoms of illness, even though the latter are couched in the vocabulary of the biosciences. This difference reflects the fact that medicine is not simply a bioscience, but an applied bioscience. Although this distinction is obvious, it is often obscured within medicine itself. The result is that the specific features and consequences of medicine as practice, as an applied science, are not fully recognized or given adequate attention.

One important issue for analysis that follows from recognition of this difference between medicine and the basic biosciences is the distinction between symptoms and illness. The presence of measurable "deviations from normal biological functioning" is only one of the conditions for illness, certainly not a necessary and sufficient condition and sometimes neither necessary nor sufficient. Proposing a broader and more naturalistic conception of illness, Engel points to the relativity of the two terms, health and disease, and to the lack of a sharp dividing line between them. On the one hand, "A person may satisfy all the criteria of health at any point in time simply because the adaptive capacity of a defective system, be it biomedical, physiological, or psychological, has not been exceeded."[25] On the other hand, patients may present with subjective complaints although no "objective" basis for them can be found. In these latter instances, "Regardless of the nature and severity of a patient's complaint, the failure to discover an abnormality on physical or laboratory examination means to many physicians that there is 'nothing wrong.' . . . The common slang is that the patient has 'no pathology,' and it carries the double implication that he is not sick and often also that he is not worthy of help or that he is 'fooling' the physician."[26] In developing his argument that many normal, naturally occurring phenomena of everyday life, such as the experience of grief, meet the usual criteria of disease, Engel notes, "The term 'pathological' is a relative one and is set by medical, scientific and even social convention. Conventions change, so that what may be considered as illness or disease at one time or by one person may not be so considered at another time by another person. . . . The heuristic value of differentiating between normal and pathological should not blind us to the fact that this is a relative matter based on ever-changing criteria."[27]

Medical sociologists and anthropologists, in their investigations of illness and medical care, have paid particular attention to this distinction between symptoms and illness. Within their sociomedical perspective, illness is viewed as one type of social deviance. One prominent theme in this work is that persons who display certain behaviors that are defined as deviant from their group's sociocultural norms come to be "labeled" as sick. (Other types of deviant behavior may lead to their being labeled as delinquent, or immature, or as heretics). An individual who is socially categorized or labeled as "sick" may then be processed into a special social role, the role of patient.

Physicians are of critical importance in this process, and the practice of medicine may be viewed within this sociological perspective, as a system of rules for making symptoms into illnesses, and for transforming persons into patients. The patient role, in turn, may have consequences that are independent of the biological components of the illness. When an individual comes to behave as a patient, certain symptoms that might otherwise remit "naturally" may come instead to be "locked in" as appropriate to this new role; thus, additional symptoms may be generated. For example, many of the behaviors of hospitalized chronic schizophrenics had at one time been viewed as characteristics of their illness. Later research indicated that their behavior was in large part a function of conditions in large custodial mental hospitals. The term "hospitalitis" appeared to be a more accurate explanation of their behavior than schizophrenia.[28]

Waxler[29] summarizes findings on levels of improvement in patients released from mental hospitals which suggest that psychiatric symptoms and social adjustment problems persist longer if an individual continues to be considered as a patient. This is a more likely eventuality in Western than in non-Western forms of psychiatric treatment. There are many other studies of the ways in which medical diagnosis and treatment, as well as course and outcome of illness, are significantly influenced by social characteristics of patients, such as their social class, ethnicity, and sex, and by the social organization and social functions of medical institutions. We shall review a number of these studies in later chapters.

The main point of this discussion is that the specification of signs and symptoms in biological terms is inadequate to the medically defined task of understanding and treating illness, because, although bodies have signs and symptoms, only people become sick. Further, the biomedical model is even less adequate to the task of understanding how diagnosis and treatment are done in actual practice, because these are socially organized activities and understanding them requires a sociological perspective. A more detailed examination of patienthood as a social role and of the labeling process is presented in Chapter 6, "The Social Construction of Illness."

One last point on the distinction between symptoms and illness deserves mention. We have been discussing this issue as if it were necessary for measurable "deviations from a norm of biological functioning" to be present in order for a person to be labeled as sick. We have also been emphasizing the role of physicians and other health professionals in the labeling process. As Engel notes, people without "objective" biological signs of disease may be viewed by physicians as having "no pathology"; they may be referred to as hypochondriacs or, more invidiously, called "crocks." A further implication of the argument we have been developing is that such people would be considered legitimate cases of illness if they and others in their social world treated them as sick. That is, given the distinction proposed between symptoms and illness, it is clear that a person may be asymptomatic in biological terms but ill in social terms. For example, individuals who have "recovered" medically from tuberculosis, a coronary attack, or an acute schizophrenic episode may continue to behave as though they were sick and continue to be treated as such by others.

In addition to the distinction between symptoms and illness, another question may be raised about the biomedical assumption of generic diseases. This is whether the taxonomy of disease constructed by Western medicine in particular social, cultural, and historical circumstances can be mapped on to the distributions of biological, behavioral, psychological, and social signs and symptoms found in other cultures. That is, would such a mapping be appropriate to and effective for the understanding and control of disease in these cultures?

This is not an easily resolvable question, and there is a lack of relevant comparative studies that address it. Even critics of the biomedical model are reluctant to adopt the position that our modern taxonomy of disease may be culture bound. Murphy, for example, reports evidence from her studies of Eskimos in the Bering Sea and the Yoruba in Africa that the patterns and frequencies of mental illness in these cultures are similar to those found in Western cultures and, further, that explicit criteria for insanity exist in these cultures. She concludes: "Rather than being simply violations of the social norms of particular groups, as labeling theory suggests, symptoms of mental illness are manifestations of a type of affliction shared by all mankind."[30] Similarly, Eisenberg, although arguing for the view that ". . . human disease inevitably and always reflects the outcome of the process of interaction between human biology and human social organization, a process in which culture occupies a central position," nevertheless concludes: "Close examination of the evidence demonstrates that, though improper care can retard recovery, psychiatric illness exists before the name assigned to it and independently of theories about its genesis."[31]

One approach is to apply standard diagnostic procedures and criteria to patients in different cultures. This has been attempted in a complex study conducted by the World Health Organization in nine cultures.[32] Psychiatrists from these different cultures were trained to follow a standard procedure for diagnosis of schizophrenia. Diagnostic information was then evaluated through the application of two different systematic statistical procedures in order to locate a group of patients with common yet distinctive symptoms. This latter group was defined as the concordant group of schizophrenics. Of the sample of 811 patients diagnosed as schizophrenics by trained psychiatrists in clinical settings in each culture, only 306 or 37 percent were found to be concordant on all criteria. This study does not deal with the issue we have raised about the cross-cultural validity of the diagnostic system of Western psychiatry. However, its findings are important in showing that even when standard procedures are applied, a considerable amount of unexplained variance remains in the diagnosis of a specific disease.

An important implication of our discussion must now be addressed. These questions about the assumption of generic diseases are of a somewhat different order than those raised earlier in our analyses of the biological definition of disease and the doctrine of specific etiologies. Those analyses, while critical of the biomedical model, stayed within the boundaries of the problems of health and illness as they have been defined by physicians. For example, although we used Ryle's work on "visible" thyroid glands to question the definition of disease as deviation from normality, his work does not directly challenge the disease model of modern medicine. Rather, his aim was to correct for one of the deficiencies of the model, namely, its reliance on average values as standards for normality, by emphasizing the range of "normal" variability. Similarly with Dubos' distinction between infection and disease and his elucidation of the complex processes through which one may, or may not, be transformed into the other. Here, too, his criticism was aimed at deficiencies of modern medicine, particularly at the oversimplified model of causation that has gained prominence. But, within his critique, one may detect a continued loyalty (albeit somewhat strained) to the biological disease model.

In raising questions about the assumption of generic diseases, we have stepped outside the boundaries of medicine. The biomedical model equates illness with biological signs and symptoms. We have argued that this is *a* conceptual model and not simply *the* representation of reality. Like any conceptual model, it defines the relevance and significance of certain aspects of reality. Within the framework of the biosciences, the biomedical model takes a class of human problems and reconstructs them as "illnesses."

The alternative perspective that we develop in this text draws on the social and behavioral sciences. It is not less "scientific" than the biomedical approach, but provides a different construction of these problems. Health and illness are defined as social rather than biological categories. This, of course, does not mean that biological processes are either irrelevant or trivial. However, there is a shift in perspective, which locates biological processes within a social context. Illnesses are made by people, we have argued, in the strict sense that giving the label of illness to certain behaviors or symptoms is an active interpretive process. This process of interpretation, through which illnesses are constructed, is guided and regulated by social rules and norms, which are central topics of inquiry in the social sciences.

Thus, in addressing the problem of generic diseases, our perspective shifts away from the study of illness as an attribute of patients. Instead, we focus on the problem of how illnesses are defined and how patients are made, particularly through the work of physicians and other health professionals. We view medicine as a subculture, with its own institutionalized beliefs, values, and practices. It may be studied and analyzed in the same way as other cultures and social institutions. Examples of such studies provide the main content in our chapter on "The Social Construction of Illness" (Chapter 6). Primary attention will be given to the "labeling" process, that is, to ways in which people with certain "symptoms" come to be defined as patients, and to the consequences of this process. Chapter 7, "Learning to Be a Leper," explores some of the complex relationships between cultural variations in responses to a particular illness and specific cultural, historical, and organizational forces.

The scientific neutrality of medicine

Physicians tend to see themselves as bioscientists. Their self-image as practitioners reflects a view of medicine as a discipline that has adopted not only the rationality of the scientific method but the concomitant values of the scientist, namely, objectivity and neutrality. Practitioners, of course, are aware of the distinction between the pure research scientist in pursuit of general truth and definitive knowledge and the applied physician–scientist with practical aims, such as the alleviation of pain and suffering and the prevention and cure of disease. Nonetheless, although they recognize that scientific research and clinical practice bear only a slight resemblance to each other, physicians tend to see the scientist as an idealized role model for themselves. Although the scientific values of rationality, objectivity, and neutrality may be difficult to achieve in practice, nevertheless they retain their force as the basis for assessing the quality of clinical work. Further, these values are used to justify the particular ways in which clinical work is done.

This "storybook image of medicine," to paraphase the analogous idealization of science itself,[33] has a number of consequences for relationships between medicine and the larger society. Of some importance is the implication that the work of physicians as practitioners is guided primarily by "objective" scientific rules and criteria and, therefore, is relatively unaffected by wider social, cultural, and political forces. The view is often phrased normatively; that is, medicine ought to be independent of and protected from these forces, because they would undermine or distort its essential features as a science.

In contrast to this, our own view is that medicine, far from being independent of the larger society, is deeply embedded within it, has been given a legitimate mandate to carry out certain tasks and perform certain functions, and has complex relationships with other social institutions. Specifically, medicine is a special type of social institution dominated by physicians as a particular profession.

Within this perspective, the principal social function of medicine is the regulation and control of one type of deviance, namely, sickness. In carrying out this function, physicians have been granted by society the right to define criteria of sickness, to determine appropriate modes of treatment and management, and to engage in practices consistent with these definitions and determinations. This is true in all societies, but specific organizational forms and practices vary as a function of relationships between medicine and other social institutions. In the village culture of the New Guinea Highlands, for example, where medical and religious practices are closely intertwined, and where "an illness has meaning for a community, not just for an individual," treatment is directed to the solution of a variety of social conflicts, ". . . social and political competition, intra-familial disputes, quarrels, conflicts, and crimes."[34] In a similar vein, Waxler reports that in the village culture of Sri Lanka, illness and the treatment rituals it evokes serve to reintegrate families and reestablish their social boundaries during periods of stress.[35]

The role of medicine in Western societies is no less central or significant to maintaining the ongoing integrity, continuity, and stability of the society. The view of modern medicine as a science, which we noted earlier, tends to obscure these connections. Glick describes this difference as follows: "In brief, whereas in Western medicine causation has no essential relationship to socio-cultural context, in most other medical systems causation and context are so intimately linked as to be the ethnographer's principal concern."[36] Fabrega makes a similar contrast: ". . . in a logical sense, disease among nonliterates is directly tied to the social behavior of the person and to his ability to function and it also has heavy social implication. . . . All types of disease raise social and personal questions about the individual and his immediate group. Thus, disease and medical care are directly woven into the social fabric. In our culture science has provided us with disease forms which, on logical grounds, are not connected to the social fabric."[37]

This "disconnection" of medicine from the social fabric is not altogether medicine's own doing; the same general point might be made about other professions and social institutions in contemporary society. On the other hand, the institutions of medicine have not been passive in this process but have been active in severing these ties. The assumption of the scientific neutrality of medicine has both reflected and reinforced this position.

We have already discussed how other assumptions of the biomedical model reflect and reinforce an approach that abstracts patients and their illnesses, and physicians and their practices, from their sociocultural contexts. We have also noted that various chapters in the text represent efforts to reinstate these contexts. Chapter 8, "The Health-Care System: Social Contexts and Consequences," and Chapter 9, "The Machine Metaphor in Medicine," are directed primarily to the task of relocating medicine as a social institution within its sociocultural, economic, and historical context. We shall, for example, examine the social functions of medicine that derive from its authority to define certain types of deviance as illness, thereby permitting physicians to certify certain people as ill and exempt from normal social obligations, for example, work or military service.[38]

Special note must be taken in this connection of the organization of physicians as an autonomous profession. Friedson[39] reviews the historical development of organized medicine and argues that its status as a profession depended on establishing a monopoly over the exercise of its work. The profession's claim for autonomy, that is, for self-regulation and control, rests in large part on the prior claim that there is a corpus of technical and esoteric knowledge that only those who are properly initiated and trained will be able to understand and apply. Friedson proposes that a sharper distinction be made between ". . . the body of scientific knowledge possessed by the profession [and] the knowledge used in applying knowledge to work situations. . . . 'pure' medical knowledge is transmuted, even debased in the course of application. Indeed, in the course of application knowledge cannot remain pure but must instead become socially organized as practice. . . . Insofar as it generically involves the practical application of knowledge to human affairs, it involves moral commitments and moral consequences neither justified by nor derived from the esoteric expertise which is supposed to distinguish the profession from other occupations. Medicine is not merely neutral, like theoretical physics . . . As a moral enterprise it is an instrument of social control which should be scrutinized as such without confusing the 'objectivity' of its applications.''[40]

As a profession, medicine must be responsive to other imperatives that bear only a tenuous relationship to the classic Hippocratic injunction, "Do no harm." Thus, the view of medicine as a science serves to justify physicians' control over technical, esoteric knowledge, and at the same time, such control supports claims for professional autonomy and self-regulation. It has been argued[41] that an increase in the general public's understanding of health issues would contribute to levels of health and that active public education efforts would be important undertakings. Such programs might reduce the "esoteric" character of medical knowledge, thereby challenging the medical profession's control of such knowledge and weakening claims for professional autonomy and self-regulation. For these reasons, we would not expect to find an emphasis on health education in either the training of students or the practice of physicians.

The impact of broader social values and forces on medicine is also illustrated by divisions within the profession itself. Despite general consensus on the assumptions of the biomedical model, with the consequences we have described, we could not expect an institution as complex as medicine to be monolithic. Divisions surface when there is competition for resources. One clear example is the conflict about funding for cancer research between basic bioscientists and clinical researchers and practitioners.[42]

This is not merely an intellectual debate, but a struggle that has economic, political, and social dimensions. The assumption of the scientific neutrality of medicine hardly seems appropriate to the rhetoric of this conflict. Witness, for example, the statements of one proponent of the clinical practitioner's view, who describes the "fundamental difference between the basic scientist and the practicing physician" as one in which the former "is trying to find the miracle pill we are all praying for," whereas the latter, with "the smallest shreds of partial knowledge, tries to relieve suffering, to prolong life, to help nature – and is sometimes able to cure."[43] He concludes: "If oncologists the world over had taken the advice that is often offered them and waited until the molecular biologists had given them the ultimate weapon, an incalculable number of patients now alive and cured or "controlled" would be dead. And we would not have the knowledge that makes it possible for us to look forward to promising developments in the near future, because that knowledge was acquired in the field, under the pressure of necessity, by those hard-working journeymen known as medical practitioners, among whom I am proud to be numbered."[44]

In discussing the assumption of the scientific neutrality of medicine, we have focused on medicine as a social institution, on its relationships to other institutions, and its functions for the larger society. It is worth noting here, as we did at the end of the previous section, that the issues addressed differ from those raised earlier in our discussions of the definition and etiology of illness. Within our overall approach, this is the broadest perspective that can be applied to the examination of problems in the health field. We are asking questions about how medicine functions within the larger society. Such an examination is necessarily comparative and takes into account historical, political, and economic factors. Because medicine in its totality is now the object of inquiry, we depart even more radically than before from the assumptions of the biomedical model. These assumptions will be viewed as interdependent with, rather than isolated from, the forms, features, and functions of society. Specific analyses within this perspective on medicine are presented in Chapters 8 and 9.

Plan of the book

We began with the premise that illness and health are social facts as well as biological facts. This first chapter was intended to set the stage for exploring the meaning and implications of this premise in the following chapters.

We have argued that the dominant perspective of modern medicine, namely, the biomedical model, has serious limitations. Its restricted and singular focus on biological disease processes and agents is unsuitable and inappropriate as a comprehensive approach to problems of health, illness, and patient care. This conclusion rests on our analysis of the context-stripping consequences of the biomedical model. That is, exclusive reliance on this model has led to the decontextualization of these problems, to the neglect in medical thought and practice of social, cultural, and institutional contexts within which health-related events are grounded and occur. Along with our critique of the biomedical model we have proposed an alternative perspective aimed at the restoration of these contexts. We intend to show that a more adequate approach may be developed when patients and their illnesses, physicians and their practices, and the institution of medicine are understood within their social contexts.

It is evident that the social and behavioral sciences are particularly germane to this task. Their subjects include the ways in which cultures and societies are organized and function. Their theoretical analyses and empirical investigations are directed to the study of how human behavior is guided and regulated by cultural values and social norms. Our review of health-relevant research is not comprehensive. Instead, we have selected particular studies and areas of research for extended analysis. We believe that detailed examination of specific studies will be instructive to health professionals in clarifying issues and in demonstrating the usefulness of this general approach.

We shall draw on work in several social and behavioral sciences, primarily anthropology, social psychology, and sociology, but work in history and economics will occasionally find a place. Each discipline has its special vantage point and its own set of concepts and methods. An anthropologist's ethnographic account of a culture or a surgical ward will differ significantly from a sociological analysis of status and power relationships among health professionals, and both will differ from a social psychological study of communication in diagnostic interviews. However, the text is not organized with reference to these distinctions. We shall present findings from various types of studies that have a bearing on issues that emerged from our critique of the biomedical model.

There are three principles of organization for the chapters that follow this introduction. First, with the exception of the conclusion, the chapters are grouped as pairs. The first chapter in each pair is more general in scope, outlines a framework of ideas for analyzing a particular problem, and reviews a small number of studies that either focus on different aspects of the problem or reflect different approaches to it. The second chapter within each pair is a more detailed examination of a specific topic. Thus, Chapter 2, "Patients in Social Contexts," addresses the general question of the role of sociocultural factors in the incidence of disease. Alternative models of social causation are discussed and studies of different types of social contexts are reviewed. Chapter 3, "Economic Change and Unemployment: Contexts of Illness," focuses on levels of unemployment as social contexts and their relation to psychiatric hospitalization rates. A similar relationship holds within each successive pair of chapters.

The second principle of organization is that each pair of chapters is oriented primarily to one of the four biomedical model assumptions examined in this first chapter. For example, in our critique of the doctrine of specific etiology, we concluded that this assumption neglects the contexts of medical practice. Thus, it excludes consideration of the process of negotiation through which patients' vague reports of symptoms are transformed into a specific illness with a specific etiology. Chapter 4, "Social Contexts of Health Care," and Chapter 5, "Physician–Patient Relationships," are concerned particularly with these issues. Again, the first chapter in the pair takes up the general problem and reports studies of the impact of hospital social organization on medical practices. The second chapter examines the microcontext of physician–patient interaction and discusses both sources and effects of typical modes of interaction in medical interviews.

In describing linkages between this chapter and the following ones, we are providing a preliminary large-scale map of the terrain we plan to cover and of the ways in which different parts are related to each other. One caution is in order, however. Although we discussed the four assumptions of the biomedical model in separate sections and emphasized each one's distinctive meaning and significance, we also found that together they constitute a unified perspective. Similarly, although each pair of chapters has a primary focus of orientation, this does not serve as an exclusive or rigid criterion of relevance. Discussions in different chapters sometimes overlap and supplement each other; studies reviewed in one chapter might equally well have been used in another.

Finally, in addition to the grouping of chapters into pairs and the primary linkage of each pair to a particular biomedical assumption, there is a third principle of organization, which reflects an ordering relationship among the assumptions and their associated successive pairs of chapters. We have already alluded to this relationship in discussing the assumption of generic diseases when we pointed out that our critique involves a progressive shift of perspective, a shift to a more radical questioning of the biomedical model.

Essentially, the text is organized so as to develop our critique in a progressive way so that each analysis, in successive pairs of chapters, departs further from and questions more radically the biomedical assumptions. Thus, although we began with an argument that the biological approach to illness is narrow and inadequate, we did not seriously question the medical definition of illness. Ryle's work on goiter, which we quoted, and the epidemiological research that will be reviewed in Chapters 2 and 3, is critical of diagnostic and clinical practice that does not take into account the sociocultural contexts of diseases; nonetheless, medical definitions of diseases are accepted. However, in our critiques of the assumptions of generic diseases and of the scientific neutrality of medicine, and in Chapters 6 through 9 on the social construction of illness and the

22   Critical perspectives on the biomedical model

social contexts and the functions of medicine, medical definitions of these problems are no longer accepted. In these latter analyses, the medical framework of concepts and practices is itself brought into question and made the object of inquiry.

This third principle is the key to the way in which the text is organized. The progression from acceptance to nonacceptance of medical definitions of problems guides the sequence in which we have treated different topics. Although, overall, the book represents an application of the social and behavioral sciences to the health field, this progressive shift in perspective has allowed us to include and to distinguish among different approaches. As health professionals become more aware of these differences in approach, they will be better prepared to undertake their own analyses and to find ways in which this perspective can be usefully incorporated into their practices.

Notes

1. Pellegrino, E. "Medicine and philosophy: some notes on the flirtation of Minerva and Aesculapius," Annual Oration of the Society for Health and Human Values. Washington, DC, November 8, 1973. Quoted in Engelhardt, H. T., Jr., and Spicker, S. F. (Eds.). *Evaluation and Explanation in the Biomedical Sciences*. Dortrecht, Holland: D. Reidel Publishing Co., 1974, Introduction, p. 3.
2. A critique of context-stripping methods in the social and behavioral sciences may be found in Mishler, E. G. "Meaning in context: is there any other kind?," *Harvard Educational Review*, 1979, *49*(1):1–19.
3. Engel, G. L. "The need for a new medical model: a challenge for biomedicine," *Science*, April 8, 1977, *196*:129–36, p. 130.
4. Cohen, H. "The evolution of the concept of disease," in Lush, B. (Ed.). *Concepts of Medicine*. New York: Pergamon Press, 1961, p. 169.
5. For a discussion of historical concepts of disease, see Reise, W. *The Conception of Disease*. New York: Philosophical Library, 1953. Essays on philosophical problems of medical concepts of health and disease are in Engelhardt, H. T., Jr., and Spicker, S. F. (Eds.). *Evaluation and Explanation in the Biomedical Medical Sciences*.
6. Quoted in Redlich, F. C. "The concept of health in psychiatry," in Leighton, A. H., Clausen, J. N., and Wilson, R. N. (Eds.). *Explorations in Social Psychiatry*. London: Tavistock Publications, 1957, p. 140.
7. Engel, G. L. "A unified concept of health and disease," in Ingle, D. J. (Ed.). *Life and Disease*. New York: Basic Books, 1963, p. 339.
8. Redlich, "The concept of health in psychiatry," p. 155.
9. *Webster's New International Dictionary of the English Language* 2nd ed., Unabridged. Springfield, MA: G. & C. Merriam, 1956.
10. Ryle, J. "The meaning of normal," in Lush, *Concepts of Medicine*, p. 146.
11. Ibid., p. 137.
12. Ibid., p. 144.
13. Dubos, R. *Mirage of Health*. New York: Anchor Books, 1961.
14. Engel, "The need for a new medical model," p. 131.
15. Ibid., p. 131.

16. Dubos, *Mirage of Health*, p. 129.
17. Ibid., p. 91.
18. Engel, G. L. *Psychological Development in Health and Disease*. Philadelphia: W. B. Saunders, 1962; See also Engel, "A unified concept of health and disease."
19. Dubos, R. J. "Infection into disease," In Ingle (Ed.). *Life and Disease*, pp. 100–101.
20. Ibid., p. 108.
21. Balint, M. *The Doctor, His Patient and the Illness*. New York: International University Press, 1957.
22. Byrne, P. S., and Long, B. E. L. *Doctors Talking to Patients*. London: Her Majesty's Stationary Office, 1976.
23. Fabrega, H., Jr. "Toward a theory of human disease," *Journal of Nervous and Mental Disease*, 1976, *162*(5):299–312, p. 299.
24. Fabrega, H., Jr. "The need for an ethnomedical science," *Science*, September 1975, *189*:969–75, p. 969.
25. Engel, *Psychological Development in Health and Disease*, p. 250.
26. Ibid., p. 252.
27. Ibid., p. 254.
28. For a review of some of this work and a report of research on the effects of changes in the social milieu of mental hospitals, see Wing, J. K., and Brown, G. W. *Institutionalism and Schizophrenia*. Cambridge: Cambridge University Press, 1970. In his *The Making of Blind Men*, New York: Russell Sage, 1969, Robert Scott describes how a homogeneous "character type" may develop in a naturally diverse population through the practice of treatment agencies.
29. Waxler, N. E. "Culture and mental illness," *Journal of Nervous and Mental Disease*, 1974, *159*(6):379–95.
30. Murphy, J. M. "Psychiatric labeling in cross-cultural perspective," *Science*, March 12, 1976, *191*:1019–28, p. 1027.
31. Eisenberg, L. "Psychiatry and society: a sociobiologic synthesis," *New England Journal of Medicine*, April 21, 1977, *296*(16):903–10, pp. 905 and 903.
32. WHO. *Report of the International Pilot Study of Schizophrenia, Vol. 1*. Geneva: World Health Organization, 1973.
33. For an analysis and critique of the "storybook image of science," see Mitroff, I. I. *The Subjective Side of Science*. New York: American Elsevier, 1974.
34. Glick, L. B. "Medicine as an ethnographic category: the Gimi of the New Guinea Highlands," *Ethnology*, 1967, *6*(1):31–56, pp. 53 and 52.
35. Waxler, N. E. "Is mental illness cured in traditional societies? A theoretical analysis," *Culture, Medicine and Psychiatry*, 1977, *1*:233–53.
36. Glick, "Medicine as an ethnographic category," p. 36.
37. Fabrega, "Toward a theory of human disease," p. 170.
38. See Waitzkin, H. B., and Waterman, B. *The Exploitation of Illness in Capitalist Society*. Indianapolis, IN: Bobbs-Merrill, 1974.
39. Friedson, E. *Profession of Medicine: A Study of the Sociology of Applied Knowledge*. New York: Dodd, Mead, 1970.
40. Ibid., p. 346.
41. For example, see Johnson, T. J. *Professions and Power*. London: Macmillan, 1972.
42. For a review of this conflict, see Epstein, S. S. *The Politics of Cancer*. Totowa, NJ: Sierra Club Books, 1978.
43. Israel, L. *Conquering Cancer*. New York: Random House, 1978, p. 11.
44. Ibid., p. 11.

2   Patients in social contexts

Elliot G. Mishler

Whoever wishes to investigate medicine properly should proceed thus: in the first place to consider the seasons of the year, and what effects each of them produces. Then the winds, the hot and cold, especially such as are common to all countries, and then such as are peculiar to each locality. . . . One should consider most attentively the waters which the inhabitants use, . . . and the mode in which the inhabitants live, and what are their pursuits, whether they are fond of drinking and eating to excess, and given to indolence, or are fond of exercise and labor.[1]

It seems appropriate to begin this chapter with Hippocrates' advice. We share his view that a "proper" understanding of disease requires study of the life contexts of patients.

Epidemiology, public health, and preventive medicine are the branches of medicine that have adopted this perspective. Emphasis in these disciplines on the health of populations and communities contrasts with the alternate medical tradition, which has focused on individual patients and the cure of specific diseases. As we noted in the previous chapter, the latter approach, now firmly based in the biosciences and the germ theory of disease, has dominated medical training, research, and practice at least since the turn of the century.

Dubos refers to this development as the modern triumph of the cult of Asclepius over the cult of Hygeia.[2] In medical thought and in the allocation of resources, priority is given to curing sick individuals rather than to promoting the health and well-being of whole communities. Modern "scientific" medicine, based on the germ theory of disease, is usually credited with the generally observed improvement in population health levels since 1900. Dubos disputes the assumption that these parallel trends are causally connected. He observes that significant decreases in death rates and major changes in levels of health antedated the germ theory of disease. He argues that these changes primarily reflected efforts in public health directed toward modifying the environment, efforts framed within a quite different conception of disease. "Clearly, the monster of infection had been reduced to a shadow of itself by the time scientific medicine provided rational and specific methods for its control. The conquest of epidemic diseases was in large part the result of the campaign for pure food, pure water and pure air based not on scientific doctrine but on philosophical faith, . . . the attempt to recapture the goodness of life in harmony with the ways of nature."[3]

Recent studies of the incidence and course of plagues and epidemic diseases from early periods of human history through the nineteenth century carry the argument a step further. McNeill[4] reports historical data showing that drastic reductions in the severity of successive epidemics occurred regularly after the initial ravaging of a population on its first exposure to a new infectious agent. He attributes this pattern to natural adaptive processes whereby survivors develop sufficient immunity to withstand successive visitations. Gradually, the population becomes "disease-experienced," epidemic illnesses become endemic, killer diseases like measles become the diseases of childhood. By the end of the nineteenth century this natural process had led, on a worldwide scale, to the effective control of many highly virulent diseases, well before the availability of the antibacterial agents spawned by the germ theory of disease. The implication of McNeill's work is that modern scientific medicine may have had even more of a secondary role than Dubos suggests in the long historical conquest of major diseases and the consequent rise in the health levels of human populations.

Dubos' and McNeill's analyses continue and extend the critique of the biomedical model we began in Chapter 1. There we drew the conclusion that a major consequence of the ascendancy of the biomedical model is the decontextualization of problems associated with health and disease. Studies of the history of medicine and of changing patterns of disease raise serious questions about the assumed relation between health levels and the current model of illness with its associated forms of treatment. These studies have helped uncover complex relationships between illness and features of larger sociocultural contexts. In this way, they lead us into the topic on which we shall focus in this chapter, namely, studies of patients in social contexts.

Epidemiological research provides a good point of entry to this set of problems. The central questions in epidemiology are these: What are the distributions, within and across populations, of incidence and prevalence rates for different illnesses? What distinctive social, cultural, economic, and historical factors characterize patient populations with particular rates and types of illnesses? Because comparisons are always involved, we might phrase the typical question in epidemiological research as follows: In what ways, besides the presence of illness, are patient populations different from nonpatient populations?

These questions mark a shift in perspective from the special angle of vision and the restricted focus of the biomedical model. The viewpoint of epidemiology enlarges the field of attention to include, in addition to disease events, the social environments of patients. We shall see that these environments are conceptualized in a variety of ways.

In an influential text, epidemiology is defined as "the study of the distribution and determinants of disease prevalence in man."[5] The authors distinguish descriptive, analytic, and experimental epidemiological studies, the type defined by whether the study permits specific etiological inferences, and the testing of hypotheses and models of causation. In their view, epidemiology is an applied discipline, to which the contributions of three other disciplines are "particularly pertinent": clinical medicine, pathology, and biostatistics. The social and behavioral sciences are notably absent from this triad of "particularly pertinent" disciplines. The omission is unfortunate and, from our point of view, mistaken. It is, at the same time, an instructive omission in that it highlights a limitation of traditional epidemiology, namely, its dependence on clinical medicine for definition of its problems.

The reliance of epidemiologic work on the biomedical model of illness is evident in the design of studies as well as in the framework of interpretation applied to findings. For example, in a typical epidemiological study, "cases" are defined by medical criteria, that is, diagnoses are based on physicians' evaluations of standard laboratory or clinical tests. Thus, epidemiologists usually select their samples of patients from clinical records; they have already been diagnosed as cases with cancer, diabetes, hypertension, or schizophrenia. Further information is collected on patients' social and cultural characteristics, either from the same records or through a separate survey. Analyses are directed to an examination of relationships between these two types of variables. In this way, social and cultural data are "added" to clinical data. The important point, from our perspective, is that this procedure does not alter or raise questions about the "received" medical definition of the problem. For this reason, we shall be particularly attentive in our review to the fact that epidemiological studies are studies of patients, that is, of people already defined as sick by physicians and diagnosed by them as having specific illnesses.

The incorporation of traditional epidemiology into the biomedical model is also reflected in the way that social and cultural variables tend to be introduced into a theory of illness. Dubos and McNeill, for example, although they emphasize the importance of sociohistorical conditions, view the occurrence and control of disease as essentially biological processes. When social variables are included in the "web of causation,"[6] they serve essentially as indicators of situations that increase or decrease biological risk factors. On the whole, epidemiology does not offer an alternative to the biomedical model either in its definition of illness or in its theory of disease causation.

We raise this issue at this point, before reviewing specific studies, because one of our principal aims is to show different approaches through which study of sociocultural variables may contribute to a fuller understanding of the problems of health and illness. Epidemiology represents one approach, and we are suggesting that its close adherence to the biomedical model entails limitations. In later chapters, particularly where we focus on the social construction of illness and the social functions of medicine, we shall describe alternative approaches that depart more radically from the biomedical model.

The classic epidemiological studies focused on diseases where the model of a specific causative agent seemed directly applicable. This was true even when the agent remained unknown until long after the disease was brought under control, as in Snow's famous studies of cholera; or when it was not an infectious disease but a dietary insufficiency, as Goldberger discovered in his studies of pellagra.[7] Many significant diseases of the contemporary world appear to have more complex patterns of causation. The same agent, for example, cigarette smoking, may be implicated in several different diseases such as lung cancer, emphysema, and hypertension. The same disease, such as hypertension, may be the end result of quite different chains of causation, some associated with the stress of particular occupations, others with diet, and still others with life-styles.

Traditional problems of epidemiological research – the definition of cases, case finding procedures, specification of populations at risk, computation of rates of occurrence – all become more difficult to resolve when a unique and singular connection between a specific agent and a specific effect cannot be established. In addition, a number of serious diseases, such as schizophrenia and diabetes, have chronicity as a principal feature and are managed or controlled rather than cured. This pattern of chronicity, with variation over time in the manifestation and intensity of symptoms, introduces further difficulties for epidemiological research. Investigators resolve these problems in different ways. We shall exploit these differences among studies to clarify some implicit assumptions about illnesses and their causes.

A list of illnesses that have been topics of epidemiologic study would undoubtedly include all the major illnesses and probably most minor and exotic ones as well. There is another source of variety as well, which is more relevant to our concerns. Investigations differ in the types of social variables, and in their conceptualizations of these variables, to which the incidence of illness is referred. Age, sex, marital status, ethnicity, social class, occupation, rural – urban residence are among the frequently used social attributes. Given our special interest in social contexts, we have selected a set of studies for detailed examination that vary in their conceptualization of this social dimension. To permit a clearer comparison across different types of studies, we have chosen to look primarily at studies of the mental illnesses.

The mental illnesses are good candidates for exploration of the critical issues with which we are concerned. The epidemiologic study of mental illnesses is an active field of research; a few years ago, 700 to 800 references per year were listed in bibliographies compiled by the Center for Epidemiologic Studies of the National Institute of Mental Health.[8] Further, all the methodological problems of epidemiologic research, such as the definition and finding of cases and the computation of rates, must be faced and resolved explicitly in studies of the mental illnesses.

Finally, some of the classic studies differ from each other in exactly that respect, namely, their context focus, which is of special relevance for our purposes. In each of the following sections, we shall examine one study in some detail. The social contexts represented are ecological units, communities, social classes, and families. In each instance, we shall review the approach to core methodological problems, assumptions underlying and implications of the resolutions adopted, principal findings, and the model of causation proposed. Other related work bearing on these findings will also be summarized.

The ecology of mental disorders

In 1939, Robert E. L. Faris and Warren Dunham published their monograph, *Mental Disorders in Urban Areas*. Subtitled, "An Ecological Study of Schizophrenia and Other Psychoses," it was described by Ernest Burgess in his Introduction as "a pioneer study in the social aspects of mental disorder," with many new and unexpected findings that "constitute a significant contribution to our knowledge of the mental life of human beings in the large city."[9] Its significance, Burgess concluded, resided in the degree to which the work opened up significant areas for further research.

Faris and Dunham framed their work within a tradition of sociological research and theory that defines the city as an ecological system consisting of "natural areas," that is, geographic areas that are internally homogeneous but different from each other with respect to a variety of social and economic features. They summarize earlier research on relationships between the city's ecological units and indexes of social and personal disorganization, which formed the background to their own work, as follows: ". . . in all of these social problems there is a concentration of high rates close to the center of the city, with the rates declining in magnitude as one travels in any direction toward the city's periphery."[10] This is the empirical side of Park and Burgess' classic model of the city as a set of concentric "zones," from the inner central business district, through transition zones and working-class neighborhoods, to the outside circle of middle- and upper-middle-class homes.[11]

Faris and Dunham applied this ecological approach to the study of mental disorders. Their principal aim was to determine if there is an association between rates of mental disorders and areas of the city that differ in socioeconomic and demographic characteristics. They reduced the 120 census-tract subcommunities of Chicago to eleven types of social areas, using type and rental level of housing as the primary index and nativity and race as secondary criteria.

Their most important discovery was the close association between type of social area and rate of mental hospital admission. Based on all admissions to both private and state hospitals for the period 1922–34, their figures show that "high insanity rates appear to cluster in the deteriorated regions in and surrounding the center of the city, no matter what race or nationality inhabits that region. . . . By far the highest rate for insanity in the city occurs in the central business district or Zone 1. In every zone, in every section of the city, with the exception of the southwest side, there is a steady decline in rates as one travels from the center of the city to the periphery. . . . This presentation definitely establishes the fact that insanity, like other social problems, fits into the ecological structure of the city."[12]

From additional analyses of rate distributions for different diagnostic groups, they report findings for schizophrenia that are consistent with those for all psychoses, and show an even stronger pattern. For example, the rates per 100,000 population for all psychoses range from about 360 in the central business district, Zone 1, to about sixty-five in the furthest-from-the-center Zone VII; this is a ratio of about 6:1. For schizophrenia, the comparable figures are from about 1020 to twenty cases per 100,000, or a ratio of about 50:1.[13] High rates for specific subtypes of schizophrenia, that is, paranoid, catatonic, and hebephrenic diagnoses, are also concentrated in deteriorated sections of the city. Rates for manic–depressive psychosis, however, show a relatively random pattern across the zones.

Another finding of interest is that rates within areas appear to be higher for those nativity groups that differ from the modal population in the area. For example, despite a generally high schizophrenia rate for blacks, their rate in the predominantly black apartment-house district is extremely low compared to rates for blacks in other areas of the city. Further, ". . . rates for the native white of native parentage and the foreign-born white for this area are the highest rates within these classifications as compared to any of the other areas of the city. It is apparent that the schizophrenic rate is significantly higher for those races residing in areas not primarily populated by members of their own groups."[14]

Before turning to their interpretation of rate differentials by area, some methodological issues deserve comment. We observed earlier that case definition is a critical problem for epidemiological studies. Faris and Dunham began with diagnostic labels found on hospital records. Although they note at one point that, with regard to subtypes of schizophrenia, ". . . there is still considerable confusion in the problem of diagnosis,"[15] they do not seriously question the psychiatric framework. Many recent studies reflect a similar unquestioning approach to hospital records, but more attention has been directed, since Faris and Dunham's work, to such problems as the reliability of diagnosis, and relationships between primary and secondary diagnosis, admission and established diagnosis, and diagnosis upon first admission and readmission. Faris and Dunham do not address these issues; at the time they were nonproblematic.

In computing insanity rates for their major analyses, they use total admissions over the thirteen-year period from 1922 to 1934, divide it by the 1930 census figures for the adult population, ages 15–64, and multiply the quotient by 13; this gives them an annual rate per 100,000. There are many problems with such estimates, particularly if the period summarized by an index based on one year is characterized by marked population change. In general, the population of all urban areas with one million or more residents, which would include Chicago, increased by about 50 percent between 1920 and 1930.[16] Differential rates of change for subpopulations of native- and foreign-born whites and blacks over this period of time would have considerable effect on the computed rates.

It should also be observed that such rapid increases in population reflect high rates of in-migration and that migration is itself a factor that has been found to be associated with rates of mental illness. For example, summarizing a series of intensive studies of migration and mental illness in the period 1949–51, Lee states that the introduction of controls for other important social variables had no significant effect on their ". . . several-time-reached conclusions – that rates for migrants within this country are considerably higher than those for nonmigrants, and that rates for foreign-born whites are intermediate between the rates for the two groups of natives. . . ."[17]

One last point about their case-counting procedure deserves mention. It appears that they include both first and readmissions in their totals. Later investigators have been concerned with the problem that readmissions may reflect a variety of other factors besides those involved in first admissions. In particular, readmissions may be sensitive to administrative rules and procedures, the relative efficacy of psychiatric treatment, and changing systems of health services in a community. These factors may have differential effects on patients from different socioeconomic classes or who differ in other respects that affect readjustment to the community or access to psychiatric care. The inclusion of readmissions with first admissions confounds the problem of interpretation, because factors that affect one cannot be disentangled from factors that affect the other. For these reasons, most comparable studies of hospitalized cases use first admissions as the best index of true incidence rates.

Our intent, in reviewing these methodological problems, is not to diminish the significance of this early and still classic study. Some of the important issues in psychiatric epidemiology only came to be recognized as a result of the study itself, through efforts of other investigators to extend and replicate the work and to test alternative explanations of the findings. Faris and Dunham concentrate on two competing models or hypotheses; these are referred to generally as social drift versus social causation explanations.

Briefly, the first proposes that the empirical association between rates of mental illnesses and social areas of the city, and the association of these rates with other socioeconomic indicators, results from the accumulation of mentally ill persons or those predisposed to mental illness in deteriorated and disorganized areas and in lower socioeconomic strata. That is, persons with psychological problems who cannot adapt well to society's demands and requirements move, or drift, into poorer sections and lower social levels. The counterargument of the alternative social causation hypothesis is that the severe and stressful conditions of life in disorganized areas and in lower social classes tends to increase the risk of mental illness.

Early in the book, Faris and Dunham suggest the direction that their argument will take. "The characteristics of the populations in these zones appear to be produced by the nature of the life within the zones rather than the reverse. This is shown by the striking fact that the zones retain all their characteristics as different populations flow through them."[18] When they come to interpreting their findings, they take note of the drift hypothesis and counter it directly. "Many of the cases of schizophrenia consist of persons who were born in and have always lived in deteriorated areas. These did not drift into the high-rate areas. . . . It is a question whether this drift process, which undoubtedly contributes something to the apparent concentration of rates, is anything more than an insignificant factor in causing the concentration."[19]

They conducted a separate analysis of young and old schizophrenics, and found that the general pattern of rates held for both groups. As they state, this is further evidence against the drift hypothesis, because "The younger cases, mostly too young to have had much time to drift, are concentrated in the central areas in much the same pattern as the older cases."[20] They also argue that the pattern of manic–depressive cases could not be accounted for by the drift hypothesis.

Faris and Dunham opt instead for a particular version of the social causation model. They propose the hypothesis that ". . . extended isolation of the person produces the abnormal traits of behavior and mentality. If the various types of unconventional behavior observed in different schizophrenic patients can be said to result from one condition, it appears that extreme seclusiveness may be that condition. The hallucinations, delusions, inappropriate action, silliness, and deterioration may all result from the fact that the seclusive person is completely freed from the social control which enforces normality in other people."[21]

They review some slight evidence from other studies bearing on the question of how the trait of "seclusiveness" might develop. In an argument that is like an advance echo of more recent social labeling theories, they propose that certain persons with a tendency to seclusiveness may be cast into the role of social outcast during their development, with the consequence that they lack effective social contacts and become increasingly isolated. Finally, they point out that conditions of life in deteriorated social areas are likely to reinforce this isolating process.

The debate between the two general models of social drift and social causation remains unresolved today. It is evident that neither is totally false or totally true and that it may be misleading to place them in opposition. A more adequate model will have to incorporate both processes. A particularly instructive effort has been made by Dunham, one of the authors of the original monograph. Thirty years later, he undertook a comprehensive study designed to assess directly the relative merits of the social causation and social drift hypotheses.[22]

For purposes of comparison, Dunham selected two different communities in an urban area that differed in their overall hospitalization rates for schizophrenia; he included cases in all types of psychiatric treatment. Many analyses later, he concludes, "The evidence provided by this study gives no support to any proposition that asserts that type of community and social class are related to the incidence of schizophrenia."[23] Coming from one of the earlier proponents of the ecological model and the social causation hypothesis, this is a strong statement, particularly because it is based on work that dealt more adequately with the methodological problems of such studies than his and Faris' pioneering effort. For example, only first admission schizophrenics are included, diagnoses are carefully assessed and confirmed, and cases from different types of psychiatric facilities are compared.

Dunham's findings strongly suggest that the different hospitalization rates for his two comparison communities are primarily a function of residential mobility. That is, persons who are hospitalized as schizophrenic tend to have migrated to certain areas of the community. These areas then produce the disproportionate rates that are found in studies of hospitalized first admissions. He goes on to argue for a more complex model of social sorting and selection, of the kind we suggested above would be necessary. ". . . The differential distribution of schizophrenic rates in a large urban community is caused by the fact that potential schizophrenics are born into families with differing life chances."[24] A combination of factors – including coming from a lower-status family, leaving home early to improve one's educational or occupational situation, the toll taken by incipient stages of schizophrenia – all interact and contribute to the excess of schizophrenics found in certain types of communities and certain social classes.

Families with adequate resources to protect their children from severe social stress are less likely to have children who end up in a treatment context diagnosed as schizophrenic. On the other hand, children from families with fewer resources, who drift out of their family and community contexts, and move downward in the social scale of occupations and residentially into lower-income and more socially disorganized areas of the city, are more likely to end up in such contexts with such a diagnosis. The empirical association between rates for schizophrenia and ecological areas, or social class, is the result of this complex sorting and selection process.

Some of the general issues discussed here will recur as we examine other types of studies of patients in their social contexts. The community study to which we now turn is similar in some respects to the ecological studies but also differs from them in certain significant ways.

Community integration and psychiatric disorders

The Stirling County Study of psychiatric disorder and the sociocultural environment is an ambitious and complex project. Reports from the project span a period of more than twenty-five years, and various substudies are still under way. We shall focus on the results of an epidemiological investigation reported by Dorothea C. Leighton and her co-workers in *The Character of Danger*, published in 1963 as the third volume in the series.[25]

Their most general finding on the relationship between community integration-disintegration and psychiatric disorder is remarkably similar to the central finding of Faris and Dunham's study: "... the degree of disintegration in the sociocultural system is associated with the prevalence of psychiatric disorder."[26] Their interpretive stance also seems closely aligned with the approach in the earlier study: namely, they adopt a social causation model and contrast it directly with the alternative social drift hypothesis. "Disintegrated social systems produce disintegrated personalities. . . . If you were to introduce a random sample of symptomatically unimpaired people into the Disintegrated Areas in numbers small enough so they produced no significant change in the sociocultural systems, we think most of these individuals would become impaired. Conversely, if you were to take people out of the Disintegrated Areas and make a place for them in a well-integrated community, we believe many would show marked reduction or disappearance of impairment."[27]

This is as strong a statement of the social causation model as one is likely to find. Before turning to the specific epidemiologic analyses offered as empirical support for this interpretation, we must discuss their approach to basic problems of measurement and definition. Without an understanding of how psychiatric cases were defined and located, how rates of disorder were computed, and how communities were classified as integrated or disintegrated, we cannot properly assess their findings and conclusions.

A typical epidemiologic study uses hospital or clinic records to locate cases with particular diagnoses. The Stirling County investigators were interested in rates and patterns of psychiatric disorder within and across communities, including untreated and previously undiagnosed cases. Hospital records would have been inappropriate to this task. Instead, sample surveys were conducted and information collected from respondents through self-report questionnaires and interviews focused on medical and psychiatric symptoms, treatment history, and features of the respondents' family and social backgrounds. Supplementary information came from community physicians, other informants, and the records of health and care-taking institutions.

All this information was assembled for each person in the sample and a judgment then made of the probability that the individual would have been considered a "psychiatric case" at any point in his or her lifetime. A case is defined as ". . . a person who, if thoroughly studied by psychiatrists, would be diagnosed as suffering from one or more of the specific psychiatric conditions described in the Manual [i.e., the Diagnostic and Statistical Manual of the American Psychiatric Association] . . . including . . . only those conditions which we believe would clearly establish an individual as a case in the opinion of most American Psychiatrists."[28] This idealization of the psychiatrist was modified by the realities of research; in practice, an individual's "caseness" was determined by the pooled judgment of the two senior investigators.

Community integration–disintegration is the other side of the Stirling County investigators' social causation equation. The communities and the criteria and methods used for classifying them are detailed in the first two volumes of the study.[29] In brief, a number of indicators of social and cultural disorganization were used, including the extent of poverty, the incidence of broken homes, rates of delinquency and crime, and the strength of social associations and networks.

All of these data were compressed by the investigators so as to permit one overall test of the community disintegration hypothesis. This was presented in the form of a complex analysis of variance, using a derived mental health status score to indicate whether a person's "caseness" rating was above or below what was to be expected of an average individual of his or her sex, age, and occupational group. The question being asked was this: Compared to other socially similar persons, is he or she more or less likely to be counted as a psychiatric case? The most critical finding is that these scores differed by type of community: individuals in the disintegrated communities had higher scores than those in the integrated communities.[30] This is the finding the authors summarize in their conclusion quoted above: ". . . the degree of disintegration in the sociocultural system is associated with the prevalence of psychiatric disorder."

Numerous other analyses are presented of specific symptom patterns, and, for example, of the effects of age, sex, occupational status, and migration across the comparison communities. Some of these are worth noting, because they indicate ways in which the general conclusion may have to be qualified. For example, rates of psychotic symptom patterns do not differ between disintegrated and integrated communities; differences are strongest for sociopathic symptoms, psychoneurotic patterns, and mental deficiency. Differences between men in the two types of community seem to be largely a function of differences between men over sixty; differences are not only slight for men under sixty but appear to reverse.

The relationship between indices of psychiatric disorder and migration is of particular interest, because the authors are aware that it bears on the competing hypothesis of social drift. No information is available on out-migrants, that is, on former residents who left these areas. There is no way of knowing whether their mental health status was better or worse than that of those who remained. Data are limited to residents of these communities at the time of the study. Although Dr. Leighton and her colleagues tend to discount its significance, the data presented show that long-term residents of the disintegrated areas have the best mental health scores and more recent migrants have the poorest scores.[31] This finding is inconsistent with the investigators' proposition that life in these areas produces psychiatric disorder.

One further point merits attention. In an elegant and detailed critique of the study, Kunitz[32] suggests that there is a lack of independence between the investigators' concepts and measures of *community* disintegration and *personality* disorganization, and further that this reflects the investigators' social values. He argues that the guiding assumptions of the study are ideologically conservative. They reflect the bias of late nineteenth and early twentieth-century social reformers that the personal and social ills of the world resulted from the advent of industrialism, urbanization, and secularism. The features the Leightons and their co-investigators use to characterize "integration" all represent aspects of the *gemeinschaft* community with a high degree of value consensus, respect for tradition, family stability, and so on. As Kunitz notes, neither this ideological perspective nor its corollary, that social disorganization leads to personal disorganization, is necessarily untrue or unsuitable as a guide to research. However, in this study, the indicators of social integration are defined in terms that are almost identical with the list of ten "basic human strivings," interference with which is expected to lead to psychological disturbance. The investigators acknowledge this, but only in passing: ". . . there is actually some correspondence between the ten essential striving sentiments and most of the ten indicators of sociocultural disintegration. Each of the sentiments can be thought of as affected by an aspect of sociocultural disintegration represented by one or a cluster of the indicators."[33] Kunitz contends, ". . . it turns out, in fact, that by definition if one is unfortunate enough to live in a disintegrated community, one has a high likelihood of having one's basic human strivings interfered with because they are both defined in the same terms."[34]

In this review of selected findings from this complex study of communities, as in our examination of Faris and Dunham's research on the ecology of mental disorders, we have tried both to indicate the relevance of sociocultural variables to problems of health and illness and, at the same time, to provide a critical reading of the work. The general trend of findings from such studies is clear and uncontested: Rates of psychiatric illnesses are socially patterned. Whether the cases counted are drawn from hospital records or represent psychiatric assessments of the behaviors and feelings of members of the community, whether the computed rates are measures of treated incidence or untreated prevalence, whether standardized diagnostic categories or general judgments of overall psychiatric difficulty are used does not alter the finding that people with illness are clustered disproportionately in certain parts of the community and in certain subpopulations.

The problem of interpretation remains unsettled. From the earliest studies on, the social drift and social causation hypotheses have been offered as contending explanations. Dunham's social selection–social drift model is another, more complex alternative. We shall return to this issue after discussing studies of social class and mental illness.

Social class and mental illness

The research collaboration between a sociologist, August B. Hollingshead, and a psychiatrist, Frederick C. Redlich, resulted in a study that has had considerable influence on later work. The published report, *Social Class and Mental Illness,* subtitled *A Community Study,* appeared in 1958.[35] Findings were based on a "psychiatric census," which included all persons from the New Haven, Connecticut, metropolitan area who were ". . . in treatment with a psychiatrist or under the care of a psychiatric clinic or mental hospital between May 31 and December 1, 1950. . . ."[36]

The study was guided by a series of hypotheses on relationships between social class position and various aspects of psychiatric disorder and treatment. The first hypothesis, which is the most general, will be our principal concern: "Hypothesis 1. The prevalence of treated mental illness is related significantly to an individual's position in the class structure."[37] Hollingshead and Redlich's summary of relevant findings will, by now, have a familiar ring: "The several procedures followed enable us to conclude that Hypothesis 1 is true. Stated in different terms, a distinct inverse relationship does exist between social class and mental illness. The linkage between class status and the distribution of patients in the population follows a characteristic pattern; Class V, almost invariably, contributes many more patients than its proportion of the population warrants."[38] This conclusion is based on two types of analysis: One compares the social class distribution of patients with the class distribution of the New Haven population; the second compares rates of mental illness across classes.

Although most of their attention is directed to prevalence rates, Hollingshead and Redlich also provide a number of instructive and critical comparisons across social classes on the several components of prevalence. They point out that their total count of patients in treatment during the six-month period of observation is made up of three different subpopulations: new cases, that is, those entering treatment for the first time during the study period, which is a measure of incidence; continuous cases, those in treatment before the beginning of the study period, who were also in treatment during some part of it; and, reentry cases, that is, those who had been in treatment at some earlier time and reentered treatment during the study period. Their totals, that is, the overall prevalence rates, are the sums of these separate groups.

The significance of this distinction between incidence and prevalence, particularly in psychiatric epidemiology, has been discussed by a number of critics and reviewers.[39] The central point is that prevalence rates confound the actual occurrence of illness with its duration. The latter may be affected by variations in remission and the relative effectiveness of different types of treatment, that is, with variation in response of different patients to different treatments. It has been shown, by Hollingshead and Redlich themselves as well as by other investigators, that social class is related to type and effectiveness of psychiatric treatment. The consequence of these relationships is that an association between social class and the prevalence of mental illness cannot be interpreted unequivocally to mean that class has an etiological or causative role in the development and occurrence of the disorder. The empirical relationship might instead be a function of class-related types of treatment received.

Hollingshead and Redlich's analyses of variations by social class in these different component rates serve to underscore the importance of this distinction and to sharpen our understanding of the ways in which social factors may be related to illness. From their comparisons of incidence, reentry, and continuous treatment rates for all cases of mental disorder, all psychoses, and schizophrenia separately, they conclude that in each instance, each component in prevalence is related significantly to class.

However, the specific form of the relationship varies across these analyses. Among incidence and reentry rates, for example, we find that Classes I–IV do not appear to differ significantly from each other; the only difference is between Class V and the other classes. In some instances, Class IV rates are lower than Class I–II or III rates. This suggests that the effects of social class are not linear but that there is a disjunction, a threshold effect, between Class V and the rest of the population. Continuous treatment rates are more orderly, but even here the sharpest break is between Classes IV and V.

In commenting on these findings for total cases, the authors state that ". . . the dramatic differences in rates from the higher to the lower classes are highlighted by the cases in continuous treatment"; and their figures ". . . provide the first clue that class position is connected with what happens to psychiatric patients in a given period of time. . . . The increase in the total patient load in Classes IV and V clearly cannot be explained on the basis of the rates for the new cases and re-entry cases."[40]

Their own caution here on the meaning of the overall prevalence findings is not always adhered to, either by the authors themselves or by later investigators; the class differences in prevalence rates have often been treated as having etiological significance. Thus, Hollingshead and Redlich propose a model of causation in which social classes are characterized as different cultures with different life conditions. These are hypothesized as leading to different patterns of personality development, for example, to class differences in ego strength and impulse control patterns, which in turn affect the differential vulnerability to mental illness in the different classes. This interpretation assumes that the prevalence rates represent incidence when, as we have seen, they are not equivalent.

Redlich is perhaps his own best critic of this tendency to overinterpret the study's findings in this way. In another context, he remarks, "The New Haven study has not really brought out anything which is of etiological significance in explaining differences in prevalence, and prevalence in itself is not a very good measure from an epidemiological viewpoint. . . . We found, as far as the accumulation of schizophrenics in the lower classes is concerned, that although not entirely, it is mostly due to the fact that the lower socioeconomic groups get different treatment and have different opportunities for rehabilitation."[41]

We shall return to this issue of the relation of treatment patterns to rates of illness in later chapters, using other specific findings from Hollingshead and Redlich's study for that purpose. It is important to recognize that this hypothesis on the effects on illness rates of class differences in treatment is a third alternative to be added to the social drift and social causation hypotheses we have already considered.

Hollingshead and Redlich provide one set of analyses directed to the assessment of the social drift hypothesis. They conclude that ". . . neither geographic transiency nor downward social mobility can account for the sharp differences in the distribution of schizophrenic patients from one class to another."[42] Unfortunately, this conclusion rests on limited data and weak analyses; only the mobility histories of schizophrenic patients in the different classes are compared with each other, and these rates are not placed in the context of the mobility rates of the social classes in the community.

The studies reviewed in this and earlier sections, and many other studies in the literature, are all consistent with each other in finding that rates of severe mental disorder are associated with sociocultural conditions. A number of reviewers have reached similar conclusions. Thus, Dohrenwend concludes, from his review of many types of studies of different types of disorder, that: "The most consistent demographic finding reported in social psychiatry field studies is an inverse relationship between social class and psychological disorder."[43] Kohn, a decade later, comments on the findings of fifty studies that focused on rates of schizophrenia in many countries including the United States: "Almost without exception, these studies have shown that schizophrenia occurs most frequently at the lowest social class levels of urban society."[44] Turner uses almost identical terms in concluding his review of epidemiological studies of schizophrenia and notes that: "Despite the conceptual and methodological difficulties attendant to epidemiological studies of schizophrenia and the related fact that results have often been importantly divergent, there are some findings that have resulted with substantial consistency across widely differing settings and procedures."[45] Finally, in a more selective review of only those studies that used incidence rates of schizophrenia, Mishler and Scotch state: "The most consistent finding, which emerges in eight of the nine studies, is that the highest incidence is associated with the lowest social class groupings used in each study."[46]

We have already referred to the somewhat ambiguous and dual relationship of epidemiological research to the biomedical model. On the one hand, the search for social correlates of illness falls outside the boundaries, or at least stretches the limits of the biomedical model. On the other hand, because epidemiologists tend to rely on medical definitions and models of disease, their findings can be incorporated with little difficulty into traditional medicine. These studies may be used to locate special populations at risk or to isolate certain disease-producing conditions; this then permits a more direct test of biologically grounded etiological hypotheses. The same findings, however, may lend themselves to social theories of disease causation. In our discussions of several classic investigations of socioeconomic factors and mental illness, we indicated that two competing models have been proposed: social drift and social causation. These continue to remain viable alternatives.

Recent studies have attempted to confront this issue directly and have moved toward more complex explanations. In addition to Dunham's work, to which we referred earlier, another instructive example is the research of Turner and Wagenfeld on social mobility.[47] They focused specifically on two types of downward social mobility, namely, the occupational status difference between fathers and sons and changes within a subject's own occupational career. Overall, they found an overrepresentation of schizophrenics in the lowest occupational category, a finding consistent with other epidemiological studies. However, this clustering of schizophrenics could not be accounted for by the social class position of the subjects' fathers. Turner and Wagenfeld interpret this as a lack of support for the social causation hypothesis. The principal factor was that "potential," or preschizophrenic, people began their working careers at a lower point than might have been expected on the basis of their background; further, they were not as upwardly mobile as a comparable cohort of people who did not become schizophrenic.

Turner and Wagenfeld distinguish between two processes of downward mobility: social drift, where people move downward within their own occupational careers, and social selection, a failure ever to attain higher levels. Their analyses lead them to conclude ". . . that social selection accounts, in largest measure, for the downward shift, with social drift making a relatively minor contribution."[48]

Despite the more recent evidence from such studies as Dunham's and Turner and Wagenfeld's, some reviewers continue to find the evidence for the social causation model relatively more convincing. For example, Kohn rejects the social drift hypothesis as an adequate explanation, arguing: "The evidence on this issue is far from unequivocal, but it seems to me that the bulk of it argues against this hypothesis providing a sufficient explanation of the class–schizophrenia relationship."[49] Others have suggested that issues of etiology must await the resolution of difficult methodological problems. Thus, Dohrenwend concludes that ". . . the substantive issue of social causation vs. social selection must yield precedence to resolution of the central unsolved problem of psychiatric epidemiology – the measurement of untreated psychological disorder."[50]

The complexity of the problem of interpretation has become clear after forty years of research on the sociocultural contexts of mental illness. Simple answers should not have been expected. With hindsight, it is too easy to fault investigators from the social sciences who attempted to apply their concepts and models of ecological structure, of community, and of socioeconomic status to the understanding of a medical psychiatric problem. In part, they took too much for granted in relying on psychiatric theories and diagnoses. In a strict sense, they were provided with their dependent variables by a psychiatry rooted in a biomedical tradition. The research objective appeared to be relatively straightforward: Find the social correlates significantly associated with the occurrence of mental illness.

In many respects, this task has been accomplished by studies in psychiatric epidemiology, as illustrated by the small sample we have selected for review. But the major accomplishment has been the opening up of new questions, rather than the closing of old ones, the elaboration of the complexity of the problem rather than its simplification. There are two more recent directions in research and theory that are particularly relevant to the newer, more complex formulations of the problem and that merit special attention: the role of the family in the relationship between larger social contexts and individual illness, and the effects of large-scale, broad currents of socioeconomic stress such as unemployment.

The family goes unmentioned in the early Faris and Dunham study, appears in shadowy form in Hollingshead and Redlich's analysis of social class life-styles, and is buried among a variety of measures of community integration–disintegration in the Stirling County study. In Dunham's more recent work,[51] although still not the object of direct study, the family plays a more critical role. In his social sorting and selection model, Dunham proposes that families with adequate resources are able to protect their children from both social and personal stresses, and are less likely to have children who end up in treatment contexts diagnosed as schizophrenic. Children in families with fewer resources are more vulnerable to these stresses, tend to drift out of their family and community contexts, and are downwardly mobile, both occupationally and residentially. Dunham argues that this complex sorting process produces the disproportionate clustering of schizophrenics in lower socioeconomic positions. His model suggests the potential importance of family studies, to which we turn in the next section.

Socioeconomic conditions have a temporal dimension as well as a structural one. Not only are individuals distributed along social gradients of income, status, and opportunity, with some groups getting more of the benefits and resources than others, but the society itself goes through periods of bad times and good times. This historical–temporal dimension was ignored in earlier epidemiological studies, but its relevance is obvious, once it has been brought to our attention, whichever model of causation we may adopt. Recent work on this topic has demonstrated the effects of cycles of unemployment on rates of mental illness; it will be reviewed and discussed in Chapter 3.

Family interaction processes and schizophrenia

Epidemiologic texts and reports do not usually include information on or analyses of family characteristics or processes. The individual is the standard unit of epidemiologic analysis; characteristics of individuals – presence or absence of illness, class position, and so on – are summed and aggregated into population rates which are then subjected to statistical analyses. As we have noted, the family has sometimes entered into interpretive models proposed as explanations of epidemiologic findings.

Our review of studies in psychiatric epidemiology has focused on several different types of context: ecological units, communities, and social strata. Clearly, the family is another significant social context. Research on the family is based on the interests and problems of clinical psychiatry. One prominent line of psychiatric theory, psychoanalytic theory and its variants, has emphasized the centrality of early family relationships in personality development and the connections between difficulties in the former and disturbances in the latter. More recently, clinical practitioners and researchers have recognized the importance of current family relationships in the lives of patients, for example, in instigating and sustaining episodes of illness.

In many important respects, the methods and concepts used in family studies contrast sharply with those of psychiatric epidemiology. Nonetheless, in the present context, we think it important to take note of an important similarity between epidemiologic and family studies, namely, that they both tend to rely on the biomedical definition of illness. There are some exceptions, but on the whole, family researchers begin with defined and diagnosed patients. They then look for characteristics of families that are associated with the occurrence of illness, and that might distinguish these families from others in which illness is not present. This is much the same approach taken by epidemiologists searching for correlates, in communities or populations, of different rates of illness. In both instances, the findings are added on to the previous description of the illness, a description provided by the biomedical model. We would expect, however, that the specific focus on internal family functioning would lead to different interpretive models and to a different set of problems for critically assessing alternative models than those we found in reviewing epidemiological studies.

Mishler and Waxler's study[52] illustrates one approach to the study of families as social contexts. They compared interaction styles in families with a diagnosed schizophrenic member, that is, a young adult child, with families whose members had no history of psychiatric problems. They based their work on theories of family relationships and schizophrenia that hypothesized specific ways of interacting and communicating in families that had etiological significance for the development of schizophrenia.[53]

Applying methods of experimental social psychology to the study of small group interactions, Mishler and Waxler used a procedure that generated discussions within a family triad of parents and one of their children; in one experimental session, the child was the diagnosed schizophrenic patient and in another session the child was one of the patient's well siblings of the same sex. These family discussions were carefully tape recorded, transcribed, and scored for a large number of variables denoting different features of language and interaction. The design included a control group of normal families in which there was no history of psychiatric hospitalization of any member. Finally, the study included families of acute and chronic schizophrenic patients, that is, patients with good and poor premorbid histories.

Only a summary of the principal findings of this study will be provided here. Mishler and Waxler grouped the large number of interaction measures into a set of five clusters, based on clinically derived hypotheses regarding special features of interaction in families of schizophrenics. These clusters were expressiveness of positive and negative feelings; strategies of control and power; disrupted or nonfluent speech, such as hesitations and repetitions; and degree of responsiveness to or acknowledgment of others.

Overall, the researchers found that the ways in which individuals talked with each other in normal families were markedly different on a variety of measures from the ways in which families with schizophrenic members talked with each other. A number of findings were consistent with clinically based hypotheses. For example, members of normal families were more responsive to and attentive to each other's contributions to the discussion than were members of patient families; relatives of poor premorbid patients were particularly low on these measures. Other findings appeared to be inconsisitent with earlier reports. For example, the investigators had expected members of normal families to be most fluent and orderly in their speech patterns, that is, to have a low frequency of speech fragments, incomplete sentences, hesitations, and pauses. The findings showed a significant difference in the opposite direction. This led to a reinterpretation of these features of speech as serving an adaptive function. That is, these apparent disruptions in speech allow for the introduction of new information, provide opportunities for changes and shifts in the discussion, and permit movement and development within the family discussion. At the other pole of relatively nondisrupted speech, family discussions approach a level of ritualistic speech, a pattern that is nonadaptive and rigid, allowing for little possibility of change and development. Families of good premorbid schizophrenic patients had the most controlled and orderly speech patterns, and this was interpreted as evidence of a more rigid and nonadaptive style of family relationships.

In addition to these and other specific findings, Mishler and Waxler found that families of good premorbid patients tended to be more different from normal families, that is, differed significantly on many more variables, than families of poor premorbid patients. This general tendency was inconsistent with initial expectations that families of the "sickest" patients, that is, those with a longer history of symptoms and a poorer prognosis, would show the most pathology in communication. The findings suggest an alternate model, namely, that the presence of early pathological signs in a child may require little pathology in family relationships for schizophrenia to develop, but where such early signs were absent schizophrenia would develop only in the context of a more severely disturbed family system.[54]

One other general finding is worth noting. Differences between patient and normal families were most significant when the comparison included discussions where the schizophrenic child was present. Although parents of patients did not change radically in their ways of interacting from the situation with their schizophrenic child to that with his or her well sibling, they changed enough for differences between them and the normal control parents to become more prominent and significant. What appears to happen is a slight exaggeration of their general style and a reduction in variability of their behavior when with their schizophrenic child. In other words, they behave like themselves, only more so, when with their schizophrenic child.

The differences between family studies and epidemiological research are apparent – in specific methods and variables, as well as in the types of theories proposed. However, we would like to indicate some similarities in problems of interpretation faced by these different approaches, because these problems reflect a shared reliance on the biomedical definition of illness. In Mishler and Waxler's study, as in other studies of relationships between family characteristics and illness, the biomedical definition of the illness serves as the basis for the work in the same way that it does in epidemiology. Thus, Mishler and Waxler drew their sample of cases from patients admitted to a psychiatric hospital and diagnosed, through routine psychiatric procedures, as schizophrenic. Further, their classification of patients as having good or poor premorbid histories was based on a review of patients' hospital records.

Mishler and Waxler propose and compare three alternative frameworks of interpretation, that is, different approaches to the explanation of their empirical findings.[55] They refer to these as etiological, responsive, and situational models of interpretation. The first model assumes that the specific features of interaction distinguishing patient families from normal control families antedated the appearance of schizophrenia; these features had causal or etiological significance. For example, this model suggests that the relatively low rate of responsiveness in poor premorbid families was a general family style, may have mystified and confused the child, made it difficult for him or her to assess adequately both inner feelings and the expectations or feelings of others, and thus led into a schizophrenic process.

The second, responsive model assumes that the direction of causality was from child to parent rather than from parent to child. That is, the specific and distinctive styles of interaction found in patient families developed in response to the strange and unpredictable behavior of a schizophrenic child. In terms of this model, the rigid and controlled style found in "good premorbid" families might reflect the defensive reaction of parents suddenly confronted with bizarre and disturbing behavior of an acutely psychotic child.

Finally, the third, situational model focuses on the possibility that the social and institutional process through which a family member has been formally diagnosed and defined as schizophrenic has affected how all family members behave with each other. That is, diagnosis, hospitalization, and treatment of a child as schizophrenic has changed the family; behaviors observed in the experimental situation reflect these changes in their relationship to psychiatric treatment systems. Their behaviors are not simply responsive to a child's symptoms but are the consequences of the labeling of the child as schizophrenic, the associated labeling of the family as including a schizophrenic, and the involvement of the family with the psychiatric treatment system.

In reviewing their findings, Mishler and Waxler pose the question of which of these alternative models provides the most adequate explanation. Their problem is similar to the one we have encountered before in trying to assess the relative adequacy of social drift and social causation hypotheses for the empirical association between social class and rates of mental illness. As was true in the case of the social drift versus social causation argument, the comparison of etiological, responsive, and situational models is inconclusive. The inconclusiveness results from the fact that although the models differ from each other primarily in terms of the assumed temporal ordering of family processes and schizophrenia, the actual sequence of these events cannot be determined from the study because observations of family behavior were made after the patient's illness had already developed and been diagnosed.

This problem of interpretation is now widely recognized in family studies. However, the solution is difficult and not yet in hand. To the point is the fact that all of the fifty-seven direct-observation studies of families summarized by Jacob,[56] in one of the most recent of several reviews of family research, collected the observations after the appearance, recognition, and diagnosis of some form of psychiatric disturbance in the child member of the family.

This problem of interpreting the direction of causal relationships is a general one in cross-sectional studies, unique neither to family studies nor to other research on schizophrenia; we have already noted its analogue in the social drift–social causation debate in psychiatric epidemiology. Several new methodologies and types of research design have been proposed as approaches to the solution of the problem. Waxler,[57] for example, used an experimental paradigm of "artificial" families in which parents of a schizophrenic adolescent interacted with a normal child and parents of a normal child interacted with a schizophrenic child. The aim of the study was to isolate and to compare more directly whether a schizophrenic child influenced the behavior of normal parents in ways that led them to act more like the parents of schizophrenics, as the responsive model would predict, or whether parents of schizophrenics would influence normal children to behave like schizophrenics, as the etiological model would predict. The complex findings provide little support for either of these models. Waxler concludes that ". . . the most consistent pattern in the findings supports a facilitating effect of normal parents upon the cognitive performance of schizophrenic children." And, further: "Within the limited domain of the present measures, we have found little evidence that shows disruptive effects of schizophrenic parents on a normal child and only minor evidence that the presence of a schizophrenic child disrupts cognitive performances of normal parents."[58]

A second research model, which has become prominent in recent years, involves the selection of samples that are of high risk for the development of schizophrenia. In these studies, subjects are selected either on the basis of attributes hypothesized as related to the later appearance of schizophrenia, for example, disturbed adolescents in outpatient treatment, or on the basis of family variables such as the presence of diagnosed schizophrenia in one of the parents. These are longitudinal panel designs in which the selected sample of subjects and families are followed over time. The aim is to determine whether there are variables that antedate the appearance of schizophrenia and that distinguish between those at high risk who develop the illness and those who do not. This is new work, and definitive findings are not yet available.[59]

Yet another direction in which investigators have moved, given the methodological difficulties of disentangling the temporal relationship of family patterns and the development of illness, is toward a reconceptualization of the problem. Rather than limiting their concern to the potential etiological role of family processes, they now propose that families may play a role in maintaining and, perhaps, exacerbating the illness. Jacob's statement, that ". . . most family investigators would suggest that there are definable family patterns and processes which are crucial to understanding the etiology, development and maintenance of abnormal behavior. . .,"[60] is an example of such an expanded perspective within which family studies remain significant even if the problem of temporal ordering cannot be resolved. In a similar vein, the authors of a special summary report of many different types of studies of schizophrenia conclude their section on family studies with the comment that their failure ". . . to provide an answer to the cause–effect question is much less critical" than their contribution ". . . in extending our descriptive horizons beyond the individual patient and thereby focusing attention on, and greatly increasing our understanding of, the broader social context within which schizophrenia develops."[61]

These new approaches in methodology and in the conceptualization of the family's role continue to depend on the biomedical model in that the psychiatric diagnosis of schizophrenia marks the beginning for both empirical and interpretive work. We shall discuss alternative approaches in a later chapter on the social construction of illness, where social processes involved in the "labeling" of persons as schizophrenic, or ill in other ways, will be examined.

Conclusion

We began this review of epidemiologic and family studies of mental illness with Hippocrates' recommendation to examine the "mode in which inhabitants live'' in order to understand the nature and significance of illness. In our critique of the biomedical model, we argued that modern scientific medicine has neglected the social contexts of patients and their illnesses. The studies discussed in this chapter represent an effort to redress this neglect and thereby contribute to a fuller understanding of illness.

The selection and organization of studies for review reflected additional considerations. It seems especially important, in introducing health scientists and practitioners to work on these topics, to distinguish among different types of social contexts and to provide, in addition to a summary of findings, a critical perspective within which this work might be understood and evaluated. Ecological units, communities, social classes, and families are different types of social context; we hoped, through a detailed and separate examination of studies directed to each of these contexts, to avoid oversimplification of the problem. There is, of course, no reason to expect that forms of social and cultural organization and their effects would be any less complex than the structure and functioning of a biological organism. Yet this work is too often presented in capsule form in such a way that a student may learn only that social class is associated with schizophrenia, but the underlying mechanisms that generate such a relationship remain obscure and mysterious.

This mystery interferes with effective incorporation into the theory and practice of medicine of such findings, and of the approach and questions that motivate these studies. The facts, that is, the empirical findings, remain alien and undigested. They are referred to casually, in passing, but do not significantly affect the clinical conception of illness or orientations to care and treatment. We have been concerned, therefore, not only with presenting certain findings but with ''demystifying'' their meaning.

To this end, we undertook in each instance a critical examination of methodological problems and alternative theories that have been proposed to account for the findings. We recognize the hazards of such an approach, namely, that the problems might appear to be so formidable and the explanations so inconclusive that the work itself might be dismissed as of little immediate value or significance. Nonetheless, it seemed to us that this risk was worth taking. Unless health professionals learn how to be informed and critical at the same time, and until they come to understand the questions as well as the answers, findings from such studies will continue to remain peripheral to their work and thought.

Although we restricted our attention to studies of mental illnesses, we believe that our analyses apply generally to epidemiological and family studies of somatic illnesses. The problems faced by investigators and the methods used are essentially the same whether the disease be schizophrenia, diabetes, hypertension, or cancer. There is one advantage to our focusing on several classic studies of mental illness, which we tried to exploit in our discussion: They include a more explicit recognition and conceptualization of different types of social contexts and, as well, an effort to develop and compare alternative models of explanation. This has allowed us to explore and clarify modes of relationship between rates of illness and social contexts and to raise questions about this relationship, which must be asked about all such studies, regardless of type of illness.

One other feature of our general approach requires further comment, although it has been noted. The text is arranged as four pairs of chapters, or sections, plus an introduction and concluding chapter. These sections are progressively differentiated from each other by the degree of adherence to the biomedical model of the studies reviewed in each section. This organization will allow us to present a number of alternative approaches within the general framework of the social and behavioral sciences. We have suggested that epidemiologic and family studies, as different as they are from each other in specific methods, concepts, and findings, share a reliance on the biomedical definition of illness. This is evidenced in investigators' acceptance of "cases" for study, as such cases are provided through standard and routine medical–psychiatric procedures of diagnosis and treatment. Further, they generally adopt biological models of illness. Although their search for the social correlates of illness leads epidemiologists and family researchers outside of traditional medical–psychiatric boundaries, the central problem to which these studies are directed, that is, the understanding of diagnosed illness, remains framed within the biomedical perspective.

Close adherence to the biomedical model has restricted the potential significance of much epidemiologic research for our understanding of the social meanings of illness. In our earlier critique of the biomedical model, we suggested a number of problems with the assumption of illness as deviation from normality, such as differences in the range of normal variability in different populations and cross-cultural variation in definitions of health and illness. We noted there that epidemiologic research might be particularly relevant to the task of restoring the social contexts of patients and their illnesses, contexts that were stripped away by the biomedical assumptions about illness. Although the studies reviewed in this chapter do serve to bring social variables back into the model, they do not directly address these basic assumptions. This restriction is not inherent to epidemiologic methods but reflects how questions have been formulated and investigated. Epidemiologic studies could be designed to examine problems of population variability in definitions and occurrences of different types of illness, but on the whole, this has not been done.

In later sections, we shall review other approaches and studies that depart in significant ways from the biomedical assumptions of illness. The following chapter is, however, linked directly to the concerns of the present one; it provides an exploration in depth of the relationship to mental illness of the social context of unemployment.

Notes

1. From Hippocrates, "On airs, waters, and places." Quoted in MacMahon, B., Pugh, T. F., and Ipsen, J. *Epidemiologic Methods*. Boston: Little, Brown, 1960, p. IX.
2. Dubos, R. *Mirage of Health*. New York: Anchor Books, 1961, chap. 5.
3. Ibid., pp. 120–30. See also McKeown, T., and Lowe, C. R. *An Introduction to Social Medicine*. Philadelphia: F. A. Davis, 1966. Studies of relationships between health levels and socioeconomic change will be discussed in Chapter 8.
4. McNeill, W. *Plagues and Peoples*. New York: Doubleday, 1976.
5. MacMahon et al. *Epidemiologic Methods*, p. 3.
6. Ibid., chap. 2.
7. For a review of early epidemiological research, see Cooper, B., and Morgan, H. G. *Epidemiological Psychiatry*. Springfield, IL: C. C. Thomas, 1973.
8. *Bibliography: Epidemiology of Mental Disorders, 1966–8*. Washington, DC: U.S. Government Printing Office, 1970 (NCMHI Publication No. 5030); and 1969–70. Washington, DC: U.S. Government Printing Office, 1973 (DHEW Publication No. HSM: 73-9043).
9. Faris, R. E. L., and Dunham, H. W. *Mental Disorders in Urban Areas*. Chicago: University of Chicago Press, 1939 (Phoenix Paperback Edition, 1965), p. IX.
10. Ibid., p. 21.
11. Park, R. E., and Burgess, E. W. *The City*. Chicago: University of Chicago Press, 1925.
12. Faris and Dunham, *Mental Disorders in Urban Areas*, pp. 35–7.
13. Ibid., p. 36, Map VI, and p. 53, Map XI.
14. Ibid., pp. 55–6.
15. Ibid., p. 109.
16. U.S. Bureau of the Census. *Statistical Abstract of the United States: 1971*, Washington, DC: U.S. Government Printing Office, 1971.
17. Lee, E. S. "Socio-economic and migration differentials in mental disease, New York State, 1949–51," *Milbank Memorial Fund Quarterly*, 1963, XLI (3):249–68, p. 267.
18. Faris and Dunham, *Mental Disorders in Urban Areas*, p. 4.
19. Ibid., p. 163.
20. Ibid., p. 164.
21. Ibid., pp. 173–74.
22. Dunham, H. W. *Community and Schizophrenia: An Epidemiological Analysis*. Detroit, MI: Wayne State University Press, 1965.
23. Ibid., p. 256.
24. Ibid., p. 161.
25. Leighton, D. C., Harding, J. S., Macklin, D. B., Macmillan, A. M. and Leighton, A. H. *The Character of Danger: Psychiatric Symptoms in Selected Communities*. New York: Basic Books, 1963.
26. Ibid., p. 368.

27. Ibid., p. 369.
28. Ibid., p. 118.
29. Leighton, A. H. *My Name is Legion.* New York: Basic Books, 1959. Hughes, C. C., Tremblay, M., Rapoport, R. N., and Leighton, A. H. *People of Cove and Woodlot.* New York: Basic Books, 1960.
30. Leighton et al. *The Character of Danger,* Table XII-I, p. 326.
31. Ibid., Table XII-8, p. 345.
32. Kunitz, S. J. "Equilibrium theory in social psychiatry: the work of the Leightons," *Psychiatry,* 1970, *33*(3):312–28.
33. Leighton et al. *The Character of Danger,* p. 371.
34. Kunitz, "Equilibrium theory," p. 322.
35. Hollingshead, A. B., and Redlich, F. C. *Social Class and Mental Illness.* New York: John Wiley & Sons, 1958.
36. Ibid., p. 19.
37. Ibid., p. 11.
38. Ibid., p. 217.
39. See especially Kramer, M. "A discussion of the concepts of incidence and prevalence as related to epidemiologic studies of mental disorder," *American Journal of Public Health,* 1957, *47*:826–40. Miller, S. M., and Mishler, E. G. "Social class, mental illness, and American psychiatry: an expository review," *Milbank Memorial Fund Quarterly,* 1959, *37*(2):174–99. Mishler, E. G., and Scotch, N. A. "Sociocultural factors in the epidemiology of schizophrenia," *Psychiatry,* 1963, *26*:315–53.
40. Hollingshead and Redlich, *Social Class and Mental Illness,* p. 216.
41. Redlich, F. C. "Discussion of papers on ecology and epidemiology of mental illness," in *Symposium on Preventive and Social Psychiatry.* Walter Reed Army Institute of Research. Washington, DC: U.S. Government Printing Office, 1958, p. 199.
42. Hollingshead and Redlich, *Social Class and Mental Illness,* p. 247.
43. Dohrenwend, B. P. "Social status and psychological disorder: an issue of substance and an issue of method," *American Sociological Review,* 1966, *31*(1):14–34, p. 15.
44. Kohn, M. L. "The interaction of social class and other factors in the etiology of schizophrenia," *American Journal of Psychiatry,* 1976, *133*(2):177–80, p. 177.
45. Turner, R. J. "The epidemiological study of schizophrenia: a current appraisal," *Journal of Health and Social Behavior,* 1972, *18*:360–9, p. 364.
46. Mishler and Scotch, "Sociocultural factors in the epidemiology of schizophrenia," p. 326.
47. Turner, R. J. "Social mobility and schizophrenia," *Journal of Health and Social Behavior,* 1968, *9*:194–203. Turner, "The epidemiological study of schizophrenia." Turner, R. J., and Wagenfeld, M. O. "Occupational mobility and schizophrenia: an assessment of the social causation and social selection hypotheses," *American Sociological Review,* 1967, *32*(1):104–13.
48. Turner and Wagenfeld, "Occupational mobility and schizophrenia," p. 113.
49. Kohn, "The interaction of social class and other factors," p. 178.
50. Dohrenwend, "Social status and psychological disorder," p. 14.
51. Dunham, *Community and Schizophrenia.*
52. Mishler, E. G., and Waxler, N. E. *Interaction in Families.* New York: John Wiley & Sons, 1968.
53. For reviews of these theories, see Mishler, E. G., and Waxler, N. E., "Family interaction patterns and schizophrenia: a review of current theories," *Merrill-Palmer Quarterly,* 1965, *11*:269–315; also in Wechsler, H., Solomon, L., and Kramer, B. M. (Eds.). *Social Psychology and Mental Health.* New York: Holt, Rinehart & Winston, 1970. Mishler, E. G., and Waxler, N. E. (Eds.). *Family Processes and Schizophrenia: Theory and Selected Experimental Studies.* New York: Science House, 1968.

54. For a similar interpretation of families of schizophrenic children with and without soft neurological signs, see Goldfarb, W. *Childhood Schizophrenia*. Cambridge, MA: Harvard University Press, 1961.
55. Mishler and Waxler, *Interaction in Families;* and, Mishler, E. G., and Waxler, N. E., "Family interaction and schizophrenia: alternative frameworks of interpretation," in Rosenthal, D., and Kety, S. S. (Eds.). *The Transmission of Schizophrenia*. New York: Pergamon Press, 1968.
56. Jacob, T. "Family interaction in disturbed and normal families: a methodological and substantive review," *Psychological Bulletin,* 1975, *82*(1):33–65.
57. Waxler, N. E. "Parent and child effects on cognitive performance: an experimental approach to the etiological and responsive theories of schizophrenia," *Family Process,* 1974, *13*(1):1–22.
58. Ibid., pp. 19–20.
59. For reviews of this approach and of studies underway, see Garmezy, N. "Children at risk: the search for the antecedents of schizophrenia. Part I. Conceptual models and research methods," *Schizophrenia Bulletin,* Spring 1974, No. 8:14–92. Garmezy, N. "Children at risk: the search for the antecedents of schizophrenia. Part II: Ongoing research programs, issues, and intervention," *Schizophrenia Bulletin,* Summer 1974, No. 9:55–125. Goldstein, M. J., and Rodnick, E. H. "The family's contribution to the etiology of schizophrenia: current status," *Schizophrenia Bulletin,* Fall 1975, No. 14:48–63.
60. Jacob, "Family interaction," p. 33.
61. Mosher, L. R., and Feinsilver, D. *Special Report: Schizophrenia*. Washington, DC: U.S. Public Health Service Publication No. (HSM) 72-9007, 1971, p. 24.

3 Economic change and unemployment: contexts of illness

Ramsay Liem

Events of special concern to the field of medicine are as much products of everyday social life as they are biological outcomes. For this reason, the scientific foundations of medicine are most appropriately derived from the social as well as natural sciences. In this book this assumption is made regarding not only physicians' practices, behaviors associated with being a patient, and professional and lay ideas about illness, but also disease processes themselves. The preceding review of psychiatric epidemiology and family research has begun to develop the argument in support of this position. It has presented evidence that the risk of psychiatric disorder differs substantially among geographic areas and subgroups within the population according to their social, economic, and interpersonal characteristics. It is unlikely that these observations would have been made had research been guided solely by the narrow assumptions of a strict biomedical model as outlined in Chapter 1. Admittedly, studies of the social distribution of health and illness have not yet been able to identify the precise characteristics of areas or populations at high risk for different disorders or to resolve competing causal hypotheses. Nevertheless, they repeatedly associate high risk for a variety of illnesses with a composite picture of related social factors including social isolation, disintegration of social ties, limited economic resources, and pandemic stresses.

A continuing challenge for research in this area is to describe with more precision these broad social contexts of disorder, for example, to identify which conditions associated with one's social class position are especially significant correlates of incidence and prevalence rates for different illnesses. Related to this task is the even more difficult problem of understanding *how* disorder and social context are related, whether by direct social causation, pure biological selection, or, as is more likely, by substantially more complex processes.

The numerous research strategies employed at one time or another to resolve these issues attest to their intransigence. Our purpose in this chapter is to introduce several areas of related research that collectively

54

illustrate a somewhat different approach to clarifying the basic epidemiological findings. These studies make two distinct but related contributions. They pay special attention to one component of the broad social context of illness, the economic sector. They also suggest how global economic conditions may have an effect on individuals through the mediation of "stress."

The first of these two emphases departs from the practice common especially in epidemiological research of measuring only global characteristics of the social context or the individual's position within it. Such an approach is useful initially to demonstrate the existence of the social distribution of illness risk. However, it fails to inform about the underlying mechanisms that bring about socially patterned rates of disorder. What is needed first is to determine more precisely which *features* of the social context are most responsible for previously observed global relationships. For example, knowing that stratifying groups by income level as opposed to educational status produces more accurate predictions of high-risk groups helps to narrow the range of plausible explanatory hypotheses for the more general social class finding. Studies examining conditions within the economy that may affect health represent one source of information that may lead to sharper definition of the relevant social context of patienthood.

This type of research activity also falls within a broader area of work on socially induced stress as a link between life conditions and personal health. Although this chapter is not intended as a general introduction to the extensive literature on social stress and health, it offers one illustration of how a social stress model can be used to describe the dynamic relation between social context and illness risk or, more precisely, the state of the economy and illness risk. The discussion of this approach will maintain continuity with the previous chapter by focusing principally, though not exclusively, on the psychiatric consequences of economic conditions.

Large-scale economic change and psychiatric hospitalization

Readers familiar with the experiences of individuals and families during the Great Depression of the 1930s may readily suspect that the incidence and prevalence of psychiatric illness increased during that time. Two kinds of research have investigated this assumption. The first attempted to determine for whole communities whether or not differences or changes in the economic strength of particular areas were associated with psychological health as measured by standard indicators of psychiatric functioning such as hospital admissions. The second investigated families experiencing the hardships of unemployment and economic losses by using intensive case studies.

The first type of study reflects more of the epidemiologist's interest in large-scale social contexts of illness. It also has a growing number of contemporary advocates whose work has stimulated serious consideration of the state of the economy as having both health-sustaining and illness-promoting consequences. We shall begin by giving some attention to this type of work. Then we shall examine studies of family and individual response to economic change for clues about the processes underlying more global relationships observed between large-scale economic conditions and institutional measures of psychiatric well-being.

The primary objective of research on the psychiatric implications of large-scale economic conditions is to establish whether or not there is a correlation between the functioning of the economic system and the individual's psychological well-being. As in the tradition of psychiatric epidemiology, this objective indicates a willingness to entertain the possibility that the risk of psychiatric disorder is not only psychologically and biochemically grounded but also linked to broad socioeconomic conditions.

In one of the earliest studies in this area, Komora and Clark[1] attempted to assess the impact of the Great Depression on mental health through examination of concurrent changes in psychiatric hospital admissions for a one-year period (1933–4). The data in this research were the personal impressions of superintendents of psychiatric hospitals regarding the role of economic hardships in producing significant changes in levels of first admissions. Relying on reports from more than half of all state psychiatric facilities in the United States, the investigators report that approximately 60 percent of the hospitals experienced increases in first admissions related to economic conditions, whereas 30 percent showed no change or an overall decrease in admissions. The authors conclude from these findings that economic recession may be an important risk factor in psychological disorder. This observation, however, is at best a reasonable conjecture.

Two major problems strain the credibility of this conclusion. The first arises from the uncontrolled variability in the judgments of hospital superintendents regarding the extent to which individual admissions as well as overall changes in admission levels resulted from the influence of the Depression. At best these diagnostic and etiologic judgments were educated guesses. A second problem pertains to the lack of information about trends in yearly changes in admissions prior to the Depression. It is virtually impossible to estimate the true health impact of that major economic crisis without systematic information regarding admission levels prior to the Great Depression.

Subsequent investigations attempted to resolve the latter problem by extending the period of data collection as much as ten years before and after the Depression.[2] By and large these analyses of hospital records of psychiatric admissions produce a mixed set of results, in some instances supporting the hypothesis that severe economic hardships are associated with a rise in first admissions and, in others, challenging it. Some of this confusion may have been the result of wide variation in either the location or scope of the areas included in these studies, for example, East Coast versus Midwest, or citywide versus statewide versus national. The absence of comparability in the areas examined in these studies is particularly problematic because no measures of economic stability for the different locations were used. Thus, there may have been substantial variation in the degree of economic breakdown in each of the areas studied.

More recently, and probably as a result of the severe economic recession of the early 1970s, similar but more sophisticated research efforts have been reported. As a whole the findings from these studies make a strong argument for substantial correspondence between large-scale economic functioning and psychiatric first-admissions, although the findings are on occasion somewhat mixed.

The most detailed of these later studies has been reported by M. Harvey Brenner.[3] He examined annual levels of psychiatric first admissions to state and private hospitals and their relationships to a standard, overall indicator of economic strength, namely, total employment in manufacturing industries. The data Brenner collected were for the entire state of New York and covered a remarkably extended period of time, from 1852 to 1967. For the first time it became possible to look at changes in hospital admissions relative to a direct measure of economic growth and decline over a long enough span of time to detect general relationships. This investigator reasoned that if employment and admissions levels are consistently correlated over such a broad span of time and economic conditions, such a finding could not be limited only to special economic circumstances, for example, periods when economic recessions are especially severe. The research strategy also involved repeated tests of the relationship of changing employment levels to psychiatric first admissions using a large number of subpopulations of first admissions. Patients were grouped by such dimensions as age, educational level, diagnosis, and marital status.

The main pattern of findings from these analyses led Brenner to report that:

relations found for the 19th century led to the conclusion that regardless of any third variable that is independent of both economic changes and mental hospital admissions, the relation between changes in the economy and mental hospital admissions in New York state was continuous for 120 years.[4]

Controlling for age, sex, and diagnosis, Brenner found exceptionally strong correlations between admissions and employment levels for the majority of years for which data were available.[5] Correlations of $r = 0.80$ or better, for example, were not uncommon in the analyses. By and large, Brenner found that an upturn in the economy is quite predictably associated with a decrease in number of psychiatric first admissions. This basic inverse relationship, measured in several ways, was found to be strongest for males versus females, married persons versus single, widowed, or divorced individuals, middle aged adults versus youths or the elderly, and grammar school and college-educated people versus high school graduates.

The relation was strongest for people diagnosed as schizophrenic and manic-depressive, although substantial correlations were found for individuals with alcoholic psychosis and general paresis. On the other hand, rates of admissions for senile psychosis and involutional psychosis were observed to increase during periods of economic growth. Finally, of the male admissions, people between the ages of thirty-five and fifty-four showed the strongest inverse relation to changes in employment levels, whereas among females, the highest negative correlations were for women aged twenty-five to fifty-four.

What is most dramatic about these findings is the overall strength of the relationship observed and its consistency across a substantial number of different patient groups. Correlations as high as those reported by Brenner are seldom found in studies of psychiatric epidemiology. These results are even more noteworthy in view of the fact that they are based on longitudinal data extending back more than a century.

It is also apparent from the pattern of findings that the relationship observed between the economy and recorded cases of psychiatric disorder is quite complex. For some groups the relation is noticeably weak, and for others it is direct rather than inverse. Thus, although the overall consistency in these results suggests a dominant mechanism underlying the basic relation, it may not be an exclusive one. The presence of variation for some groups is an indication that there may be several distinct processes, each involving moderating or facilitating conditions linking the economy to psychiatric outcomes for different groups.

We shall return to a discussion of the implications of these and related findings shortly. Before we do so, however, it is important to note that several additional studies similar in design to the work of Brenner have been reported. To a significant degree these studies corroborate his findings. They also suggest that overall economic functioning may be associated with other aspects of health and well-being. In one recently reported study, for example, outpatient psychiatric admissions in a single catchment area were analyzed using unemployment rates from the *same* geographic region as the economic indicator.[6] Reasoning that psychological response to changes in overall unemployment rates is most likely to occur in less than a year's time, the investigators used monthly estimates of outpatient admissions and unemployment rates over a twenty-year period rather than annual estimates. They observed a similar but even stronger relationship between the status of the economy and psychiatric service utilization than the one first reported by Brenner. The pattern for male and female outpatients in this study also closely parallels Brenner's observation of a stronger psychiatric response to economic downturn by men as opposed to women.

The similarity of these findings to those reported by Brenner is especially significant in view of the different methods employed in this research. In the earlier work employment and psychiatric admissions were measured for the entire state of New York. The unbiquitous inverse correlations between them, therefore, indicate that psychiatric admissions throughout the state are likely to increase when statewide employment decreases. This "ecological" relationship, however, does not necessarily mean that *individuals* who lose their jobs are also those who ultimately seek psychiatric help. Although this is a plausible hypothesis, the methods used by Brenner do not permit this conclusion. In the research to which we are presently referring, the geographic unit is much smaller, a single mental-health catchment area. The investigator sought to increase the probability that the economic measure would be sensitive to the actual experiences with the economy encountered by the potential patient population. Even though this single-catchment-area procedure does not rule out the possibility that those experiencing economic losses will not be the same as those entering psychiatric hospitals, the data it produces add to our confidence that there may be a direct relationship between these events. The only adequate means for handling ecological correlations is to collect economic and psychiatric information for each individual rather than for a geographic area. In a later section we shall examine several studies employing such a procedure.

One additional point worth noting about this research is that unemployment and admissions data collected monthly appear to produce as strong if not stronger correlations than data collected annually. This comparative observation suggests that unemployment or other economic losses associated with a downturn in the economy may have relatively immediate psychological repercussions. This characteristic of economic events is consistent with the kind of temporal relationship commonly reported between crisis events and onset of psychological symptomatology in the more inclusive literature on crisis intervention.[7]

The emerging picture of a patterned community response of greater utilization of psychiatric services during periods of economic decline is modestly supported by two additional studies, one focusing on the Standard Metropolitan Area as the unit of analysis[8] and the other, on the state.[9] In the former, correlations in the area of $r = 0.70$ were observed between inpatient psychiatric first admissions and overall employment rates. In the latter study, only correlations for male first admissions confirmed the general pattern and then only to a moderate degree. Those for females were largely nonsignificant. Although there is no clearcut explanation for these differences, it may be noteworthy that the period of analysis in this study coincided with large-scale deinstitutionalization of state hospitals and a structural shift in the economy from manufacturing to service industries. These structural changes may have weakened the validity of the measures of employment in manufacturing industries and first admissions to state hospitals as representative of true overall economic functioning and need for psychiatric services.

In spite of some inconsistency in the findings from these studies, it is difficult to dismiss the strong suggestion they make that the macroeconomy has some bearing on overall patterns of utilization of psychiatric services. At the same time it would be unwarranted to assume that fluctuations in the economic system are specifically targeted to psychiatric outcomes. Although researchers have yet to devote substantial attention to other indicators of well-being in the population, some work has begun in this direction. One recent study[10] has reported higher levels of child abuse during periods of overall economic tightening, and another[11] has found a strong relationship between economic change and suicide rates. What is particularly interesting about the latter finding is that suicide rates, in contrast to rates of psychiatric admissions, appear to increase not only during periods of economic decline but also during periods of significant growth. This finding is interpreted as demonstrating that economic change per se, whether for apparent gain or loss, can be disruptive in ways that lead to uncertainty and insecurity. The finding also lends itself to Durkheim's classic interpretation of the origins of the social rate of suicide.[12] In this work anomie, defined as a societal state of norm-lessness accompanying social change and instability, is a major contributor to suicide rates.

It should finally be noted that Brenner has recently extended his basic methodology to a broad range of indicators of well-being.[13] In a special study for the U.S. Congressional Joint Economic Committee, he used an array of economic indicators, weighting unemployment rates heavily, to examine relationships on a national scale between the economy and several health and social indicators. He found negative changes in the economy to be closely related on an annual basis to increases in total mortality rates, deaths from cardiovascular diseases, prevalence rates for cirrhosis, suicide rates, and rates of penal incarceration as well as rates of psychiatric first admissions. These data confirm the basic finding not only for a variety of negative outcomes but also for a very large geographic unit of analysis.

The problem of causality

The studies we have reviewed establish some confidence that a significant relationship exists between the state of the economy at large and standard indicators of mental health in the population. They provide us with a concrete set of referents for exploring how social context and illness vulnerability are related. At least four basic causal patterns are possible: Economic change causes illness; illness causes economic change; economic change and illness are mutually determining to some degree; and economic change and illness are both determined by a common third factor such as wars, population changes, and the like.

None of these alternatives can be ruled out definitively on the basis of existing data, especially the explanation involving reciprocal causation. However, there are several reasons for favoring the position that economic change as measured by overall rates of employment or unemployment is more a determinant than an outcome of mental illness measured in terms of service use.

First, it is difficult to conceive how the relatively small population of people who experience a first admission to a psychiatric hospital could create a set of circumstances leading to a decline in overall employment levels. This point is especially apparent if we consider that some research has used total rates of employment or unemployment for the national economy, figures that are hard to imagine as affected by changes in the population due to psychiatric hospitalization. Second, all studies report either concurrent changes in unemployment levels and psychiatric admissions or, more commonly, a delayed reaction where a downturn in the economy always *precedes* an upturn in admissions. Although this "lagged" relationship is not definitive evidence that the economic variable has greater causal significance, it clearly lends itself to this interpretation. If the critical economic factor is unemployment itself, and not some other correlated economic disturbance, this conclusion is even more likely to be valid.[14]

Each of these arguments on the side of economic change as a determinant of psychiatric disorder, however, would be negated if the indicators of both economic change and mental illness were systematically responsive to some third, yet unspecified, factor. An obvious example is the event of war, which might trigger both an economic recession and an increase in psychiatric hospital rolls. The evidence against this position, albeit indirect, is that in those studies covering substantial spans of time, the basic relationship is not limited to particular blocks of years where such "third-factor" determinants might be expected to occur, such as war years. In fact, where data are available, it does not appear that the economy–mental illness relationship is noticeably more robust for the three periods of time during this century when other events might be expected to have had most influence on this relation, that is, the years of World Wars I and II and the Great Depression.

The causal links between macroeconomic change and psychiatric disorder are probably not limited to only one of the four alternatives we have posed. Causality in the social world rarely operates in a simple, unidirectional, and linear fashion. For the remainder of this chapter, however, we shall assume that some of the variation in psychiatric hospital admissions rates is produced by negative changes in the economy. This is done with the understanding that there may well be other causal pathways that deserve equal attention.

Unemployment as an intervening event

How, then, are psychiatric admissions influenced by the state of the economy? What is the underlying process? Some investigators have taken the event of unemployment as an obvious starting point for examining this process. Although only one of the many possible contributing factors, unemployment is the event most directly and consistently reflected in the economic indicators used in the studies previously cited. Where multiple indicators have been used, unemployment or employment rates have been by far the best predictors of health outcomes.[15] Furthermore, the pattern of findings reported by Brenner and others for different patient subgroups indicate greatest sensitivity to economic change among those groups either most likely to experience job loss during an economic downturn (e.g., males versus females) or to suffer the greatest material losses from unemployment (e.g., males between the ages of thirty-five and fifty-four, presumably at the height of their careers; or college-educated males, who probably occupy the higher-income and -status positions). Those groups least likely to be directly vulnerable to unemployment (e.g., youths and the elderly – those diagnosed as senile psychotic or involutional melancholia) actually experience substantial increases in psychiatric admissions during economic upturns rather than declines.

This reading of longitudinal studies of economic and mental-health indicators finds another source of support in the work of several early researchers conducted during the Great Depression. A common theme in these richly detailed case studies is the loss of self-esteem following unemployment and an accompanying decline in contact with others outside the home.[16] The latter observation is reminiscent of Faris and Dunham's hypothesis that social isolation is an especially important characteristic of urban areas with high rates of psychiatric hospitalization.[17]

Efforts have also been made to locate more precisely the period of most significant psychological disorganization following unemployment. Several investigators note that the threat to esteem and security immediately following job loss is often less severe than the ensuing despair that typically follows an initial period of highly motivated job hunting.[18] They argue that it is failure to find reemployment after this temporary optimism and continuing depletion of financial resources that can lead to such outcomes as prolonged depression, loss of occupational identity, apathy, and disorganization in time and place. The latter observation has also been noted in a recent study of forty unemployed men.[19] The investigator reports that the loss of a stable, daily routine for these men frequently appeared to disrupt their ability to judge the passage of time, not only in days and weeks, but also minutes and hours. She believes that the work routine provides one standard by which other daily activities are ordered. When this structure is eliminated, the absence of a behavioral routine is accompanied by distortions in the perception of time.

This observation suggests a more general consideration or guideline for examining job loss as a precursor of psychiatric disorder. The basis for unemployment as a stressful life event is to be found in the contributions of work to the personal and social requirements of the individual. From this point of view, unemployment derives its stress value from the negation of socially and culturally grounded experiences and goods associated with working. One widely accepted formulation of these functions of work in this society describes work as providing the basis for sustaining material life, organizing and structuring daily activity, and serving as a primary resource for meaningful life experiences.[20] To this list we would add access to social relationships and, more broadly, a sense of membership in society. It is our primary dependence on work for these goods that makes unemployment a devastating experience that can threaten health. The following quotation captures this sentiment well:

By forcing him to come to grips with his environment, with his livelihood at stake, it [work] confronts man with the actuality of his personal capacity – to exercise judgement, to achieve concrete and specific results. It gives him a continuous account of his correspondence between outside reality and the inner perception of that reality as well as an account of the accuracy of his appraisal of himself. . . .In short a man's work does not satisfy his material needs alone. In a very deep sense it gives him a measure of his sanity.[21]

The argument that unemployment is an aspect of the mechanism accounting for the relation between the macroeconomy and mental illness is, thus, both empirically and conceptually based. Although there are without doubt other factors that determine this relation, it would make little sense not to give some priority to job loss as one point of departure for explaining this observation.

Those who propose that unemployment may serve to mediate between the economy and mental illness in the population tend also to adopt a particular set of basic assumptions about how the social context influences health. We shall examine next this general explanatory model and its application to the particular circumstance of job loss.

Social stress as an explanatory model

Discussions of unemployment as a threat to health invariably make extensive use of the concept of stress. In medical circles stress generally refers to unusually high or sustained levels of activation in the body often associated with the neuroendocrine and cardiovascular systems. The source of activation is generally assumed to be a physical stimulus external to the body, for example, dramatic shifts in the temperature to which the individual is exposed or uncommonly intense auditory stimulation. The recognition that stress defined in these terms may play a role in the etiology of disease is due in large part to the early work of such principal contributors as Hans Selye[22] and Walter Cannon.[23] These pioneers of stress research focused mainly on physiological responses to physical stressors, for example, the influence of physical restraint on secretion of adrenalin in dogs and mice. Extensive laboratory experimentation along these lines indicates the presence of a generalized stress reaction in many higher-order species, comprising anticipatory, protective physiological responses that appear to aid the organism in resisting diverse types of stressors. Selye observed that if these responses are prolonged by unyielding stressors, "diseases of adaptation" can occur in which elevated levels of hormonal secretions result in a variety of cardiovascular, renal, and musculoskeletal diseases.

More recently a social stress version of this model has been explored. Greater attention has been paid to social rather than physical stressors, and investigators have been equally interested in psychological (e.g., anxiety) and physiological responses.[24] Although the current evidence is equivocal regarding how such responses may be induced by social circumstances,[25] the hypothesis that some social experiences do in fact function as stressors has considerable currency at the present time.

One example of recent research guided by this point of view is the study of stressful life events. For our purposes this relatively new area of research both illustrates the social stress perspective and provides some limited findings bearing on the issue of unemployment as a link between the economy and health. Life events research begins with the hypothesis that everyday life frequently exposes the individual to a wide variety of stressful experiences that are potential contributors to the onset or maintenance of illness. A related assumption is that the individual's coping resources can be taxed by continual exposure to such events. Under such conditions exhaustion of resistance capacities increases the person's vulnerability to physiological and psychological dysfunction.[26]

In theory many different kinds of events could precede or even "trigger" an episode of psychological illness. The birth of a baby, loss of a job, and death of a loved one are examples of life events that often appear in the records of psychiatric and medical patients. More systematic investigations of the impact of such experiences have been aided by the development of instruments to assess the occurrence of critical life events. A crude taxonomy of critical life experiences based on Adolph Meyer's life chart[27] served as the initial basis for developing what is now the most widely used measure of stressful life events.[28] The life chart contains a wide variety of commonly occurring experiences that Meyer observed often accompany the onset of psychological problems. It was used by Thomas Holmes and Richard Rahe as a guide to examine numerous clinical records of psychiatric and medical patients and to conduct large numbers of patient interviews. The primary objective was to identify common life events in these populations that regularly preceded the onset of illness. Forty-three such events were subsequently chosen on the basis of clinical judgment and comprise the primary life events measure. These events can be crudely grouped as entrance and exit events (birth of a child, death of a family member), events within and outside the individual's control (increased problems with spouse, injury to spouse), and desirable and undesirable events (promotion at work, loss of a job). They can also be grouped according to the substantive domains of work, school, family, and personal life.

Research employing this measure or one of several recent modifications indicates a moderate but consistent relationship between prior exposure to life events and the appearance of such physical disorders as myocardial infarction, respiratory illness, and general physical symptomatology. Other studies have noted a similar relationship between the experience of life events and basic physiological reactivity in the form of elevated levels of epinephrine, serum cholesterol, and the cathecholamines.[29] Psychological reactions to life events include depression, anxiety, schizophrenia, psychiatric hospitalization, and general psychiatric symptomatology.[30] In much of this work the basic research strategy is to use retrospective reports of life events that occur over a year's time to predict symptomatology measured either at the same time that life events are assessed or at a future point in time.

There is a remarkable degree of consistency in the overall findings from studies of this sort, about which even the general public is now informed. Nevertheless, there is some controversy regarding a number of issues. One unresolved question pertains to the etiological significance of life events. Some investigators point out that current research designs do not permit us to rule out the possibility that illness precedes life events and influences both their recall and the likelihood of their having occurred in the first place.[31] For example, if you cannot concentrate on your work because of crippling migraine headaches, you may run a high risk of losing your job. A second issue is more conceptual and involves inconsistent findings regarding the appropriate method for scaling life events. Some argue that any event that creates demands for readjustment in one's life circumstances can be stressful.[32] Others provide data indicating that events which are commonly perceived as undesirable or threatening and not simply as making demands for life change are the best predictors of illness.[33] This debate resembles the question raised by the research on suicides cited earlier about whether or not *any* change in unemployment rates, not just increases, can be accompanied by increased numbers of suicides. As one contributor has suggested, the resolution of this issue partly requires taking into consideration the fact that different etiological processes are associated with different health outcomes.[34] Thus, psychological impairments involving a large component of anxiety may be more responsive to any event that presses for life readjustments, whereas clinical levels of depression may be more susceptible to life events that involve unwanted separations from important others.

These opposing views of what makes an event stressful have direct implications for how we view any particular event, such as unemployment, as a potential source of stress. The life-change argument suggests that unemployment need not be perceived as undesirable in order for it to induce stress. It need only create demands for readjustment. On the other hand, others would consider job loss a risk factor for disease mainly when its occurrence is unwanted or perhaps involuntary. In fact, with this particular event it is highly likely that both criteria for social stress are met in a majority of instances. Our discussion of work as a primary source of multiple resources for the individual implies that unemployment often creates significant demands for life change and in many cases substantial threat. Unemployed workers often report both major changes in their lifestyles over the time they are without work and pervasive insecurity and fear. Which of these factors is most critical for the experience of stress remains a question to be resolved by future research and more refined methodologies that take into account the variability in etiological processes for different disorders.

Life events research primarily gives us a concrete example of the use of a social stress model in research that attempts to specify broadly some of the social context of illness. Few studies have compared the relative importance of different domains or types of life events for predicting stress reactions. Most research focuses instead on the cumulative effects of a broad range of external stressors; it treats them as different only in the amount of threat or life change they induce. Three investigations, however, do make some distinctions among categories of events predictive of psychiatric symptomatology in ways especially relevant to our principal interest in the problem of unemployment. One research group, in a follow-up of an earlier study, examined people whose "life event–symptom" scores deviated from the usual pattern.[35] They discovered that persons with few life events and yet substantial symptom scores were more often single or divorced *and* unemployed or dissatisfied with their jobs than "high-event–low-symptom" individuals. More to the point Coates, Moyer, and Wellman found that 61.5 percent of subjects experiencing a demotion or loss of job reported clinically significant levels of psychiatric distress compared to 22 percent of those not experiencing demotion or job loss.[36]

Similar factors were also found to distinguish rates of psychiatric disability and suicide among a group of more than three thousand urban workers.[37] People in this sample who missed at least one month of work for psychiatric reasons were more likely than others to have had thirty or more consecutive days of unemployment or a change in jobs during the preceding year. This group also had an unusually large number of suicides and suicide attempts.

The data from these studies are, thus, supportive of the hypothesis that job loss can be a stressful experience with implications for psychiatric disorder. Very little direct attention has been paid in these studies, however, to controlled comparisons of the predictive power of different domains of events in relation to specific health outcomes. Consequently, for our purposes life events research remains primarily a body of work that demonstrates the viability of a general model of social stress as one way of describing the relation between social context and health. Secondarily, that unemployment in particular may affect health by generating or exacerbating stress is suggested by its frequent appearance as one of a number of work-related events that discriminate levels of psychiatric symptomatology.

Unemployment and its health consequences

The data from life events studies are one modest source of evidence that unemployment can have significant effects on health and, thus, serve as a link between changes in the economy and psychiatric illness. They are not, however, the kind of findings that one would choose for the sole defense of this proposition. Besides the early Depression research that we have already cited, only one full-scale study of the health consequences of unemployment has been reported in the recent literature, although several others are currently in progress.[38] The one exception is a longitudinal study by Stanislav Kasl and Sidney Cobb with a number of other contributors.[39] These researchers made considerable effort to examine a variety of health outcomes in a large number of blue-collar workers laid off as the result of two major plant closings. Workers were interviewed before, at the time of, and twice subsequent to the factory closings. A control group of employed workers from four similar plants was also interviewed.

The findings are quite complex and deserve a closer reading than is appropriate here. Nevertheless, several general trends in the results are especially noteworthy. First, significant differences between unemployed and employed workers are most substantial for physiological symptom measures, although some expected findings are also reported for psychiatric symptomatology. Seven of thirteen physiological measures (e.g., levels of cholesterol, serum creatinine, norepinephrine, epinephrine, serum uric acid) discriminated the two groups in the predicted direction. As interpreted by Kasl and Cobb, the particular pattern of physiological response to job loss suggests a greater probability of coronary heart disease, dyspepsia, joint swelling, hypertension, and alopecia among job losers as compared to employed controls.

The results for measures of psychological functioning indicate that only tension related to anxiety distinguished unemployed from employed persons over the entire course of the twenty-four-month study period. However, depression, anomie, anger and irritation, and suspicion were significantly more descriptive of workers who experienced extended as opposed to short periods of unemployment. No direct measures of psychiatric treatment are reported in this study. The discussion of the relatively weak psychological effects, however, suggests that probably few cases of severe psychiatric symptomatology occurred in the unemployed group.

Thus, although this research adds strength to the view of unemployment as a source of physiological stress, it apparently fails to give a definitive answer regarding the mental-health implications of job loss. One further comment about the psychological findings is appropriate, however. For six of the nine measures of psychological functioning, effects in the predicted direction are found when estimates of workers' perceived supportiveness from their spouses and neighbors are taken into account. In other words, men who describe their wives and neighbors as highly supportive are least distressed psychologically by the experience of job loss. This observation resonates with earlier findings by Komorovsky.[40] Reporting on in-depth interviews with husbands and wives during the Depression, Komorovsky notes substantially greater distress among men whose marital relationships were more overtly utilitarian rather than based on mutual caring.

This finding of a potential moderating effect of some marital relationships is an especially important observation. In addition to hinting at a special set of conditions that may influence how much of a psychological impact is created by unemployment, it has broader implications for the basic social stress model. It requires us to elaborate the model to incorporate social and perhaps individual factors that serve to moderate the stress of life events in general.

Concerning the event of job loss specifically, we earlier made the assumption that the loss of work is a potential source of significant stress because of the multiple resources commonly associated with work. People differ, however, in the extent to which they rely on work for these goods and in the degree to which they are able to tolerate their loss. A variety of factors can account for these differences. For example, in a study of unemployment and its effects on family life currently in progress, a recently unemployed first-class machinist reported negligible changes in his network of close relationships following his job loss.[41] For this person the source of important social ties is principally his residential neighborhood and extended family. Consequently, he experienced no immediate loss of relationships following a change in his status in the workplace. For him and others like him this structural characteristic of his social network directly influences the degree of interpersonal loss created by unemployment. Other things being equal, job loss can be expected to be initially less stressful under these circumstances than in situations where work and social relationships overlap substantially. This example is one illustration of the role of the social context in determining the degree and quality of stress created by unemployment.

A related issue involves systematic differences in the capacity to handle stress created by job loss. A recently reemployed truck driver in the same research project commented that his most important support throughout his unemployment was the closeness among the members of his immediate family and their ability to be open and "truthful" about how they were reacting to the job loss. The implication is that the buildup of resentment and blame were minimized in this family by the open sharing of feelings and anxieties. Although formal analyses of health outcomes for workers with and without this kind of family support are not presently available, we suspect that the presence of these and other interpersonal and material resources will be associated with the degree of medical and psychiatric difficulties experienced. This example may capture some of the dynamics of what Komarovsky and Kasl and Cobb refer to as the moderating influence of supportive marital and family relationships.

These considerations substantially alter the basic, more straightforward social stress model with which we began. Stress is still retained as an aspect of the process intervening between economic change and illness mediated by the occurrence of unemployment. However, both its initial intensity and the individual's capacity to handle it are dependent on other characteristics and resources of the social context of the job loser. The model requires modification to accommodate a more complex picture of the social grounding of stress and its ultimate significance for the individual's health.

In this elaborated model illness emerges clearly as a social as well as biomedical fact in two respects. First, although the model treats illness as a medical phenomenon, etiology is not assumed to be limited to organic processes. Events such as unemployment are taken to be social occurrences that generate stress rather than mere indicators of prior psychological and biochemical states which give rise both to behaviors that eventuate in job loss and to disease itself. In other words they are not treated as symptoms of illness. Interpersonal and material resources that condition the impact of stressful life events are also viewed as conditions of the person's life circumstances rather than as further manifestations of an incipient disease process.

Some indirect empirical evidence for these assumptions has already been presented in the discussion of causal relationships in the longitudinal studies of broad economic change and psychiatric admissions. Unemployment measured in the aggregate tends to precede changes in psychiatric admissions for large and small geographic areas. It is difficult to imagine that these unemployment levels are the sole product of the personal characteristics of job losers to the exclusion of market and political forces. Less can be said in this regard about the conditions that moderate the effects of social stressors. Research is first needed to establish more definitively which factors have the strongest mitigating effects given different classes of stressors and illnesses. However, there is nothing in the social psychological literature currently indicating that supportive marital relationships or neighborhood-situated social ties, for example, are principally *traits* of healthy individuals. Structural properties of social networks in particular appear to be related to other characteristics of the social context, such as the organizational structure of the workplace, occupational status, and social class position.[42] Furthermore, as Liebow points out, the benefits derived from work and, thus, the kinds of losses produced by unemployment, are determined as much by the objective characteristics of occupations as they are by the values held by workers.[43] No amount of valuing self-expression in one's job can produce a strong sense of self-actualization in a routinized, fragmented, and authoritarian workplace. Job loss and the conditions that may serve to soften its impact are *both*, thus, social realities for which recent research suggests a significant role in the development of medical and psychiatric illness.

The social production of stress, however, is only one aspect of the social basis of illness. A second, related issue is the distribution of stress-producing events such as unemployment and the social circumstances that modify its effects. In other words, is there a socially structured pattern of vulnerability to the stress of unemployment among different groups in the society? There is substantial documentation that the risk of unemployment varies systematically according to workers' geographic location, industry, and occupation, and age, race, sex, and social class membership.[44] For our purposes a review of this literature and the com-

plex interdependencies among these factors is not important. It is sufficient to note that formal analyses of who becomes unemployed confirm
everyday journalistic and media reports of the unequal distribution of job
loss in this society. At this time we can only guess that as we learn more
about the conditions that moderate or exacerbate the stress of losing
one's job we shall discover that for some of them there is also a social
basis of distribution.

Concluding remarks

This book encourages the conceptual relocation of medicine, medical
practice, and problems of health and illness in the society to which they
are in actuality bound. The contributions from the social sciences we have
described in this chapter illustrate one aspect of this social grounding. We
began with some provocative findings strongly suggesting that health in
general and psychological well-being in particular are closely related to
the fate of local, state, and national economies. We then reviewed early
and more recent work offering some evidence that the event of unemployment is an important intermediary in the broader relation between the
economy and illness. Finally, we noted the applicability of a model of
social stress for describing one aspect of the intervening process in this
relation and an important elaboration of it to accommodate greater complexity in the social production of stress than is generally assumed in
stress research.
    The image of the social context that emerges in this discussion is one of
an autonomous reality that can act on the individual in ways detrimental
to health and not an epiphenomenon of events and conditions dictated
largely by underlying disease processes. We may have overstated this
distinction and appeared to be advocating a social deterministic conception of the relation of social context to illness. On the contrary, unlike
some perspectives presented in subsequent chapters, the social stress approach does not require a radical transformation of the biomedical perspective. Instead, it augments that perspective by pointing to factors in
the society that may stimulate, sustain, or enhance the physiological processes underlying illness. Thus, both social and biomedical processes have
integrity in this approach to the etiology of disease. Neither simple social
determinism nor biomedical reductionism can do justice to the empirical
evidence we have examined in this chapter.
    The inappropriateness of relying exclusively on either of these posi-
tions for interpreting the data on the economy, unemployment, and mental illness is a concrete example of the limitations of the more general

social causation – social drift opposition in psychiatric epidemiology. The question, for example, of whether social class causes mental illness or whether mental illness or its psychobiological precursors produces a sorting of patients by social class is clearly framed too simply. An alternative to both of these points of view is the social selection hypothesis, which adopts a more interactional perspective.

The applicability of the social selection hypothesis to research on unemployment is most clearly exemplified when job loss occurs during periods of significant economic downturn. Recessionary market forces alter the criteria for evaluating the utility of workers in different areas of production. Under these conditions keeping one's job may be a function of the structural necessity of one's position, the seniority one enjoys, or one's capacity to increase his output. Each of these conditions can also be substantially related to a worker's present or past health status. In such cases, job loss would be both a consequence of broad market forces and symptomatic of prior states of well-being. Although this example presumes broad depression throughout the economy, it is reasonable to expect that under most market conditions there is a continuous interaction between external factors and personal dynamics in the determination of the assessed quality of work performance and hence, one's vulnerability to job loss. The stress of unemployment, therefore, can be externally imposed on the worker and simultaneously continuous with the person's underlying state of well-being. Thus, if we chose to focus either on health as a predictor of the probability of losing one's job *or* the obverse, we would in each case discover statistically significant relationships. This is what happens when advocates of the social causation and social drift hypotheses confront one another. Often, such data lead to an impasse. However, as our example makes clear, these kinds of findings are not irreconcilable. They can be accommodated if the investigator makes a conceptual leap from simple, undirectional causal reasoning to more complex, multidirectional models. The social selection hypothesis has been advocated in the preceding chapter to explain the distribution of mental illness by social class, and the specific mediating event of unemployment allows us to illustrate some possible aspects of the underlying process.

The implications of this interpretative framework for future research on the relationship between economy and mental illness are direct. Research designs are needed that permit longitudinal measurement of the macroeconomy, together with the individual's status in the workplace, health, and resources for resisting stress. Such research is both costly and painstakingly slow. However, the complexity of the underlying processes we seek to understand requires this kind of investment. The potential payoff is also substantial, given that research on unemployment has relevance to our ability to understand the more global social class–mental illness relation.

What is less straightforward are the implications for the practitioner of the major findings and hypotheses in this area of work, especially in view of the fact that all the results are not yet in. A conservative reading of this literature suggests at the very least that unemployment should be considered as a social indicator of illness risk, particularly in people with a previous history of mental disorder. Case finding and preventive health care would be enhanced by routine monitoring of local economies and planning of services in areas especially vulnerable to plant closings and industrywide layoffs. This research also suggests that, given such economic events, efforts to support and strengthen familial relationships as well as broaden social network ties should help to minimize the occurrence of health-related problems. Direct treatment of illness, therefore, is only one of several ways in which the physician could respond to economic threats to health in light of what is currently indicated by research on unemployment and mental illness.

A more fundamental issue is raised by this body of research, however: the manner in which the physician construes the problems that define the domain of medical concern. This research clearly supports a growing awareness in the public at large as well as the medical professions that health and illness are conditions not simply of the person but also of the person in relation to a broad range of life circumstances. This wider social context now appears to encompass the economic sector. The implication is that the social processes that regulate the economy also play a significant role in determining the health of the population. Physicians, to be sure, are not accustomed to commenting on state and national economic policies in their professional capacities as doctors. However, studies like the ones we have reviewed have begun to stimulate concern within the social sciences about the general lack of attention to social costs in the economic planning process. As physicians become more sensitive to the very real significance of events such as unemployment in the immediate experience of their patients, they may come to view active resistance to such contemporary economic myths as the "5 percent unemployment-full employment economy" as a legitimate public health function.[45]

Notes

1. Komora, P. O., and Clark, M. A. "Mental disease in the crisis," *Mental Hygiene*, April 1935, *19*: 289–301.

2. Dayton, N. A. *New Facts on Mental Disorders*. Springfield, IL: Charles C. Thomas, 1940. See also Malzberg, B. *Social and Biological Aspects of Mental Disease*. New York: State Hospital Press, 1940, chap. XI; and Pugh, T. F., and MacMahon, B. *Epidemiologic Findings in United States Hospital Data*. Boston: Little, Brown, 1962, p. 70.
3. Brenner, M. H. *Mental Illness and The Economy*. Cambridge, MA: Harvard University Press, 1973.
4. Ibid., p. 36.
5. The statistical analyses in this work are based on traditional econometric procedures such as time-series analysis. Their use in this research represents the first extensive application of econometric techniques in the field of psychiatric epidemiology. For a technical discussion of their suitability to mental health data, see ibid., chap. 2, and Liem, R. "Economic change and individual psychological functioning," Final Report, Research Grant No. R03MH27443, Center for Metropolitan Studies, National Institute of Mental Health, September 1977, app. A.
6. Sclar, E., and Hoffman, V. *Planning Mental Health Services for a Declining Economy*. Final Report to the National Center for Health Services Research. Waltham, MA: Brandeis University, 1978.
7. The earliest outlines of crisis theory were formulated in Lindemann, E. "Symptomatology and management of acute grief," *American Journal of Psychiatry*, 1944, *101*:141–8. For a more general discussion of crisis theory, see Caplan, G. *Principles of Preventive Psychiatry*. New York: Basic Books, 1970.
8. Catalano, R., and Dooley, D. "Economic predictors of depressed mood and stressful life events," *Journal of Health and Social Behavior*, 1977, *18*:292–307.
9. Liem, "Economic change and individual psychological functioning."
10. Garbarino, J. "A preliminary study of some ecological correlates of child abuse: the impact of socioeconomic stress on mothers," *Child Development*, 1976, *47*:178–85.
11. Pierce, A. "The economic cycle and the social suicide rate," *American Sociological Review*, 1967, *32*:457–62.
12. Durkheim, E. *Suicide: A Study in Sociology*. New York: The Free Press, 1951.
13. Brenner, M. H. *Estimating the Social Costs of National Economic Policy: Implications for Mental and Physical Health, and Criminal Aggression*. Prepared for the Joint Economic Committee of Congress. Washington, DC: U.S. Government Printing Office, 1976.
14. The strength of the economy is generally assessed on the basis of a standard set of leading economic indicators such as number of new housing starts, the consumer price index, and the prime lending rate. Unemployment levels are considered a "lagging" indicator that tend to follow rather than precede a significant change in the functioning of the economy. Thus, the fact that changes in hospital admissions rates tend to follow changes in rates of employment or unemployment suggests that changes in other economic conditions also precede changes in admissions rates.
15. Several studies have used multiple indicators of economic functioning to predict health outcomes. Commonly they include indices such as annual rate of inflation, consumer price index, and rates of new housing starts in addition to unemployment rates. See Brenner, *Estimating the Social Costs of National Economic Policy*.
16. Angell, R. *The Family Encounters the Depression*. New York: Scribner & Sons, 1936. See also Bakke, E. *Citizens Without Work*. New Haven, CN: Yale University Press, 1940; and Jahoda, M., Lazarsfeld, P., and Zeisel, H. *Marienthal, the Sociography of an Unemployed Community*. Chicago: Aldine, Atherton, 1971.
17. Faris, R., and Dunham, H. W. *Mental Disorders in Urban Areas*. Chicago: University of Chicago Press, 1939.

18. A five-stage response to unemployment was first suggested in Bakke, *Citizens Without Work*, and later corroborated by Powell, D., and Driscoll, P. "Middle class professionals face unemployment," *Society*, 1973, *10*:18–26.
19. Levin, H. "Work, the staff of life." Paper presented at the Annual Convention of the American Psychological Association, Chicago, September 1975.
20. Tausky, C. "Meaning of work among blue collar men." Paper presented at the Annual Meeting of the American Sociological Association, San Francisco, 1968. See also Morse, N., and Weiss, R. "The function and meaning of work and the job," *American Sociological Review*, 1955, *20*:191–8.
21. Jacques, E. *Equitable Payment*. New York: John Wiley & Sons, 1961. Quoted in *Work in America: Report of a Special Task Force to the Secretary of Health, Education and Welfare*. Cambridge, MA: The MIT Press, 1976, p. 6.
22. Selye, H. *The Stress of Life*. New York: McGraw-Hill Book Company, 1956.
23. Cannon, W. *Bodily Changes in Pain, Hunger, Fear and Rage*. Boston: Charles T. Branford Co., 1953.
24. Levine, S., and Scotch, N. (Eds.). *Social Stress*. Chicago: Aldine Press, 1970. See also Dohrenwend, B. P., and Dohrenwend, B. S. (Eds.). *Stressful Life Events: Their Nature and Effects*. New York: John Wiley & Sons, 1974, chaps. 1 and 10.
25. Curtis, G. "Physiology of stress," in Ferman, L., and Gordus, J. (Eds.). *The Consequences of Work Transition: Resource Papers in Mental Health and The Economy*. Kalamazoo, MI: UpJohn Institute, 1980.
26. The concept of resistance resources is discussed in Antonovsky, A. "Conceptual and methodological problems in the study of resistance resources and stressful life events," in Dohrenwend and Dohrenwend, *Stressful Life Events*, chap. 15. See also Lazarus, R. *Psychological Stress and the Coping Process*. New York: McGraw-Hill Book Company, 1966.
27. Meyer, A. "The life chart and the obligation of specifying positive data in psychopathological diagnosis," in Winters, E. E. (Ed.). *The Collected Papers of Adolph Meyer, Vol. III, Medical Teaching*. Baltimore, MD: The Johns Hopkins Press, 1951, p. 52–6.
28. Holmes, T., and Rahe, R. "The social readjustment rating scale," *Journal of Psychosomatic Research*, 1967, *11*:213–18.
29. The basic measure of life events has been modified a number of times to suit the characteristics of different populations. See Holmes, R., and Masuda, M. "Life change and illness susceptibility," in Dohrenwend and Dohrenwend, *Stressful Life Events*, 1974, chap. 3; and Wyler, A., Masuda, M., and Holmes, R. "The seriousness of illness rating scale: reproducibility," *Journal of Psychosomatic Research*, 1970, *14*:59–64. Life events and myocardial infarction have been studied by Rahe, R., and Paasikivi, J. "Psychosocial factors and myocardial infarction. II. An outpatient study in Sweden," *Journal of Psychosomatic Research*, 1971, *15*:33–9; and respiratory illness by Jacobs, M., Spilken, A., Norman, M., and Anderson, L. "Life stress and respiratory illness," *Psychosomatic Medicine*, 1970, *32*:233–42; and general physical symptomatology by Holmes, R., and Masuda, M. "Life change and illness susceptibility"; and biochemical reactivity by Theorell, T. "Life events before and after the onset of a premature myocardial infarction," in Dohrenwend and Dohrenwend, *Stressful Life Events*, chap. 6.
30. Life events and depression have been studied by Paykel, E., Myers, J., Dienelt, M., Klerman, J., Lindenthal, J., and Pepper, M. "Life events and depression: a controlled study," *Archives of General Psychiatry*, 1969, *21*:253–60; and anxiety by Laver, R. "The social readjustment scale and anxiety: a cross-cultural study," *Journal of Psychosomatic Research*, 1973, *17*:171–4; and schizophrenia by Brown, G., and Birley, J.,

"Crises and life changes and the onset of schizophrenia," *Journal of Health and Social Behavior*, 1968, 9:203–14; and psychiatric hospitalization by Fontana, A., Marcus, J., Noel, B., and Rakusin, J. "Prehospitalization coping styles of psychiatric patients: the goal directedness of life events," *Journal of Nervous and Mental Disease*, 1972, *155*:311–21; and general psychiatric symptomatology by Myers, J., Lindenthal, J., and Pepper, M. "Social class, life events, and psychiatric symptoms: a longitudinal study," in Dohrenwend and Dohrenwend, *Stressful Life Events*, chap. 12.

31. Fontana et al., "Prehospitalization coping styles."
32. Dohrenwend, B. S. "Life events as stressors: a methodological inquiry," *Journal of Health and Social Behavior*, 1973, *14*:167–75.
33. Gersten, J., Langner, T., Eisenberg, J., and Orzeck, L. "Child behavior and life events: undesirable change or change per se?" in Dohrenwend and Dohrenwend, *Stressful Life Events*, chap. 10.
34. Gersten, J., Langner, T., Eisenberg, J., and Simcha-Fagan, O. "An evaluation of the etiologic role of stressful life changes in psychological disorders," *Journal of Health and Social Behavior*, 1977, *18*:228–44.
35. Myers, J., Lindenthal, J., and Pepper, M. "Life events, social integration, and psychiatric symptomatology," *Journal of Health and Social Behavior*, 1975, *16*:121–7.
36. Coates, D., Moyer, S., and Wellman, B. "Yorklea study: symptoms, problems and life events," *Canadian Journal of Public Health*, 1969, *60*:471–81.
37. Theorell, T., Lind, G., and Floderus, B. "The relationship of disturbing life changes and emotions to the early development of myocardial infarctions and other serious illness," *International Journal of Epidemiology*, 1975, *4*:281–93.
38. The final stages of a longitudinal study (1975) of psychological and physical consequences of unemployment are being completed by Ferman, L., Director, Institute of Labor and Industrial Relations, University of Michigan and Wayne State University. A longitudinal study of the impact of unemployment on workers and their families is currently in progress (1978) by Liem, J. H., and Liem, R., Co-Directors, Work and Unemployment Project, Boston College and the University of Massachusetts at Boston. A one-year longitudinal study (1978) of individual, family, and community impacts resulting from the closing of a major steel mill is being directed by Redburn, S., and Buss, T., Center for Urban Studies, Youngstown State University.
39. Cobb, S., and Kasl, S. *Termination: The Consequence of Job Loss.* Cincinnati, OH: OHEW (NIOSH) Publication No. 77–224, 1977. See also Kasl, S., Gore, S., and Cobb, S. "The experience of losing a job: reported changes in health, symptoms, and illness behavior," *Psychosomatic Medicine*, 1975, *37*:106–22; and Gore, S. "The effect of social support in moderating the health consequences of unemployment," *Journal of Health and Social Behavior*, 1978, *19*:157–65.
40. Komarovsky, M. *The Unemployed Man and His Family.* New York: Dryden Press, 1940.
41. Liem and Liem, *op. cit.*, 1978.
42. The influence of the organizational structure of the workplace on characteristics of workers' social networks is discussed in Howard, L. "Workplace and residence communities of Indian factory and non-factory workers." Paper presented at the Annual Meeting of the American Sociological Association, Chicago, September 1977.
43. Liebow, E. *Tally's Corner: A Study of Negro Street Corner Men.* Boston: Little, Brown, 1967.
44. Readers can establish for themselves the disproportionate distribution of unemployment by social groups by reviewing monthly statistics reported in *Employment and Earnings*, U.S. Labor Department, Bureau of Labor Statistics. Patterns of unemployment within

states are also regularly documented as, for example, in McLaughlin, M., and Sum, A. "Interrelationships between unemployment and poverty in Massachusetts," Massachusetts Department of Manpower Development, n.d.
45. Part of the research cited in this chapter was supported by the Center for Metropolitan Studies, National Institute of Mental Health, Research Grant Numbers RO1-MH 31316-01 and RO3-MH 27443.

4   Social contexts of health care

Elliot G. Mishler

We have been looking at patients and their illnesses. By drawing on various studies, we have documented significant effects on illness rates of such social contexts as ecological areas and communities, social classes, families, and economic conditions. In this chapter, we shift our attention to treatment and health-care practices. In particular we shall be interested in the ways in which the social organization of health-care institutions affects health-care practices and outcomes.

Within the framework of the biomedical model, the practice of medicine tends to be viewed as an applied technology. Thus, medical care and treatment are defined primarily as technical problems, and the aims of medicine are framed in terms of technical criteria, such as validity of diagnosis, precision of disease-related treatment, symptom relief, and termination of the disease process. This view reflects the key assumptions of the biomedical model as we discussed in Chapter 1. For example, the doctrine of specific etiology, which proposes a determinate relationship between discrete diseases and specific causal agents, both expresses and reinforces a technical conception of medicine.

Evidence is omnipresent that a technological perspective dominates modern medicine. Reiser's historical study of the impact on medicine of technical developments is aptly titled, *Medicine and the Reign of Technology.*[1] He sets the stage for his analysis by asserting that "the physician has become a prototype of technological man."[2] This technological orientation is embedded in the standard medical curriculum and students are introduced to it early. The first stage of training, the preclinical curriculum, focuses on the technical knowledge, concepts, and procedures of the biosciences. Biochemistry and physiology are the core disciplines. Analysis and description of normal and deviant biological structures and processes provide the basic tools students are expected to bring to their work with patients in the second, clinical stage of their training. Thus, it is made clear to physicians-to-be that treating patients is an application of scientific – technical skills and knowledge. The further fact that medical train-

79

ing takes place in teaching hospitals with the full armamentarium of large-scale medical technology accentuates this tendency. The intense demands of work with seriously ill patients combined with the requirements of senior attending physicians for rapid and precise information press students, interns, and residents into dependence on laboratory tests, electronic monitors, and the elaborate machinery of modern treatment.[3]

With this increased dependence on technology, there has been a subtle but significant shift in the criteria for determining adequacy and effectiveness of treatment. This is a shift for assessment based on outcome to assessment based on the competence displayed in performance, that is, from ends to means. This situation is captured ironically by the joking comment, "The operation was a success, but the patient died." As Friedson argues,[4] emphasis on technical, often esoteric, expertise serves the further function of legitimating claims by the medical profession for monopolistic control over health-related issues by medically trained persons, namely, physicians.

This approach, which gives primacy to the technical aspects of medicine, is also reflected on the larger screen of health policy discussions. Population differentials in levels of health, for example, are often viewed as a function of differences in the organization of the scientific technology of medicine. As a consequence, inequities in the geographic distribution of physicians, or the expense of sophisticated equipment for diagnosis and treatment, are the basic problems that occupy the attention of health-policy makers and administrators. It often appears that the general aim of progressive health policies is to ensure the more equitable distribution of the technical resources of modern medicine to all sectors of the population. On the whole, issues of health education, of preventive medicine, and of environmental health hazards receive considerably less attention.

This emphasis on medicine as an applied technology is associated with the prevailing assumption that overall increases in levels of health over the past one hundred years have depended on the growth of scientific medicine, particularly on the germ theory of disease with the consequent discovery of specific etiologies and treatments. As we showed earlier in our discussion of the doctrine of specific etiology, recent historical analyses have found that general improvements in social and environmental conditions provide a more adequate explanation of these changes than the rise of scientific medicine.[5]

These introductory comments on the dominant view of medicine as an applied technology serve as a frame for our alternative approach. In reviewing studies of patients in social contexts, our aim was to relocate the occurrence of illness within the concrete social conditions of patients' lives. Our aim, in this chapter, is similar. We shall review studies of the social organization of medicine and show that the ways in which medical care is provided, as well as its outcomes, cannot be described adequately or understood simply as the application of technical-scientific knowledge, skills, and procedures. Rather, these are complex social acts that involve a division of labor among many specialists, require the coordination and integration of information from many sources, reflect the traditional stratification of health institutions, and depend on normative standards that regulate relations between physicians and patients. The central question becomes: How is clinical practice affected by particular features of social organization?

As we shall see, one major thrust of these diverse studies is their demonstration that the realities of medical practice do not match the ideal formulation. That is, ideal norms intended to guide role performance, such as universalistic criteria, affective neutrality, and so forth,[6] are not realized in practice. For example, the health-care delivery system is characterized by marked inequities in that services are provided differentially to different socioeconomic groups within the society, so much so that the system is often described as a dual system of health care, one for the rich and one for the poor. Clearly, the ideal norm of universalist criteria in the selection of patients does not apply in practice.

Although many studies of health-care institutions are critical of medical practice, for example, as inequitable or impersonal, investigators tend to accept the assumptions of the biomedical model. Thus, studies of hospitals may emphasize how bureaucratic and hierarchical forms of organization interfere with and undermine "good" medical care and treatment. Nonetheless, "good" medical care is implicitly assumed to reflect the bioscience model of health and illness. On the whole, these studies do not question medical definitions of good or adequate treatment.

For these reasons, one might think of these studies as liberal in intent. They provide a more socially realistic picture of medicine than is found in the idealized abstract image of scientific medicine. They are aimed at correcting inequities and at modifying current arrangements so that better care can be provided. However, neither the underlying medical model of illness nor the ideal norms for medical role performance are brought into question. This approach is analogous to what we found in our review of studies of patients in social context, where the biomedical model of illness was taken for granted.

Nonetheless, although they do not challenge the assumptions of the biomedical model of illness and treatment, these studies of the social organization of medical practice demonstrate the inadequacy of a conception of medicine as an application of technical – scientific procedures. The ways in which physicians function depend as much on features of health-care institutions as social systems as they do on levels of technical – scientific knowledge and skill. Indeed, a full understanding of the effects of practice on the health of patients requires knowledge of the particular ways in which practice is socially organized.

This emphasis on the realities of medical practice rather than on the abstract idealization of medicine as an applied technology has led to a specification of critical variables that affect treatment and its results. These variables tend to be ignored in the more traditional conception. For example, rates of staff turnover on psychiatric hospital wards appear to have marked effects on suicide rates,[7] but this variable has no place in the technical – scientific model of medicine. Or, to use another example, the problem of patient compliance with recommended or prescribed treatments does not arise within a conception of medical care where the physician's work is over when he or she has successfully performed the technical tasks of diagnosis and selection of the appropriate treatment. However, studies of patient noncompliance indicate that it ranges from a low of 19 percent to a high of 72 percent.[8] The critical factors that affect noncompliance are found in the ways in which physicians and patients communicate with each other, and these become important topics for study when the perspective shifts to medicine as a practice.[9]

Finally, this alternative approach suggests that relationships between patterns of health care and levels of health are a function of how health-care systems are organized and not of the level of scientific knowledge achieved or the expertise of physicians as applied scientists. Implications of this view for medical education and health policy will be discussed in the concluding section of this chapter.

Studies of medical practice cover a wide range of topics, including the structure of the total system of health care, features of medicine as a profession, the social organization of hospitals and other health-care institutions, and patterns of interaction between physicians and patients. These represent different contexts, from the macrocontext of the system as a whole, through mesocontexts of institutions, to the microcontext of physician and patient in interaction with each other. We have organized our review of studies in terms of these different contexts. We shall give most attention to mesocontexts, that is, to hospitals as health-care institutions. Studies of the microcontext of physician – patient interaction will be discussed in detail in the following chapter.[10]

The macrocontext: the dual system of health care

In popular dramas about medicine, individual physicians and their patients hold center stage. The scene may be a hospital corridor, operating room, or office, but these are only stage sets for the main action between the two actors in the leading roles. The large and sophisticated array of modern medical technology – X-ray machines and isotope counters, computers and vital sign monitors – are stage props. Other health professionals are extras – nurses, interns, residents, and technicians provide additional human interest and allow for secondary story lines.

This popular view of an individual physician and patient as the essential and basic unit of health care is consistent with the view held by the medical profession itself. Other health professionals traditionally have been referred to as ancillaries and, more recently, paramedical personnel have joined the cast; the labels mark their subordinate roles. The scenes and props are passive, and little attention has been paid to the dynamic interdependence between a physician's performance and the active setting of his or her work.

We shall be discussing some specific aspects of these complex relationships at later points in this and succeeding chapters. It is important to begin, however, by noting that this emphasis on the physician – patient unit interferes with a clear view of the overall system of health care. The underpinning of medicine in the biosciences, the definition of illness as a biological process, the tradition of ultimate authority for physicians in matters of diagnosis and treatment, the solo practice model and the fee-for-service basis of American medical practice – all of these, and other characteristics of modern medicine, strengthen further the view of physician and patient as the basic unit. The net result is that health care is abstracted from its larger social context and the ways in which health services are organized into a social system are obscured.

Among observers of the health-care scene, however, there is common recognition that there is a health-care system, even though its main characteristics may be ". . . separation by function, fragmentation by process, and segregation by payment."[11] Faced by the daily problems of their work with patients, physicians may remain relatively unaware of how their work is affected by characteristics of the larger system. In fact, they may be surprised and, one hopes, dismayed by a general consensus among critics that ". . . the medical care sector, while costing more, is not performing any of its functions well for all those who could benefit by them, a nearly ubiquitous view that there is a 'health care crisis.' "[12]

It is not unusual for a view of social practices as systematically organized to come from outside observers rather than from members of the system. Further, the significance of system properties is more often recognized when there are problems rather than when the system is running smoothly. The evidence of trouble is all around us. Principally, it consists in the maldistribution of health-care services usually referred to as a dual system of health care. That is, available providers and resources are socially distributed, and there is a ". . . high incidence of remediable conditions together with low rates of utilization for the poor, the black and the other socially disadvantaged population groups."[13]

In sketching the broad outlines of the overall system of health care, we are taking a first step in locating physicians within their social context. The reciprocal nature of this relationship between physician and context must also be underscored. The way in which medicine is organized as a profession is itself a critical feature of the context within which physicians practice. That is, differential access to and utilization of health services cannot be understood as a function of the social characteristics of patients, although patient characteristics provide one of the principal empirical ways of describing the system. Rather, differences in accessibility and utilization reflect how the delivery of health care is organized. Thus, the dual system of health care describes how physicians practice and the consequences of their mode of practice; this dual system, in turn, becomes an important context within which they work.

Rates of health-service utilization are a complex function of many different variables, including the incidence of disease, the availability of services, and attitudes toward the use of such services. For example, as is suggested by epidemiological findings, illness rates may generally be higher for lower socioeconomic classes; however, health services may be less available to them than to higher socioeconomic classes, and, further, social classes may vary in their dispositions to seek medical care. In addition, standard measures such as physician visits or hospital admissions usually do not distinguish among types of services received, in terms of adequacy and quality. Finally, economic changes, such as increases in medical insurance coverage, may drastically alter differences found in utilization rates at any one time.

Despite these methodological problems, the weight of the data ". . . would support the conclusion that health service utilization in the United States based on consumer decisions (that is, on cases where patients decide whether or not to seek care) is directly related to socioeconomic status. The lower the social status of the person, the less likely he is to utilize medical facilities."[14] Studies conducted by the National Center for Health Statistics in the 1960s, for example, show that physician visits per year were 4.6 for those with family incomes under $4,000 and 5.7 for those with family incomes above $7,000. Differentials were particularly marked for children: For those under fifteen years of age, the respective rates were 3.0 for families earning less than $2,000 per year, compared to 5.7 for those earning over $7,000.[15] Secondary analyses of these data reveal that the direct relationships of physician utilization rates with income and education hold within different age – sex groups and that there is a similar relationship between socioeconomic indicators and the use of preventive services.[16]

A more direct examination of this pattern of social discrimination in how the health-care system functions is provided by investigations that compare types of treatment and associated outcomes for patients from different social classes who present with the same problems to the same institutions. A number of studies demonstrate that type of treatment received in psychiatric outpatient clinics varies by social class. For example, Myers and Schaffer[17] found that the likelihood of receiving extended psychotherapy decreased radically with a decrease in social class. Thus, whereas 18 percent of their upper-class group were seen for only one visit and 53 percent for ten or more therapy sessions, 45 percent of Myers and Schaffer's lowest social class were seen only once and the proportion having ten or more sessions dropped to 12 percent.

In addition to the epidemiological findings we reviewed earlier, Hollingshead and Redlich's study of social class and mental illness[18] also brought together materials on social class differentials in treatment. When these researchers controlled for diagnosis and treatment setting, they found that lower-class patients tended to receive custodial care and less active methods of treatment than did patients from higher social classes. For example, among neurotic patients in treatment with private practitioners, they found that the "standard" fifty-minute hour was standard only for patients from Classes I and II, but not for patients in Class V. More than 90 percent of the former had sessions of that length, whereas this was true of less than half of the patients in Class V; fully a third of those from Class V were in and out in less than half an hour.[19] Similar differentials appeared for patients with more severe illnesses: Among schizophrenic patients in state and Veteran Administration hospitals, between 30 and 40 percent of patients from Classes III and IV received custodial care as the principal form of treatment, whereas the percentage receiving such limited treatment rose to 58 percent for Class V patients.[20]

The effects of these differences in treatment are neither trivial nor transitory. A ten-year followup of the sample of patients hospitalized in public institutions in Hollingshead and Redlich's original study showed that the percentage of each class group still in the hospital a decade later increased steadily from 39 percent for the highest social class to 57 percent for Class V.[21]

These studies of social class differentials in utilization, treatment, and outcome underscore the general point that the health-care system is not autonomous. It reflects the structure of the larger society, and health care, like other resources, is distributed along the main lines of social stratification. We shall have more to say about this relationship in Chapter 8, on the social functions of medicine.

Here, we wish to take note of another implication of these analyses, namely, their bearing on the validity of the biomedical assumptions about illness and etiology. The inequities of a dual system of health care are apparent. There is a concomitant of this pattern of care that has important consequences for theories of illness based on clinical practice, that is, on diagnostic and therapeutic work with patients. As we have seen, patients are a highly selected sample of the population of people with symptoms. The utilization data, for example, indicate that patient samples disproportionately underrepresent disadvantaged social groups. There are several other lines of evidence that are consistent with this conclusion that patients are unrepresentative of the "true" population of sick people. First, it appears that patients are not a particularly high percentage of this total group. In one study of medical symptoms in a nonpatient population, it was found that the number of people with symptoms who did not seek medical attention equalled those who did.[22] Thus only half the population of "potential" patients by medical criteria became actual patients.

Further, whether an individual with symptoms is found in the patient or nonpatient subpopulation is a function of such variables as social class or education. Middle-class persons, for example, are much more likely than lower-class persons to view their symptoms as physicians do and are, therefore, more likely to seek medical attention.[23] At the next stage along the path to treatment, once symptoms have been recognized and the appropriateness of medical care acknowledged, other factors such as the family's role in the referral process and treatment planning may influence whether the person actually enters the medical setting.[24] Finally, diagnosis and prescribed treatment may vary as a function of ethnic styles in presenting complaints and reporting symptoms.[25]

These brief comments bring our discussion of the dual system of health care back to our more general critique of the biomedical model. An important implication of these studies is that patients' signs and symptoms, on which theories of disease and etiology rely, are only one among many characteristics that distinguish diagnosed patients from nonpatients;

many of the latter may have the same symptoms, which go unreported and untreated. In these circumstances, such assumptions as the doctrine of specific etiology must be considered as problematic. Thus, the dual system of health care has consequences for medical theory and practice as well as for patients.

Mesocontexts: institutional settings

We have been suggesting that a dual system of health care is a salient characteristic of the macrocontext within which physicians and other health professionals practice. The effects of this system on practice are often indirect and mediated through another level of social organization, which we shall refer to as mesocontexts. These are the institutions of health care, such as hospitals, clinics, and other settings within which the work of care and treatment is undertaken.

Studies of hospitals as social organizations represent a major research area in medical sociology.[26] We have selected several studies that demonstrate the impact on medical practice and patient care of certain organizational features. An additional criterion in our selection is emphasis on structural characteristics whose significance may not be directly evident to those working within the system. That is, although health-care professionals know that one hospital is larger than another and that relationships between physicians and nurses may be more authoritarian on one ward than on another, the systematic consequences for patient care of these differences are often not clearly recognized. An important contribution of studies of hospitals as social systems is that these relationships are analyzed and made explicit.

Hospital size and staff–patient ratios

The size of an organization or group, in terms of number of members, is a highly visible and differentiating characteristic. It also significantly influences forms of organization, processes of communication and coordination, member attitudes and perceptions, and levels of productivity. Studies of industrial and office settings tend to be in agreement with the conclusion reached some years ago by Worthy from his large-scale study of Sears, Roebuck and Company units and employees: "Our researches demonstrate that mere size is unquestionably one of the most important factors in determining the quality of employee relationships: the smaller the unit the higher the morale, and vice versa."[27] Worthy proposes that this effect may be a function of the increased complexity of large organizations, which require a much more elaborate hierarchy of supervisory levels as well as the institution of more formal controls.

Ullman quotes Worthy and many other investigators in his review of studies of the effects of size in nonhospital settings; he summarizes the overall thrust of findings as follows: " . . . increasing size usually (but not always) is associated with increased absenteeism, turnover, accidents, and labor disputes, and decreased job satisfaction and productivity. To this list we would add as of prime importance decreased participation of members."[28]

A more recent summary of this literature by Moos[29] reaffirms these conclusions and extends them to school and correctional settings. From his own study of a large sample of American and British psychiatric wards, using standard questionnaires to elicit perceptions of the social climates of wards from both staff and patients, Moos reports that: "As size increases and/or staff-patient ratio decreases, there are decreases in the encouragement of patients to be helpful and supportive toward other patients and in the supportiveness of staff to patients. Moreover, patients are less strongly encouraged to act openly and to freely express their feelings."[30] In addition, patients feel that staff use more methods of formal control in large and/or poorly staffed wards. In a further analysis, he found that with increased size there was less agreement between patients and staff about characteristics of the treatment milieu.

Moos suggests several ways in which increased size affects the social climate of a ward: "(1) it creates pressure toward a more rigid structure, (2) it increases staff need to control and manage, (3) it decreases the degree of patient independence and responsibility and the amount of support and involvement which staff are able to give patients, (4) it leads to less spontaneous relationships among patients and between patients and staff, and (5) it results in somewhat less emphasis on understanding patients' personal problems and the open handling of their angry feelings."[31]

Ullman[32] conducted an extensive study of the effects of hospital size on patient outcome. Using a sample of thirty Veterans Administration psychiatric hospitals, he examined relationships between differentials in hospital size and staff–patient ratio to both rates of early release of patients and proportions of long-term hospitalized cases. Size of hospital, defined as the average daily patient load over a two-year period, ranged from 604 to 2,390 patients, with a mean of 1,453. A principal dependent variable was a patient's "First Significant Release" (FSR), that is, " . . . leaving the hospital within 274 calendar days of admission and remaining in the community at least 90 consecutive days."[33]

Ullman found a significant correlation of -0.37 between hospital size and early FSR, which dropped only slightly to −0.34 when staff–patient ratio was introduced as a control. That is, small size is significantly associated with early release, and this remains true even when staffing is held constant. Because the FSR measure was corrected for age and marital status, the relationship with size is also independent of these two variables.

When hospital size is held constant, rate of early release is not associated with staff–patient ratios. With size constant, however, staff–patient ratio is highly correlated with several measures of patient turnover. For example, there is a correlation of −0.65 between staff–patient ratio and the percentage of patients in the hospital for two years or longer. That is, long-term hospitalization is associated with lower staff–patient ratios, regardless of the size of hospitals.

These findings point to effects on the course and outcome of illness of organizational characteristics such as size rather than to generic features of the illness itself. To account for these findings, Ullman proposes a model of bureaucratic functioning in large hospitals, similar in its thrust to the ideas noted earlier of Worthy and Moos on the effects of increased size. In Ullman's model, pressures toward hierarchical organization, combined with an emphasis on formal rules and procedures for defining and assessing patient behavior, lead to a displacement of goals from the care and treatment of patients to the satisfaction of administrative requirements. Ullman makes a number of key proposals to reduce the negative consequences of large size. These include the partitioning or "unitizing" of large hospitals into smaller functional units and changes in the basis of funding so as to emphasize treatment rather than custodial objectives.

Some of the specific organizational processes that Ullman infers as mediating relationships between size or staff–patient ratios and treatment effectiveness will be examined more directly in the following sections on other features of the institutional contexts of practice.

Social stratification on hospital wards

All social organizations may be characterized, at a minimum, as having a division of labor with members specializing in different tasks and a system of authority and control. The familiar "table of organization" is a schematic representation of these features. Organizations vary in the specific ways in which they accomplish the tasks of differentiation, coordination, and control of member activities; they also vary in goals and purposes. When organizations are classified in terms of their different purposes, it is commonly recognized that they will also differ systematically in structure, that is, in the specific forms taken by the division of labor in the horizontal plane and the lines of authority in the vertical plane. Thus, we all know that military organizations differ from educational institutions, administrative systems from production systems, and so on. In addition to distinctive characteristics of any one type of organization, such as hospitals, there is also room for considerable variation within the type. Thus, in one hospital the exercise of authority may be coercive and authoritarian, whereas in another hospital there may be a more egalitarian and participatory mode of decision making.

Students of hospital social organization have attended both to their distinctive characteristics as special types of social institutions and to variations in structure among hospitals and between services within the same hospital. A general text on medical sociology summarizes findings on the salient characteristics of hospital social structure as follows: "Among the more outstanding characteristics are: (1) a dual authority system prevails in which the administrative organization is based on the principles of a bureaucracy and invested with rational–legal authority while the medical staff is organized along collegial lines and has a charismatic authority. . . . (2) Extreme division of labor . . . not only among the medical staff members, but in regard to the administrative staff as well. . . . (3) A third feature of the modern hospital is its authoritarian nature."[34]

This summary reflects the prevailing view among medical sociologists. Studies and analyses have focused less on efforts to confirm these broad generalizations than on the consequences of such a system for its members and for patients, that is, on how it functions as a health-care system. Some have examined the problems generated by the dual system of authority;[35] others have discussed the inadequacy of a collegial pattern of authority for maintaining adequate standards of performance and imposing sanctions;[36] and others have studied the effects of such highly stratified systems on patterns of contact and communication among different groups.[37] The importance of negotiation among different groups under these conditions of multiple lines of authority with an elaborate division of duties and responsibilities, in decision-making situations with high risk and much uncertainty, has also been investigated.[38]

In a study that is especially relevant to our purposes here, Seeman and Evans compared the effects on various indices of medical performance of differences among hospital wards in their degree of stratification.[39] They found that variation in such stratification was related to quality of medical care. Their sample consisted of eight surgical and six medical wards in a large university-affiliated general hospital. Basing their measure of stratification on nurses' responses to a series of items that tapped such dimensions as the degree of power concentration over decisions by the attending physician, social distance among personnel, and emphasis on prestige distinctions by the attending physician, they defined differences among the wards as follows: "... when we speak of wards that are high in stratification, we mean those wards on which the head physician tends to maximize these status differentials between himself as the occupant of the key position and the occupants of other positions on the ward."[40]

Interns who rotated through the various wards on one-month rotations were asked to describe their own performance and the quality of medical care on a ward when they finished their assignment there. In addition, the researcher used the regular performance ratings of interns by chief residents and senior staff physicians. Seeman and Evans found that wards differing in degree of stratification also differed on these judgments of performance and medical care. From the perspective of interns, the two major functions of communication and teaching are significantly affected by stratification: "Where staff stratification is low, the communication to and about the patient appears to be, relatively speaking, full and clear ... and the teaching function is said to be well performed. ... The reverse, of course, holds on the high stratification wards."[41] Ratings by chief residents of intern performance also reflect degree of stratification: The quality of interns' performance is rated more highly when they are on wards with low stratification; the most marked difference is in the rating of interns' "patient relations."

Going beyond these "subjective" measures of medical performance, Seeman and Evans examined medical records for objective indicators of patient treatment and outcome. In these analyses they also controlled for and compared medical and surgical wards, and clinic and private patients. Two of their findings are of particular interest. First, rates of medication errors, as noted in nurses' reports, were significantly higher in the more egalitarian medical wards; differences were slight among surgical wards. Second, differences between private and clinic patients in length of stay were related to stratification: The difference in length of stay between the two classes of patients was greater on the low-stratification wards. On the whole, clinic patients stay longer than private patients, but it appears that "... the highly stratified ward keeps its private patients considerably longer and thereby narrows the gap between the two types of patients."[42]

In summarizing their findings on the impact on medical performance of different degrees of stratification, Seeman and Evans argue that they have demonstrated an important set of relationships between the structure and functioning of the hospital as a health-care system. Interns rate the teaching function as being performed more poorly on highly stratified wards, and in turn their performance there is rated as poorer by their chief residents. Further, less use is made of consultation on these wards. Other personnel do not remain unaffected: The rate of turnover among nurses is relatively high on high-stratification wards. Finally, patient medical care as reflected by frequency of medication errors and patient outcome as measured by length of stay are both significantly associated with differences in degrees of stratification.

Staff turnover and suicide in a psychiatric hospital

We have already referred to rates of staff turnover in organizations in discussing effects of size and stratification. We noted that high turnover rates are among the consequences of large size, the bureaucratization of administration, and high levels of stratification. In studies of work organizations, staff turnover is usually treated in similar fashion as a consequence of other organizational features – a consequence that managers and administrators are attentive to because of its costs, for example, in productivity, recruitment, and retraining. Frequently, the interpretation of rates of turnover is framed in terms of employee dissatisfaction, itself a result of other system problems. As one recent text concludes: "All the major reviews of research on satisfaction and turnover indicate that high turnover is associated with job dissatisfaction. . . . The consistency of this relationship is emphasized in a recent review of research in this area. Of thirteen studies reviewed, including populations of insurance salesmen, student nurses, lower-level managers, retail store employees, and Air Force pilots, only one failed to find dissatisfaction related to turnover."[43]

Less attention has been paid to the effects of turnover on the functioning of systems, and it is this direction of effect that is of particular significance for health care. It is a common observation that effective management of illness and treatment of patients requires continuity of care. In debates about national health policy, this is often phrased as the patient's right to his or her own physician. In hospitals, however, many more persons are involved with patient care than physicians. Effective nursing care should require a similarly high level of continuity of relationship between nurses and patients. At a more complex level, the better a treatment agent knows a patient, the more adequately will he or she be able to interpret the significance of a symptom or of diagnostic information. In all these respects, high rates of turnover can be expected to disrupt relationships and to interfere with the essential requirements of good health care.

There are other turnover processes that are particularly evident in hospitals that operate twenty-four hours a day, seven days a week. Such systems require different shifts for the daily cycle of activities and staggered weekend and holiday arrangements. In addition, many hospitals serve as training centers for all types of health-care professionals, and there is a regular turnover of students – nurses typically on a three- or four-month rotation, medical students moving from one service to another every four, six, or eight weeks, residents changing on a half-yearly or yearly basis, and new interns arriving annually.

The ubiquity of these several types of turnover processes and the resultant problems for patient care are obvious to those who work within these systems. However, they have been relatively neglected in theory and research. With the exception of Kahne's study, which we shall review in detail later, we have been able to find only two instances where the problem was addressed directly. Rapoport observed that the "premature discharge" of psychiatric patients from a therapeutic community was closely associated with the turnover of doctors, specifically the arrival of new doctors. He concludes ". . . that the coming and going of doctors has an especially important effect on the problem of holding new patients in the Unit . . . [and] many of the peaks in the premature discharge rate seem associated with the turnover of key staff . . ."[44] Ravenscroft developed a more elaborate model of the "summation" of different calendar rhythms – ward, training cycle, holiday, and seasonal rhythms. He argued that "mood swings" on a psychiatric ward were associated with the overlap among these different rhythms: "Such periods of synchrony, or multiple rhythm coincidence, have a massive impact on the entire community in terms of the global level of tension."[45] The tension, in turn, is associated with increases in acting out and suicide attempts on the part of patients, and increased conflict among the staff.

Kahne[46] provides a detailed analysis of the association between rates of personnel and patient turnover and suicides among hospitalized psychiatric patients. He attributes pathogenic effects on patients to the difficulties of integrating new members into the ward social system, with consequent disruption of effective patterns of care. Kahne examined rates of turnover among patients and different categories of personnel over six years and compared these rates for periods preceding, during, and following a suicide period with rates around times when suicides did not occur. He was particularly interested in evaluating two alternative theories of suicide: a psychological theory of loss, in which suicides are expected to follow the departure of persons with whom relationships had been established; and a sociological theory of social anomie, derived from Durkheim's work, in which suicides are expected to follow the arrival of new persons with the consequent difficulties of integrating them into the ongoing system.

The data are most consistent with the sociological model. "Thus, the main effects appear to be due to the influx into the social system of relative strangers, both among patients and personnel. Increased patient discharges or personnel terminations show no such association."[47] In more detailed analyses of subcategories of personnel, Kahne found that whereas the arrival of psychiatrists decreases the likelihood of a suicide in subsequent periods, the influx of more than the usual numbers of aides and nurses increases the probability of a suicide. He observes that "At times personnel seemed so completely absorbed in the mundane details of simply maintaining the functioning of the hospital bureaucracy in the face of the continuous high personnel turnover . . . that it is questionable whether there was much time to familiarize themselves with anything more than the grossest of patient signals of distress."[48]

Kahne points to the paradox that administrative attempts to improve coverage on the wards, sometimes in response to a suicide, may further aggravate rather than mitigate the problem. The combined effects of rapid turnover of patients and of staff make it difficult for a stable set of social processes to develop that can support the efforts of people already under stress to cope with their problems. He concludes: "Epidemics of suicide among patients in mental hospitals bear an intimate relationship to the stability of the social milieu."[49]

Hospital milieu and chronicity

The potentially damaging effects on patients of traditional mental hospitals became a focus of major concern in the decade after World War II. Studies of state mental hospitals in the United States documented their typical features as custodial, coercive, and dehumanizing.[50] Goffman's essay, "On the Characteristics of Total Institutions," in his book, *Asylums*,[51] was particularly influential and widely cited among other observers. Goffman's description of the "mortification" of the self as an essential and typical process undergone by hospitalized mental patients captured the general view of the pernicious quality of these institutions. He notes that, upon admission, the person is "stripped" of the normal social arrangements that have provided support for a stable sense of the self. "In the accurate language of some of our oldest total institutions, he begins a series of abasements, degradations, humiliations, and profanitions of self. His self is systematically, if often unintentionally, mortified."[52]

In addition to these studies of traditional custodial institutions, characterized by the relative absence of medical–psychiatric staff and appropriate treatment, and run primarily by ward aides and attendants with an emphasis on custody and control, social scientists also investigated the organization and functioning of smaller, highly staffed, treatment-oriented hospitals. Here, attention was directed to the effects of microprocesses such as conflicts and disagreements among the staff[53] and to the cultural norms and values of the hospital community.[54] Recognition of the importance of the social environment, combined with a suddenly vigorous humanitarianism and a sense of responsibility and newly developed competence among mental health professionals, led to proposals and programs for change. The social milieu was to be made more therapeutic. There were reports on how custodial systems had been changed into therapeutic ones,[55] and studies of how the therapeutic potential of ward personnel could be activated through retraining and appropriate forms of reward and encouragement.[56] In an influential monograph, Jones[57] proposed the creation of therapeutic communities. In such institutions, in contrast to usual mental hospitals, traditional norms of authority, control, and coercion would be replaced by norms of egalitarianism between staff and patients, with democratic participation by patients in decisions both about their treatment and the organization of their lives in the hospital, and with an emphasis on the community rather than on individual problems.[58]

In many hospitals, new programs were introduced aimed at activating the therapeutic potential of the social environment. The intent was to diminish the negative effects of institutionalization, to utilize more effectively the nursing service and ward personnel who were in closest direct contact with patients, and to reduce the sharp discontinuity between the hospital and the outside community.[59] It would be difficult to assess the full long-term impact of these changes, and no survey of institutional changes is available on which to base an assessment. Nonetheless, it is clear that it is difficult to sustain such programs. Some were dependent on the force of a particular charismatic leader, whose departure was followed by the demise of the program. Other changes in treatment policies and programs also affected the degree to which these new milieu programs continued to be emphasized. For example, the emphasis during this past decade on community mental health centers, accompanied by the massive and largely successful effort to reduce the number of hospitalized patients, has shifted attention to short-term treatment methods and to outpatient and community facilities for long-term care.

With all these changes, nevertheless, hospitals remain a critical component of the overall treatment system, and a significant proportion of the psychiatric patient population remains in long-term care. For these reasons, the effects of the social milieu merit systematic investigation. Wing and Brown[60] compared three British mental hospitals and found consistent effects on the clinical condition of patients of the degree of relative "poverty of the social milieu." The quality of the social environment, that is, the poverty or richness of the social milieu, was assessed in terms of degree of contact patients had with the outside world, amount of personal possessions, amount of constructive activity within the hospital, and other factors. Both primary clinical conditions such as social withdrawal and secondary disabilities such as attitudes to discharge were measured for patients.

Wing and Brown's general finding, across all three hospitals, was of a consistent relationship between the poverty of the social milieu and the clinical condition of patients. "Patients who were living in the most understimulating social environment were likely to show the greatest clinical poverty, and this complex was likely to be more severe the longer the patient had been in hospital."[61] Wing and Brown examined the basis for this relationship in some detail, through comparisons of the three hospitals with each other at one time and through an analysis of effects on patients of program changes over time.

They found that in the first period of their study, 1960, the three hospitals provided quite different social environments on this dimension of the poverty of the milieu. Most important, they found that the clinical condition of patients, in terms of both primary symptoms and secondary disabilities, paralleled milieu differences between the hospitals. For example, 56 percent of the patients in the hospital with the most impoverished environment showed severe flatness of affect or poverty of speech, compared to 39 and 26 percent in the less-impoverished environments. Further, patients in hospitals with better-quality milieus showed less disturbed social behavior on the ward than did those in the hospital with the poorest milieu.

Wing and Brown attempted in several ways to assess the directionality of effect, that is, the question of whether the quality of the milieus reflected differences in the level of pathology of their patient populations, or whether the patient populations were similar to each other in terms of pathology with differences in clinical conditon an effect of the different milieus. On the whole, their analyses are more consistent with the latter hypothesis. They were able to test this more directly by comparing changes in hospital social environments between 1960 and 1964 with changes in patient conditions. They found that these changes paralleled each other: "Poverty of the social environment did lessen between the 1960 and 1964 surveys and poverty of clinical condition decreased concomitantly. . . . Clinical improvement occurred significantly more often in patients whose social environment had improved."[62] Further, they conclude: "Improvement of the social environment of a hospital was always accompanied by a decrease in social withdrawal in the patients there. Clinical and social deterioration also always occurred together."[63]

Finally, Wing and Brown were able to test the direction-of-effect hypothesis in a more elegant and precise way. Whereas the hospital with the most impoverished environment in 1960 continued through 1968 to show improvement in the quality of the milieu and a parallel and continuous increase in the clinical state and social behavior of patients, the other two hospitals underwent a "reversal of fortunes" and "social conditions, after an initial improvement, returned to approximately their previous level. At both hospitals the process of clinical improvement was also reversed, and patients became more socially withdrawn. One cannot suppose that the curves representing social and clinical change, . . . which move in phase with each other, but which show concomitant improvement and deterioration at different times in different hospitals, are describing the natural history of an illness."[64]

Wing and Brown conclude their discussion of their several sets of findings on institutionalism and schizophrenia with a cautious but firm assertion: "The various stages of this study point towards a conclusion which is very difficult to resist – that a substantial proportion, though by no means all, of the morbidity shown by long-stay schizophrenic patients in mental hospitals is a product of their environment."[65]

Microcontexts: physician–patient interaction

In Chapter 1, in our discussion of the doctrine of specific etiology, we referred to Balint's concept of the "negotiation of illness." Through examples from physicians' diagnostic interviews with patients we illustrated how vague and diffuse patients' reports of symptoms could sometimes be and noted the problems posed by such accounts for definitive diagnosis. In introducing the studies reviewed in this chapter, we referred to findings on patient compliance with medical prescriptions: Degree of compliance is highly variable, but at best only three-fourths of patients follow doctor's orders. This suggests that the process of negotiation is more pervasive than is implied in Balint's concept.

The specific context within which negotiation proceeds, which has marked and significant effects on patient compliance, is the clinical interview. Studies of this microcontext, of interaction between physician and patient, will be reviewed in detail in the following chapter. Here, some brief comments are in order to introduce the topic and to relate it to our discussions of macro- and mesocontexts.

Studies and analyses of these three different contexts have proceeded in relative independence of each other. That is, in research on institutional features such as size or ward stratification, both macro- and microcontextual features tend to be neglected. Whether, for example, styles of interaction between physicians and patients tend to be consistent with different degrees of stratification on hospital services remains an unexamined problem. The distinction we have made among these different types of context, however, is intended to suggest that there may be significant relationships among them; this is a nested set of contexts, the smaller ones fitting within the larger ones with the larger ones serving as "supracontexts" for the smaller ones. When studies of macro- and mesocontexts are put side by side, as we have done in this chapter, a general theme becomes apparent. In brief, the health-care system is highly stratified and authoritarian in its mode of functioning. This is evident in its overall characteristics as a dual system of health care as well as in the organizational features of hospitals.

These larger contexts of medical practice are of special significance for understanding findings from the microcontextual studies of physicians interacting with patients. If, as we shall show in the next chapter, there are "gaps" in the communication between physicians and patients, if physicians seem overconcerned with issues of dominance and control, and if they do not try to make themselves understood to or to understand patients from disadvantaged social groups, these ways of relating to patients should be understood within the larger framework of a stratified and authoritarian system of health care.

In other words, interaction between physicians and patients must be placed in context, and this context has particular features. The medical examination, whether conducted in a private office or an outpatient clinic, is part of an institutional context that, in turn, is a component of the overall health-care system. These work settings, and their constituent norms, values, and structural features, are as significant for the clinical performance of physicians and other health-care professionals as their levels of training, technical knowledge, and technical skill. A fuller understanding of clinical practice and of the interaction between physicians and patients depends on the study of these different social contexts and their relations to each other in much the same way that an understanding of illness depends on the study of the life contexts of patients.

Contexts of practice: toward a new perspective

We have already remarked on the fact that studies of the impact on medical practice of institutional and societal contexts are often themselves carried out within the perspective of the biomedical model. Thus, the dual system of health care, the rigid stratification of medical wards, the custodial environment of mental hospitals, and the inadequacies of communication between physicians and patients are all treated as malfunctions that interfere with effective and "good" medical practice. The studies are critical of how health-care systems and practitioners actually function but not of the biomedical assumptions that are intended to guide practice. We have referred to these studies as liberal in that their policy recommendations focus on proposals to "correct" various system problems so that physicians and other health-care providers will then be able to perform in ways that are closer to the ideal of medicine as an applied bioscience. For example, a more equitable distribution of physicians may be proposed as a way to bring high levels of technical medical expertise to underserved groups in the population; or training physicians in effective interviewing skills may be seen as helping them to elicit relevant information from patients in order to make more accurate diagnoses.

These proposals are useful for correcting marked inequities and deficiencies in health care and, if implemented, may have considerable and significant benefits on the quality of care provided. Nonetheless, it is important to recognize that these proposals are limited in aim and scope because they retain the framework of and do not seriously question the underlying biomedical assumptions of the present health-care system.

An alternative perspective, to which we have alluded and which we shall develop as we proceed further with our analyses, begins with a conception of medicine as socially organized practice rather than as an application of scientific knowledge. In this view, the health-care system is not simply a source of problems for practitioners, but modes of practice are an integral part of the system. Thus, the hierarchical organization of ward service personnel is not an aberration but a component feature of medical care. The hierarchy of health professionals does not interfere with "good" clinical practice, but the system is organized that way so as to be consistent with the functions of a particular mode of practice. In other words, the system is functionally integrated: A hierarchical relationship among different types of health-care professionals is intimately connected with the emphasis placed on control and dominance in relationships between physicians and patients; in turn, this pattern of authority among professionals and between them and patients functions to support the monopolistic control over matters of health by physicians as a profession in the society.

By emphasizing the importance of technical expertise and bioscientific knowledge to improvements in health levels, policy makers, medical educators, and health administrators thereby also support the continued dominance of the medical profession. Proposed changes in the health-care system are guided primarily by instrumental concerns; for example, they are directed to ensuring a more equitable distribution of physicians or a more effective application of scientific medicine. A more radical approach might focus on the social organization of treatment systems and would place its emphasis elsewhere. For example, more attention might be given to health education so that patients would be better able to participate in treatment decisions and control their own programs of treatment. Physicians might then be seen primarily as health educators and health consultants rather than as technical experts with the right of final authority over medical decisions. The notion of patient compliance, a concept that itself contains the view that the essential task of a patient is to obey doctor's orders, might be inverted; we might instead ask, and study, the extent to which physicians attend to patients' definitions of their problems and design treatment plans accordingly. In other words, do physicians "comply" with patients' requests for help?

These suggestions go beyond recommendations to "correct" troubles in the present health-care system. They depend on a shift in the ways in which we think about health and illness, a shift away from the biomedical model that both expresses and reinforces the system. The doctrine of specific etiology, for example, which we have seen as particularly relevant to the tendency to idealize and abstract clinical practice from its social contexts, implies that what is "wrong" with the patient can be determined by the application of technical knowledge and skills. Access to and control of this knowledge is the basis for the physician's role as an expert and an authority. A patient's tasks are to listen and comply. The jobs of ancillary and paraprofessional health personnel are to implement physicians' decisions. In questioning the grounds for this assumption as a guide to clinical practice, by pointing to such processes as the negotiation of illness and the impact of organizational variables on treatment outcomes, we have been arguing that many other factors than those included in the biomedical model have significant consequences for patient care. Proposed remedies for the "crisis in health care" must be based on a more comprehensive model of health and illness that includes these factors. These brief comments are intended to raise questions that remain unasked when studies of social and institutional contexts such as those reviewed in this chapter remain bound to the biomedical model. Implications of an alternative perspective, which focuses on the social construction of illness and on the social functions of medicine, will be explored in more detail in later chapters.

Notes

1. Reiser, S. J. *Medicine and the Reign of Technology.* Cambridge: Cambridge University Press, 1978.
2. Ibid., p. x.
3. For discussion of these pressures for precise and up-to-the-moment technical information on the status of patients, see Bosk, C. L. *Forgive and Remember.* Chicago: University of Chicago Press, 1979. The impact of the reliance on technology for students and practicing physicians is discussed in Reiser, S. J. "The medical student and the machine," *Harvard Medical Alumni Bulletin,* September–October 1978, *53*(1):14–16.
4. Friedson, E. *Profession of Medicine: A Study of the Sociology of Applied Knowledge.* New York: Dodd, Mead, 1970.
5. See Dubos, R. *Mirage of Health.* New York: Anchor Books, 1961; McKeown, T., and Lowe, C. R., *An Introduction to Social Medicine.* Philadelphia: F. A. Davis, 1966; and McNeill, W. *Plagues and People.* New York: Doubleday, 1976.
6. For an influential formulation of these norms, see Parsons, T. *The Social System.* Glencoe, IL: The Free Press, 1951, chap. X.
7. Kahne, M. "Suicides in mental hospitals: a study of the effects of personnel and patient turnover," *Journal of Health and Social Behavior,* 1968, *9*(3):255–66.
8. Stimson, G. V. "Obeying doctor's orders: a view from the other side," *Social Science and Medicine,* 1974, *8*:97–104.
9. For example, see, Hayes-Bautista, D. E. "Modifying the treatment: patient compliance, patient control and medical care," *Social Science and Medicine,* 1976, *10*:233–8; Korsch, B., and Negrete, V. F. "Doctor–patient communication," *Scientific American,* 1972, *227*:66–74; and Vida, F., Korsch, B., and Morris, M. J. "Gaps in doctor–patient communication," *New England Journal of Medicine,* 1969, *280*(10):535–40.
10. This distinction among different types of context is borrowed from Bronfenbrenner, U. "Toward an experimental ecology of human development," *American Psychologist,* 1977, *32*(7):513–31.
11. Berki, S. E., and Heston, A. W. "Introduction to: The Nation's Health: Some Issues," *The Annals of the American Academy of Political and Social Science,* January 1972, *399*:IX–XIV, p. XIII.
12. Ibid., p. IX.
13. Ibid., p. X.
14. Mechanic, D. *Medical Sociology.* New York: The Free Press, 1968, p. 267.
15. National Center for Health Statistics. "Medical care, health status, and family income: United States," *Series 10, No. 9.* Washington, DC: U.S. Government Printing Office, May 1964, pp. 24–5.

16. Ross, J. A. "Social class and medical care," *Journal of Health and Human Behavior*, 1962, *4*:35–40; also White, E. L. "A graphic representation on age and income differentials in selected aspects of morbidity, disability, and utilization of health services," *Inquiry*, 1968, *5*:18–30.
17. Myers, J. K., and Schaffer, L. "Social stratification and psychiatric practice: a study of an out-patient clinic," *American Sociological Review*, 1954, *19*(3):307–10.
18. Hollingshead, A. B., and Redlich, F. C. *Social Class and Mental Illness*. New York: John Wiley & Sons, 1958.
19. Ibid., p. 270, Table 29.
20. Ibid., p. 292, Table 37.
21. Myers, J. K., and Bean, L. L. *A Decade Later: A Follow-Up of Social Class and Mental Illness*. New York: John Wiley & Sons, 1968.
22. Pearse, I. H., and Crocker, L. H. *The Peckham Experiment*. London: Allen & Unwin, 1943.
23. Koos, E. L. *The Health of Regionville*. New York: Columbia University Press, 1954.
24. See, for example, Mishler, E. G., and Waxler, N. E. "Decision processes in psychiatric hospitalization: patients referred, accepted and admitted to a psychiatric hospital," *American Sociological Review*, 1963, *28*:576–87; Waxler, N. E., and Mishler, E. G. "Hospitalization of psychiatric patients: physician-centered and family-centered influence patterns," *Journal of Health and Human Behavior*, 1963, *4*:250–7.
25. Zola, I. K. "Culture and symptoms: an analysis of patients' presenting complaints," *American Sociological Review*, 1966, *31*:615–30.
26. For a review and representative selection of hospital studies, respectively, see Perrow, C. "Hospitals: technology, structure and goals," in March, J. G. (Ed.). *Handbook of Organizations*. Chicago: Rand McNally, 1965; and Friedson, E. (Ed.). *The Hospital in Modern Society*. New York: Free Press of Glencoe, 1963.
27. Worthy, J. C. "Organizational structure and employee morale," *American Sociological Review*, 1950, *15*(2):169–79, p. 173.
28. Ullman, L. P. *Institution and Outcome: A Comparative Study of Psychiatric Hospitals*. New York: Pergamon Press, 1967, p. 173.
29. Moos, R. A. *Evaluating Treatment Environments*. New York: John Wiley & Sons, 1974.
30. Ibid., p. 132.
31. Ibid., pp. 136–7.
32. Ullman, *Institution and Outcome*.
33. Ibid., p. 54.
34. Coe, R. M. *Sociology of Medicine*. New York: McGraw-Hill Book Company, 1970.
35. Goss, M. E. W. "Patterns of bureaucracy among hospital staff physicians," in Friedson, *The Hospital in Modern Society*.
36. Friedson, *Profession of Medicine*.
37. Mishler, E. G., and Tropp, A. "Status and interaction in a psychiatric hospital," *Human Relations*, 1956, IX:187–205.
38. Strauss, A., Schatzman, L., Ehrlich, D., Bucher, R., and Sabshin, M. "The hospital and its negotiated order," in Friedson, *The Hospital in Modern Society*.
39. Seeman, M., and Evans, J. W. "Stratification and hospital care: I. The performance of the medical intern," *American Sociological Review*, 1961, *26*(1):67–80; "Stratification and hospital care: II. The objective criteria of performance," *American Sociological Review*, 1961, *26*(2):193–204.
40. Seeman and Evans, "Stratification and hospital care: I," p. 69.
41. Ibid., p. 73.
42. Seeman and Evans, "Stratification and hospital care: II," p. 197.

43. Reitz, H. J. *Behavior in Organizations*. Homewood, IL: R. D. Irwin, 1977, p. 278.

44. Rapoport, R. N. *Community as Doctor*. London: Tavistock, 1960, p. 143.

45. Ravenscroft, K. "Multiple Integrated Group (MIG) theory: a model for milieu rhythms and cycles," unpublished, April 1970, p. 13. For an analysis of stress and adaptation processes associated with residency turnover, see the same author's "Milieu process during the residency turnover: the human cost of psychiatric education," *American Journal of Psychiatry*, 1975, *132*(5):506–12.

46. Kahne, "Suicides in mental hospitals."

47. Ibid., p. 262.

48. Ibid., p. 264.

49. Ibid., p. 265.

50. For examples of such studies, see Belknap, I. *Human Problems of a State Mental Hospital*. New York: McGraw-Hill Book Company, 1956; and Dunham, H. W., and Weinberg, S. K. *Culture of the State Mental Hospital*. Detroit, MI: Wayne State University Press, 1960.

51. Goffman, E. *Asylums: Essays on the Social Situation of Mental Patients and Other Inmates*. New York: Doubleday Anchor, 1961.

52. Ibid., p. 14.

53. Stanton, A. H., and Schwartz, M. S. *The Mental Hospital*. New York: Basic Books, 1954.

54. Caudill, W. *The Psychiatric Hospital as a Small Society*. Cambridge, MA: Harvard University Press, 1958.

55. Greenblatt, M., York, R. H., and Brown, E. L. *From Custodial to Therapeutic Patient Care in Mental Hospitals*. New York: Russell Sage Foundation, 1955.

56. See the reports assembled in Greenblatt, M., Levinson, D. J., and Williams, R. H. (Eds.). *The Patient and the Mental Hospital*. Glencoe, IL: The Free Press, 1957.

57. Jones, M. *The Therapeutic Community*. New York: Basic Books, 1953.

58. For an analysis of how a therapeutic community functioned when developed in accord with these norms, see Rapoport, *Community as Doctor*, 1960. The histories and programs of several therapeutic communities is reviewed in Hinshelwood, R. D., and Manning, N. (Eds.). *Therapeutic Communities: Reflections and Progress*. London: Routledge and Kegan Paul, 1979.

59. For a review and discussion of several of these programs, see Schwartz, S., Schwartz, C. G., Field, M. G., Mishler, E. G., Olshansky, S., Pitts, J. R., Rapoport, R., Vaughan, W. T., *Social Approaches to Mental Patient Care*. New York: Columbia University Press, 1964.

60. Wing, J. K., and Brown, G. W. *Institutionalism and Schizophrenia*. Cambridge: Cambridge University Press, 1970.

61. Ibid., p. 87.

62. Ibid., p. 110.

63. Ibid., p. 129.

64. Ibid., p. 180.

65. Ibid., p. 177.

5   Physician–patient relationships

Stuart T. Hauser

. . . our knowledge of the dynamic factors active in the doctor–patient relationship is uncertain and scanty, and . . . we do not even know whether we are aware of all the important factors. Here, at any rate, is a sample of them. In the first place the patient is nearly always frightened, though to a varying degree, and he is in the dark. He comes to the doctor, who knows. Then the patient is afraid about the future, and expects comfort. Often he is suffering and hopes for relief. Patients have to face the fact that they are ill . . . temporarily or perhaps permanently incapacitated. Some are really gratified when the doctor, so to speak, allows them to be ill; others deeply resent it. The doctor has often to be the umpire in a difficult reality situation, such as when a patient is overdriving himself to cope with his responsibilities and his family expects this from him, or when a seriously ill patient is not properly looked after, or a patient with a non-incapacitating chronic condition demands inordinate attention and care from his relatives, and so on, *ad infinitum*.[1]

In this chapter we look in some detail at interpersonal components of physician–patient relationships. Our focus is on those processes that link physicians and patients as they proceed in their work together. Specifically, we are interested in communications during, and feelings associated with, the initial evaluation, history taking, diagnosis, and negotiation of a treatment plan. The topics addressed in previous chapters clearly impinge on physician–patient interaction. For example, the biomedical model, social class, and the social organization of medical practice affect relationships between physicians and patients. However, the primary thrust of this chapter differs from those of the preceding ones in that we concentrate more directly on processes *within* the medical relationship.

The opening passage from Balint, with its rich "sample" of factors, alerts us to the complexity of the physician–patient relationship. There are numerous pressures and demands, and many opportunities for both participants to err in their judgments, mistrust each other, and be dissatisfied with the outcome of their relationship. Events that influence interaction between physicians and patients occur on many levels – ranging from the individual psychological (the physician's personal goals for helping and "cure," his or her "apolistic mission,"[2] the patient's anxiety and expectations) to the social (the medical setting, social class, language). We shall review a diverse array of studies as we work toward answering two broad and related questions: (1) What are the significant factors that influence cognitive and affective aspects of physician–patient relationships? and (2) What is the impact of the physician–patient relationship on treatment and its subsequent outcome?

We turn first to studies that detail typical features of physician–patient relationships. Underlying these studies are psychological or social psychological perspectives. These perspectives are the dominant ones in this chapter. It is important, however, to keep in mind the fact that the relationship between physician and patient unfolds in social and historical contexts. Many interaction studies themselves do not take these contexts into account. Following our presentation and discussion of empirical studies of physician–patient relationships, we shall review analyses of the social matrix within which the medical relationship exists. Several key issues will emerge as we proceed through the empirical studies. Our plan will be to return to these recurrent concerns in later sections and then consider how broader, more theoretical analyses might resolve dilemmas raised by the empirical observations.

Empirical studies of physician–patient interactions

A growing trend in recent empirical studies has been to use direct observations from a variety of medical settings as the basic data for systematic, usually quantitative, analyses of physician–patient interactions. A second group of studies is based on clinical observations, often coupled with retrospective analyses. Taken together, these investigations cover many aspects of physician–patient relationships: communication of medical information, distortions of understanding, patients' compliance with physicians' instructions, and affective behavior. As we consider the different sets of studies, it will become apparent that their findings often converge. These points of convergence will become an important motif in the discussions, as we attempt to determine what features of the medical relationship itself, and the social context, may underlie such prominent recurrent findings.

Information exchange and disclosure: communication

A large number, perhaps most, empirical studies have addressed the topic of "communication" between physician and patient, taking up such variables as information disclosure and "gaps" in communication between physician and patient.[3] In one of the earliest investigations, in England and Wales, Cartwright[4] found many difficulties and much dissatisfaction surrounding the flow of information and explanations from physicians to their patients. This is also reported in several other studies and discussions.[5-7] Almost half of the 739 patients in Cartwright's sample considered physicians the main source of information about their illness and treatment. Other, smaller proportions, of patients relied on nurses and associated medical personnel for their information. Among the large number of patients who relied on physicians as their major source, only 32 percent found them to be helpful and 21 percent described them as clearly *not* helpful along these lines.

As we shall also see in several other studies, social class was an important factor. Sixty-five percent of the patients who were professionals asked about their illness and treatment, whereas only 40 percent of the working-class patients inquired about this. In addition, professional patients were more critical of the information they were given about their illness and treatment.

A serious limitation of these early studies is that they relied on followup interviews, which are sensitive to retrospective distortions, to provide evidence for communication (or noncommunication). More recent studies use data drawn *directly* from ongoing physician–patient interactions. Key questions addressed within the direct-observation literature include: What features of the medical setting may contribute to "gaps" in physician–patient communication? How, and where, in the interaction do impediments to communication take place?

In one of the largest direct-observation studies, Barbara Korsch and her colleagues investigated aspects of communication "gaps" in 800 emergency room visits.[8] Participating in these medical consultations were physicians who were members of a university hospital staff, patients ranging in age from under six months to ten years, and the patients' mothers. Analyses were based on tape recordings of the medical consultation, followup interviews with the mothers, and a review of the medical records. The results parallel Cartwright's conclusions (based on British adult patients). Once again, the findings were that sufficient medical information was *not* made available to the patient or mother by the physician.

Nearly a fifth of the 800 mothers reported that they had not received a clear statement of what was "wrong" with their child. And "almost one half of the entire group were wondering when they left the physicians what had caused their child's illness."[9] Korsch and Negrete comment on the disturbing impact of these omissions: "The absence of an explanation of the cause is unnerving in such a situation, because the mother of a sick baby has a tendency to blame herself for the occurence, and needs specific reassurance."[10] Actual tapes of the consultations corroborated the mothers' reports, showing that in many cases the physician had failed to provide a clear diagnostic statement and often offered no prognosis.

A second type of communication gap was the physician's disregard of the mother's account of what worried her about her child's illness. Korsch gives an example of this nonattentiveness and its outcome through her account of a mother who repeatedly tried "to interest the physician in the fact that her child had been vomiting, he ignored her remarks and persisted in asking about other symptoms, which she did not realize related to the same basic problem – dehydration of the child."[11]

The taped interviews provided many instances of how these "gaps" appear within physician–mother interactions. One strong set of differences involved "making statements and asking questions." The physicians gave almost all of the instructions, while the mothers asked for few instructions. In addition, physicians did little to encourage mothers to take a more active role in solving the medical problems, as they asked for suggestions from mothers in only 6 of 285 taped interviews.

Mothers expressed more "negative affect" (tension, disagreement, hostility) than the physicians, but their negative feelings were tension, fear, or helplessness rather than any direct attack on or rejection of the physician. Within the individual interviews, expressions of tension accounted at times for close to half of the mother's statements. Moreover, Freeman notes that "the outstanding negative feelings experienced during the acute consultation were experienced and expressed by the mother."[12] Only occasionally was there reciprocal antagonism between the physician and mother. To index the degree of emotional involvement that the patient and pediatrician had during the visit, the proportion of affective (positive and negative) statements to neutral statements was calculated for each person: Mothers' scores were double those of the physicians. Finally, less than 6 percent of the physicians' talk with the mother was rated as friendly or warm conversation. This minimal degree of expressed warmth between physician and mother is especially problematic in light of the fact that effective pediatric outpatient care requires cooperation and understanding by the responsible parent.[13]

There is an additional surprising and intriguing finding in this series of studies. An assumption frequently held by both physicians and patients is that the more time a physician can spend with a patient, the more satisfactory will be the results. Korsch's findings provide no support for this seemingly obvious belief. The many analyses revealed no significant associations between length of the consultation and (1) the patient's satisfaction or (2) the clarity of the diagnosis of the child's illness.[14]

These observations focus explicitly on problems of communication between doctor and patient. Not covered in these studies is recognition of, and attention to, social factors. Data about patients' social class, race, and ethnicity were available, yet none of the analyses were taken in this direction. This omission reflects an important bias in many of the detailed analyses of physician–patient interaction. With their dominant interest in the intricacies of the actual interaction, investigators frequently overlook the relationship of their results to the broader social context in which the interaction is located.

Conceivably, the dissatisfactions and gaps so apparent to Korsch were manifestations of the probably wide differences between white, middle-class physicians and predominantly nonwhite, working-class patients. Such social differences may involve differing cognitive styles, language variations, and values.[15] The multiple impacts of social class on one type of physician–patient relationship (psychiatric) is reviewed in a recent paper by Jones.[16] Duff and Hollingshead[17] present the most extensive discussion of links between social class and medical relationships. However, with the exception of these two reports, the literature on physician–patient interactions rarely takes account of social class variables. In later sections we shall consider the influences of social class as well as other social context dimensions (institutional setting, roles) on physician–patient relationships.

Another group of communication studies have examined the disclosure of diagnosis and prognosis to dying or terminally ill patients. Glaser and Strauss[18] describe several patterns of information disclosure that occurred between physicians and such a group of patients, patterns that varied with the patient's family structure and type of illness. Despite this diversity of patterns, the dominant configuration was one of *nondisclosure* ("do not tell") by the physician. Several other observers present similar descriptions of physicians communicating with seriously ill and dying patients.[19] Many of these reports are discussed by McIntosh[20] in his survey of studies about information seeking and control in cancer patients. This comprehensive review is especially interesting because of its emphasis on how psychological and sociocultural dimensions shape the informing of cancer patients with respect to their diagnosis and prognosis.

Taken together, the disclosure studies highlight the fact that significant medical information is often withheld from seriously ill and dying patients. Even though this pattern has by now been amply documented, we remain uncertain as to how psychological processes, for example, physicians' styles and ideologies about information disclosure, and patients' means of coping with illness actually influence these important communications.

In thinking about issues of disclosure, still another, perhaps obvious, point must be added. We know, from clinical experience and many of these studies, that dilemmas over communicating crucial medical information cannot be resolved by simple principles of "openness," "honesty," "truth," and "secrecy." As anyone who has cared for seriously ill patients understands, the problems of *how* and *when* to disclose such information are complex and subtle, influenced by individual differences among patients as well as the state of the doctor–patient relationship at these crucial times in a patient's life.[21] Knowledge in this area is most likely to advance through continued clinical and other carefully designed studies that take this complexity seriously, using observations of the medical setting, physician, and patient experience.

Distortions of meaning and language differences

Another approach in physician–patient studies has been to examine varying language styles and distortions of understanding. Stated most simply, these studies take up the problem of how "doctor talk" or "patient talk" facilitates or blocks the exchange between physician and patient. One important feature of the language and distortion investigations is that they include the dimension of level of awareness. For instance, whereas research on terminal illness is usually about conscious decisions to withhold information, meaning/language research is more apt to look at "blind spots" and momentary lapses of which the physician and/or patient may be unaware. Some of these lapses may be a consequence of emotional experiences, such as the patient's or physician's anxiety; others may be a by-product of fundamental differences between the languages used by patients and physicians.

The extent of patients' "nonunderstanding" in outpatient clinics was studied by Plaja and colleagues.[22] In analyzing interviews between physicians and their patients in three outpatient clinics in Colombia, they found a range of distinct physician–patient interaction styles and associated communication problems. By far the most common orientation of physicians was "bureaucratic task-oriented," a style characterized by "efficient, limited sensitivity. . . ." A basic aspect of this style was a standard manner of questioning, which showed little or no variation from patient to patient. Eighty percent of the patients interviewed by "bureaucratic task-oriented" physicians responded with a "matter of fact collaboration" style, answering questions in the exact order asked and expressing little initiative or apparent concern with the way in which the physician guided the interviews. The remaining patients interviewed by these physicians responded in ways that were "rambling and elusive; vague and difficult to pin down." A second large group of physicians was classified as "insecure and detailed." These were physicians who held very long and mechanically detailed interviews. Not surprisingly, their patients responded in one of two ways: with vagueness, imprecision, and minute irrelevant detail; or in a style that was "detached and matter of fact."

Few of the physicians were classified as "amiable, person-oriented," with individualized approaches to patients not tied to a mechanical format or a narrow medical focus. Empathy and explicit awareness of patients' feelings together with their medical complaints were important features of interviews conducted by this small group of physicians. These interviews were very full ones, as they included discussion of clear symptoms as well as more covert emotional conflicts.

Half of the patients seen by "person-oriented" physicians responded in ways that were "pleasantly collaborative." The other half were "detached and matter of fact." *None* of the patients interviewed by these physicians was classified as "vague, or difficult to pin down." Most striking is the fact that all but one of the "amiable, person-oriented" physicians were medical students. This finding leads to questions about later phases of medical training, and the impact of new (nonmedical school) settings on physicians. For example, how do experiences following medical school influence the interviewing style and associated listening capacities of the physician? Does this later experience in some way interfere with the development of the broader sensitivities and listening capacities shown by the "person-oriented" physicians?[23]

Rather than observing different interview styles, some studies have looked closely at the actual language used by physicians and their patients. Analyzing transcribed physician–patient interviews selected from private practice, clinic, and emergency room settings, Shuy[24] found that the largest portion of the medical interview was dominated by the physician's language and perspective. During an interview, patients would often strain to speak in a way that would approximate the physician's "medical" language. These attempts were usually unsuccessful, and patients would then frequently revert to their own language, which may even have become more vague or "regressed" as a result of the failure of expression. These points are illustrated in the following excerpt from one of the interviews:

DR: Chest Pains? OK. Do you use any medications?
PT: I was on, uh, what you call it? Diagrens – they call Diag . . . Diagrens, like little pink pills.
DR: Hmmm. Have you ha . . ., have you taken them during this pregnancy?
PT: No.
DR: Anything that you've taken during this pregnancy?
PT: I had some Dia. . . . They gave me some vitamins, some green pills and I had some little, bitty white pills and some red pills.[25]

The most serious breakdowns in communication between a physician and a patient occurred "when patients would (or could) not speak the doctor language and doctors could (or would) not understand the patient language.[26] These patterns of limited comprehension between physician and patient parallel Plaja's observations, where the majority of physicians interviewed their patients in a style that was "efficient," with "limited sensitivity"; their interviews were characterized by a predominance of physicians' standard questions and patients' "matter of fact, passive collaboration."[27] Shuy also conducted followup interviews that revealed likely consequences of the physician-dominated medical consultations: Almost 40 percent of the patients described feeling "extremely uncomfortable about understanding what physicians had told them" and "about making themselves clearer to doctors." An equal number of patients felt that their physicians were "generally unfriendly and intimidating." The possibility that a medical setting, such as a busy outpatient clinic, might be an important influence in creating these difficulties is suggested by Shuy's observation that those physicians who were the exception to the tendency of not speaking or understanding patient language were those private physicians who saw patients (who did not differ by social class) in their hospital offices rather than at the outpatient clinic. This group of physicians did not reveal signs of the "general expectation that the patient was to learn doctor talk."

Problematic physician–patient communications are not limited entirely to outpatient clinics. Golden and Johnston[28] spoke with and taped patients with their doctors on various medical and surgical services of a general hospital. Using many instances taken from taped physician–patient interviews, Golden and Johnson concluded that ". . . the most dramatic findings related to the massive amounts of anxiety experienced by patients and, lamentably, the lack of recognition of their anxiety by the doctors."[29] This is one of the few empirical interaction studies that raises and then explores the possibility that emotional experience (anxiety) may be an important source of distortion in physician–patient communications.

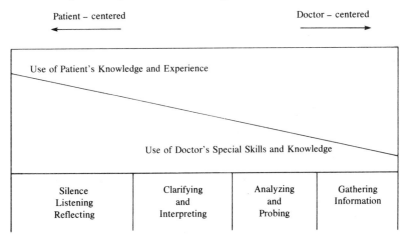

Figure 1. Doctors' styles in the diagnostic phase of the interview.[31]

A fourth study of interaction and language in medical interviews is de-scribed by Byrne and Long.[30] Drawing on a sample of 2,500 interviews conducted by more than sixty British general practitioners, Byrne and Long conceptualize several modes of physician–patient interaction, rang-ing from "patient-centered" to "doctor-centered." The range is reminis-cent of the spectrum implied in Shuy's analysis, where "patient talk" and "doctor talk" were the contrasting polarities. Similarity of the two studies is even more specific. Whereas Shuy found a predominance of "doctor talk," Byrne and Long report that most of their physicians used "doctor-centered" style. Figure 1 outlines the four basic styles elabo-rated by Byrne and Long. The most common doctor-centered pattern was "gathering information." The following dialogue illustrates this style:

DR: "Come in, please, come in and sit down. No better?"
PT: "I don't know what was the matter, but I've had a fortnight in bed."
DR: "With what?"
PT: "With 'flu.'"
DR: "Flu?"
PT: "I lost my balance."
DR: "And how did this 'flu' affect you?"
PT: "I was sweating and sneezing, I couldn't stop sneezing."
DR: "Any aches and pains?"
PT: "Well, I was aching, all over."
DR: "Any cough?"
PT: "Yes, I had a cough."
DR: "Bad?"
PT: "Well, it was really like bronchitis, I got a lot up, it was that greeny color."
DR: "No blood?"
PT: "Oh, no."

DR: "Has that cleared now? The phlegm."
PT: "Well, no, not quite, it's still loose on the chest."
DR: "You still get it up? Still green?"
PT: "Yes."
DR: . . .
PT: "Rusty again."
DR: "Are you taking those tablets I gave you?"
PT: "Oh yes, I'm still taking those tablets."
DR: "Have you got any pain in your chest?"
PT: "No, there's no more pain."
DR: "Are you short of breath?"
PT: "Oh, yes, I get that. You see, when I was short of breath before, I used to get the pain."
DR: "Gone, completely, has it?"
PT: "Yes."
DR: "That's something."
PT: "But during the night, sometimes, I can feel it like catarrh at the back of my throat. But that looks brown."
DR: "Does it wake you? Your chest?"
PT: "Well, it's not this last few nights."
DR: "These little white tablets, have you any left?"
PT: "No. . . ."[31]

Byrne and Long comment that by this time the physician was clear about the diagnosis and his treatment strategy. The ensuing dialogue, which they report in great detail, reveals his increasing insensitivity to various requests made by the patient.

This physician was well aware of the tight control and associated unresponsiveness that he imposed on the dialogue. He strongly endorsed his approach for its efficient, time-managing properties. In commenting on his approach, the physician reflected:

The doctor's primary task is to manage his time. If he allows patients to rabbit on about their conditions then the doctor will lose control of time and will spend all his time sitting in a surgery [outpatient appointments] listening to irrelevant rubbish. Effective doctoring is characterized by a "quick, clean job."[32]

The majority (more than 75 percent) of the physicians used either this "gathering information" style or an "analyzing-and-probing" style. Often a physician would shift from one to the other of these styles in any given interview. What is common to both styles is that they do not allow for the entry of patient-initiated concerns or feelings, once the initial complaint has been presented. When engaged in these styles, then, the physician is essentially unresponsive to those patient feelings and thoughts that are not related directly to the symptoms under investigation. Most of the other physicians used a "clarifying-and-interpreting" style while with their patients. Characterizing this mode were responses such as "broad questions," "repeating information," "challenging," "offering observations," and "summarizing to open up." Here the focus of the physicians' interest includes patients' concerns that are not tied directly to medical diagnosis, symptoms, or treatment plan. But there remain many ways in which the physician still actively structures the interview and does not allow the interaction to become "too free." Only three physicians interviewed patients in the mode that was most clearly at the patient-centered pole, "silence, listening, reflecting."

Two themes are interwoven and frequently alluded to in the studies of language as well as of information disclosure. The findings describe physicians as (1) narrow in their sensitivity to patients' feelings and more subtle requests for help, and (2) withholding in their disclosure of relevant medical information. These related conclusions suggest that many physicians' interactions with patients may be seriously limited.

There are various labels applied to this pattern of constriction. One study terms it "doctor-dominated" behavior, another describes it as "doctor-centered," whereas still a third analysis labels it as "bureaucratic task-oriented." The analyses all converge in their conclusions concerning limitations in physicians' awareness and understanding and the consequent distortions of medical information by patients. One source of "doctor-dominated" style may be the physician's orientation to a purely biomedical approach to understanding disease. An implication of strict adherence to this orientation is that only specific signs and symptoms are of relevance for diagnosis and treatment. Emotional factors or more subtle social requests are thus irrelevant unless they mask the "basic" data. Less apparent is the contribution made by the social systems within which the physician–patient relationship exists. For example, what features of the surroundings – the outside community and the immediate medical setting itself – might sustain or even encourage "doctor-centered" interviews and styles? An important unanswered question, then, is why the "doctor-dominated" styles are so prevalent. What are the adaptive functions of this type of physician–patient relationship? What psychological and social processes underlie the pervasive and, in many ways, problematic doctor-centered interactions? These are broad and critical questions, which clearly cannot be readily or simply answered. In Balint's view, with which we began this chapter, emphasis is on psychological aspects of the doctor–patient relationship, the demands experienced by both participants, the threats felt by each.

In addition, there are social processes that impinge on both physician and patient. These factors, too, must be considered in any attempt to grasp what underlies the pattern of limitation and constriction repeatedly described in the studies we have reviewed so far. After reviewing several other psychologically oriented approaches to the study of physician–patient interactions, we shall turn to sociological analyses that suggest other determinants of the doctor-centered relationships.

Compliance and the physician–patient relationship

Except for the evidence that doctor-dominated interactions are associated with patient dissatisfaction and distortions in understanding, we have not yet dealt with the various *consequences* of physician–patient interactions. In this section we consider studies that examine one important potential consequence, patients' compliance with (or adherence to) medical recommendations.

Compliance is usually defined as the extent to which patients follow through on their physicians' advice. The concept has been used in two ways to refer to: (1) the patient's attitude, "an orientation of willing readiness to do what the doctor prescribes," and (2) the patient's behavior, his or her *actual* carrying out of the doctor's orders. The recent studies we shall be discussing have generally explored the behavioral aspect of compliance. In the previous chapter we noted that patients vary widely in their degree of compliance. It is clear that this "following through" can be highly variable, as Davis'[33] review indicates. In their recent analysis of 165 studies, Dunbar and Stunkard report that "when the clinician begins to measure adherence he can . . . expect to find that between 20 and 82 percent of his patients are not following their regimens."[34] This broad range reflects the several factors that influence compliance: medical setting, type of illness, characteristics of the patient, characteristics of the clinician, and characteristics of the treatment regimen. Finally, no completely reliable measure of compliance has been identified. The many measures, together with the numerous influences, clearly contribute to the varied, seemingly inconsistent findings that have been reported in the literature that has developed around this problem. A few of these studies have looked at the influence of physician–patient relationships on patient compliance.

One extensive study looked at how different medical consultations might be associated with patient compliance.[35] Patients first seen by fourth-year medical students and senior physicians in a university hospital medical clinic were followed for two successive interviews with a content analysis procedure and a special compliance index (using patients' *and* doctors' perceptions of compliance together with medical record information). The interviews that were studied systematically included (1) the physician's presentation of his formulation (diagnosis and medical regimen) to the patient during the first visit; and (2) the interview between the physician and the patient when the patient returned for the next clinic appointment.

In the initial interview, the findings indicated that patients were highly accepting, submissive, and passive. In contrast, patients were more active and authoritative with their physicians in the following appointment. This reversal of "within-interview" patient behavior is intriguing when viewed beside the relationships between interview content scores and compliance index scores. There were no links between any of the initial interview content ratings and compliance scores. But there were several associations between return-visit content scores and the measures of patient adherence. Patients who expressed much tension release or were passive and accepting in the second interview usually had higher compliance scores. And those patients who took the initiative in "asking the doctor for his opinion" also had higher compliance scores. On the other hand, patients who during the interview evaluated or attempted to analyze their diagnosis, therapy regimen, or illness in general were less likely to have followed the recommended treatment plan. The patients with the very lowest compliance scores were those who observers rated as having the most "unreleased tension" in the second interview.

Several kinds of physician responses also contributed to patient adherence or its absence. The patients with the lowest compliance scores had physicians who (1) passively accepted the patient's active participation in the interview; (2) gathered information without feedback to the patient; and (3) were highly formal or distant while with their patients. The patients with the highest compliance scores were those paired with physicians who were characterized as "giving orientation and suggestion." This last set of findings about physician responsiveness suggests that one significant consequence of markedly "doctor-dominated" interactions may be noncompliance – a consequence that from the medical perspective obviously is most undesirable for both physicians and their patients.

This apparent impact of doctor-centered interviews is consistent with many of Korsch's observations. She reports that the type of affect expressed by the physician in the medical interview was strongly associated with the patient's later compliance.[36] The greater the number of positive affect statements made by the physician, the more likely was the child's mother to be satisfied and to comply with the physician's recommendations. In addition, the "proportion of negative affect" (disagreements, tension, antagonism) was inversely related to compliance. High negative affect scores for *either* mother or physician were associated with low compliance. A third finding by Korsch is most pertinent to one of the potential pitfalls of doctor-centered interviews. Those mothers who received sought-after information from the physician were also most compliant. When the balance of the interview tilted in the opposite direction – the patient being pressed for information by an increased number of questions from the physician – the patient was more likely to be noncompliant.

The subjects in most compliance studies have been working-class patients attending teaching hospital clinics. The Korsch and Davis studies are both in this tradition. Because of the sampling bias, questions can be raised: How, if at all, do the results apply to middle-class patients, or to patients seen in settings different from the clinic, such as a private office? Two studies are relevant to these questions concerning social class. Charney[37] and Hulka[38] also found variations in compliance in middle-class patients. Using large samples of children with acute infections and adults with chronic illnesses (diabetes and congestive heart failure), they observed that factors such as previous experience with the prescribing physician and information availability enhanced compliance.

Apart from these two investigations, the most detailed work concerning compliance and physician–patient relationships is based on working-class clinic populations. Consequently, the influences of medical setting (clinic, office, hospital) and social class on compliance is not clear. As we have just seen, however, the two studies that followed middle-class patients in office settings came up with findings similar to the other investigations. The most salient, and recurrent, observation in all of these analyses is that patients are less compliant when there has been limited information exchange, dissatisfaction in the interview, and restricted responsiveness by the physician.[39]

Affective components of physician–patient relationships

Our review of many studies indicates that there are a variety of distortions and difficulties in verbal physician–patient communication. In addition, several sets of findings show that these distortions and difficulties appear to influence subsequent patient compliance with medical regimens. Clinical observation and more recent research suggests that much communication, especially of feelings, between doctor and patient occurs through *nonverbal* channels.[40]

One approach, then, to the investigation of the feeling states and personality styles of physicians as well as patients may be through systematic analysis of these subtle behavioral cues.

Milmoe's[41] study of nonverbal cues in physician–patient relationships indicates that physicians' feelings about alcoholic patients may be expressed by "how" they speak rather than "what" they say. Analyzing relationships between physicians' feelings as expressed in their speech patterns and their success at referring alcoholic patients for treatment, Milmoe found that when physicians' voices conveyed anger, patients did not follow through on referrals.

The physician sample consisted of residents who had been responsible for the diagnosis and disposition of patients seen in the emergency room of a large university hospital. The resident was required to offer the services of the hospital alcoholism unit to each diagnosed alcoholic.

The speech analyses were performed on tape-recorded interviews held with each of the physicians one year after their emergency room rotations. Physicians' replies to the question, "What had been your experience with alcoholics?" were excerpted from all of the tapes and content-filtered. The filtering allowed a listener to discern pitch and volume variations but not the interview content. (Voices sounded as though heard through a wall.)

These "normal" (nonfiltered) and the content-filtered excerpts were then rated along four emotional dimensions. Ratings on two dimensions were associated with physicians' referral success. One link has already been noted. In the content-filtered speech Milmoe found a negative association between anger and referral success. Analyses of the normal speech uncovered another significant association, this time between anxiety and referral success. In contrast to their apparent response to the physician's anger, Milmoe found that patients were *more likely* to comply with the referral to the alcohol clinic when their physician's speech expressed anxiety, perhaps interpreted as concern. Despite the small sample and the indirectness of the interview data, Milmoe's findings are suggestive. Her observations and analyses point out again that there are relationships between physicians' expressed feelings and patients' compliance patterns, a conclusion strongly implied in several compliance and communication studies.

A second approach in this area focuses on the influence of patients' feelings on their understanding of medical information. Through carefully following sequential interviews between seventeen patients and their physicians over a four-year period, Raimbault and his associates[42] located where and how particular difficulties, such as gaps, ruptures, and dead ends, were entered into and maintained during these sessions. The patients all had Turner's syndrome, which includes a number of well-known malformations, such as growth retardation and gonadal dysgenesis. The interview analyses revealed that it was around potentially threatening topics – growth status, chromosomal abnormalities, absence of gonads – that problems in the interaction appeared. Often the difficulties involved the physician's unawareness of how his or her particular responses might be triggering conflicted feelings and covert fantasies in the patient. The following dialogue and commentary reveal the evolution of such serious difficulties, set off by events in one interview and seen in the next:

DAISY: "Is it [Turner's Syndrome] hereditary?"
DOCTOR: "No. . . . What do you mean by hereditary?"
DAISY: "From birth."
DOCTOR: "Then yes."
DAISY: "I mean, did it come from previous generations?"
DOCTOR: "No, it doesn't come from previous generations. Both the father and the mother give one half of each part of the chromosomes that is necessary to make an individual . . . ."
DAISY: "Yes."

The physician goes on to give a technical and one-sided explanation of how one chromosome is lost. Some unexpected, and distressing, effects of such an explanation are revealed a year later:

DAISY: "There has been a misunderstanding when you explained the story of chromosomes. You told me that one out of two is missing; one doesn't know why. I've deduced that it was either my father's or my mother's that was missing. During my nursing studies I've learned that each chromosome is represented in every cell of every organ, and so as I look very much like my father, I have concluded this."
DOCTOR: "You have concluded what?"
DAISY: "That it's my father's which I have. I resemble him so much that I've imagined lots of things."
DOCTOR: "Finally, what does it feel like when one thinks that one has lost a half?"
DAISY: "I feel that I was the same as him."
DOCTOR: "Yes."
DAISY: "Then I thought a lot. When I was small I was a real tomboy. Everybody always said so. So it began to worry me."
DOCTOR: "What worried you?"
DAISY: "It seemed odd to look like my father, like two peas in a pod, while in fact, I'm a girl."
DOCTOR: "Yes . . . (silence) . . . You say that this has worried you? What else did you think about?"
DAISY: "I don't know – I don't want to talk about it."
DOCTOR: "About what?"
DAISY: "About the fact that I was exactly like him."
DOCTOR: "And your mother, how does she fit in all this?"

DAISY: "I was wondering since I don't look at all like her. We haven't got the same temperament. I have nothing in common with her."

The doctor's explanation had been understood in such a way that it allowed for the developing of the girl's hidden belief that she was like her father – perhaps a man. In fact, the doctor had given this information in an objective way. He had not taken into consideration that the girl's utilization of these explanations was to rationalize her own fantasies.[43]

This is a very powerful example of the linking of a patient's feelings and individual fantasies in her understanding.[44]

In a recent clinical paper, Groves[45] also vividly portrays how patient *and* physician feelings interpenetrate the medical relationship. Describing the intense, not fully conscious response that physicians have toward certain highly dependent and angry patients, Goves details the anger – "hate" – that may be evoked in physicians. Most pertinent are Groves' observations of how the physician's experience so often goes on to influence crucial aspects of the medical relationship through such behaviors as unavailability, discouragement, or reluctance to meet with the patient.

Ben-Sira's[46] study of Israeli urban patients offers additional observations about emotional aspects of physician–patient relationships. He reports strong associations between measures of patient satisfaction and general practitioners' affective behavior. "Affective behavior" was defined as the "type of behavior directed by the physician toward the patient as a person rather than as a case." "Showing devotion" to the managment of the patient's problems was most highly correlated with satisfaction. On the other hand, patient satisfaction had weak or no relation to administrative factors such as waiting, or clinic staffing, and was also unrelated to patient judgments of technical competence.

These studies touch on a number of by-now-familiar themes. For example, one implication of the language and distortion studies was that careful perception of affect might have led to diminished distortion.[47] Other results of the language studies suggest that the dominant-physician style is insensitive to nonverbal cues signaling emotional responses.[48] And there is in several compliance studies the idea that a physician's greater awareness of a patient's affect and engagement with him or her is related to greater compliance.

What is different about the group of studies discussed in this section is their direct attention to *how* affective processes become manifest in physician–patient interactions, and their influence on patients' understandings as well as physicians' behaviors. Many of the studies we have reviewed make it clear that affective processes have multiple and strong influences on physician–patient interactions. It is likely that much emotional meaning is conveyed through nonverbal modes (voice tones, intensity and rhythm, posture, body motion). To probe more deeply and systematically into emotional aspects of physician–patient relationships, we shall have to shift our attention toward videotaped observations and other means of measuring nonverbal dimensions. This focus is present in recent analyses of psychiatric interviews[49] but not in other analyses of physician–patient interaction.[50] An important direction for future investigations will be to examine emotional aspects of physician–patient relationships while at the same time attending to cognitive (communication, language) and social (medical setting, class, role) dimensions.

Social contexts and physician–patient relationships

Until this point we have concentrated primarily on empirical studies of physician–patient interaction, and we have surveyed a broad range of variables, including compliance, language, distortions of meaning, expressed emotion, and information disclosure. For the most part, findings from these studies converge in supporting the general point that serious limitations in listening, understanding, and, overall, effectively exchanging information exist in many physician–patient relationships.

As we noted earlier, there is an important question that is rarely raised or seriously discussed in the interaction studies: Are there ways in which these limitations are formed or sustained, by the training of the physicians, by their social roles, and by the social organizations within which physicians work and into which patients come for health care? In this section we look at the interface between these social contexts and physician–patient relationships. First we shall review theoretical and empirical analyses directed toward understanding physician socialization and physician–patient social roles. We shall then examine a second group of studies that focus on medical interactions within large acute-care hospitals.

The socialization of physicians

One vantage point for understanding context influences on physician–patient interaction is developmental, exploring the question of how students *become* physicians. Analyses of medical education reveal that it is not simply skills and knowledge that students begin to master as they pass through medical school. Besides facts and competencies, specific values and attitudes are associated with the social *role* of the physician. These values and attitudes have pervasive, often hidden, effects on the feelings, thoughts, and behaviors of the future doctor. There are no formal courses in such role-related attitudes or values. Such learning takes place within the overall medical curriculum, starting with the "basic science" courses and clinical introductions, and then even more fully in the clinical rotations and postgraduate years, where the medical apprenticeship relationship becomes the major teaching vehicle.

Studies of medical students locate many and diverse stresses experienced by students beginning with the very first year of medical school when they are simultaneously disappointed by the near absence of patient contact and overwhelmed by the volume of knowledge they are expected to learn.[51] The values learned during this period of medical training have important consequences for physician–patient relationships.

One consequence is described in some detail by Lief and Fox.[52] From their observations of medical students, they describe a dynamic, yet precarious, balance between detachment and concern. In the first years of medical school, students are encouraged to develop greater emotional detachment as a means of coping with the helplessness and vulnerability they feel when new, potentially threatening demands are made on them: cadaver dissections, autopsies, first clinical interviews, and physical examinations of patients. During their later phases of training the direction of encouragement shifts toward the development of concern, as students are given increasing degrees of patient responsibility. One outcome of this mix of experiences and pressures is that the student evolves a combination of attitudes and feelings expressed as "detached concern." Lief and Fox consider this to be the typical, and most desirable, consequence. If all goes well, the stance of detached concern changes into what is usually termed empathy. The physician or medical student is ". . . sufficiently detached or objective in his attitude towards the patient to exercise sound medical judgment and keep his equanimity, yet . . . also has enough concern for the patient to give him sensitive, understanding care."[53]

Some students may develop a less positive orientation. The combination of the strains in the first medical school years together with disenchantment and discouragement in the clinical years contributes to a stance of "overdetachment":

. . . beginning with the anatomy laboratory for some students a pathologic process of over-detachment begins, which may eventually lead them as mature physicians to perceive and treat their patients mechanistically. The process of over-detachment may not stop at the failure to see the patient as a person but may go on to the unconscious fantasy that the best patient is the one who is completely submissive and passive; and the most cooperative patient is inert, anesthetized, or even dead.[54]

Although Lief and Fox report that overdetachment was infrequent among the medical students they studied, the studies we reviewed earlier suggest that it may be a more prevalent pattern among practicing physicians. Through a variety of ways, physicians frequently maintain considerable distance from their patients; reports of "doctor talk," "communication gaps," and "doctor-centered" interviews all refer in part to the dimension of emotional distance. A recent study of medical training, *The Doctor Tree*,[55] also cites the "gap" and "distance" patterns in describing the oscillation between empathy and objectivity in medical student development.

The emphasis on "objectivity" during medical training is striking and is observed in several studies. It would be an oversimplification to view these socialization experiences as the primary, or only, determinants of "communication gaps" in physician–patient relationships. Nonetheless, it is not far-fetched to conclude that the complex and intense socialization experience of becoming a physician does contribute in important ways to the physician's later style and approach with patients. Highly valued "objectivity" can function as one way in which the graduate physician maintains emotional distance from patients in various clinical encounters.

There are other aspects of medical training that influence later physician–patient relationships. Medical training occurs over a prolonged period of time, and certain values and ideals may be specific to particular phases. For example, one relatively well-demarcated phase of training is in the last two years of medical school. In this second half of American medical school training, most teaching occurs through direct clinical experience with patients in hospitals and outpatient clinics. The didactic teaching about interviewing, and examples shown by physician–instructors, are important influences in shaping students' later outlook toward direct interviewing, through history taking and consultations. Reiser and others[56] have observed a decreased emphasis on history taking, which has accompanied increased reliance on technology for gathering seemingly precise information through "tests" and specialized examination techniques (for example, ascultation and cardiography). Speaking of this trend, Reiser notes that "young physicians increasingly tended to neglect history-taking, in some cases because their teachers had not emphasized the diagnostic importance of sitting down with the patient and questioning him about his illness."[57]

The theme of value changes and the development of new values during the passage through medical school is also an important one for Becker[58] and Fox.[59] Becker notes the increasing cynicism and diminishing idealism that he found among medical students as they moved from their first to their senior year. Fox describes the development of certain basic values, such as affective neutrality, tolerance for uncertainty, and medical responsibility. A broad conceptualization of the medical school experience and its potential outcomes is presented in *The Doctor Tree*.[60] The Zabarenkos depict five "lines of development" the medical student must traverse and in so doing struggle with five difficult dilemmas: objectivity versus empathy, nurturance versus executive necessity, omnipotence–omniscience versus toleration of uncertainty, the foundation of the physician ego ideal, and the maturation of an operational professional identity. Although these developmental lines clearly overlap and interpenetrate, the authors argue that they also occur in a specific sequence: the objectivity–empathy dilemma is at its peak earliest in medical training, whereas professional identity issues become most salient for the developing physician at a much later point in training.

The socialization experience continues in perhaps an even more accelerated and intense form during several years immediately following graduation from medical school (internship and residency training). Although most observers recognize the importance of these phases in physician development, there are few systematic studies to draw upon. In an empirical investigation based on interviews with forty-six interns in two urban hospitals,[61] the interns described a number of regulations, "norms," that had evolved to govern their relations with patients, particularly those who were very ill. These rules were directed toward such problems as modulating feelings, diminishing "intensive involvement" with patients, and the place of emotions in the treatment of various types of patients. In one interview, an intern described his disturbing predicament over feelings for a very ill patient:

You are interested in human welfare and the alleviation of suffering, but this interest is directed to one patient at one moment, and another later. Today, for instance, there was a man admitted with cancer of the larynx. He will never talk again after it is removed. . . . You can say, "I am sorry, old chap" or something of that nature, or think the same, but inwardly you cannot become too personally involved.[62]

Two other accounts treat the complex and difficult internship year. Mumford[63] followed the unfolding experience of internship in two very different settings, a university hospital and a community hospital. Her monograph highlights the different orientations between these two settings, particularly in terms of the alternative values, for example, academic advancement versus community participation, they impart to new physicians who pass through them. She offers many observations of these differences and, more powerfully, the numerous pivotal points in both systems, where strong influences are brought to bear on the developing

physicians' orientations and medical relationships. The second, more bit-
ing account of internship appears in a recent novel, *House of God*,[64]
where many of the issues touched in the empirical studies are elaborated
in fictional form, such as the frequently conflicting values of academic
knowledge and patient care, and the dilemmas over empathy, nurturance,
and objectivity.[65]

These descriptions and studies of medical training suggest important
developmental factors that contribute to problematic aspects of physician–patient relationships. But as the next section points out, there are
still other social dimensions we must consider.

The social roles of physician and patient

A second approach to the study of how social and cultural processes contribute to the physician–patient relationship focuses on the influence of
socially defined roles on each participant. Parsons' sociological analysis
of the "sick role" is an early and influential statement of this orientation.[66] Parsons' position is that society has specific expectations for people who play the role of "doctor." Doctors learn this role long before
medical school, and through a variety of experiences, patients also learn
the rules governing the "patient" role. These learned roles serve as significant determinants of physician–patient relationships.

Although the theoretical perspective is similar to that adopted in the
socialization studies, Parsons' approach adds other components. First,
the social-role perspective cites experiences that clearly precede medical
school; and, second, it indicates that the development of the *patient* as
well as the physician is highly relevant in any analysis of physician–patient interaction. For physicians, the patterns of attitudes, expectations,
and values have been learned during the entire course of growing up,
though in their most concentrated form during the passage through medical school. For the individual who becomes a "patient," cultural rules
applying to this new, usually temporary, role have also been internalized
during the course of development. Learning to assume the future patient
role occurs within the family setting, as the child and young adult observes various relatives moving in and out of this status during different
points in their life cycles. This learning continues even after one becomes
a patient. There are many cues, for instance, within medical interviews
and in hospitals or clinics as to what is appropriate "patient behavior." In
Parsons' analysis of the role of the physician, he describes the physician
as "an agent of social control." By this he means that physicians are
implicitly charged by society with "the job of returning the affected per-

son to full functioning, of reversing the withdrawal so that the patient may again take up with threads of social obligations."[67]

At the most general level, then, the physician "is the symbol of the well and normal, or the non-ill encountering the ill . . . symbol of health."[68] In this theoretical framework there are three facets of the physician's role. The central dimension is "affective neutrality." This is the distancing mechanism that helps prevent the physician from becoming so enmeshed in the patient's illness that he or she no longer has objective judgment and therapeutic leverage. Dilemmas surrounding this attitude were noted earlier in discussing studies of medical students and interns. The concurrence of Parsons' theoretical analysis, these socialization studies, and the numerous empirical physician–patient interaction findings may reflect the fact that "detached concern" or "affective neutrality" is a basic, salient, and potentially troublesome tension inherent in the work of the physician.[69]

Two other aspects of the physician role identified by Parsons are its "universalism" and "functional specificity." Universalism refers to the norm for physicians to view all ". . . patients as in some sense equal members of a universe of health and illness. Judgments are guided by technical medical factors; and criteria that lie outside the field of health and illness are considered irrelevant to the medical treatment."[70] For instance, physicians are expected to treat all pregnant women in the same way, regardless of whether one is poor and single or another the wife of the richest man in the community.

Norms of functional specificity, the third aspect of the medical role, prescribe a limitation on the physician's attention and activities to a rigidly circumscribed sphere – to those things that are defined as "medical." Thus, physicians are not expected to offer religious or political counsel, or to intrude into the patient's private life other than as required by the medical problems at hand. This formulation of the physician's role is particularly controversial. A number of recent contributions[71] and the position taken by proponents of "holistic medicine"[72] challenge the value of this restriction on a physician's role; they argue that such an orientation may seriously limit the effectiveness of physicians.

Parsons' analysis of physician and patient roles focuses on social norms that govern appropriate behavior for participants in medical transactions. Other investigators have emphasized the importance of the physician's authority and power, and the influence of medical settings as social organizations.[73]

Szasz and Hollander[74] discuss three theoretical models of physician–patient relationships and propose that the relationship that prevails at any given time is a function of *both* the medical setting and the particular medical problem at hand. These points are illustrated in the following summaries of their three models.

1. Activity–passivity. In the activity–passivity relationship the physician is active and the patient is passive. Szasz and Hollander note that such a mode is most appropriate for the treatment of medical emergencies. In these acute situations, the physician "does something" to the patient. An important characteristic of this medical orientation is that "treatment" takes place regardless of the patient's contribution or active participation.

2. Guidance-cooperation. Szasz and Hollander argue that the guidance–cooperation relationship is the most pervasive in ongoing medical practice. It is usually present in situations that are less desperate than acute emergencies. Although the patient is ill, he or she is still conscious and expresses wishes and feelings. The patient is nonetheless suffering, seeking help, and ready to "cooperate." In turning to a physician, patients place themselves in a position of less power; the physician has knowledge and skills, resources the patient does not possess. The patient, in turn, is expected to "obey," "follow orders," comply with the medical regimen prescribed by the doctor. Although patients are no longer viewed as helpless children, they are expected to be dependent and cooperative in the relationship. The guidance–cooperation mode is probably identical with the "doctor-centered" interaction described by Byrne and Long.[75]

3. Mutual participation. Mutual participation is favored by patients who "want to take care of themselves."[76] Socially, and psychologically, it is the most complex of the three relationships to sustain, because both physician and patient must be aware of each other's needs, wishes, and individuality. Szasz and Hollander suggest that mutual participation may be most appropriate in the treatment of chronic illnesses such as diabetes mellitus and chronic heart disease, where patients are required to carry out much of the treatment program themselves with only occasional medical consultation.

The potential benefits of a relationship based on mutual participation is highlighted in two recent articles by patients who have survived severe illnesses.[77] Both men depict the significance of the collaborative relationship with their physicians that evolved over long periods of time. These moving descriptions portray physicians who were highly responsive to new inputs from their patients concerning points of diagnosis as well as medical management. These patients were highly educated and articulate, a fact that is consistent with Szasz and Hollander's suggestion that conditions of relatively equal status will be most conductive to the flourishing of a mutual participation relationship.

In many of the studies we reviewed earlier, mutual participation is often notable by its absence. A number of authors advocate the desirability of mutual participation as the ideal form of physician–patient interaction, arguing that such a mode might alleviate many of the problems associated with the more usual "guidance–cooperation" medical relationship. For example, Lazarre[78] discusses a "customer approach" to the patient, describing a "negotiation where the participants (physician and patient) simultaneously influence one another, hopefully leaving the clinician better educated to make a more valid formulation, and leaving the patient more willing to consider the clinician's suggestion."[79] Lazarre and Reader[80] specifically underscore the importance of collaboration and negotiation between doctor and patient. As we have already seen, empirical studies detailing problematic aspects of physician–patient relationships often conclude with discussions about the potential advantages of a greater mutuality between physician and patient.[81]

As we have suggested throughout this chapter, physician–patient relationships occur within contexts, and are significantly influenced by them. In the next section, and the concluding discussion, we shall look more fully at how medical and social settings constrain and contribute to these interpersonal relationships.

The hospital setting and physician–patient relationships

The negotiation of mistakes and trust

Drawing on her two years as a participant observer in several university hospitals, Millman[82] explored the closely related topics of physician mistakes and patient trust. Her account is of much interest because it deals with ways in which important issues between individual patients and physicians are shaped by influences from surrounding hospital environments. In her analysis, Millman elaborates in some detail several strategies physicians use to cope with these issues that are central to their interactions with patients.

1. Mistakes. Medical errors are upsetting to physicians for a number of reasons. To begin with, there is the self-doubt and frequent loss of self-esteem that may accompany awareness of a mistake. There is the distress of anticipated consequences, which may include serious medical ramifications such as a patient's death, or potential disruptions in physician–patient or physician–family relationships, as through the choice of a new physician. There is an additional lurking threat of malpractice suits. In terms of professional impact, mistakes carry the risk of tarnished reputation in the eyes of colleagues, as well as formal sanctions or punishments. Within hospital environments, particularly academic ones, the possibility of mistakes coming to the awareness of medical colleagues and associated personnel is even greater than in private office practice.

In light of these multiple dangers, how do physicians cope with the anticipation and effects of errors? Millman elaborates three lines of defense that physicians employ. The primary mode is withholding of information. Although there may be many reasons to withhold information about a patient's illness, Millman argues that the strongest reason has to do with limiting the power and autonomy of the patient. With less knowledge of their condition, patients are in a poorer position to recognize that a mistake has in fact occurred. Another form of withholding is the refusal of physicians to evaluate the competence or performance of others who are caring for the patient, or to comment on the "wisdom" of treatment recommended by other physicians. Within the hospital treatment system, this second form of withholding is especially important and prevalent.

Millman observes that these withholding practices are often justified as serving to "protect" patients from undue stress or confusion. However, she maintains that their crucial function is to protect physicians from awareness of as well as results of their mistakes. The hospital system tends to support these practices. For example, the nursing staff generally exercises much caution over sharing information about a patient's illness, or their judgments of the competency of involved physicians.

The third way in which physicians cope with mistakes is to "discredit" the patient. That is, the patient is made responsible for diagnostic or treatment errors. For example, the patient may be described as "a turkey," "chronic," unreliable, or alcoholic. The onus of overlooking a physical finding or not admitting a seriously ill patient is thereby shifted from the physician to the patient. Such discrediting is also engaged in and supported by nurses and attendants who work in emergency room and ward settings.

Discrediting is a process we have not yet encountered in other studies of physician–patient interactions. Many studies refer to nondisclosure or the withholding of information and their multiple ramifications and possible functions. But Millman's analysis differs in two basic ways. First, it is based on a long period of naturalistic observations including attendance at daily rounds, the emergency room, and postmortem conferences. The other important departure in Millman's analysis is her attribution of individual and group motivation underlying the strategy of withholding information. Other investigations note the patient dissatisfaction associated with nondisclosure; and some[83] offer the interpretation that the nondisclosure functions as a means of social control exercised by physicians over their patients. Millman goes beyond these interpretations in arguing that there are specific "protection" motivations behind information/evaluation withholding. The physician's withholding is in the service of masking anticipated mistakes and repairing the damage that so often follows the making of mistakes.

2. *Trust.* Closely related to the issue of medical mistakes is that of trust. Just as mistakes are distressing events that physicians seek to minimize awareness of, and consequences from, so too are indications of patient mistrust. One obvious means of physicians' handling signs of patient mistrust is to allay their anxieties over revealed mistakes by using discrediting and nondisclosure techniques. More directly, evidence of mistrust can be diminished through avoidance. Millman gives many instances of how assertions, questions, and direct emotional expressions of distrust were frequently ignored or responded to in ways that clearly discouraged further pursuit. Sustaining the patient's anxious questioning concerns may lead the physician, and staff, to experience more vulnerability themselves should a planned surgery or medical procedure go poorly. Besides the greater vulnerability there are the additional burdens of greater time and energy demands that ensue when worried questions and concerns are taken seriously.

In addition to avoidance, signs of distrust can be coped with through what Millman terms "neutralization," where questions and concerns are redefined in such a way that the inherent doubts are somehow removed, replaced by mechanically direct reassurance. Finally, there is the practice of shielding patients from hearing potentially upsetting information. This can be carried out by such limited or overly technical explanations as Golden and Johnson[84] and Korsch[85] describe. Or the shielding of patients can occur as the ward staff cautiously communicates with the patient in such a way that few facts are conveyed about the patient's current medical situation. Consistent with these ways of avoiding and minimizing awareness of distrust are the forms of self-deception that Millman also observed, as the medical personnel, assuring themselves of unquestionning trust, "act as if they assume that patients are thoroughly trusting and they do not hear, see, think about, or notice anything which is not directly addressed to them."[86]

Millman's analyses and interpretation add to our understandings of physician–patient relations on several counts. They take place in complex hospital environments rather than in clinics or private offices. Even more important, they are attuned to facets of physician–patient relationships that may come to light only through long-term, longitudinal, observations of physicians and their patients. Millman followed unfolding medical relationships as they moved through diagnosis, treatment, surgery, and death. Most of the other empirical studies have been based on briefer (one or two visits) interactions in emergency room or acute clinic settings. The significant and subtly masked problems of trust, mistrust, and mistakes may be particularly difficult to discern and elucidate through these other, more cross-sectional methods. Millman's interpretations are provocative ones, suggesting ways in which we can understand the findings of the communication, language, and distortion studies. Yet it is essential to keep in mind the fact that her conclusions and interpretations are in the end focused almost completely on nuances of physician–patient interactions. The ways in which hospital systems sustain, and sometimes shape, these interactions are attended to, but clearly they are not her principal points. This is not the case in the next hospital study. The matrix of relationships between community, hospital, physician and patient is, without doubt, central to the interests of Duff and Hollingshead.[87]

The sponsorship of the patient

In following the hospital course of 225 patients, Duff and Hollingshead concentrate on the interplay between the physician–patient relationship and two settings, the hospital and the family. In their analysis they introduce an aspect of physician–patient interaction that we have not yet directly encountered: The form, and degree of responsibility, that a physician takes for his or her patient. Duff and Hollingshead term this dimension "sponsorship," ". . . the method through which the physician assumes responsibility and discharges obligations to care for the patient."[88] Sponsorship is highly responsive to numerous pressures within hospital as well as community settings. Duff and Hollingshead found that the most important determinant of a patient's sponsorship was his or her social class. Other factors that influenced the sponsorship included type of illness and age. There were four types of sponsorship, discussed in the following paragraphs.

1. Committee sponsorship. The fundamental feature of committee sponsorship was that the patient had no single continuous physician on whom he or she could depend. Instead, "care was vested in an ever-present, ever-changing committee,"[89] whose members were house staff (interns and residents), medical students, and senior academic physicians from the medical school. Patients who had this type of sponsorship were from the lowest socioeconomic classes (working class). The overriding consideration in the committee's approach to its patients was "learning"; consistent with this emphasis, patients were generally viewed as representing diseases, not people. Diseases were dealt with rigorously and scientifically, but the patients as people received less attention. Duff and Hollingshead describe numerous instances of misunderstandings, disappointments, and lowered self-regard among the patients who had this type of sponsorship by their physicians. Contributing to these difficulties was the fact that physicians and students "rotated" among the many hospital wards and services; this led to routinely discontinuous relations between physicians and patients.

2. Semicommittee sponsorship. Semicommittee sponsorship included a private physician who was nominally involved in the patient's care; but a large segment of the responsibility for diagnosis and treatment, and communication with the patient, was assumed by the house staff. Although the patient paid for the services of one or more private physicians, this sponsorship scarcely differed from the committee type. The private physician simply served as another member of the committee.

3. Casual sponsorship. With casual sponsorship the private physician was clearly in the foreground of the patient's care. The focus of their interaction was the disease symptoms, the diagnosis, and the treatment procedures. The technical medical knowledge of the physician was applied to understand the patient's disease. Little time was allowed for patients to ask questions about their illness; and when concerns were raised, the patient was told that "the best of science was being applied."[90] Patients in this form of sponsorship were from middle- and upper-middle-class groups.

4. Committed sponsorship. Committed sponsorship differs most sharply from committee sponsorship. The relationship was one of "determined assumption of responsibility for the patient by the physician," a responsibility extending beyond his or her interest in the disease. In contrast to the first form of sponsorship, the social class gap between physician and patient was minimal or absent. Although Duff and Hollingshead comment that this form of sponsorship offers the greatest possibility of collaboration between physician and patient, it also presents significant problems.

In one-quarter of the committed sponsorship cases they found that the physician–patient relationship posed a threat to the patient. In their effort to maintain a congenial continuing collaboration and often broader friendship, both physician and patient became vulnerable to social influences such as concern about the importance of "pleasantry and good manners" as opposed to solving the patient's medical problems. These instances may be examples of what Parsons[91] means in his warning of the danger of equality in the medical relationship. Such difficulties are discussed further in our final section.

The findings about the consequences of sponsorship touch on several of the results from the cross-sectional studies we reviewed earlier. The "communication gaps" discussed by Korsch and others are likely to be most prevalent under conditions of committee sponsorship and are probably closely related to patients' social class. Language difficulties and distortion may also be more common under committee and semicommittee sponsorship, because these problems are tied to class and ethnic physician–patient differences. The physician–patient interactions in the committed group may be closest to what Szasz and Hollander term "mutual participation." That the physician has a limited grasp of the patient's language, understandings, and conflicts is reiterated by Duff and Hollingshead. This limitation is not simply a function of social class membership. Duff and Hollingshead refer to it in their discussions of all forms of sponsorship with the qualified exception of the committed type.

Because their observations spanned longer periods of time and a greater variety of places, it is not surprising that both studies reviewed in this section call attention to new facets of physician–patient interactions. The two analyses offer concepts that place many of the diverse, more microscopic findings (from the social psychological studies of language, communication, and distortion) in a broader social context. Thus, Millman, and Duff and Hollingshead, bring together a range of observations about problematic features of physician–patient interactions, such as physicians' self-protective strategies and the varying structures for patient care within teaching hospitals.

Doctor-talk and mutual participation

In this chapter we have stressed the complexity of physician–patient relationships as well as their many problematic features. In several sections we discussed a specific type of relationship, that of "mutual participation," involving a high level of collaboration between physician and patient. Several of the interaction studies emphasize the absence of such collaboration; their findings detail doctor-dominated, "doctor-talk" interviews. Millman, and Duff and Hollingshead, document patterns that clearly diverge from ones based on mutual participation.

A significant question raised, but unanswered, in the studies is what conditions impede, or enhance, the development of the mutual participation mode. Or, from another perspective, what factors underlie the more frequently found medical relationships, with their strong orientation toward patient dependence and physician domination? Responses to this question are offered by three important sociological analyses. The models presented in these analyses take us back to considerations raised at the start of the chapter: influences of the social matrix on physician–patient relationships.

Three views of how these influences operate are offered by Parsons and Friedson:

1. The learning of the "sick role" and the "doctor role": A tenet of Parsons' model, elaborated on in several more recent analyses, is that the guidance–cooperation relationship is a direct consequence of socialization, of the cultural expectations inculcated in both physicians and patients. In this perspective, the significant infuences on the current physician–patient relationship are belief structures or orientations, governing the enactment of roles that have been acquired by the participants in the course of their development within the culture. This approach assigns relatively less importance to the immediate setting, because it does not significantly shape the physician–patient relationship.

2. The structure of the relation between physician and patient: In his earlier work, and even more emphatically in a recent paper, Parsons[92] argues that an asymmetry is *inherent* in and necessary to the physician–patient relationship. The patient may be an active participant; yet there is a fundamental, irreducible, inequality based primarily on the special responsibilities and competence of the physician. Although Parsons acknowledges that there may be many variants of this essential medical relationship, in the final analysis it is crucial to maintain the inequality in the interest of maximizing effective health care:

. . . with respect to the inherent functions of effective care and amelioration of conditions of illness, there must be a built-in institutionalized superiority of the professional (physician) roles, grounded in responsibility, competence, and occupational concern . . . the lines should be shifted from time to time in the light of new knowledge and changing conditions. I fail, however, to see how it is at all possible to eliminate the element of inequality. To go too far in attempting to do so would surely jeopardize the therapeutic benefits of the vast accumulation of medical knowledge and competence which our culture has so painfully built up over a very long period.[93]

From this perspective, the "costs" of a physician–patient relationship that veered toward an ideal of mutuality and equality – jeopardizing medical care – would outweigh its benefits. In short, from Parsons' analysis, the goals of medical care ("the prevention of illness, the mitigation of its severity and disabling consequences, and its cure . . .")[94] demand an asymmetric relationship between physician and patient.

3. The social networks and conflicting interest of physicians and patients: Elliot Friedson[95] proposes an alternative to the Parsonian formulation. His argument is that the crucial influences on physician–patient interactions come through the social networks and power positions in which physicians and patients are situated. Expectations, in themselves, cannot explain how physicians and patients interact with and influence one another:

Attention must be paid to the social structure in which those perspectives (expectations, attitudes) are located, and there must be systematic specification of the variable situations and positions of influence in which doctors and patients find themselves. Furthermore . . . it is realistic to see the relationship as a form of conflict, the compromise of practice shifting now one way, now another, as the influences of the participants' positions shift.[96]

Instead of a fixed structure of expectations and of roles, Friedson stresses the *conflict* between the competing interests of physician and patient, the various forces for and against the smooth carrying out of physicians' orders. An important implication of this conceptualization is that, given the current organization of health care, there are many reasons to conclude that the mutual-participation relationship, while desirable, may not be realizable. In Friedson's view, physicians expect patients to accept their recommendations unquestioningly, whereas "patients seek services on their own terms." These conditions of opposing interests lead to conflict instead of mutual participation.[97]

In his investigation of patients from three different medical settings, Friedson describes patients' "lay referral systems." Consultation with other laymen was found to be a strong determinant of patients' initial opinions and subsequent consultations with physicians and other medical-care professionals. The influence of this nonmedical interpersonal network is underestimated, or missed entirely, when physician and patient are seen as playing out culturally patterned, socialized roles. From these findings, Friedson argues that direct influences on the physician–patient relationship derive from the "interpersonal networks that are part of everyday life."

Clearly, these three theoretical models – socialization, inherent structural constraints, and social networks – offer alternative explanations of what underlies the prevalence of "doctor-centered," "guidance–cooperation" physician–patient relationships. It seems most likely that any given physician–patient relationship is influenced by *both* the social setting *and* the internalized expectations of participants. A comprehensive understanding of the influences on physician–patient interaction requires identification of the relevant variables – both those having to do with the social system (medical setting, conflicting interests, structural constraints) *and* those having to do with socialization (of patient and physician). It requires, as well, conceptualization of how these complex processes weave together to determine the form of physician–patient relationships. Although we cannot yet provide a full answer to the broad question of what factors interfere with the development of mutual participation between physician and patient in health care, the analyses discussed suggest a spectrum of important determinants, which we must thoughtfully consider.

Notes

1. Balint, M. *The Doctor, His Patient and the Illness.* New York: International University Press, 1957, pp. 247–8.
2. Ibid.
3. Consistent with the strong emphasis on communication is Waitzkin and Stoeckle's extensive study analyzing the elaborate communication in physician–patient relationships in terms of multiple factors that influence these various exchanges. The ongoing study is reported in Waitzkin, H., and Stoeckle, J. D. "Information control and the micropolitics of health care: summary of ongoing research project," *Social Science and Medicine,* 1976, *10*:263–76; and Waitzkin, H., Stoeckle, J. D., Beller, E., and Mons, C. "The informative process in medical care: a preliminary report with implications for instructional communication," *Instructional Science,* 1978, *7*:385–419.
4. Cartwright, A. *Human Relations and Hospital Care.* London: Routledge and Kegan Paul, 1964; and Cartwright, A. *Patients and Their Doctors.* London: Routledge and Kegan Paul, 1967.
5. Ambuel, L., Cebulla, J., Watt, N., and Crowne, D. "Doctor–mother communications, a study of information communicated during clinic visits for acute illness," Columbus: Ohio State University, unpublished, 1964.
6. Reeder, G., Pratt, L., and Mudd, M. "What patients expect from their doctors," *Modern Hospital,* 1957, *89*:88.
7. Bergen, B. "Psychosomatic disease and the role of the physician: a social view," in Lipowski, S. J., Lipsitt, D. R., and Whybrow, P. C. (Eds.). *Psychosomatic Medicine.* New York: Oxford University Press, 1977.
8. Korsch, B. M., and Negrete, V. F. "Doctor–patient communication," *Scientific American,* 1972, *227*:66–74; Korsch, B. M., Gozzi, E., and Francis, V. "Gaps in doctor–patient communication: doctor–patient interaction and patient satisfaction," *Pediatrics,* 1968, *42*:855–71; Francis, V., Korsch, B. M., and Morris, M. J. "Gaps in doctor–patient communication," *New England Journal of Medicine,* 1969, *280*:535–40; Freeman, B., Negrete, V., Davis, M., and Korsch, B. "Gaps in doctor–patient communication: doctor-patient interaction analysis," *Pediatric Research,* 1970, *5*:298–311.

9. Korsch and Negrete, "Doctor–patient communication."
10. Ibid.
11. Ibid. Several of the discussions of the different languages spoken in the medical interview are relevant to this second, "communication gap." These language issues are discussed more fully in the next section of the chapter.
12. Freeman et al., "Gaps in doctor–patient communication."
13. Korsch and Negrete, "Doctor–patient communication."
14. Ibid.
15. Kohn, M. *Class and Conformity*, 2nd ed. Chicago: University of Chicago Press, 1977; Bernstein, B. *Class, Codes, and Control, Vol. 2, Applied Studies Towards a Sociology of Language*. London: Routledge and Kegan Paul, 1973.
16. Jones, E. "Social class and psychotherapy: a critical review of research," *Psychiatry*, 1974, *37*:307–20.
17. Duff, R., and Hollingshead, A. *Sickness and Society*. New York: Harper & Row, 1968.
18. Glaser, B., and Strauss, A. L. *Awareness of Dying*. Chicago: Aldine, 1965.
19. Sudnow, D. *Passing On: The Social Organization of Dying*. Englewood Cliffs, NJ: Prentice-Hall, 1967; Racy, J. "Death in an Arab culture," *Annals of the New York Academy of Science*, 1964, 871–9; Abrams, R. "The patient with cancer – his changing pattern of communication," *New England Journal of Medicine*, 1966, *274*:317–22; Oken, D. "What to tell cancer patients: a study of medical attitudes," *Journal of the American Medical Association*, 1961, *175*: 1120–8; Artiss, K., and Levine, A. "Doctor–patient relations in severe illness," *New England Journal of Medicine*, 1973, *288*:1210–14; Millman, M. *The Unkindest Cut*. New York: Morrow, 1977; Roth, J. *Timetables*. Indianapolis, IN: Bobbs-Merrill, 1963; Haan, N. "Psychological meanings of unfavorable medical forecasts," in Stone, G., Cohen, F., and Adler, N. (Eds.). *Health Psychology*. San Francisco: Jossey-Bass, 1979.
20. McIntosh, J. "Processes of communication, information seeking, and control associated with cancer," *Social Science and Medicine*, 1974, 8:157–87.
21. Fiore, N. "Fighting cancer: one patient's perspective," *New England Journal of Medicine*, 1979, *300*:284–9; Lipkin, M. "On lying to patients," *Newsweek*, June 4, 1979, p. 13.
22. Plaja, A., and Cohen, S. "Communication between physicians and patients in out-patient clinics: social and cultural factors," *Milbank Memorial Fund Quarterly*, 1968, *46*:161–213.
23. Mumford, E. *Interns: From Students to Physicians*. Cambridge, MA: Harvard University Press, 1970; Shem, S. *House of God*. New York: Marek, 1978, have addressed these questions through their very different examinations and reflections on the internship experience. For the most part, however, medical socialization studies have concentrated on the medical school years.
24. Shuy, R. "Problems of communication in the cross-cultural medical interview," *Working Papers: Sociolinguistics #19*, Washington, DC, mimeo, 1974.
25. Ibid.
26. Ibid.
27. Plaja and Cohen, "Communication between physicians and patients."
28. Golden, J. S., and Johnston, G. D. "Problems of distortion in doctor–patient communications," *Psychiatry in Medicine*, 1970, *1*:127–49.
29. Ibid.
30. Byrne, P. S., and Long, B. E. *Doctors Talking to Patients*. London: Her Majesty's Stationary Office, 1976.
31. Ibid., pp. 91–92.
32. Ibid., p. 93.

33. Davis, M. S. "Variation in patient's compliance with doctor's advice: empirical analysis patterns of communication," *American Journal of Public Health*, 1968, *58*:274–88. In this section we shall discuss "selected" compliance studies. The interested reader can find a highly inclusive review in Dunbar, J., and Stunkard, A. "Adherence to diet and drug regimen," in Levy, R., Rifkind, B., Dennis, B., and Ernst, N. (Eds.). *Nutrition, Lipids, and Coronary Heart Disease*. New York: Raven Press, 1979.
34. Dunbar and Stunkard, "Adherence to diet and drug regimen," p. 398.
35. Davis, "Variation in patient's compliance with doctor's advice."
36. Korsch and Negrete, "Doctor–patient communication." The index of compliance was similar to the one constructed by Davis, except for the additional components of using objective behaviors such as checking patients' medicine bottles for labels, as well as number of pills remaining.
37. Charney, E., Bynum, R., Eldredge, G., Frank, D., MacWhinney, J., McNabb, N., Scheiner, A., Sumpter, E., and Iker, H. "How well do patients take oral penicillin? A collaborative study in private practice," *Pediatrics*, 1967, *40*:188–95.
38. Hulka, B., Cassel, J., Kupper, L., and Purdette, J. "Communication, compliance and concordance between physicians and patients with prescribed medication," *American Journal of Public Health*, 1976, *66*:847–53.
39. Those readers who wish to pursue further the subject of compliance can see comprehensive reviews of this important area by Blackwell, B. "Drug therapy: patient compliance," *New England Journal of Medicine*, 1973, *289*:249–52; Mortson, M. "Compliance with medical requirements: a review of literature," *Nursing Research*, 1970, *19*:312–23; Gillam, R. F., and Banshy, A. "Diagnosis and management of patient noncompliance," *Journal of the American Medical Association*, 1974, *288*:1563–7. In addition, the most recent review and thorough discussion by Dunbar and Stunkard has already been cited in note 34.
40. Studies in nonverbal processes cite a variety of "expressive cues" in spoken language and bodily movements that convey the emotions of those who are speaking together: Mahl, G., and Schulze, G. "Psychological research in the extralinguistic area," in Sebeok, T. A., Hagnes, A. S., and Bateson, M. C. (Eds.). *Approaches to Semiotics*. London: Mouton, 1964, pp. 51–124; Kramer, E. "Judgment of personal characteristics and emotions from nonverbal properties of speech," *Psychological Bulletin*, 1963, *60*:408–20; Knapp, M. *Nonverbal Communication in Human Interaction*. New York: Holt, Rinehart, 1972; Hinde, R. A. (Ed.). *Nonverbal Communication*. Cambridge: Cambridge University Press, 1972; Friedman, H. S. "Nonverbal communication between patients and medical practitioners," *Journal of Social Issues*, 1979, *35*:89–99.
41. Milmoe, S., Rosenthal, R., Blane, H. T., Chafetz, M. E., and Wolf, I. "The doctor's voice: postdictor of successful referral of alcoholic patients," *Journal of Abnormal Psychology*, 1967, *72*:78–84.
42. Raimbault, G., Cachin, O., Limal, J., Eliacheff, C., and Rapaport, R. "Aspects of communication between patients and doctors: an analysis of the discourse in medical interviews," *Pediatrics*, 1975, *55*:401–5.
43. Ibid.
44. The failure of physicians to anticipate such misunderstandings is taken up by Bergen, "Psychosomatic disease and the role of the physician," in his discussion of the "two languages" in medical interviews.
45. Groves, J. E. "Taking care of the hateful patient," *New England Journal of Medicine*, 1978, *298*:883–7.
46. Ben-Sira, A. "The function of the professional's affective behavior in client satisfaction: a revised theory," *Journal of Health and Social Behavior*, 1976, *17*:3–11.

47. For instance, see Golden and Johnston, "Problems of distortion."
48. Shuy, "Problems of communication"; Golden and Johnston, "Problems of distortion"; and Byrne and Long, *Doctors Talking to Patients.*
49. Ekman, P., and Friesen, W. "Nonverbal language and clues to deception," *Psychiatry,* 1969, *32*:88–106; Ekman, P., and Friesen, W. "Nonverbal behavior and psychotherapy research," in Shlien, J., Hunt, H., Matarazzo, J., and Savage, C. (Eds.). *Research in Psychotherapy, Vol. 3.* Washington DC: American Psychological Association, 1968; and Mahl and Schulze, "Psychological research in the extralinguistic area."
50. In his current review of this area, Friedman also draws this conclusion (Friedman, "Nonverbal communication.").
51. Becker, H., Geer, B., Hughes, E., and Strauss, A. *Boys in White: Student Culture in Medical School.* Chicago: University of Chicago Press, 1961.
52. Lief, H. I., and Fox, R. C. "Training for 'detached concern' in medical students," in Lief, H. I. (Ed.). *The Psychological Basis of Medical Practice.* New York: Harper & Row, 1963.
53. Ibid., p. 12.
54. Ibid., p. 21.
55. Zabarenko, R. N., and Zabarenko, L. M. *The Doctor Tree.* Pittsburgh, PA: Pittsburgh University Press, 1978.
56. Reiser, S. J. *Medicine and the Reign of Technology.* Cambridge: Cambridge University Press, 1978; Oppenheimer, R. H. "Significance of symptoms in medical teaching," *Southern Medical Journal,* 1930, *233*:58; Engel, G. L., "Are medical schools neglecting clinical skills," *Journal of the American Medical Association,* 1976, *236*:861–3.
57. Reiser, *Medicine and the Reign of Technology.*
58. Becker et al., *Boys in White.*
59. Fox, R. "Training for uncertainty," in Merton, R. K., Reader, G., and Kendall, P. L. (Eds.). *The Student Physician.* Cambridge, MA:Harvard University Press, 1957.
60. Zabarenko and Zabarenko, *The Doctor Tree.*
61. Daniels, M. J. "Affect and its control in the medical intern," *American Journal of Sociology,* 1960, *66*:259–67.
62. Ibid.
63. Mumford, *Interns.*
64. Shem, *House of God.*
65. Except for the two studies cited here (Mumford, Daniels), we have been unable to locate any other *empirical* accounts of the internship experiences. An additional aspect of postgraduate medical socialization, not taken up in this section but worth noting, is the influence of new medical settings on physicians. This point is well developed by Jones, M., and Rapoport, R. "The absorption of new doctors into a therapeutic community," in Greenblatt, M., Levinson, D., and Williams, R. (Eds.). *The Patient and the Mental Hospital.* Glencoe, IL: The Free Press, 1957.
66. Parsons, T. *The Social System.* Glencoe, IL: The Free Press, 1951; Parsons, T. "The sick role and the role of the physician reconsidered," *Milbank Memorial Fund Quarterly,* 1975, *53*:257–78; Levine, S., and Kozloff, M. A. "The sick role: assessment and overview," *Annual Review of Sociology,* 1978, *4*:317–43.
67. Wilson, R. N., Bloom, S. W. "Patient–practitioner relationships," in Freeman, H., Levine, S., and Reeder, L. *Handbook of Medical Sociology.* Englewood Cliffs, NJ: Prentice-Hall, 1972, p. 321.
68. Ibid.
69. Rich and thoughtful discussions about this dimension, and associated issues, can be found in Balint, *The Doctor, His Patient and the Illness.*

70. Wilson and Bloom, "Patient–practitioner relationships."
71. Cousins, N. "Anatomy of an illness (as perceived by the patient)," *New England Journal of Medicine*, 1976, *295*:1458–83; Fiore, "Fighting cancer"; Duff and Hollingshead, *Sickness and Society*.
72. Hayes-Bautista, D., and Harveston, D. "Holistic health care," *Social Policy*, April 1977:7–13; Relman, A. S. "Holistic medicine," *New England Journal of Medicine*, 1979, *300*:312–13.
73. The recent review by Levine and Kozloff, "The sick role," elaborates problematic aspects of Parsons' formulation. Readers interested in this theoretical area may also find Parsons' recent "The sick role" of interest.
74. Szasz, T., and Hollander, M. "A contribution to the philosophy of medicine: the basic models of the doctor–patient relationship," *Archives of Internal Medicine*, 1956, *97*:585–92.
75. Byrne and Long, *Doctors Talking to Patients*.
76. Szasz and Hollander, "A contribution to the philosophy of medicine."
77. Cousins, "Anatomy of an illness"; Fiore, "Fighting cancer."
78. Lazarre, A., Eisenthal, S., and Wasserman, L. "The customer approach to patienthood: attending to patients' requests in a walk-in clinic," *Archives of General Psychiatry*, 1975, *32*:553–8; Lazarre, A., Eisenthal, S., Wasserman, L., Harford, T. C. "Patient requests in a walk-in clinic," *Comprehensive Psychiatry*, 1975, *16*:466–77.
79. Lazarre et al., "Patient requests," p. 467.
80. Reader, L. G. "The patient-client as a consumer: some observations on the changing professional client relationship," *Journal of Health and Social Behavior*, 1972, *13*:406–12.
81. Shuy, "Problems of communication"; Byrne and Long, *Doctors Talking to Patients*; Millman, *The Unkindest Cut*; Friedson, E. "Dilemmas in the doctor–patient relationship," in Rose, A. (Ed.). *Human Behavior and Social Process*. Boston: Houghton-Mifflin, 1962; Wilson and Bloom, "Patient–practitioner relationships."
82. Millman, *The Unkindest Cut*.
83. Waitzkin and Stoeckle, "Information control," 1976; McIntosh, "Processes of communication."
84. Golden and Johnston, "Problems of distortion."
85. Korsch and Negrete, "Doctor patient communication."
86. Millman, *The Unkindest Cut*.
87. Duff and Hollingshead, *Sickness and Society;* readers may also find of interest the critique of this research written by one of the senior physicians in the hospital under study: Beeson, P. "Review of R. Duff and A. B. Hollingshead, *Sickness and Society,*" *Yale Journal of Biology and Medicine*, 1968, *41*:226–41.
88. Duff and Hollingshead, *Sickness and Society*, p. 124.
89. Ibid., p. 127.
90. Ibid., p. 139.
91. Parsons, "The sick role," 1975.
92. Ibid.
93. Ibid., pp. 271–2.
94. Ibid.
95. Friedson, E. *Patients' views of medical practice*. New York: Russell Sage, 1961; Friedson, E. *Profession of medicine: a study of the sociology of applied knowledge*. New York: Dodd, Mead, 1970.
96. Friedson, E. *Patients' views*, p. 191.
97. This and the subsequent discussions of Friedson's perspective are drawn from Friedson, *Patients' views*.

6   The social construction of illness

Elliot G. Mishler

While it is possible to say that man has a nature, it is more significant to say that man constructs his own nature, or more simply, that man produces himself. . . . it is important to emphasize that the relationship between man, the producer, and the social world, his product, is and remains a dialectical one. That is, man (not, of course, in isolation but in his collectivities) and his social world interact with each other.[1]

This quotation is from Berger and Luckmann's influential text, *The Social Construction of Reality*. The title summarizes a major tradition of socio-logical thought, often referred to as "constructivism" or "social constructivism." The implications of constructivism are profound and far-reaching because its theorists propose that reality is constructed through human action, and does not exist independently of it. This does not mean that the world exists only in our heads; rather, that the world as a *meaningful* reality is constructed through human interpretative activity.

This tradition has been a prominent one among social science investigators in the health field. We shall review several studies that represent variants of this approach. At this point, it may be useful to outline some of its general implications, because they underly and guide particular studies. This will also permit us to clarify the differences between this perspective and others that we have discussed in previous chapters.

First, to a constructivist, health, illness, and medical care are social facts; that is, they are socially constructed categories that define and give meaning to certain classes of events. Whether or not a particular behavior or experience is viewed by members of a society as a sign or symptom of illness depends on cultural values, social norms, and culturally shared rules of interpretation. This approach is in contradistinction to the biomedical model of diseases as defined by reference to universal, culture-free criteria. We pointed to this difference in our critique of the biomedical model, particularly in discussing the assumption of generic diseases.

A second and related implication of the constructivist approach follows directly from its denial of the assumption of generic diseases. Given the view that illnesses are culturally defined, one would expect cultural variation in the specification of behaviors as signs of illness, and in taxonomies of disease. The definitions provided by the biosciences in modern Western medicine are considered to represent only one such culturally based set of diseases. This does not mean that the same biological processes would not be observed in different cultures, but that they will be given different meanings. Thus, a sharper distinction is made than in the biomedical model between biological signs and diagnosed illness. Consistent with this emphasis is a view of diagnosis as active interpretive work rather than solely, or principally, as technical procedure. That is, rather than seeing diagnosis as the measurement and assessment of specific deviations from biological norms, constructivists regard it as a process through which certain signs are evaluated as having cultural significance and, in particular, as having the "meaning" of disease.

This distinction between signs and their meaning as disease is, in part, a difference between the experiences of patients and the definition of their problems by health professionals, particularly physicians. Several critics of the traditional biomedical model have proposed that this difference be acknowledged explicitly by the use of different terms. For example, Eisenberg asserts: "To state it flatly, patients suffer 'illnesses'; physicians diagnose and treat 'diseases.' "[2] Eisenberg points out that a principal reason for making this distinction is that "illness" and "disease," defined in this way, do not stand in a one-to-one correspondence. Differentiation of terms would, he believes, avoid unnecessary confusion between the two realms of culturally defined and medically defined problems.

For our purposes, where the principal contrast being made is between the biomedical and constructivist approaches, it has not seemed useful to attend in a systematic way to differences within the constructivist camp. Nonetheless, there are important subvariants of the basic position that should be noted. One important dimension of variation is the degree of relativism adopted by the investigator. Some, like Eisenberg, retain a view of disease as a biomedical reality while at the same time recognizing the existence of alternative views of the problem; the latter are the nonmedical or "folk" theories of illness. Other investigators are more drastically relativistic and view the biomedical definitions as only one of a number of alternative frameworks with no higher claim to ultimate "truth" than any other. For some investigators, "objective" signs of illness must be evident, which may then be interpreted in different ways; other investigators take the position that the actual presence of such signs is irrelevant and that individuals may be labeled as sick even in their absence. Differences in emphasis among studies of these problems tend to reflect these dimensions of variation within the constructivist approach.

A further consequence of the constructivist approach to illness is that it shifts attention away from the medically defined signs which are seen as representing the condition of the patient to the processes, that is, the socially organized activities of health professionals and others, through which these signs come to be defined, interpreted and responded to as having the "meaning" of illness. This is a critical shift in focus, and it has led investigators to study health professionals and their practices as well as the institutional and cultural settings of their work. The question changes from "What are the characteristics of patients?" to "How does a person come to be defined as ill and diagnosed as a patient?" And, further, "What factors influence these processes and what are the consequences for persons to be labeled as patients?" The studies that we shall discuss in later sections of this chapter and in Chapter 7 are addressed to these questions.

These introductory comments may help to clarify an observation made previously that epidemiological studies of patients and institutional studies of medical practice, although they introduce social factors as contexts for understanding problems of health and illness, do not raise serious questions about the biomedical definition of illness. The constructivist approach departs more radically from the biomedical model and proposes alternative definitions of health and illness. In the specific form that this approach has usually taken, referred to as the "social labeling" or "societal reaction" theory, illness is defined as one type of social deviance. Definitions of and responses to deviance are a function of social rules.[3] A frequently quoted statement of the position makes this point directly: ". . . social groups create deviance by making the rules whose infraction constitutes deviance, and by applying these rules to particular people. . . . From this point of view, deviance is not a quality of the act the person commits, but rather a consequence of the application by others of rules and sanctions to an 'offender.' "[4] If one substitutes the term "illness" for "deviance" in this quotation, the relationship of this approach to the general constructivist perspective is evident, as are the general implications noted in this section of this approach for studies of health and illness.

We shall be reviewing studies of diagnosis as a social process through which individuals are labeled as having a particular illness: diabetes, alcoholism, hyperkinesis, mental retardation, blindness, and, in the following chapter, leprosy. These studies examine the features of diagnostic practices, cultural and institutional influences on them, and the consequences for persons labeled as patients. It seems useful, however, to place these studies in the context of the general problem of diagnosis within medicine, and we shall begin with that.

The problem of diagnosis

Establishing a correct diagnosis is one of the chief aims of medical practice. Its importance is stated clearly by Feinstein in his monograph on clinical judgment: "Diagnosis is the focal point of thought in the treatment of a patient. From diagnosis, which gives a name to the patient's ailment, the thinking goes chronologically backward to decide about pathogenesis and etiology of the ailment. From diagnosis also, the thinking goes chronologically forward to predict prognosis and to choose therapy. . . . The taxonomy used for diagnosis will thus inevitably establish the patterns in which clinicians observe, think, remember and act."[5]

Attention to problems of diagnosis appears to be coterminous with the origins of medicine. For example, the earliest known writings on medicine, Egyptian papyri dating from 1900 to 1550 B.C., include a classification of diseases.[6] On the basis of these early accounts, a historian of medicine states that he is confident " . . . that classification existed in medicine long before it became scientific in any sense of this word."[7] The long and continuous history of interest in the classification and diagnosis of disease underscores their central place in medical theory and practice. It might, therefore, seem surprising that the process of diagnosis has received little systematic study. As one researcher remarks, "The activity known as 'diagnosis' is central to the practice of medicine but is studied less than its importance warrants."[8]

The aims of diagnosis, and the procedures for arriving at an accurate diagnosis, are among the taken-for-granted "silent" assumptions of medicine. As is true in everyday life as well as in areas of specialized practice, such assumptions do not become topics of reflection and questioning in the ordinary, practical circumstances of the work done in accord with them. That is, diagnosis is integral to the physician's work with patients and is the principal objective of much research in medicine, both pure and applied. For physicians to raise questions about what they do, and why, would involve questioning the enterprise of medicine as a whole. This point is evident to those who have examined the problem. For example, Engle and Davis, in their review and analysis of the history and current status of diagnosis, state: "Diagnosis is such an established part of medical practice that few physicians consider whether there is general agreement about what is meant by the term diagnosis; whether diagnosis is an art, a science, or both; whether diagnosis is an essential prerequisite to medical management; and even whether diagnoses are clearly defined disease entities."[9]

We begin with these observations on diagnosis, as a central yet relatively unexamined feature of medicine, because we see diagnosis as intimately linked to the key assumption of the biomedical model that we have referred to as the assumption of generic and universal diseases. Engle and Davis point out that "Diagnosis is intimately related to our concepts of disease."[10] They then note that "At the present time there is no unified concept of disease," but they and others attribute the problems of diagnosis to certain technical and practical difficulties in the specification and differentiation of disease entities from each other. Thus, they distinguish several "orders" of diseases on the basis of the certainty with which a diagnosis can be made. The essential criteria turn out to be the degree of consensus about etiology and the invariance of symptoms and signs across persons and environments. These produce a hypothetical ordering of certainty from physical traumas such as fractures through diseases with less certain diagnosis where etiology is clear but there is clinical variability, such as infections and allergies, to symptom constellations or syndromes where etiology in unknown and the disease picture is highly variable.

Underlying this ordering of diseases on a dimension of "certainty of diagnosis" is the assumption that diseases are real entities and that the problems of ascertaining the presence or absence of a specific disease in any particular case reflect a current lack of knowledge about causation and/or the lack of sufficiently precise tests. There are, of course, other views within medicine about the nature of diagnosis. For example, diagnosis has sometimes been referred to as an art rather than a scientific procedure.[11] One clinician describes diagnosis as a process of synthesizing key features of a case into a ". . . 'clinical picture' in much the same way that a landscape painter on viewing nature chooses and combines, for his purpose, the elements that are necessary for his work of art."[12] For others, diagnosis includes an assessment of the particular and unique significance of specific signs and symptoms for the individual patient, that is, what the symptoms mean in terms of each patient's personal characteristics and life patterns. Engle and Davis comment that this way of formulating a diagnosis approaches "the point where no two patients have precisely the same diagnosis."[13]

The polarities of art and science cover widely divergent approaches to diagnosis within medicine. Nonetheless, whether a clinician leans toward one or the other pole, the assumption is retained that there is a real "disease" to be found. Its signs may perhaps be obscured by other biological processes, symptoms may be masked or distorted by psychological states or cultural values, but is assumed that underneath this "noise" is a specific disease with its own distinguishing and differentiating features. In this way, practitioners and medical scientists, whether they adopt a broad artistic or a narrow scientific approach to the problem of diagnosis, tend to isolate their work from its social surroundings and from its social consequences. We shall, in later sections of this chapter, approach the problem from another perspective, one from which the nomenclature of diseases is viewed as a system of social categories although defined primarily by biological features. Further, as we have already suggested, the work of diagnosis will be examined as a social process through which illness is constructed and certain persons are cast into the role of patients.

In our earlier comments on the assumption of generic diseases in the biomedical model, we noted that the critical connection made in modern medical thought between biological processes and diseases is itself a product of a particular history and cultural tradition. Thus, we quoted Fabrega, who pointed out that, although to modern medicine, "disease is given a biomedical reality insofar as its chemical and physiological attributes are emphasized," within a broader cross-cultural and historical frame of reference, "biomedicine, the prevailing orientation of the contemporary physician, is but another view of disease."[14] This does not mean, of course, that biological structures and processes have no reality. It does mean, however, that the degree to which they are "emphasized" in the definition of diseases and the significance attributed to them for diagnostic purposes reflect more general sociocultural norms, values, and purposes.

In this connection, it is instructive to examine how problems in the reliability of diagnosis are approached within medicine. First, it is noteworthy that the reliability of diagnosis has not been a central topic for research. A recent review concludes: "The reliability of many signs, procedures, and diagnostic and therapeutic judgements has never been studied."[15] Given the centrality of diagnosis for clinical practice (and its equal importance for research on the etiology of different diseases), we might have expected more attention to the problem. We believe that one plausible reason for this inattentiveness is that the issue of reliability does not arise naturally when there is a deep belief in the real equivalence between biological signs and specific diseases. That is, biological signs are assumed to be determinate indicators of disease, and because biological signs are observable and measureable, the issue becomes one of accuracy, not of reliability. As a consequence of this view, the problem is defined in terms of the calibration and precision of instruments rather than as a problem of agreement between observers, the users of the instruments.

Koran remarks that although it is often assumed that in clinical practice clinicians can reach a level of good agreement on diagnoses, his review of many reliability studies of a variety of illnesses leads him to conclude that the evidence does not justify such confidence. In summary, he states: "The physicians studied almost always disagreed at least once in 10 cases, and often disagreed more than once in five cases. . . . Disagreements of this magnitude, if characteristic of clinical practice in general, cannot safely be regarded as inconsequential."[16] Koran's recommendations, like those of Engle and Davis, also reflect a view of diagnosis as a technical problem, in the sense we noted above: They focus on clearer definitions of terminology, criteria, and procedures, with some attention to factors that might interfere with efficient performance and accurate perception, such as physician fatigue.

Problems in the reliability of diagnosis have received more attention in psychiatry than in other areas of medicine.[17] The difficulties in arriving at valid and reliable diagnoses of the different mental illnesses are widely recognized. The basic issues, however, are not more different here than in the diagnosis of physical illnesses, and approaches to the problem of reliability rest on the same assumptions of the biomedical model of disease. Thus, one widely cited paper, which proposes specific diagnostic criteria for many of the major mental illnesses, notes a number of difficulties in establishing the validity of diagnoses. These include the "absence of known etiology or pathogenesis . . . [for] the more common psychiatric disorders," the fact that "unfortunately, consistent and reliable laboratory findings have not yet been demonstrated in the more common psychiatric disorders," and the relatively low level of reliability, precision, and reproducibility of clinical descriptions.[18]

These several deficiencies in psychiatry have led to recommendations for increased standardization of terms, signs, and procedures. Kramer, for example, points to the difficulty of interpreting variations in reported rates of mental disorder such as "the extraordinary differences between the patterns of first admissions specific for diagnosis to the mental hospitals of England and Wales as compared to the United States."[19] He argues that "the major need for assuring reliable diagnostic data on the mental disorders is the development of diagnostic methods and instruments that would lead to greater precision and consistency in the way psychiatrists utilize diagnostic terms."[20] He proposes: "What is needed to get at the problem of observer variability is a method for allowing a set of observers to arrive at an independent assessment of the same patient. These ratings must be based on identical anamnestic and clinical data and a standard clinical interview."[21]

The rationale for such standardization seems to be clear and self-evident. The assessment of treatment effectiveness, the interpretation of research findings, and the development and evaluation of health-care programs all depend on a consistent use of standard methods and criteria. Nonetheless, Kramer's and others' similar recommendations merit further examination because they rely on the biomedical assumption of the universality of specific generic diseases. That is, the problem to which these recommendations is addressed is observer variability. Clinicians, it is argued, differ in their diagnoses because they vary among themselves in their definitions of diagnostic categories, in the significance they attach to different signs and symptoms, and in their methods for assessing the presence of these signs and symptoms. For example, psychiatrists in England and Wales may have a narrower conception of schizophrenia and a broader conception of manic-depressive psychoses than their American counterparts. This would help account for the findings of consistently higher rates for schizophrenia in the United States than in England and Wales and the reverse ordering of rates for manic-depressive psychoses.[22] The recommended solution to this problem of marked cross-national differences in the rates of different mental disorders is to have British and American psychiatrists use the same criteria and methods.

This approach assumes that there is a real entity to which the label of schizophrenia ought properly to be applied, and another real entity to which the label of manic-depressive psychosis is to be applied. By emphasizing the application of standard methods, the basic problem of validity is sidestepped and obscured. An alternative approach, more consistent with the critique of the biomedical model we have been developing, would begin by recognizing the reality of the different definitions of schizophrenia rather than treating variation as a sign of error and unreliability. That is, if diagnosis is a social process and illness is a social category, then we should expect to find variation across cultures and over time. In this view, illness is not a fixed reality waiting to be discovered by the application of more and more precise and standardized methods; rather, illness is socially constructed, and any definition and diagnosis depends on the selection of particular signs and symptoms as relevant. These selection decisions depend on the complex interplay of many factors, including general cultural norms and values as well as the norms and values that are specific to medicine at a particular time and in a particular place.

Descriptions of diseases in standard texts and handbooks of medicine are richly detailed and include criterial and differentiating symptoms and signs. Discussions of the reliability of diagnosis, on the other hand, tend to be more abstract and usually reflect the viewpoints of researchers and administrators rather than of clinicians. Studies of the reliability of diagnosis tend to be shaped by research and administrative perspectives. In a typical study some standard item of information, such as an X-ray or electrocardiogram, is given to several physicians who are then asked to make a specific diagnosis on the basis of this information; their agreement is used as the measure of reliability.[23] Studies of the reliability of diagnosis in actual clinical practice are relatively rare. However, there are a number of reports from observations of the diagnostic process that provide a more adequate picture of this aspect of clinical work. We shall review some of these studies, directing attention to the general problem with which we are concerned, namely, the ways in which nonmedical factors enter into the diagnosis and treatment of patients.

Studies of the social construction of illness

Diabetes

It is not uncommon for a physician to diagnose an illness in a clinically asymptomatic patient when some key biological sign or indicator of the illness is found in a physical examination or laboratory test. One example is an elevated blood sugar level, often used as a principal criterion in the diagnosis of adult-onset diabetes. Nowadays, relatively few adult patients appear in a physician's office with the overt clinical syndrome of diabetes, "characterized by polyphagia, polydipsia, and polyuria, loss of weight and other signs and symptoms attributable to hyperglycemia, glycosuria, and other consequences of a disordered metabolism of carbohydrate fat and protein."[24] The case is different for children, but adults may come to be diagnosed as diabetic when sugar is found in their urine during a routine medical examination. Typically, the finding is unanticipated, because the person has been asymptomatic. Sometimes referred to as "chemical" diabetics or as having "subclinical" diabetes, these patients will then usually be placed on a treatment regimen that may include a special diet, tablets, or insulin injections. The essential aim of the treatment is to reduce blood sugar levels so that they approximate "normal" levels, and thereby prevent development of the clinical symptoms of diabetes listed earlier. It is also believed by some diabetologists that other complications of the disease, such as microvascular disorders, may be diminished or prevented through strict control of blood sugar levels.

Although this approach to the control of adult diabetes is quite wide-spread, one investigator argues that the grounds for both diagnosis and treatment are not particularly definitive. Posner,[25] an anthropologist whose report is based on observations and interviews in a British diabetic outpatient clinic, cites a number of specialists to the effect that a high blood sugar level by itself is an inadequate index of diabetes. Among the difficulties in evaluating the clinical significance of this index are the following: blood sugar levels are subject to considerable fluctuation, with the amount of variation between successive tests in the same person often as great as variations between people; even high levels require reference to other physiologic systems and metabolic processes for adequate inter-pretation; finally, a strong correlation has not been established between the severity of diabetes as measured by blood sugar levels and the development of complications.

The efficacy of treatment is also far from being well demonstrated; Posner cites one commentator as follows: "In general the treatment of mature diabetes would seem to be an example of the large-scale use of ineffective and possibly dangerous therapies in a particularly inefficient way."[26] In addition, although treatment is prescribed to reduce the risk of complications and symptoms that may result from chronic hyperglyce-mia, hypoglycemic attacks from taking insulin appear to be more common than the effects of hyperglycemia among adult diabetics under treatment. One of Posner's respondents told her of one survey that reported hypo-glycemia as "the most common complication" in long-term diabetic pa-tients.[27] These results suggest that a significant complication of adult-on-set diabetes may be iatrogenic, that is, treatment-induced.

On the basis of her study, Posner argues that the evidence is equivocal with regard to the link between high blood sugar levels and the serious sequelae of diabetes. Nonetheless, active treatment with insulin injec-tions or tablets is commonly prescribed, often in conjunction with diet recommendations. Posner then asks why the hypothesis guiding the diag-nosis and treatment of diabetes has not been seriously challenged or re-placed in clinical practice. She proposes that when physicians are faced with a situation of great uncertainty and the unpredictability of onset of serious and life-threatening complications, it is understandable that they "need to feel that they can at least control it (i.e., blood sugar levels), and that there is something they can do which will help prevent complica-tions."[28] One physician whom she quotes suggests the degree to which the hypothesis' acceptance is a matter of faith: " . . . we all secretly feel that this is in fact the case, . . . we all secretly believe this and hope about it, but there is no outstanding evidence that it is true."[29] Posner concludes that "the medical theory of the treatment of diabetes is a belief system which is sustained by certain medical assumptions and, like any other, by social, structural and cultural factors.''[30]

Posner's analyses and interpretation must be qualified in some obvious ways. In particular, she studied only one clinic, and we recognize that there is considerable variation and controversy among diabetologists as to the proper treatment of this complex illness. Nevertheless, despite our reservations, her study helps to illustrate some features of the constructivist perspective we outlined earlier. In addition, we have suggested that the biomedical model with its assumption of generic diseases underlies the act of faith she describes, and what she refers to as "magical elements" in clinical practice. Posner points to one set of factors that serves to sustain these practices, namely, the uncertainty and unpredictability of the disease in the context of a physician's commitment to reduce risk and to alleviate suffering. The influence of broader sociocultural values and of the specific definition of physicians' role obligations are evident. For example, there is the general view in medicine that once a technique that can provide some control over a problem is available, it should be used. Thus, when it was found that insulin could reduce blood sugar levels, physicians came to feel that it would be "unethical" not to prescribe it even though it has remained unclear that an elevated blood level is the principal and criterial factor in producing the complications of diabetes.

This example suggests the importance of general social norms and cultural values in the orientation of physicians to their work. They are morally obligated to treat persons who show signs of illness. In the case of diabetes, when an individual is labeled as having this disease on the basis of an elevated blood sugar level, which is a deviation from a biological norm, then treatment of the disease appears to be required by the sociocultural standards of professional practice. In an otherwise asymptomatic person, the biological sign in and of itself would not seem to require medical intervention. Further, as Posner's respondents suggest, there are risks of both insulin treatment and tablets, risks that provide a sufficient basis to question their routine prescription. Thus, although both diagnosis and treatment might appear on the surface to be primarily technical matters, it is clear in this instance that their determinants reflect the sociocultural context of medical practice. In the sections that follow, we shall examine other examples of sociocultural and institutional influences on diagnosis, treatment, and outcome.

Alcoholism

A specific treatment, insulin, is available for reducing elevated blood sugar levels and, as we have seen, this appears to be related to the practice of diagnosing diabetes on the basis of this specific biological indicator. It is instructive to examine diagnostic practice in an instance where a specific mode of treatment is not available. Blaxter[31] studied how physicians use the diagnosis of "alcoholism." She points out that such new "social" diagnoses do not fit well within the medical disease model. From her review of various rationales proposed for the importance of diagnosis in clinical practice, she concludes that the primary purpose is "instrumental"; that is, a diagnosis is made when a physician knows what to do.

Blaxter suggests that difficulties arise in the diagnostic process if no practical and effective treatment is known or available, as is the case with alcoholism. She hypothesizes several consequences of these difficulties: reluctance to make the diagnosis, use of the diagnosis only if channels exist for formal referral to nonmedical agencies that deal with the problem, a translation of alcoholism into a medical category, and a tendency to stereotype patients. Her analysis of records, by diagnosis, of all discharges during one year from all nonpsychiatric hospitals in one region in Scotland "showed quite clearly that in this setting the formal category of 'alcoholism' is, on the whole, meaningless."[32]

Blaxter bases her conclusion on findings that indicate considerable variation in the use of the several diagnostic categories for alcoholism and alcohol-related diseases in the International Statistical Classification of Diseases (ICD) Manual. There were several reasons for this variation in diagnosis. For example, clerks who coded physicians' notes into patient records used specific diagnostic categories only if a physician had specifically done so, and physicians varied in their use of these categories. More than three-fifths of the alcohol diagnoses were secondary rather than primary and, thus, would not be counted in official diagnostic statistics, with the result that the extent of alcohol involvement would be severely underestimated. Many of those diagnosed as alcoholic had sustained injuries after drinking or had added alcohol to an overdose of drugs, and for many of these the label of "alcoholic" is likely to be inappropriate. More than half of the diagnosed alcoholics were placed in the residual category of "other and unspecified alcoholism." Finally, for those classified as having alcoholism as a disease, the majority were chronic cases with a psychiatric diagnosis of alcoholism somewhere in their history: " . . . in this general hospital setting, doctors preferred to rely upon a previously applied psychiatric diagnosis, and to avoid raising the question of such a diagnosis themselves." And, even in the case of patients diagnosed as having the disease of alcoholism, " . . . in two-thirds of the cases, no reference whatsoever was made to the alcohol problem in the treatment notes or in the summary sent to the patient's general practitioner."[33]

In her summary, Blaxter points out that dictionary classification systems such as the ICD Manual cannot give instructions to users for situational and contextual use. Therefore, when " . . . the categories and the process get out of step – if the classificatory system no longer matches the generally accepted concepts of disease – then the result may be arbitrary choices of label and perhaps inappropriate action. . . .Medical categorizations of "alcoholism" not only illustrate confusion concerning the concept of disease, but (if diagnosis is process) unease and uncertainty about the clinician's proper work."[34]

There are obvious differences between the processes through which alcoholism and diabetes are diagnosed. In the latter, the "instrumental" function of diagnosis is evident; insulin treatment and diagnosis of diabetes are linked together through the presence of elevated blood sugar levels. There is a lack of such a connection in the case of alcoholism; a specific diagnosis does not require a specific treatment, because an effective treatment is unknown. In these circumstances, diagnoses are variable and, as Blaxter asserts, "meaningless." Nonetheless, in both instances we recognize the significant influence of nonmedical factors on the diagnostic process. With regard to alcoholism, diagnosis depends on several social variables: organizational practices of record keeping and the use of the ICD Manual, local medical customs, cultural definitions and views of alcoholism. We would expect, of course, that these factors would vary in their particulars from setting to setting and, as a consequence, that diagnoses would appear to be highly unreliable and incidence rates would differ markedly from one locale to another. However, these are not merely technical problems that would be solved by clearer definitions in a revised ICD Manual. Variations in diagnosis are a function of real differences in sociocultural contexts.

By examining a new diagnostic category for an "illness" that did not fit easily and clearly within the traditional disease model, namely, alcoholism, Blaxter was able to specify some general problematic features of the diagnostic process. These features, such as the connection between diagnosis and the availability of treatment, and the process through which physicians' notes are translated into diagnostic category codes, are usually hidden in the routine practices through which nonproblematic "typical" cases are diagnosed. Her analyses are based on information recorded in patients' charts, that is, on the end products of the diagnostic process. It is useful to examine the process itself.

Hyperkinesis

Conrad's studies[35] of the introduction and use of hyperkinesis as a diagnostic category include such process observations. In his review of the history of this newly discovered disease, he points out that a period of twenty years elapsed between the original observations, in 1937, that amphetamine drugs " . . . had a spectacular effect in altering the behavior of school children who exhibited behavior disorders or learning disabilities,"[36] and the naming of these varied problems by a specific diagnostic term, "hyperkinetic impulse disorder." Another ten years passed before the diagnostic category, "minimal brain dysfunction" or MBD, was selected by a task force of experts and professionals from more than three dozen diagnoses then in use as the "overriding diagnosis that would include hyperkinesis and other disorders."[37] During this same period of time, hyperkinesis became the most commonly diagnosed childhood psychiatric problem, and Ritalin, a drug synthesized in the mid-1950s, became the treatment of choice. As Conrad notes: "Hyperkinesis is no longer the relatively esoteric diagnostic category it may have been twenty years ago, it is now a well-known clinical disorder."[38]

Like alcoholism, hyperkinesis and the generic category of MBD are new types of illnesses. In both, diagnostic signs and symptoms are behaviors that are deviant from normative requirements and expectations rather than deviant biological processes. This distinction is a strong one in the case of MBD, because this diagnosis depends on the absence of clear organic signs. A further similarity to alcoholism is that the co-presence of symptoms of other diseases excludes a primary diagnosis of hyperkinesis. Within the frame of reference provided by the biomedical model, one might think of alcoholism and hyperkinesis as diseases that have been discovered. The history of medicine abounds with instances where previously unrelated symptoms came to be recognized as going together and therefore as representing a single disease. As one example, Temkin refers to Bright, who " . . . associated morbid changes in the kidney, edema, and albumen into an entity that came to be named after him."[39]

Within a sociological perspective, on the other hand, the emergence of new disease categories may be viewed as instances of the social construction of reality, in particular, as the social construction of medical realities or medical meanings. Conrad proposes that a critical problem in understanding " . . . the construction of medical reality is how signs and symptoms are given medical meaning and interpreted as evidence for a medical disorder," and contends that " . . . the central issue in the construction of the medical reality of hyperactivity is the minimization of uncertainty."[40] Many observers have noted the omnipresence of uncertainty in clinical medicine; there is, for example, a frequently cited classic paper on the training of physicians which argues that its key function is "training for uncertainty."[41]

Conrad[42] lists a set of specific conditions at a clinic he observed that created a situation of uncertainty. These include: (1) disagreement over the concept of hyperactivity itself, with widely varying opinions as to what it is, its major signs and symptoms, and when it is actually present. He quotes one resident who says that "it has no real hard and fast criteria"; (2) the lack of a major reliable diagnostic method or tool, with EEG findings and evidence of "soft neurological signs" viewed an inconclusive, contradictory, and difficult to interpret although tests for these signs and others are part of the routine screening and diagnostic process; (3) the ambiguity and unreliability of reports from teachers and parents on behavioral and developmental history; (4) the rapid turnover of the clinic's pediatric residents, who do much of the diagnostic screening and who have neither the training or experience to evaluate critical nonmedical data, such as behavioral reports from parents and teachers; (5) the relative unpredictability of drug response, where only 60 percent of children diagnosed as hyperactive show a modification of hyperactive behavior after being placed on medication; finally, (6) various myths, stereotypes, and local lore enter into evaluations, adding further to the general problem of uncertainty, such as the comment from an old to a new resident, "Hockey tends to be their favorite sport and they are generally goalies."

In the situation of uncertainty that results from these conditions, the clinic staff relies on "routines of evaluation," which produce data that can then be interpreted as "evidence" for or against a diagnosis of hyperactivity. These routines include developmental and behavioral reports from parents and teachers, pediatric and psychiatric interviews of the child and parents, and a neurodevelopmental examination focused on the detection of soft neurological signs. The results of the neurodevelopmental examination appear to be critical to the diagnosis; other information is used, if at all, in a supplementary way. "Doing well" on the examination generally precludes a diagnosis of hyperactivity, whereas "doing poorly" leads to the diagnosis of hyperactivity, associated with the assumption that the problem is "constitutional," that is, organic. If results of the examination are equivocal, or unavailable for case presentation, and uncertainty remains about the diagnosis, the staff may use a number of other strategies. Essentially, they will try to negotiate a consensus, often with reference to shared typifications about "normal cases" of hyperactivity or by specifying another problem as the "major" diagnosis, such as sexual acting out or mild mental retardation, using hyperactivity as a secondary diagnosis.

In summary, Conrad states: "The social construction of hyperactivity is the creation of a medical definition of deviant behavior. The diagnosis of hyperactivity is as much a product of the social process in which medical reality is constructed as it is a product of any objective physiological reality. The physicians construct a reality for a diagnosis of hyperactivity and yet construe this reality of hyperactivity as something that exists independently from their construction of a medical reality."[43]

It is evident from the studies reviewed thus far that many complex factors enter into the diagnostic process. Variations in general social norms and cultural values, as well as differences in the local subcultures of particular hospitals and clinics, result in different judgments as to the diagnostic significance of specific signs and symptoms. Given the influence of all these factors, and the far from adequate knowledge about many disease processes, the relatively modest reliabilities reported in studies of diagnosis[44] are not unexpected. We are not suggesting that high reliability is in itself a sufficient index either of secure and determinate knowledge about a particular disease or of the general validity of the biomedical model as an approach to understanding illness. The example of diabetes, where a high reliability may be assured by the use of the single criterion of elevated blood sugar levels, suggests that reliability may sometimes be purchased at the cost of validity. Further, in this instance, it appears that nonmedical assumptions play as strong a role as they do when reliabilities are low, as in alcoholism. Our main point, repeated and documented through these observational studies of the diagnostic process, is that diagnosis is an interpretative practice through which illnesses are constructed.

Mental retardation

Patients who arrive at a medical treatment setting have already passed through a number of other decision points. Analyses of the "path to treatment"[45] suggest a variety of factors that affect whether and how symptoms are recognized as indicators of illness and, if so, how individuals then move through a referral network into patient status in a diagnostic-treatment context. To this point, we have focused on processes involved in formal medical diagnosis. This is well along the path, and we shall now look more carefully at some of the earlier steps.

Mercer's research[46] on the ways in which children in the public school system come to be labeled as mentally retarded is particularly relevant to our discussion. In addition to detailed analyses of critical decision points, she explicitly contrasts "clinical" and "social-system" perspectives as alternative approaches to the study and interpretation of mental retardation. This contrasting pair of perspectives is closely related to the biomedical and constructivist approaches that we have been counterposing in this chapter. Further, by showing how teachers, principals, and clinical psychologists make their diagnostic decisions, Mercer demonstrates that the biomedical model has ramifications beyond the borders of medicine itself.

Mercer lists a number of differences between the clinical and social-system approaches.[47] She observes that educators and mental health professionals tend to view mental retardation as an individual pathology that can be defined and diagnosed with reference to medical-pathological and/or statistical models of normality. Within this framework, retardation is approached in a straightforward way as one type of intellectual deficit. Because retardation is viewed as a characteristic of the individual, it is assumed that it may be measured and diagnosed by certain tests of intelligence. Although it is recognized that such tests may have some degree of measurement error, they are considered to be relatively independent of cultural and social variables. This approach is analogous to the biomedical approach to diagnosis and rests on the same assumption, namely, that pathology is in the person.

Mercer's analysis of implications of the clinical perspective is similar to our own critique of the biomedical model. She points out that adherents of this view, because they assume that mental retardation has an "objective reality," tend to study the problem within an epidemiological framework with the aim of determining "true" incidence and prevalence rates and their social correlates. Research problems come to be defined primarily as technical ones, for example, as problems in the operational definition of criteria for determining cases, the reliability of instruments, and the representativeness of study samples. These are the issues of epidemiological research that we reviewed earlier in Chapter 2.

The social-systems perspective is framed by alternative and contrasting assumptions. The mental retardate is viewed as an occupant of a particular social role that she or he achieves and to which she or he is assigned through a complex sorting-selecting process. Whether or not a person is labeled as a mental retardate depends on particular social norms and expectations, the extent to which the person fails to perform adequately or deviates from such expectations, and cultural responses to such deviance. In this perspective there is no one "true" incidence or prevalence rate, and retardation is culture-specific. Research problems, such as determining whether or not a person is a "case," are conceptual and not merely technical.

Guided by both perspectives, Mercer carried out several different but overlapping studies. One is particularly close to our interests. She tried to answer the following question: How is the status of mental retardation achieved in the public schools? Approaching the problem in almost the same way one might design a computer program, she specified the steps on a path through which an individual would have to pass in order to end up labeled a mental retardate. This approach leads to a flowchart, or a decision-tree diagram, which shows a sequence of choice points through which a child moves from "normal student" status, through "academic problem" status, to points of being tentatively labeled as and finally achieving the status of being a mental retardate.[48]

Mercer directs her analysis to the processes involved and the criteria used at each of these choice points that determine whether a child is channeled along the path to the status of mental retardation or is returned to normal student status. One of her critical analyses focuses on the empirical association between ethnicity and mental retardation. Her data show that black and Mexican-American children are heavily overrepresented in the population of mental retardates. The distribution of different ethnic groups in the public school system that Mercer studied was as follows: Anglo, 80 percent; Mexican-American, 11 percent; black, 8 percent. The distribution of children placed in the status of mental retardation was markedly different: Anglo, 32 percent; Mexican-American, 45 percent; black, 22 percent.[49]

Clearly Anglos are underrepresented, and Mexican-American and black children are overrepresented in the population of mental retardates. There are four times as many Mexican-American children classified as mentally retarded as would be expected from their numbers in the overall population, and almost three times the number of black children expected. Mercer argues, and we concur, that an epidemiological study conceived by researchers oriented to the clinical or biomedical model would be likely to stop with these findings. From the perspective of that model, two populations "at risk" have been discovered, that is, Mexican-Americans and blacks. Theories might then be proposed to account for high rates of pathology in these groups. These might be genetic theories, or environmental theories implicating the effects of nutritional deficiency in these groups on intellectual functioning, or perhaps sociological theories suggesting the negative consequences of fatherless families on intellectual development.

Mercer adopts a different approach. She asks: How does the first distribution of ethnic groups in the population get transformed into the final distribution? What happens at different stages in this process? Are any of these stages, or choice points, particularly critical?

She begins by noting that the function of the public school system in this process is of special importance, because it is the most significant formal community organization for the designation of persons as retarded. Not only are schools the principal agents in labeling, but many other institutions use the school's classification as the basis for their own assignment of individuals to this status. Thus, in her analysis, enrollment in school is the first decision point. She states: "The first step in becoming retarded in the public schools is to enroll in the public school system rather than one of the private schools available in the city."[50]

Only two children were reported to the study by private schools as mentally retarded. However, independent psychological testing conducted by the project staff found that 1.1 percent of the private school population had IQ scores below 79; this would have made them clinically eligible for the status of mental retardation if they were attending public school. The equivalent percentage of the public school population with IQ scores below 79 is 0.8 percent. In brief, children who test at these levels are at higher risk of being labeled retarded if they are enrolled in the public schools than if they are in private schools.

Following through the various steps in the flowchart of decisions, Mercer points to the importance of the elementary-grade teacher in the labeling process, particularly to the teacher's role in the critical event of a pupil's being held back rather than promoted to the next class. Mercer finds the role of the psychologist particularly significant in that the stage of psychological testing is the single most crucial step in the process. In California, where the study was conducted, an individual cannot be classified as mentally retarded without having been given an intelligence test by a trained and certified professional, namely, a psychologist. Mercer shows that the ethnic distributions of children referred for testing and actually tested by psychologists are roughly the same as the overall ethnic distribution in the school population. In other words, ethnicity is not a significant variable up to this point in the path. These distributions change radically after testing: Significantly more Mexican-American and black children than Anglo children score below 79 and thus fail the test.

The test results account for much of the difference in the ethnic distribution of children found in special classes for the mentally retarded. A recommendation for assignment to a special class is made on the basis of the test results. Ethnicity, however, plays a role in both the recommendation made and in the actual placement of a child in such a class. For example, of all children who "fail" the IQ test, only 49 percent of those with Anglo backgrounds are recommended for placement, whereas 70 percent of the Mexican-American and black children receive such a recommendation. The average IQ test scores do not differ among these three "failing" ethnic groups. Finally, of those who are recommended for placement, only two-thirds of the Anglo children achieve this status, that is, are actually enrolled in these classes; but nearly all of the Mexican-American and black children who receive such recommendations do end up in these classes.

Mercer concludes this part of her study with the following statement: "Anglocentricism, institutionalized and legitimated by the diagnostic procedures used in the formal organizations of the community, appears to be the most pervasive pattern in labeling the mentally retarded in the community. . . . institutionalized Anglocentricism is a recurring pattern in the labeling process, a pattern that is closely linked with the statistical definition of 'normal' and the IQ test."[51]

Blindness

The social and psychological consequences of being labeled as a patient with a particular disease or disorder are often implied, as they are in Mercer's research where we all have a general understanding of what it might mean to be diagnosed as a mental retardate. Scott's study, *The Making of Blind Men*,[52] is unusual in its attention to these consequences. Blindness may be thought of as a more objective condition than mental retardation, or even than diabetes. Scott demonstrates that becoming a blind person involves a labeling process that is similar in essential ways to processes we have seen at work in other illnesses.

First, blindness, like mental retardation, has an administrative and quasi-legal definition that has grave consequences in our society, because the label of blindness entitles the person to claim a variety of special services. We are already familiar, through our examination of diabetes and mental retardation, with the use of specific tests for such determinations. In the case of blindness, the Snellen chart serves the function that the IQ test does for mental retardation. Although there are some supplementary criteria on the scope of the visual field, there is one essential criterion that determines whether or not a person is considered to be blind, namely, central visual acuity of 20/200 or less in the better eye, with correcting lenses. Clearly, this is only one aspect of visual impairment, but it is the only one used. Further, the Snellen test is particularly crude and imprecise in the impairment range; for example, there are no gradations between 20/100 and 20/200, although there are gradations between 20/20 and 20/100. In sum, people who come to be diagnosed/labeled as blind are heterogeneous in degree and type of visual impairment. Scott states: "The overwhelming majority of people who are classified as blind can, in fact, see . . . [they] are not sightless; they are sighted people who experience difficulty seeing."[53]

Despite this diversity and some degree of vision for most of them, blind people tend to be viewed as a homogeneous group with certan personal and social characteristics that are presumed to result from their "common" affliction of blindness. Scott describes widely held commonsense views and stereotypes that are believed to set the blind apart from normal-sighted people. These include "helplessness, dependency, melancholy, docility, gravity of inner thought, aestheticism."[54] These views appear to be shared by professional workers in agencies that serve the blind. Further, there are important consequences of this labeling process. Because these stereotypes enter into both interpersonal relationships and professional contacts, defined blind persons are pressed toward adapting to these attributions and expectations. In behavior and self-concept, they come to resemble the stereotype, and thus the myth perpetuates itself.

Services offered to the blind by medical and social agencies are double-edged. In order to receive these services, an individual must discard whatever view she or he may have about the nature of the problem – most often self-defined as "trouble seeing" – and adopt the official view, which is that "blindness" is one of the most severe handicaps, that it is long-lasting, pervasive, and difficult to ameliorate. As Scott states, "the client's views about the problems must be discredited."[55]

Professionals' efforts are directed at changing what they regard as their clients' unrealistic and simplistic understanding of their problems. Pressures on clients to accept the professional definition of their situation are powerful and very difficult to resist. Some clients become "true believers." They accept the agency's redefinition of their problem and organize their identities and their lives around their blindness, and around the agency itself. This group becomes a highly visible part of the blind population, although we do not know the proportion they actually represent, and thus continue to reinforce and perpetuate stereotypes about the blind. Other clients adopt the role as a facade, an expedient that permits them access to needed services, but drop the facade when they are out of sight of professionals. Finally, there are resisters who attempt to maintain their independence, and who may actually refuse the help offered because it requires the redefinition of themselves as persons. This position requires substantial personal resources and a supportive interpersonal and social environment in order to override the stigmatizing effects of attributions to persons with this handicap.

Special studies of the independent blind, that is, those living outside the embrace of special agencies for the blind, reveal that they do not have the attitudinal and behavioral characteristics attributed to the blind. For example, findings from a study of blinded veterans who receive financial assistance, and where rehabilitative efforts are directed to their return to the community, show them to be in good health with few symptoms of anxiety or depression commonly associated with chronic impairments. They were found to be more highly educated than a comparable sighted population, were reading at twice the rate as the general population norm, and visited friends and joined associations at higher rates than the general population.

Scott concludes that "Blind men are not born, they are made."[56] Further, it is the service systems established to help them that determine the experience of being blind, that "make" blind men.

Implications: constructivism and humane medical care

We began with a brief statement of the constructivist approach to social reality, an approach that locates social meanings in the active interpretive work of human actors. In showing how this general perspective has been applied to the study of health-related issues, we pointed to the critical distinction between symptoms and illness as a medical category. We focused on the problem of diagnosis and reviewed studies that developed this perspective in terms of a particular model, namely, the labeling of deviance as illness.

A principal aim of the chapter has been to document the proposition that medicine, although viewed as an applied technology within the biomedical framework of assumptions about illness as generic and universal, may more adequately be understood as a social practice. That is, like all other human action, medicine is active interpretive work through which a particular social reality is constructed, a "reality" constituted by diagnosed illnesses and prescribed treatments. The clinical tasks of diagnosis and treatment cannot be understood as involving only the application of standardized technical biomedical criteria and procedures. Rather, clinical practice is based on and guided by sociocultural values and assumptions, organized and regulated by social norms and institutional requirements, and socially consequential in its effects on the rights and responsiblities of those labeled as sick and assigned the social role of patient.

In addition to demonstrating the responsiveness of clinical practices to various features of the social settings of these practices, we have also tried to clarify the distinction between the argument advanced in the constructivist approach and our earlier discussions of the social and institutional contexts of patients and physicians. In those analyses, for example, of epidemiological and hospital organization studies, we reintroduced social contexts that had been stripped away through the narrow application of the biomedical model. Our purpose was to understand how these contexts affected the occurrence and course of illness. Thus, we reviewed studies showing how the incidence and development of illness reflected community and family contexts and how treatments and their consequences were affected by features of hospital social organization. Although findings from these studies represent a significant contribution of the social sciences to problems in the health field, the research does not seriously question assumptions about illness within the biomedical model. In sum, these studies retain the biomedical definition of illness and rely on standard medical practices for the determination of cases, the characterization of treatments, and the evaluation of course and outcome.

As we have seen, labeling studies and other research within the constructivist framework do not rest on biomedical assumptions nor rely on routine medical practices to define their objects of study. Instead, these assumptions and practices become the main topics of investigation. In this approach, illnesses are not viewed as "objective" attributes of patients separate from and independent of the clinical methods used to detect their presence. The work of physicians and other health professionals is considered integral to the definition and diagnosis of illness, and hence to its production. For this reason, physicians are not treated in these studies as expert informants, as those who "know" what diabetes is or how hyperkinesis is manifested behaviorally. Rather their beliefs and practices with regard to diagnosis and treatment are topics of inquiry and require further analysis and interpretation. Therefore, the focus of investigation shifts from patients' symptoms as criteria for the diagnosis of diabetes or mental retardation to the ways in which such criteria are applied, to institutional factors that affect clinical practice, and to broader socio-cultural forces and values that influence the choice and use of particular criteria.

Clearly, this is an alternative and competitive model of illness. Its implications are evident in how such problems as variations in rates of illness are approached. Although a labeling theorist may begin by examining the association between differentials in incidence or prevalence rates and the social characteristics of population groups, these findings are not treated as the basis for etiological hypotheses as they are in the epidemiological studies we reviewed in Chapters 2 and 3. Rather, this "finding" is treated as an empirical observation, which must be understood through an analysis of how the health system operates. That is, analyses are directed to the socially organized features of clinical practice that produce this association between, for example, the prevalence of mental retardation and ethnicity as in Mercer's work.[57] Mercer's study exemplifies this approach, and her comparison between social system and clinical perspectives on mental retardation, which we summarized, expresses the distinction we are making between the biomedical and constructivist models of illness.

Variations in medical practices are themselves associated with broader historical, sociocultural, and economic forces. These relationships will be examined in more detail in the following chapter, "Learning to Be a Leper." Here we want to note the general point that societies vary in both the definition and scope of deviant behaviors that are labeled as illness. Sociologists have used the phrase, the "medicalization of deviance,"[58] to refer to the tendency within a society to define a wide range of deviant and problematic behaviors as illnesses.

The trend toward enlarging the category of illness is particularly apparent in modern Western society, where medicine has achieved a high level of dominance among professions with legitimate mandates to manage and control deviance. This has led one critic to expand the phrase into the "medicalization of life," and to assert: "Medicine always creates illness as a social state. The recognized healer transmits to individuals the social possibilities for acting sick. . . . Medicine has the authority to label one man's complaint a legitimate illness, to declare a second man sick though he himself does not complain, and to refuse a third social recognition of his pain, his disability, and even his death. It is medicine which stamps some pain as 'merely subjective,' some impairment as malingering, and some deaths – though not others – as suicide. . . . The physician decides what is a symptom and who is sick."[59]

We shall return to Illich's critique of modern medicine when we discuss the social functions of the health-care system in Chapter 8. It is important at this juncture, however, to make explicit another implication of the constructivist approach. Criticism of the health-care system, based on studies of patients and physicians in social contexts that we reviewed in earlier chapters, leads to recommendations for improvements in the system that would reduce social inequities or minimize institutional problems that interfere with good medical care. These might include changes in how health-care costs are financed to reduce social differentials in accessibility to care or changes in hospital social organization to decrease staff turnover so as to improve patient care. Physicians and other health professionals may feel uncomfortable with such criticism or believe that the evidence is not as strong as critics claim it to be, but they understand the grounds on which the criticism is made and are likely to share the aims of the proposed recommendations. That is, they too believe that inequities in health care should be reduced.

A critique mounted from the constructivist position is more difficult to understand and more troubling to health professionals, because it questions the basic assumptions of medical practice, namely, the biomedical model. Whether the critique is broad-based and phrased in terms of the "medicalization of life," or more narrowly framed as the "medicalization of deviance," the usual image of the physician as healer of the sick is inverted. Rather than being viewed as fighters against pain and conquerers of disease, as followers of the norm to "do no harm and heal the sick," physicians appear to be accused of making people ill. Illich refers sweepingly to the practice of medicine as iatrogenic; within the more restricted constructivist perspective, physicians are viewed as closely implicated in and essential to the "production" of illness.

Our review of these criticisms is intended to help physicians and other health professionals understand their sources. Given the essential incompatibility of the biomedical and constructivist models of illness, it would be naive to expect any easy resolution of the conflict between them. Nonetheless, in addition to recognizing the nature of the challenge, a few points merit consideration. First, although many of the studies focus on medical practices, the overall perspective is a broader one and includes a role in the production or labeling of illness for patients, their significant others, and other members of the society. That is, health professionals are not alone in the definition and control of illness but are participants in a larger social process. The constructivist approach, seen in this way, may help to enlarge the perspective of health professionals so as to include more than is contained within the frame of the biomedical model and, at the same time, heighten their awareness of their specific roles within this larger social process.

When the constructivist model is pitted against the biomedical model, as is often done by constructivists and as we have tended to do in this chapter in order to sharpen the contrast, health professionals may feel that this enlargement of perspective would have serious costs. To see illness as socially produced, as the result of interaction among a number of participants including physicians, implies that a wider range of information and interests must be taken into account in making medical decisions than is required by the biomedical model. The result appears to be a restriction in the scope of medical authority and a loss of the social benefits of status and power that are the accompaniments of medical dominance.

There are, however, potential benefits from the recognition that others, including the patients themselves, are full participants in the complex process of labeling, diagnosis, management, and treatment of illness. The cost of absolute authority and responsibility has been a narrowing in the conception of illness to fit the biomedical model and the isolation of the health-care system from the natural social communities of patients in which these problems are seen more fully and faced in contexts of mutual support. These others are not adversaries, interfering with "good" medical care, but potential allies in providing more humane and more socially responsive care. In the terms we have been using throughout this text, we are suggesting that clinical practice be restored to its social context. In this way, health professionals may be able to join together with their patients and significant others in their lives in working on the shared task of finding a new direction for health care, away from the medicalization of life to the resocialization of medicine.

Notes

1. Berger, P. L., and Luckmann, T. *The Social Construction of Reality.* New York: Doubleday Anchor Books, 1967, chap. II, pp. 49 and 61.
2. Eisenberg, L., "Delineation of clinical conditions: conceptual models of 'physical' and 'mental' disorders," in *Research and Medical Practice: Their Interaction,* CIBA Foundation Symposium 44 (New Series). North-Holland: Elsevier/Excerpta Medica, 1976. Clinical implications of this view are developed in Kleinman, A., Eisenberg, L., and Good, B. "Culture, illness, and care: clinical lessons from anthropologic and cross-cultural research," *Annals of Internal Medicine,* 1978, *88*(2):251–8. For another examination of this distinction and its implications, see Fabrega, H., Jr., and Manning, P. K. "Disease, illness and deviant careers," in Scott, R. A., and Douglas, J. D. *Theoretical Perspectives on Deviance.* New York: Basic Books, 1972.
3. For a general introduction to this perspective, see Schur, E. M. *Labeling Deviant Behavior: Its Sociological Implications.* New York: Harper & Row, 1971. For a critique of this approach, from within sociology, see Gove, W. R. (Ed.). *The Labeling of Deviance.* New York: John Wiley & Sons, 1975.
4. Becker, H. S. *The Outsiders.* Glencoe, IL: The Free Press, 1963, p. 9.
5. Feinstein, A. R. *Clinical Judgement.* Baltimore, MD: Williams & Wilkins, 1967, p. 73.
6. Clendening, L. (Ed.). *Source Book of Medical History.* New York: Dover Publications, 1960.
7. Temkin, O. "The history of classification in the medical sciences," in Katz, M. M., Cole, J. O., and Barton, W. E. (Eds.). *The Role and Methodology of Classification in Psychiatry and Psychopathology.* Washington, DC: U.S. Government Printing Office, 1968 (PHS Publ. No. 1584), p. 11.
8. Blaxter, M. "Diagnosis as category and process: the case of alcoholism," *Social Science and Medicine,* 1978, *12*:9–17, p. 9.
9. Engle, R. L., and Davis, B. J. "Medical diagnosis: present, past, and future. I. Present concepts of the meaning and limitations of medical diagnosis," *Archives of Internal Medicine,* 1963, *112*:512–19, p. 512. Also, see Engle, R. L. "Medical diagnosis: present, past, and future. II. Philosophical foundations and historical development of our con-

cepts of health, disease, and diagnosis," *Archives of Internal Medicine*, 1963, *112*:520–43.

10. Engle and Davis, "Medical diagnosis I," p. 516.
11. See Blaxter's discussion of these opposed ideas in "Diagnosis as a category and process," pp. 12–13.
12. Quoted in Engle and Davis, "Medical diagnosis I," p. 514.
13. Ibid., p. 515.
14. Fabrega, H., Jr. "Toward a theory of human disease," *Journal of Nervous and Mental Disease*, 1976, *162*(5):299–312, p. 200.
15. Koran, L. M. "The reliability of clinical methods, data and judgments: I and II," *New England Journal of Medicine*, 1975, *293*(13):642–6; 1975, *293*(14):695–701, p. 700.
16. Ibid., p. 700.
17. Extended discussion of various approaches to problems of psychiatric diagnosis may be found in Katz et al. (Eds.). *The Role and Methodology of Classification.*
18. Feighner, J. P., Robins, E., Guze, S. B., Woodruff, R. A., Winokur, G., and Munoz, R. "Diagnostic criteria for use in psychiatric research," *Archives of General Psychiatry*, 1972, *26*:57–63, p. 57.
19. Kramer, M. "Classification of mental disorders for epidemiologic and medical care purposes: current status, problems, and needs," in Katz et al. (Eds.). *The Role and Methodology of Classification*, p. 107.
20. Ibid., p. 109.
21. Ibid., p. 110.
22. Ibid., p. 109, Figure 2.
23. For a review of many studies of this type, see Koran, "The reliability of clinical methods, I and II."
24. Posner, T. "Magical elements in orthodox medicine," in Dingwall, R., Heath, C., Reid, M., and Stacey, M. (Eds.). *Health Care and Health Knowledge.* New York: Prodist, 1977, p. 152.
25. Ibid.
26. Cochrane, A. L. *Effectiveness and Efficiency: Random Reflections on Health Services.* Nuffield Provincial Hospitals Trust, 1972; quoted in Posner, "Magical elements in orthodox medicine," p. 150.
27. Posner, "Magical elements in orthodox medicine," p. 145.
28. Ibid., p. 155.
29. Ibid., p. 154.
30. Ibid., p. 154.
31. Blaxter, "Diagnosis as category and process."
32. Ibid., p. 14.
33. Ibid., p. 15.
34. Ibid., pp. 16–17.
35. Conrad, P. "The discovery of hyperkinesis: notes on the medicalization of deviant behavior," *Social Problems*, 1975, *23*(1):12–21; and "The social construction of hyperactivity: uncertainty and medical diagnosis," chap. 6 in Conrad, P. *Identifying Hyperactive Children: The Medicalization of Deviant Behavior.* Lexington, MA: Heath, 1978.
36. Conrad, "The discovery of hyperkinesis," p. 13.
37. Ibid., p. 14.
38. Ibid., p. 14.
39. Temkin, "The history of classification in the medical sciences," p. 15.
40. Conrad, "The discovery of hyperkinesis," p. 1.
41. Fox, R. C. "Training for uncertainty," in Merton, R. K., Reader, G., and Kendall, P. L. (Eds.). *The Student Physician.* Cambridge, MA: Harvard University Press, 1957. The

theme of uncertainty is prominent also in Posner's analysis of diagnosis in diabetes, "Magical elements in orthodox medicine."

42. Conrad, "The discovery of hyperkinesis."
43. Conrad, Identifying Hyperactive Children, p. 14.
44. Koran, "The reliability of clinical methods, I and II."
45. A model for analyzing social influences on "paths to treatment" is presented in Mishler, E. G., and Waxler, N. E. "Decision processes in psychiatric hospitalization: patients referred, accepted, and admitted to a psychiatric hospital," *American Sociological Review*, 1963, *28:*576–87. See also the studies of the prepatient stage reported in Spitzer. S. P., and Denzin, N. K. (Eds.). *The Mental Patient: Studies in the Sociology of Deviance.* New York: McGraw-Hill Book Company, 1968.
46. Mercer, J. R. *Labelling the Mentally Retarded.* Berkeley: University of California Press, 1973.
47. Ibid., pp. 36–7.
48. Ibid., pp. 98–9.
49. Ibid., p. 112, Table 7.
50. Ibid., p. 97.
51. Ibid., pp. 120–3.
52. Scott, R. A. *The Making of Blind Men.* New York: Russell Sage, 1969.
53. Ibid., pp. 42–3.
54. Ibid., p. 4.
55. Ibid., p. 77.
56. Ibid., p. 121.
57. Mercer, *Labelling the Mentally Retarded,* 1973.
58. For example, see Conrad, "The discovery of hyperkinesis."
59. Illich, I. *Medical Nemesis: The Expropriation of Health.* New York: Bantam Books, 1977, pp. 36–8.

7   Learning to be a leper: a case study in the social construction of illness

Nancy E. Waxler

People who feel ill often first discuss their symptoms with family members or friends and then later go to a physician who questions, evaluates, and perhaps prescribes treatment. In the course of this exploration the "trouble" itself is transformed from vague and disconnected symptoms to a labeled condition, that is, an illness that others in the society understand to have a particular explanation and social meaning. Thus, social negotiations turn symptoms into social facts that may have significant consequences for the sick person.

In this chapter we shall look at several aspects of this "social labeling" process.[1] In particular, we shall stress that the definition of a specific disease and associated social expectations often depend as much on the society and culture as on the biological characteristics of the disease itself. People diagnosed as having a particular disease learn "how" to have it by negotiating with friends and relations as well as with people in the treatment system; this process is affected by society's beliefs and expectations for that disease. Finally, society's definition of and expectations for a particular disease are sustained by social and organizational forces that may have little to do with the disease itself as a biological process.

Leprosy is a disease in which the process of social transformation is clear. Leprosy has a known cause, an effective treatment (but no cure), and thus a predictable outcome. From the perspective of the medical model, if the patient is treated quickly and regularly, the bacillus is controlled and the patient will recover; routine and scientifically neutral treatment is all that is required. But Westerners and many Asians– even those who have never seen a leprosy patient– may suspect that scientific treatment of the biological phenomenon misses the point. Often leprosy is feared; lepers are shunned; we say of a deviant community member, "He's like a leper." Doctors in Indian hospitals refuse to see cases; attendants in Ceylonese hospitals refuse to change dressings; wives begin divorce proceedings when husbands are diagnosed as lepers; patients leave their villages to become urban beggars. In some societies, then, routine treatment is neither given nor received. Responses to the disease by patient, family, and doctor are strongly influenced by social expectations and not simply by the biological characteristics of leprosy.

If the social transformation of the disease has such profound effects on those who experience it, then we must ask how a biological phenomenon has taken on such a definition. Is there some inherent quality of the disease – perhaps its communicability, threat to life, its disfiguring effects – that determines social expectations? Or are social definitions of particular diseases specific to certain societies and historical circumstances? Finally, why are certain social definitions perpetuated, for example, the terrible fear of leprosy, in the face of a known cause and effective treatment?

One way to consider these questions is to examine disease and illness cross-culturally. A cross-cultural analysis of leprosy controls for the nature of the disease but varies societal and historical factors, giving us an opportunity to ask whether the stigma of leprosy is universal (thus perhaps associated with biological phenomena) or whether social definitions differ from society to society. In this chapter we shall document the truth of the second alternative, that there is considerable variation in the social and moral definition of leprosy across cultures, and speculate that this variation may be linked to specific historical events.

We shall also ask how patients respond when caught up in their own society's definition of the disease, and we shall show that the career of the diseased person reflects society's expectations. American lepers, though stigmatized, tend to respond aggressively, "taking on" the disease and the society; Ethiopian and Indian lepers stigmatize themselves and withdraw, complying with society's definition even before others recognize the disease.

Finally, we shall question how and why particular moral definitions of disease continue unchanged. Why are the stigma and fear of leprosy still prevalent in many countries when an effective treatment is readily available? In this regard we shall examine the organizational and social context in which care is offered and shall show that the medical organizations that treat leprosy may have had an important although inadvertent part in perpetuating the stigma of the disease.

Leprosy is an exotic disease, one that most of us have never seen. We examine it here for the same reasons that many anthropologists examine exotic cultures, to reflect on common phenomena. Studies of diseases such as leprosy that have clear and strong moral definitions in some societies provide insights into the moral component of all diseases. We can expect, then, that similar analytic principles might be useful in understanding our own society's definitions of tuberculosis, heart disease, schizophrenia, and cancer.

Some medical facts about leprosy

Leprosy has been known for thousands of years as a chronic and communicable disease affecting the skin, eyes, internal organs, peripheral nerves, and mucous membranes. Not until 1873, however, did Hansen report the discovery of *Mycobacterium leprae*, now thought to be a causal factor in the disease, and only recently has an agent, the nine-banded armadillo, been discovered in which the bacteria can be cultivated experimentally. Pending effective cultivation and experimental tests, the exact relationship between the bacterium and the disease is not clear, although researchers assume that the bacterium plays a part in the disease.

Leprosy is assumed to be only mildly communicable, even though the mode of transmission is not entirely understood. It is usually suggested that long-term skin or respiratory contact of ten or fifteen years' duration is required for transmission. Alternatively, however, a long incubation period is also known. American soldiers, who presumably were infected abroad during World War II, became symptomatic 2.9 years later (for tuberculoid leprosy) and 9.3 years later (for lepromatous leprosy).[2] Further, some immunity factor also is hypothesized.

The common stereotype of the disease, in novels, films, even in fundraising literature, is of a person whose fingers have fallen off, without a nose, with terrible ulcers on the skin. In fact, the most common symptoms of leprosy, especially in the early stages, are mild and unremarkable. Anesthetic skin (causing secondary problems such as accidental burns), raised patches resembling eczema, skin ulcers that do not heal, for example, are usual; the unremarkability of the symptoms often contribute to late treatment. Only after many years without treatment do leprosy patients experience severe malformation and dysfunction of the kind that might be readily recognized by the layperson.

Currently the most common treatment is sulfone drugs administered over a long period. In Sri Lanka, for example, leprosy patients are expected to continue treatment for a minimum of five years following diagnosis. No one terms these drugs a "cure," and presumably no cure will be known until the causal factors are understood more clearly. These drugs are known to arrest the growth of the bacteria, however, and to cause a drop in the bacteria count in most but not all patients; after three months the disease is usually no longer communicable. For patients whose disease has progressed to the stage of physical malformation, surgery is also used.

The World Health Organization[3] estimates the worldwide prevalence of leprosy to be about 10 million cases or 0.8 per thousand. Ninety-four percent of these cases are in tropical Africa and Asia. Of the total number of estimated cases, only one-third are registered with a health agency and only one-fifth are being treated. Although Westerners usually think of leprosy as a problem "over there," an average of 100 new cases of leprosy was reported each year in the United States during the twenty-year period following World War II; of these, approximately one-half were foreign-born residents.[4] In the Commonwealth of Massachusetts, an average of one case of leprosy per year has been reported since 1970.

If we construct a picture of the "typical" leprosy patient from the medical facts, then, we see a man or woman whose symptoms are mild enough to be unrecognizable to the layperson, who sometime in the past may have lived or worked closely with a leper. During the time the disease was harbored it is relatively unlikely that it was passed along to others. If the disease is diagnosed early and treated regularly with the appropriate drugs, the patient's symptoms will disappear and the disease will be arrested if not cured, leaving no visible signs.

This should be the "medical career" of the typical leprosy patient today. Even in many African and Asian countries, treatment is available and known to ordinary villagers, and thus it is quite possible for a leprosy patient to receive early outpatient treatment, exhibit few visible symptoms, and carry on ordinary social activities. Why is it possible, then, for lepers in Nigeria to follow this career and for Indian lepers, on the other hand, to experience profound changes in their whole life, to lose their occupations, their wives, their children, their very identities? That is, how and why does the moral definition of the disease vary across cultures?

Is leprosy universally stigmatized?

It is easy for Westerners to assume that leprosy is stigmatized in all societies. If we attend to Conrad's novels, the Bible, even "Jesus Christ Superstar," we could conclude that, everywhere, lepers are shunned. This assumption has been made without question by a number of authors who have then offered a functional hypothesis about stigma. These authors suggest that because leprosy is universally stigmatized, stigma must function as a sort of social protection device. That is, the moral definition of leprosy was developed to explain and justify society's need to isolate lepers from the majority group that the communicable disease threatened. The assumption, then, is that the disease is indeed inherently life-threatening, that society must protect itself from such a disease by isolating those who are afflicted, and that the moral ideology regarding leprosy is society's justification for its own self-protection.

But does the moral definition of the disease come from the quality of the disease itself or from the social and historical conditions in which the disease exists? One way of answering this question is to investigate the extent to which the stigma of leprosy differs across societies. If we assume that the basic biological characteristics of leprosy are much the same everywhere in the world and we find that social and moral definitions are not, then we must conclude that these social definitions cannot be explained simply in terms of the biological nature of the disease itself. Reflecting on this hypothesis, we shall look at the social definitions of leprosy in India, Sri Lanka, and Nigeria.

The Indian definition of leprosy can be quickly understood by reference to one set of facts. Of 100 people with leprosy being treated in the city of Lucknow, 53 percent had been born and raised in rural villages; after their leprosy was discovered, all but 18 percent of this group had migrated to the city, away from home and family; 66 percent of these migrants never returned to visit their homes; many became beggars.[5] As Kapoor reports, "The attitude of the society towards these unfortunate people is so cruel and cynical that the victim of the disease feels isolated, despised and virtually excommunicated."[6] Such rejection of people with leprosy is also apparent in Indian leprosy hospitals themselves, where it has been reported that doctors in charge sometimes refuse to touch the patient's body when treatment or diagnosis is required.[7]

These informal norms were formalized in Indian law. Before the 1950s in India, all pauper lepers were segregated regardless of the level of infectiousness. Lepers were excluded from all inheritance in the joint family, were barred from traveling in trains with nonlepers, were not eligible for insurance, and were not allowed to serve in the military. In the 1950s the laws were changed to allow normal inheritance of property by leprosy patients but at the same time to provide for judicial separation and divorce when leprosy appeared in a married man or woman. A proposal has also been made for compulsory sterilization of all infectious male patients.[8]

From all reports, then, lepers are often physically and socially rejected in Indian society; some modern laws perpetuate these norms. There is great fear of contagion (an Indian friend advised, "If you talk to a leper, put your handkerchief in front of your nose and mouth"), and repulsion at the sight or even thought of a leper. Those who discover that they have the disease often leave or are pushed out of their homes, to migrate to the cities to the "normal" role of a beggar.

In India, then, we see in reality the novelist's picture of stigma. Lepers are shunned and isolated, removed from family and larger society, relegated to the bottom of the hierarchy, treated as outcastes. If we used India as a sample of one, we might be tempted to conclude that the moral definition of leprosy derives from the threatening and contagious nature of the disease itself and that stigmatization is self-protective.

But if we look at Sri Lanka (formerly Ceylon), we see a different picture. Here, again, the general population fears leprosy, believes it to be extremely contagious, and to result in hideous deformities; few have seen a leper, however, even in a population where best estimates indicate that the prevalence is 0.37 per thousand.[9] One might expect that the Sri Lankan leper's life experience would be similar to the Indian's, including rejection and mobility. Our interviews of lepers receiving outpatient treatment indicate that this is not so.[10] Instead, we found that leprosy patients, after diagnosis, remain in their own homes and carry on the same occupation that they had before the disease appeared. The schoolteacher continues teaching; the housewife continues cooking and caring for children; only one man, a baker, left his job, he reported, because the physical symptoms prevented him from doing his work.

Families of patients remain intact as well. Those who were married before diagnosis remained married; several more were married after the disease appeared. Only one man reported, "When I went to the Kurunegala hospital they said I had leprosy and sent a telegram to my wife saying that I was being transferred to the leprosy hospital. When people at home read the telegram my mother-in-law wanted my wife to get a divorce but my brother-in-law said, 'Wait and see.' Then the hospital sent some booklets about leprosy saying it was O.K. and they changed their minds about the divorce."

Thus, there is little of the overt rejection reported in India. Yet life is not entirely unchanged for Sri Lankan lepers. Most patients, in fact, withdraw from society to some extent; they stigmatize themselves. When asked what advice they would give to other patients, our leprosy patients said, "Do not move around the village," "Do not visit others' homes unless it is absolutely necessary." They apply similar advice within their own families (and usually follow this advice), saying, "Use separate eating utensils and sleep separately." And there is general but not unanimous agreement that it is better *not* to tell nonfamily members about the illness; "Others will be afraid," "Others might stop visiting, even stop working with us." Leprosy patients, then, are fully aware of the stigma of the disease; their response is to avoid possible rejection by mild with-drawal and secrecy.

Yet often the secret of leprosy cannot be kept forever. When villagers discover that someone they know has leprosy, their first response is fear and rejection; but that often disappears over the years and relationships return to normal. One patient reported that when the villagers found out about his illness, "They went to the Montessori school my son was at-tending and asked the teachers to separate him from the others. Then the children began to harass my son. So I wrote a letter to the rural develop-ment society telling them they could call any doctor and give me an exam-ination. They didn't do that but the harassment of my son stopped after that. I know the doctors would not say I had leprosy because the treat-ment is kept secret and they wouldn't tell what it was." For this man stigmatization early in the course of his illness also meant that villagers stopped using his well for bathing. "But now (seven years later) they use the well again and relations are back to normal."

Although the general population in Sri Lanka seems to favor rejection and isolation of lepers, the actual experience of many of these patients is quite different. Families accept the patient, marriages continue, and, over the years, neighbors who might have been afraid at first resume normal relations. Patients themselves sometimes withdraw into their families and avoid unnecessary nonfamily contact. This is not true, naturally, for all those with leprosy, but the general pattern, relative to the Indian one, is of acceptance or at least tolerance.

Nigeria provides an even more benign example.[11] Among the Hausa of Northern Nigeria, leprosy is highly prevalent, as it is in India. In this peasant agricultural, largely Muslim, society, indigenous beliefs about the cause of leprosy include gluttony, swearing falsely by the Koran, washing in the water a leprosy patient has used. Treatments may consist of burn-ing and scraping the skin, purges, and potions. Although leprosy is com-mon, modern methods and theories not understood, and traditional treat-ments probably ineffective, no one is afraid. "The Hausa, in contrast to the West, exhibit little fear or disgust concerning leprosy. They do not seem to regard it with any special apprehension; it is not necessarily more unusual than any other of the great range of diseases that assail them."[12] Lepers continue to reside with their families, living a normal life until the very advanced stages of the disease. "At this point there seems to be a distinct change in vocation with many of the victims becoming beg-gars,"[13] but begging itself is an accepted, nonstigmatized role among Mus-lims.

The East African situation echoes that in Nigeria. In northern Tanzania, in a sparsely settled agricultural and herding population, " . . . the attitude of the people toward leprosy patients is rather benevolent, and leprosy seldom leads to complete segregation of patients from their families or villages. In fact most of the afflicted are accepted as members of the community."[14] The majority of adults have no objections to a leprosy patient sharing food and sleeping with his or her family or to marrying or continuing a marriage.

Variation in the degree to which leprosy is stigmatized is apparent across Africa, with reports from Ethiopia[15] that resemble the experiences of Indian lepers (divorce, migration, begging), and mild rejection or none at all in Nigeria and Tanzania.[16]

How can we account for differences in the moral definition of leprosy that are apparent in different cultures? Perhaps the incidence of the disease, variations in subtypes, patterns of immunity, or effectiveness of treatment contribute to a society's perceptions. But these may play a minor role in comparison with the culture norms and historical circumstances in which the disease is found. Lepers in India may easily be rejected because a clear and elaborate hierarchical caste structure, justified by the ideology of impurity and sin, is available into which a threatening person may be placed. Caste beliefs and caste practices (not eating with, not touching, not sitting with) serve very well to handle society's fear of the leper. It is easy, then, for normal people in Indian society to equate leprosy with punishment of sins and to treat lepers as outcastes. The cultural background of Sri Lanka is quite similar to that of India, but with two crucial differences. The caste structure is less hierarchical (more than half of the population belongs to the high cultivators' caste), and the majority of the population is Buddhist, not Hindu. The Sinhalese experience with low-caste, and particularly outcaste groups, is relatively small; traditional caste obligations of family to family have generally disappeared, and the concern with who is who and how to behave in the company of other castes is narrowing. Further, Buddhism's stress on tolerance of differences and on compassion for others contrasts with Hindu values. These cultural and structural differences, then, may help explain why the general population in Sri Lanka fears and wants to reject lepers but the family and neighbors of leprosy patients actually accept them with little permanent stigma.

By examining leprosy in India, Sri Lanka, and Africa we have shown that lepers are not universally stigmatized. Thus it is unlikely that the social definition of leprosy arises entirely from biological qualities of the disease itself, that is from its degree of contagion or visible symptoms.

Instead, stigma may be linked to particular historical and cultural conditions, specific to each society.

How does the moral definition of leprosy develop?

How does a disease come to be feared and stigmatized in some cultures, yet remain an unremarkable fact of life in others? This is obviously a complicated question to which there can be no single answer. We might, however, find some answers in historical conditions or in the cultural and social matrix in which the disease is embedded. Many explanations are buried in the past; in India the extreme stigma of leprosy is certainly not new. Nineteenth-century Hawaii, however, provides one well-documented case in which the moral definition of leprosy is related to specific historical, economic, and social circumstances.[17]

In the 1840s in Hawaii, and elsewhere in the West, leprosy had almost disappeared, and when it did occur was considered to be a hereditary household disease. It was of minor importance, not stigmatized, a disease that most people did not encounter. Soon after mid-century, however, Hawaii's economic and social situation began to change, reflecting the worldwide movement of people at the height of colonialism. Europeans moved out to the colonies; Americans traveled for purposes of trade. Chinese began to move the other way, to Hawaii to work on the plantations and to the American West during the gold rush. In 1851 the first group of 180 Chinese immigrants arrived in Hawaii, and by the 1860s the movement of Chinese to Hawaii had become a flood.

The Hawaiians believed that the Chinese had brought leprosy. In the 1850s Hawaiian authorities noted an increase in leprosy, but newspaper reference to leprosy "was purposely omitted . . . for fear of injuring . . . commercial development."[18] By 1862 it could not be ignored and was publicly described as a major outbreak of the disease. This raised several questions in the minds of Hawaiians, and in the minds of health officials around the world. If Hawaii had suddenly experienced a serious increase in leprosy, could one still cling to the idea that leprosy was hereditary? And if it were not hereditary, who carried the disease?

In 1865 Hawaii's official response to the outbreak of leprosy was quarantine of lepers, implying a belief in contagion. This was confirmed in 1874 by Hansen's discovery of the bacillus, *Mycobacterium leprae*. Within one or two decades, at a time of vastly increasing population movements, world opinion shifted from belief in inheritance to belief in contagion.

The Chinese who were believed to have brought leprosy to Hawaii and the western United States were "industrious, painstaking, persevering and frugal – qualities which in Caucasian Protestants undoubtedly would have been considered virtues."[19] Yet they were also viewed by white people, in that age of social Darwinism, as natural cultural inferiors. Further, they provided cheap labor, and their industriousness perhaps threatened poor Westerners who wanted work. Thus, "while there were many demographic – environmental factors at work other than the coincidence of Chinese immigration with the leprosy outbreak in Hawaii that might have triggered the epidemic, the Chinese, nevertheless, almost immediately came to bear the full brunt of responsibility, a stigmatization of them that soon reached monstrous proportions."[20]

The strength of anti-Chinese feeling in the Pacific is apparent in an Australian newspaper article of 1888, during the period when Australia was experiencing the same increase in leprosy as Hawaii. "We take great precautions to prevent the introduction of hydrophobia among our dogs. But we have no safeguard against the importation and spread of leprosy in the persons of Chinese colonists. The danger to human life in Australia is far greater in the latter than in the former case and leprosy is a far more terrible complaint than even hydrophobia. Leprosy is far more common among Chinamen than is generally known and it often first makes its appearance on their hands. That the disease is transmitted by contagion is undoubted."[21]

The outbreak of leprosy in Hawaii "indicted a whole foreign population, in this instance Chinese wage laborers, as a contaminating source."[22] In 1880 Hawaii enacted its first laws to exclude Chinese; these were followed closely by American laws to exclude Asians from California. At the century's end not only did Westerners believe that leprosy was contagious, but attempts to treat it had led to the conclusion that it was incurable. Thus, there was even greater concern with self-protection against the disease carriers.

The Chinese were blamed, stigmatized, and excluded. Yet if we look more carefully at Hawaiian Board of Health records, it is not at all clear that the Chinese actually brought leprosy. Writing in 1886, the then superintendent of the Molokai Leprosy Hospital inquired about early cases to discover that leprosy was recognized by missionaries in 1823 and by a physician familiar with the disease in 1840, a decade or more before the great influx of Chinese laborers.[23] Health data support the conclusion that the Chinese were not an important source of leprosy. In the period 1866–85, the Molokai Hospital admitted 3,076 patients, 2,997 of whom were native Hawaiians, 22 Chinese, and the remainder Europeans, Americans, and Africans.[24] Leprosy, however, was called "Mai Pake," or "China-men's disease." Why? Another observer (Meyer, 1886) explains: "It was recognized (in the 1850s) by the few Chinese then on the islands (who knew of it in China) and this has given it the name of "Mai Pake" here, and not because it was introduced by Chinese. It is much more likely that it came to the islands through the mixed crews of whale ships which had negroes, black and white Portuguese, and men of other races, coming from countries where leprosy was, and still is, prevalent."[25]

In analyzing this phenomenon a hundred years later, we might conclude that the Chinese became convenient scapegoats for Western society. Whether they actually brought leprosy – and it is not clear that they did – the presence of the disease in Hawaii provided a rationale for rejection that in fact had other basic causes. First was the potential or real economic threat that native Western workers may have felt from Chinese laborers. If Chinese could be believed to have leprosy, that fact made a convenient excuse for excluding economic competitors. Second was the nineteenth-century belief in the inherent inferiority of nonwhite people. If the Chinese could be believed to have a threatening contagious disease, so much the better because that would confirm the Westerner's sense of superiority.

If the Chinese were stigmatized ostensibly because they brought leprosy, then the association could also work the other way; leprosy became stigmatized because it was common among the Chinese. This phenomenon may have occured in the Western world, and particularly in Hawaii. The result, by the end of the nineteenth century, was the transformation of a relatively unknown disease into a socially and morally threatening phenomenon. In this case the moral definition of the disease came from and was reinforced by the moral and social definition of those believed to carry it.

The association between particular historical events and the appearance of leprosy in Hawaii may explain why leprosy became a stigmatized disease there. In other cultures quite different circumstances may influence the moral definition of the disease. We can look again at Africa for evidence of another definitional process, the introduction of stigma by Western medicine.

In northern Tanzania, as we have indicated, there was traditionally little stigma attached to leprosy; patients lived with, ate with, slept with their families. Leprosy was an unremarkable disease. But in 1966 the Geita Leprosy Scheme was inaugurated, focusing not only on case finding and treatment but also on public education. Talks were given to school children in grades 5, 6, and 7 once every two years; key members of the community were also reached, although the general public was not directly educated about the disease. Information on cause, symptoms, mode of transmission, treatment, and social problems was included in each additional effort; thus Western medical notions about leprosy were introduced into the traditional system, largely through the children.

A survey conducted five years later showed how effective this educational effort had been. In response to almost all information questions about the disease, "The majority of the school children expressed the modern view of leprosy as being caused by certain bacteria and by physical contact with a patient, whereas the adult population and the leaders associated leprosy more frequently with such factors as heredity, witchcraft. . . . "[26] Whereas the educational program "stressed that there is no need to isolate the patient provided certain basic rules of hygiene are maintained, and that there is no reason to discontinue marriage to a leprosy patient,"[27] there was a surprising finding. School children, targets of this education, opposed the idea of leprosy patients sharing food and sleeping space with family members, and objected to leprosy patients marrying. "Another illustrative example of attitudes derived from health education is that of the sellers at the Sengerema market who, after a health education session by the Geita Leprosy Scheme some years ago, for the first time in Sengerema's history, urged their colleagues suffering from leprosy not to enter the market again."[28] Thus, together with scientific medicine's facts about causation and treatment, other attitudes had inadvertently been added to the society; the new idea of infection had presumably led Tanzanians to recommend avoidance and even rejection of people with leprosy.

In Tanzania, we see what could be the beginning of a new moral definition of leprosy, introduced without intent by public health educators. A somewhat similar phenomenon seems to have occurred in Nigeria[29] and elsewhere[30] when Western modes of treatment – isolation in leper colonies – were introduced by Christian missionaries. In neither instance is there evidence that the general public's attitude toward leprosy underwent a radical shift toward stigmatization. Yet what we see in this century in Tanzania and Nigeria may appear, in the next century, in a more institutionalized form.

The cases of Hawaii and Africa provided examples of two different processes through which an ordinary disease may take on a particular social and moral definition. In Hawaii it appears that the status of those believed to carry the disease – the inferior yet economically threatening Chinese coolies – may have been transferred to the disease itself. In Africa a new moral definition may have been inadvertently suggested by scientific medicine's public health educators. Thus, depending on specific historical/economic/cultural/medical "accidents," leprosy, and by implication perhaps all diseases, are transformed into illnesses having culture-specific social and moral definitions.

Learning to be a leper

A society's expectations for lepers, its beliefs about them, have a significant influence on their experiences as sick people. If we examine what a particular patient does when he discovers he has leprosy, we find that his response to leprosy is consistent with society's expectations for lepers. In fact, he learns to be a leper, the kind of leper his family and neighbors, even his doctors, expect him to be.

Ethiopia provides one example of the leprosy patient's confirmation of his society's beliefs about his disease. Leprosy there is feared and stigmatized. "People entering the bus which links the area around the leprosy hospital to the center of town will cover their nose and mouth. When there is an important visitor to the hospital . . . the patients may be confined to their wards."[31]

Those who discover that they have leprosy respond to this social definition in the way we might expect. Often they stigmatize themselves. In a sample of 100 leprosy patients interviewed in the leprosy outpatient clinic in Addis Ababa, Ethiopia, a fairly common patient career was apparent. One-fifth of the patients had been rejected by their families or had voluntarily left their homes. Half of the lepers continued to attend church, "although this does not mean that they actually entered the building. Seventeen refrained from going, mainly out of fear of being rejected."[32] Of those who remained married, one-third stopped having sexual relationships. But many marriages did not continue. One-half of all lepers who were married at the outbreak of the disease were later divorced; of these divorces, one-half were actually initiated by the patient. (This divorce rate is much higher than that of the general population.) Finally, one-fifth had migrated to the city to become beggars.

"The interviews provided ample evidence of the inclination of patients to self-isolation and withdrawal from normal activities, disguised as fear that these activities might enhance the disease. This was most obvious in the abstention from sexual activities. Anticipating a change of social identity the patient tries to overcome his anxiety by withdrawal, at the same time demonstrating a striking degree of fatalism and resignation with regard to his changed self-identity."[33] Thus, in a situation where the symptoms of leprosy cannot be concealed (bathing and clothing practices prevent this), where the stigma of leprosy is strong and the belief that it is incurable pervasive, the response is acceptance of society's definition. Lepers, often voluntarily, take on the stigmatized social identities expected of them.

The response of Ethiopian lepers to their predicament is consistent with the fatalism of the Ethiopian peasant. Many American lepers, on the other hand, take a role that is almost a caricature of American values: They "fight back."

Leprosy patients treated at the U.S. Public Health Service hospital at Carville, Louisiana, begin with the assumption that the public fears and stigmatizes lepers. Some report experiences with families or communities that confirm the existence of fear and even rejection. And some leprosy patients accept the public definition of the disease by withdrawing to the haven of the Carville hospital, where they are allowed to live the remainder of their lives. Yet those who make this choice do not willingly accept the beliefs about leprosy that are associated with stigma, beliefs about extreme contagion, deformity, and incurability.

Instead, patients who voluntarily withdraw from society support another segment of the patient population, those whom Gussow and Tracy call "career patients."[34] It is these career patients who take on a peculiarly "American" role, one that is undoubtedly respected by the public. They become professional educators, acting as representatives of all lepers in an attempt to change the public's view of the disease. They give talks at Rotary clubs, organize seminars, speak about leprosy on the radio, conduct tours of the leprosy hospital, publish *The Star*. The content of their educational attempts is a new set of beliefs about leprosy, beliefs that are designed to replace the "old" ideas that justified stigma.

The career patients' educational program about leprosy "attempts to demythologize leprosy by emphasizing the historical, social and medical errors and confusions which surround it."[35] They suggest that the leprosy of the Bible and the leprosy of today have been erroneously linked. To support this argument, educational materials refer only to the new name, Hansen's Disease, officially applied to leprosy by the International Congress of Leprosy in 1948. In fact, the word "leprosy" appears nowhere in *The Star* which, instead, is liberally sprinkled with *HD*s. Suggestions of communicability are downplayed, with leprosy usually described as being only mildly contagious. Those patients who tend to become the educators are usually not incapacitated and thus provide good evidence that leprosy is not the horrible affliction the Bible describes. The assumption behind this new ideology, promoted by the career patients, is that American society's fear of leprosy will wither away as the public learns the "truth" about the disease. No longer will lepers feel wrongly labeled and no longer will they be stigmatized.

In a sense, these career patients are America's version of the Ethiopian beggar. Their response to leprosy is consistent with American values on activism, self-sufficiency, and change; when they see a problem, especially a problem for themselves, they try to solve it. They do not respond like the Ethiopian fatalists. At the same time, however, from the point of view of the public, they are not "normal." They are still lepers, whose role as educators depends on existence of the disease itself. "At the present time this status [as career patient] appears to be the only legitimate one the leprosy patient has available to him for life in open society."[36]

Lepers in the United States learn to be the kind of lepers Americans expect. To confirm the lay American's fears of leprosy, they withdraw, avoid, protect themselves, and protect others. But they do these things reluctantly and temporarily, until their active educational efforts succeed in changing public opinion. In the meantime, those who go openly into the outside world go labeled as "leper," fulfilling our expectations that lepers are indeed "different."

There is a world of difference between the Ethiopian leper begging in front of the train station and the American leper showing a film to the Lions' club. But underlying that difference is a more basic similarity: Lepers learn how to be lepers from the beliefs and expectations their society has for them. In every society the sick person is socialized to take a role the society expects.

How is the moral definition of leprosy perpetuated?

Even though leprosy is sometimes feared and lepers stigmatized, and even though leprosy patients often willingly take on the deviant role that society expects, why do such moral definitions continue far beyond the time when effective treatment is readily available? Wouldn't one expect that as the disease becomes easily treatable the fear and threat would subside?

To examine this question we must return to the situation at the end of the nineteenth century, when although a pandemic of leprosy was feared by European and American observers, it did not occur. The public at the time believed leprosy to be highly contagious, but very few people actually contracted the disease. The panic died down. Leprosy was limited to tropical people, usually the poor, and did not become a threat to colonial settlers. Although an official statement was made in 1909 that leprosy was incurable,[37] by the 1920s a moderately successful treatment had been instituted, and by the 1940s a more effective one. We must ask why fear of leprosy and rejection of lepers continued in many societies when, in reality, most people in those societies had discovered that leprosy was relatively nonthreatening. Here, again, we shall look at social and organizational contexts in which the disease exists rather than at the biological qualities of the disease itself.

In the second half of the nineteenth century, when it was believed that leprosy was not only highly contagious but life-threatening, the churches acted. Father Damien established the leper hospital at Molokai, Hawaii, in 1860 and died there, from leprosy, in 1889. The Mission to Lepers was established in Great Britain in 1874. The Louisiana Home for the Lepers, now the U.S. Public Health Service Hospital at Carville, was founded by the Catholic church in 1894. During this time, of course, numerous missionaries were sent out, to Africa, India, Oceania, to treat lepers. Not until the 1920s did nonreligious organizations enter the field, and they still remain of minor importance compared with the worldwide involvement of missionaries. Even today the nursing staff at the U.S. Public Health Service Hospital at Carville is provided by the Sisters of Charity of St. Vincent de Paul.[38] Also today the American Leprosy Missions and the Leprosy Mission (of Great Britain), foundations that finance treatment centers all over the world, integrate Christian ideology with treatment goals. "The main object of the Mission is to minister in the name of Jesus Christ to the physical, mental and spiritual needs of sufferers from leprosy, to assist in their rehabilitation, and to work toward the eradication of leprosy."[39]

Thus certain groups, church groups in this case, came to "own" the disease. They set up hospitals, trained staff, searched for patients, collected and disseminated information, and spoke and acted "for" the lepers. Because leprosy was in many places greatly feared, those who did this work took on an aura of saintliness. "This care of such people by the religious was perceived as devoted and altruistic – an extraordinary service analogous to Christ's ministry to the unfortunate."[40] The linkage between ancient Biblical notions about the horrors of leprosy and current missionary work were thus natural and easily made.

We have introduced two important facts about leprosy since 1920. First, private church-related organizations became the main providers of treatment to leprosy patients, collecting funds mainly from the industrial West and funneling money to nonindustrial tropical countries. Second, in many (but not all) of these nonindustrial countries, leprosy was strongly stigmatized. One might expect that, once an effective treatment became known and once the missionary organizations began to provide this treatment, the stigmatization of leprosy would decline. Changes in definition of the disease might be slow, might take decades, but with effective and available treatment fear and thus stigma would disappear, even in India and Ethiopia.

Yet they have not disappeared. In fact we suspect that the organizations most committed to treating and curing may have, inadvertently, had a part in perpetuating the stigma of leprosy, through a complex and circular relation between the expectations that some societies have for people with leprosy and the organizational constraints and requirements for the leprosy organizations' own survival.

"Normals" in the community prefer to have deviant people of many sorts removed from view and cared for by others. Just what threatens the community varies with the form of deviance. For example, the mentally ill may threaten us because they behave in ways that make interactions with them unpredictable and stressful. Blind people threaten us because they may become inconveniently dependent on the sighted. People with leprosy threaten us not only with (supposed) infection but also with the terrible sight of their malformed faces and hands. The stigma of disease, then, is a convenient belief for communities that would prefer to rid themselves of "abnormal" and sometimes difficult people.

Leprosy organizations have taken the responsibility for the care of lepers from "normals" and have in many societies done just what the community wants, removed the leper from view. Inpatient facilities are often completely contained villages providing not only treatment but also employment, education, and recreation. There is often no need for a leprosy patient to leave this "asylum" and, in fact, it is sometimes physically difficult to do so because leprosy hospitals are often found on islands (e.g., in Sri Lanka and the Philippines) or in the remote countryside. In fact, organizations justify the isolation of leprosy patients by reference to the community's stigmatization of lepers. "Some are rejected by their homes and families . . . for some there is, humanly speaking, no hope; their disabilities mean that they will be dependent for the rest of their lives. The Mission cares for such as these also."[41] Removal of lepers from the "normal" community serves to confirm the idea of stigma. People in Sri Lanka may say, "If lepers must be sent to a remote island for treatment then there must be something very terrible about them and their disease." Stigma is thus confirmed.

Leprosy organizations have not only removed threatening people from community view, they have also demanded little change on the part of "normals" by focusing their work largely on treatment and rehabilitation rather than on prevention or on public education to reduce stigma. The

American Leprosy Mission for example, made its largest allocation of funds (43 percent of its $1 million budget) for medical and rehabilitation work.[42] Treatment of lepers particularly in inpatient facilities places no burden on the community to change its image of the threat of leprosy.

Thus, leprosy organizations, by building permanent inpatient hospitals and stressing treatment of stigmatized patients rather than change in the public's view of the disease, have acted "for" the normal community. In many cases leprosy patients, even in the United States, remain permanently under organizational control and do not return to their communities.[43] We expect that so long as these organizations continue to remove leprosy patients, they will be supported by the community. Scott, in discussing comparable functions of agencies for the blind, has suggested that " . . . the blindness agencies sponsoring programs compatible with community need to minimize awareness of the blind have had the most success in raising funds for their operations, while the agencies adopting a restorative approach to rehabilitation have experienced the most serious financial problems. This lesson of history in the blindness field has not been forgotten; indeed, it has probably been overlearned."[44]

Once organizations are established, they tend to perpetuate themselves. In the case of leprosy foundations, continued maintenance is stressed because large capital investments have been made in hospitals, clinics, even jeeps and planes, and commitments have been made to people, both staff and patients. The tendency to self-perpetuation is reflected in the organizational ideology as well. There is always more work to be done and even new problems to tackle. Until recently, leprosy organizations argued that the work must go on because innumerable cases of leprosy remained undetected and/or untreated: "The leprosy problem in most countries, however, is usually far out of proportion to the actual number of cases registered. Not more than 20 percent of estimated cases are under regular treatment."[45] Within the past two or three years, however, the argument has changed with the growing awareness of immunity to standard treatments. As the American Leprosy Mission *Bulletin* reports: "But more distressing than all this is the fact that today, more and more people are being found who are infected with a form of leprosy bacillus which is resistant to treatment with this drug. . . . Before long the resistant variety or strain of bacilli outnumber the normal type and it quickly becomes apparent that the customary treatment of the disease is ineffective."[46] Thus, when one problem becomes close to being solved, another appears. Rather than calling for increased involvement by government public health agencies to deal with new problems, the new problems become justifications for increased activities and thus greater demand for funds by the private leprosy organizations themselves.[47]

Leprosy organizations, like many medical foundations, are dependent on public donation of funds. As Scott has suggested, funds may be contributed more generously if such organizations confirm popular beliefs by medical and social science. Spokespersons for these foundations have suggested as much, in discussions of the change from "leprosy" to "Hansen's disease," when they say: "There is a case for retaining the substance of current terminology related to *leprosy* particularly because of its value to fund-raising." They explain that appeals for "overseas" charity, for Asian and African patients, must compete with 77,000 charities at home and "the evocation of a reaction to the word *leprosy* is an essential factor."[48] Thus, leprosy foundations may, to sustain themselves, find it necessary to allude to the idea of threat and to support the community in its willingness to stigmatize.

If we look at fund-raising and public relations materials, often distributed to Sunday schools and Ladies' Missionary Societies, we see the perpetuation of the idea of stigmatization. In these instances, several messages are implicit. One, leprosy is a frightening phenomenon. Phrases such as: " . . . leprosy is already assuming alarming proportions," " . . . it is nothing short of terrifying . . . ," "the situation is truly menacing," and "we must rid the world of this scourge . . . " are common descriptors. In the brochure that reports the change of name from "leprosy" and "leper" to "Hansen's disease," to avoid "a cruel pejorative term that does grave injustice to the dignity and worth of a person," the term "Hansen's disease" is nowhere used; instead, consistent reference in all Foundation materials is to "leprosy." Second, not only is leprosy terrible, but in some vague way it may touch upon Westerners (the donors). For example, "Leprosy is found in almost every country of the world, a world made small by modern means of travel. . . . Tourists, students, businessmen, government officials freely intermix on the highways of the world. No longer can the well-being of mankind in one part of the globe be separated from the well-being of men everywhere."[49] Thus, the terrible disease may not be confined to the poor of the tropics and out of our sight, but may attack our neighbors, relatives, even ourselves.

These brochures show what the foundations are doing. Their service is described as extraordinary, requiring devotion and great risk. Numerous articles in *The Star*, the publication of the U.S. Public Health Service hospital at Carville, describe people like "Dr. Emilia Ode, . . . a woman who has given seventeen years of devoted service to a hospital in the heart of African Equatorial forests."[50] There are people, therefore, who have taken on the special burden of working with leprosy patients. As the American Leprosy Mission brochure suggests, "Christians have pioneered leprosy work. From the days of Jesus and the Apostles, Christians have had a special concern for victims of this disease and have ministered to those so afflicted when no one else would. Even today, in many places, patients are dependent upon the Christian Church for medical care."[51] In fund-raising brochures many pictures and vignettes describe the unusual people who have chosen to carry on the unending and often unrewarding work with leprosy patients.

Westerners, vaguely threatened by a terrible disease, and certainly somewhat guilty about but very willing to turn the care of such patients over to others, can do only one thing: give donations. As the American Leprosy *Bulletin* suggests, the fact that immunity to standard drugs is occuring more frequently " . . . is nothing short of terrifying, simply because, to date, there is absolutely no other drug which is readily available, as free of negative side effects, as inexpensive and as effective as DDS has been up until now. . . . The quality of care must be raised until a high proportion of cases are found early and treated regularly. Five dollars per year is not enough. Thirty dollars is a more reasonable figure, but in many areas adequate care cannot be given for less than fifty to sixty dollars per patient per year."[52] All one needs to do, then, to be relieved of the burden of dealing with stigmatized people, is to give money, in this case, to keep the disease out of sight in the poor tropical countries.

Much of what is stated in these messages is, according to current scientific knowledge about leprosy, factually wrong. Leprosy is not a terrible or life-threatening disease, nor a real threat to Westerners. Service to lepers, like all service, requires devotion, but the degree of risk is not great. In fact, in a growing number of countries service to lepers is provided by government health service employees in the same way as it is for other diseases. It is apparently true that the immunity of some bacilli has become a problem that must be handled by greater expenditure and/or better planning based on epidemiological knowledge.[53]

Why do foundations dealing with leprosy arouse fears and suggest stigma – particularly in the face of scientific and experiential knowledge that leprosy is not highly contagious and can be treated effectively on an outpatient basis while the patient carries on normal activities? We have suggested that the economic and social commitments of the organizations, justified by an ideology about "important work that remains undone," requires continued financial and other support. To sustain financial support these organizations have learned that they survive only if they confirm society's preference for removal of deviant people from view. Thus, the organizations whose goals are "to assist in their [leprosy patients'] rehabilitation and to work toward the eradication of leprosy" at the same time perpetuate, through their actions (building inpatient hospitals and providing long-term care) and words (public education programs and fund-raising brochures) the community's ideas of stigma. It is not insignificant that the 1978 brochure of the Leprosy Mission is entitled *Set Apart*.

Conclusion

We began with a bacillus, mildly communicable, treatable, not life-threatening nor even deforming if treated early. Now we see that the bacillus itself is only a minor actor in the drama of leprosy. Instead, surrounding the disease in many societies is a set of social beliefs and expectations that profoundly affect the patient's experience and the doctor's work.

First we showed that the stigma of leprosy is not universal. In many societies, even where leprosy is common, leprosy is believed to be just another of the debilitating illnesses that many families must tolerate. Patients remain at home and marriages continue. In other societies, lepers are quickly divorced, pushed out of their homes, to end up as beggars. This cross-cultural variation in the stigma of leprosy led us to conclude that the source of a particular response is in the social and cultural matrix in which the disease exists.

In many societies beliefs about leprosy developed and stabilized long before written records were kept. In nineteenth-century Hawaii, however, we saw the economic and social threat of the Chinese immigrants become transformed into the social threat of the disease they were believed to carry. In Africa, we pointed to the very beginning of what could be a new, and stigmatized, notion of leprosy inadvertently introduced by public health educators. Thus, the moral definition of leprosy may arise from particular historical/social/medical circumstances, different in each society.

Second, we showed that the ideology surrounding leprosy provides a map for the leper. Moral definitions tell the leper how to "have" the illness. We contrasted Ethiopian and American experiences, profoundly different, but each exemplifying the effect of society's expectations on the leper's career.

Finally, once the moral definition becomes established, it is often perpetuated for reasons having very little to do with the disease itself. In the case of leprosy, even though effective treatment is available in the tropical countries where the disease is prevalent, and even though the Christian missionary organizations that are often the main providers of treatment certainly do not intend to stigmatize, the stigma of leprosy continues. We have suggested that this moral definition of leprosy is often perpetuated by the very organizations that treat the disease through a complex and circular relationship between the community's preference for removing deviant people and the leprosy organizations' needs for society's support in order to survive. Both the organizations' actions (removing leprosy patients from society) and their ideologies (in the form of public educational materials) sustain the idea that leprosy is horrible and threatening, requires treatment by "special" people, and is an enormous, often hidden, and unending problem. These actions and beliefs, though not based on medical facts, are consistent with the normal community's definitions of the disease and thus receive most sympathy from prospective donors. To continue their work, then, the organizations that "own" leprosy must sustain the stigma of leprosy.

We have examined leprosy because it provides a clear example of the social transformation of disease. In some societies leprosy is transformed into an illness that has serious implications for the social career of the sick person. Similar transformations might occur with other diseases. The effects may be milder and the social transformations less obvious, but if we examine the beliefs, practices, and experiences of patients who suffer from other diseases, we should see similar processes.

One such medical problem is blindness. Using either medical or legal definitions, most "blind" people can actually see, yet we tend to think of all blind people in stereotypical categories, often as "helpless," and we find it personally much easier not to have to interact with a blind person because "relationships with the blind are often strained and infused with ambiguity."[54] The lack of nonverbal communications through gestures and reciprocal smiles, etc., makes such interactions tense. The constant threat that the blind person will become overly dependent on the sighted leads us to fear such contact, even to stigmatize the blind. Just as with leprosy patients in India or Ethiopia, the normal community finds it more convenient and comfortable to avoid contact with blind people by providing funds for agencies that will remove the blind from view and take charge of the problem.

As Scott suggests, although agencies for the blind "uphold the desirability of the restorative approach to rehabilitation, most of them follow an accommodative approach in practice."[55] Thus, rather than helping blind people by offering mechanical devices or training that might allow them to return to their former jobs, they are often retrained for jobs originally devised for the totally blind. In time, blind people may be effectively removed from society, to participate in sheltered workshops, special "blind" social activities, even segregated homes. Agencies succeed, then, in transforming people from sighted people who have trouble seeing to blind people with residual vision. And ideologies develop around this accommodative approach justifying continued resocialization and even removal from normal society. As one theory suggests: ". . . with the death of the sighted man the blind man will be born."[56] The agencies that survive are the ones that confirm the community's willingness to stigmatize blind people. They provide services and accompanying ideologies that justify removing "difficult" people from our midst.

The social definition of illness has an obvious effect on doctors. For example, not only must they treat the leprosy bacillus, they must also recognize and deal with the culture's beliefs about the disease. In India and Sri Lanka they must find the hidden patients and convince those in treatment to return for more. In Hawaii and Louisiana doctors must care for and also justify the continued hospitalization of large proportions of leprosy patients with inactive diseases who do not want to go home.[57] The social and cultural context in which the disease exists must be seen as part of the disease process itself.

Our understanding of leprosy can move beyond this "conservative" analysis of the relationship between social factors and disease. It is not simply that doctors are waiting outside the society with neutral values, waiting to step in to treat and to take into account society's peculiar transformations of disease. Instead the medical institution is part of society itself, and thus is implicated in the social and moral definition of disease. We have seen that missionary doctors who went to Africa and India took with them a particular conception of leprosy that required isolation hospitals, and this new treatment method implied that it was right and good that lepers be taken from their homes and isolated from their families. New threats and fears – even the idea of stigma – were thus introduced. These threats and fears, predominant in the West, have been strengthened over the years by medical and missionary organizations whose basic needs are to survive.

Chapter 8 will examine this perspective on the institution of medicine in more detail. Here, in our case analysis of the leprosy treatment organizations, we have shown that the medical system operates within, not outside of, the society; it acts for its own interests and seeks to fulfill its own needs. While doing so medicine itself contributes to the social and moral definition of disease.

Notes

1. Schur, E. M. *Labeling Deviant Behavior: Its Sociological Implications.* New York: Harper & Row, 1971.
2. Feldman, R. A. "Leprosy surveillance in the USA: 1949–1970," *International Journal of Leprosy,* 1968, *37*:458–60.
3. World Health Organization Expert Committee on Leprosy. *World Health Organization Technical Report Services,* No. 459. Geneva: World Health Organization, 1970.
4. Feldman, "Leprosy surveillance in the USA."
5. Kapoor, J. N. "Lepers in the city of Lucknow," *Indian Journal of Social Work,* 1961, *22*:239–46.
6. Ibid., p. 239.
7. Ryrie, G. A. "The psychology of leprosy," *Leprosy Review,* 1951, *22*:1, 13–24.
8. Kapoor, "Lepers in the city of Lucknow," p. 245.
9. Heffner, L. T. "A study of Hansen's disease in Ceylon," *Southern Medical Journal,* 1969, *62*:977–85.
10. Waxler, N. E. "The social career of lepers in Sri Lanka." Unpublished study, 1977. The fact that our sample of leprosy patients was obtained from the outpatient leprosy clinic means that we have no information on half of the group estimated to remain untreated. Our conclusions may be biased but in ways that we cannot determine.
11. Shiloh, A. "A case study of disease and culture in action: leprosy among the Hausa of northern Nigeria," *Human Organization,* 1965, *24*:140–7.
12. Ibid., p. 143.
13. Ibid.
14. van Etten, G. N., and Anten, J. C. "Evaluation of health education in a Tanzanian leprosy scheme," *International Journal of Leprosy,* 1972, *40*:402–9, p. 407.
15. Giel, R. and van Luijk, J. N. "Leprosy in Ethiopian society," *International Journal of Leprosy,* 1970, *38*:187–98.
16. Hertroijs, A. R. "A study of some factors affecting the attendance of patients in a leprosy control scheme," *International Journal of Leprosy,* 1974, *42*:419–27; van Etten and Anten, "Evaluation of health education."
17. For some of the analysis presented, the author is indebted to Gussow, Z., and Tracy, G., "Stigma and the leprosy phenomenon: the social history of a disease in the nineteenth and twentieth centuries," *Bulletin of the History of Medicine,* 1970, *44*:424–49; Gussow, Z., and Tracy, G. "The use of archival materials in the analysis and interpretaion of field data: a case study in the institutionalization of the myth of leprosy as 'leper,' " *American Anthropologist,* 1971, *73*:695–709.
18. Gussow and Tracy, "Stigma and the leprosy phenomenon," p. 433.
19. Ibid., p. 441.
20. Gussow and Tracy, "The use of archival materials," p. 706.
21. Ibid.
22. Gussow and Tracy, "Stigma and the leprosy phenomenon," p. 433.
23. Mouritz, A. "Report of the Superintendent of the Molokai Leprosy Hospital," in *Appendix to the Report on Leprosy of the President of the Board of Health to the Legislative Assembly.* Honolulu, Hawaii, 1886.
24. Ibid.
25. Meyer, R. W. "Report of the Agent, Board of Health at the Leper Settlement, Molokai, Hawaii," in *Appendix to the Report on Leprosy of the President of the Board of Health to the Legislative Assembly.* Honolulu, Hawaii, 1886, p. CXXXIX. Mouritz makes a similar observation: "The name 'Mai Pake' may, no doubt, have originated on the interrogation by a native of a Chinaman, 'What is this disease?' The Chinaman would proba-

bly answer, 'I don't know the Hawaiian word but there are plenty of people sick with the disease in my country.' I think this origin of the word is more probable than the explanation given that the disease was called 'Mai Pake' because the Chinese brought it." Mouritz, "Report of the Superintendent," p. XXXIX.

26. van Etten and Anten, "Evaluation of health education," p. 405.
27. Ibid., p. 417.
28. Ibid., p. 408.
29. Shiloh, "A case study of disease and culture in action."
30. "There was . . . no stigma attached to the disease amongst the Austrailian Aboriginals until segregation became law and sufferers were taken from their families and isolated. It seems that the Aboriginal people have known and coped with the disease at least since the influx of immigrants from leprosy endemic areas in the middle of the last century – and had no fear of it." Editorial, *The Medical Journal of Australia,* 1977, 2(11):345–7.
31. Giel and van Luijk, "Leprosy in Ethiopian society," p. 194.
32. Ibid., p. 190.
33. Ibid., p. 196.
34. Gussow, Z., and Tracy, G. "Status, ideology, and adaptation to stigmatized illness: a study of leprosy," *Human Organization,* 1968, 27:316–25, p. 322. These authors assert that in the West the stigma of leprosy is a myth perpetuated by treatment agents. This "myth" is taken quite seriously by the patients themselves; whether it is actually true is not important for our analysis here.
35. Ibid., p. 320.
36. Ibid., p. 324.
37. Gussow and Tracy, "The use of archival materials," p. 700.
38. Ibid., p. 703.
39. "Set apart." London: *The Leprosy Mission,* 1978.
40. Gussow and Tracy, "The use of archival materials," p. 702.
41. "Set apart."
42. American Leprosy Missions. *Annual Report,* 1977.
43. Bloombaun, M., and Gugelyk, T. "Voluntary confinement among lepers,"*Journal of Health and Social Behavior,* 1970, 11:16–20.
44. Scott, R. A. *The Making of Blind Men.* New York: Russell Sage, 1969, p. 93.
45. Hassleblad, O. W. "Leprosy . . . present-day understanding." *American Leprosy Mission,* n.d.
46. American Leprosy Missions. *Bulletin,* Fall 1978.
47. Because most leprosy hospitals have church and missionary affiliations, their organizational goals are mixed, combining concern with provision of medical care with interests in teaching Christian values and doctrine. However, as more Asian and African countries have obtained independence and as nationalistic feelings have become strong, negative reaction to the presence of missionaries has increased. In India and elsewhere it is now necessary for missionary groups to show that they provide concrete medical (or other) services in order to remain in the country. Thus continued control of leprosy (and other) hospitals is crucial if the Christian missionary work of these organizations is to continue.
48. *Hansen: Research Notes,* 1975, 6(1–2):202.
49. Hassleblad, "Leprosy."
50. *The Star,* 1976, 35(3):4.
51. Ross, W. F. "Questions people ask about leprosy." American Leprosy Missions, n.d.
52. American Leprosy Missions, *Bulletin,* Fall 1978.
53. Some have suggested that drug-resistance requires development of a new treatment strategy that will interrupt transmission in large populations of leprosy patients. One

part of this strategy, ironically, may be the need to provide "facilities for the hospitalization of a larger number of patients than at present during the first few months of treatment. This will require building or remodeling of facilities. . . " Lechat, M. "Sulfone resistance and leprosy control," *International Journal of Leprosy,* 1978, *46*:64–7.

54. Scott, *The Making of Blind Men,* p. 17.
55. Ibid., p. 90.
56. Ibid., p. 81.
57. Bloombaum and Gugelyk, "Voluntary confinement among lepers."

8 The health-care system: social contexts and consequences

Elliot G. Mishler

New perspectives on the health-care system and society

Among the many recent books and monographs on medicine and health care, an increasing number bear titles that suggest a new and distinctive formulation of issues. Representative examples of this new genre of criticism, all published during the past decade, are the following: *The American Health Empire: Power, Profits, and Politics;*[1] *The Cultural Crisis of Modern Medicine;*[2] *The Exploitation of Illness in Capitalist Society;*[3] *Medical Nemesis;*[4] *Power and Illness: The Political Sociology of Health and Medical Care.*[5]

These volumes vary in their particulars, but they share an orientation marked by their use of such key terms as power and politics. These terms position health care as a topic within those social science disciplines concerned with the structure of political power in society and reflect the central question of these disciplines, "Who gets what?" The referent of "what" is not restricted to the standard goals of health care, such as the cure of illness and the remission of symptoms, but is expanded to include, and often to focus on, such social and economic benefits as status and profits. The distribution of these benefits among various health professionals and between them and other groups in society becomes a principal focus of attention.

Within this framework, we turn to a set of questions that differ in significant ways from those we have discussed in earlier chapters. Although those seeking to answer them draw on studies of the social correlates of illness or of organizational effects on clinical practice, they do not treat the results as findings about disease and treatment but as indicators of the political and economic consequences of how the health-care system functions. Questions of primary interest include the following: Which social groups or classes benefit economically and politically from how the health-care system is organized and functions? How are health-care institutions and professions related to other social institutions, in terms of socioeconomic dominance and power? In what ways do the forms of

195

health care serve the interests of and incorporate the ideology of powerful groups in the society? How do these relations between society and health care vary across different cultures with different types of economic and political organization? In sum, the general question is this: What are the social, economic, and political functions of the health-care system?

It is evident that the tone of these questions is critical, and recent interpretations of the data are correspondingly so, particularly those on health-care systems that have achieved a high level of power, such as modern scientific medicine in highly industrialized societies. Not all of the investigators sharing this broad perspective agree with Illich's assertion that "the medical establishment has become a major threat to health,"[6] or with Ehrenreich's formulation of the key question about "the real value of scientific medical care" as "what the price of that care is, in terms of physical harm, social dependency, and political impotence."[7] Nonetheless, these positions are taken seriously by the new critics, and they provide major points of entry for their analyses of the health-care system.

Within the framework of the biomedical model, the assumption of the objective neutrality of scientific medicine incorporates a view of medicine as an applied science that is value-free. There is the implication that the practice of medicine may be understood with reference to the current state of scientific knowledge and assessed by scientific methods and criteria. There is the further corollary of this view that the primary determinants of advances in health care and of increases in levels of health lie within the boundaries of medicine itself. That is, it is assumed that medical progress depends on developments in scientific and technical knowledge that are then translated into practice. Medicine is thus considered to be relatively autonomous of other large forces within the society – historical, economic, political, social, and cultural.

This assumption of the relative autonomy of medicine and its neutrality with regard to conflicting interests and values within society is challenged directly by the new critics. Their argument begins with the counterclaim that medicine is not insulated from the larger society but is embedded within and responsive to sociocultural, economic, and political forces. Our analyses in previous chapters of the social contexts of patients, physicians, and medical views of illness could be understood as examples of this general proposition. However, the new critics carry the argument further. Not only is medicine influenced by society, but medicine has consequences for society. Even more specifically, because these critics view society as an arena of conflict over power and resources, they assert further that the health-care system not only pursues its own special interests but, at the same time, aligns itself with dominant groups and classes in the society, thus serving their special interests as well.

Various features of the health-care system, such as its form of organization and the roles of health professionals, the relative availability of services for different population groups, health levels and associated rates of morbidity and mortality for different diseases, resource allocations for preventive health measures as compared to treatment and rehabilitation, and the effectiveness of medical interventions and treatments, are all viewed as intimately connected to and consequential for the larger society.

Analyses of the health-care system undertaken on the basis of these assumptions cut across our own earlier analyses of the social contexts of patients, physicians, and medical care. Some of the new critics might argue that they undercut these analyses by raising more basic and more radical questions: Their critiques are directed not only to the assumptions of the biomedical model but to assumptions traditional in the social sciences on which we have so far relied. For example, in Chapter 2 we used epidemiological studies of relationships between socioeconomic status and schizophrenia to demonstrate the necessity for taking into account social conditions and social characteristics of patients. The aim was a fuller understanding of disease than that provided by the biomedical model with its assumption of illness as deviation from normal biological functioning. We did not ask, however, if a disproportionately heavy rate of illness among lower socioeconomic groups is "functional" for a stratified society, in which social class is a critically important dynamic in the struggle for economic and political power. The new critics do raise this question and further propose that the answer is "yes." Specifically, they maintain that such differentials in levels of health work to the advantage of classes in power, and are therefore functional to their interests in maintaining the status quo. The reasoning is that people whose deviance is labeled as "sickness" are removed from their normal social roles and are less likely to be available for and less effective in organizing and acting for their own economic and political interests as members of disadvantaged social groups.

Another example comes from Chapter 6, in which labeling studies were used to support criticism of the biomedical assumption of generic diseases. Here, too, although we cited Mercer's findings that the labeling of children as retarded was socially discriminatory in that it depended on ethnicity, we did not ask whether and how such a pattern might be functional for current structures of social, economic, and political power. The new critics want to look at such consequences, at the way in which this labeling process serves to deny access to educational channels of mobility for Mexican-Americans and other disadvantaged ethnic minorities, thereby maintaining the competitive advantage of Anglos in the job market.

In contrasting our earlier analyses and the approach we shall discuss in this chapter, our intent is not to undermine the former or give precedence to the latter. Our principal objective in this text is to present alternative frameworks to the biomedical model, frameworks based on the formulations and findings of the social and behavioral sciences. The questions raised by those we have referred to as the new critics extend far beyond the framework of the biomedical model itself. In an important sense, their critique is directed to the larger society within which the biomedical model functions and through which it is legitimated as an approach to problems of illness and health care. The work of the new critics represents an effort to place the entire health-care system in context, to examine the interdependence of definitions of disease, diagnostic practices, and institutional forms, and of relationships between the complex system of health care and the social system of which it is one part.

This chapter is directed to a clarification of the perspective of these critics. It is evident from these introductory comments that the topic is too broad for more than limited coverage. Our examples have been selected to convey the diversity of approaches to the general issue of the social functions of medicine. Now, examining cross-cultural and historical studies, we shall focus on relationships between the health-care system and broader cultural, economic, political, and social forces.

The medicalization of life

In the contemporary world, ideas about good health and proper medical care are so closely linked that we may easily forget that these are not simply two alternative terms for the same phenomenon. The tendency to identify health with medicine, a tendency widely shared by both lay persons and health professionals, carries the further implication that an extension and expansion of health-care services will be accompanied by rises in population health levels. Stated in its strongest form, this view is that health is a function of the quality of medical care; that is, the latter determines the former.

To raise questions about this presumed connection requires a wrench to our ordinary ways of thinking about health and the influences promoting and maintaining it. Among those who have begun to raise such questions are a number of medical historians who have been reexamining relation-

ships between increases in levels of health through the nineteenth and into
the twentieth century and parallel advances in scientific medicine. In previous chapters, we referred to Dubos' argument[8] that the historic declining trend in mortality and morbidity rates reflected the work of sanitation
engineers more than that of physicians, and to McNeill's thesis[9] that
epidemic diseases ceased to be major killers as they became endemic
and populations became, as it were, self-immunized. Both Dubos and
McNeill challenge the standard interpretation of the relationship between
improvements in health and the development of a scientifically based theory and practice of medicine. Their findings demonstrate that in this instance, as in others, correlation does not necessarily signify causation.
Other investigators have provided detailed analyses of changes over time
in socioeconomic conditions that appear to bear a more causal relationship to changes in health.

For example, using the progressive decline in mortality rates since the
early decades of the nineteenth century as an index of gradual improvement in health levels of the population of England and Wales, McKeown
and Lowe[10] examined a variety of factors to ascertain the determinants of
this long-term downward trend in mortality. They provide separate analyses of three time periods: the eighteenth century through 1838, 1838–
1900, and post-1900. The middle period is examined in most detail, and
they state that there is "no doubt" that the reduction in mortality "was
due almost entirely to a decrease in deaths from infectious disease."[11]
From their review of changes in death rates associated with five major
groups of diseases, which together accounted almost entirely for the decline of mortality in this period, they conclude that the following factors,
in order of importance, were the primary influences in the decline in mortality: "(1) a rising standard of living, of which the most significant feature
was probably improved diet (responsible mainly for the decline of tuberculosis and less certainly, and to a lesser extent, of typhus), (2) the hygienic changes introduced by sanitary reformers (responsible for the decline
of the typhus-typhoid and cholera groups), and (3) a favorable trend in the
relationship between infectious agent and human host (which accounted
for the decline of mortality from scarlet fever and may have contributed to
that from tuberculosis, typhus, and cholera). The effect of specific medical measures was restricted to smallpox and hence had only a trivial effect
on the total reduction of the death rate."[12]

McKeown and Lowe's review of trends in both the eighteenth and
twentieth centuries leads to a similar conclusion. They note that the advance in health that began in the eighteenth century "initially appears to
have been due to changes in the environment, of which the most impor-

tant feature was probably an improvement in the standard of living"[13] associated with the Industrial Revolution. For the recent past, since 1900, where the decline in infant mortality is the most striking feature of the trend, they argue that the relative importance of different factors remained as it had before that point. In summary, they assert: "Without denying the value of personal health services, or of the specific therapy which has been a notable achievement of the past forty years, it seems right to conclude that in descending order of importance the main influences responsible for the decline of mortality – our best index of improved health – since deaths were first registered in 1838 have been: a rising standard of living, hygienic measures, and specific preventive and curative therapy."[14]

It is a big jump from McKeown and Lowe's demonstration of the relatively minor role played by specific medical practices in the long-term improvement in health levels to Ivan Illich's thesis in his book, *Medical Nemesis*,[15] that the advance of modern scientific medicine has actually had a negative impact on health. A key term in Illich's argument is iatrogenesis, referring to diseases and other individual and social problems resulting from the practice of medicine itself.

Illich begins his critique with a review of studies of clinical iatrogenesis, that is, of "doctor-made" diseases. Not only is specific medical treatment "never significantly related to a decline in the compound disease burden or to a rise in life expectancy,"[16] asserts Illich, in a more extreme version of McKeown and Lowe's conclusion, but iatrogenic illnesses are now a major epidemic. "The pain, dysfunction, disability, and anguish resulting from technical medical intervention now rival the morbidity due to traffic and industrial accidents and even war-related activities, and make the impact of medicine one of the most rapidly spreading epidemics of our time."[17] These negative consequences include the side effects and addictions associated with drugs, unnecessary surgery, accidents, injuries, and infections resulting from hospitalization; Illich cites one study, for example, which reports that one out of five patients admitted to a typical research hospital acquires an iatrogenic disease.[18]

For Illich, the specific diseases resulting from deficiencies in medical practice, that is, "clinical iatrogenesis," are only a small part of the problem with which he is concerned. The major problem is the "medicalization of life," a function of "social" and "cultural" iatrogenesis. "Medicalization of life" refers to the extension of medical definitions of health, illness, and treatment into all areas of life. Given the monopoly control of such issues by the medical profession, this means that many ordinary and normal problems of life that were traditionally dealt with through natural social, community, and personal activities are now taken over by health-care professionals. In Chapter 6 we quoted Illich's view of the dominant and special role of physicians in the social construction of illness. Essentially, he argues that in all societies the social state of illness is created by medicine, and that socially recognized "healers" have the right and authority to define normality. In modern society, physicians have the power to decide what symptoms merit treatment and which persons are legitimately sick.

In some respects, this restates the general theme that we have been developing progressively in this text, namely, that concepts and practices with respect to health and illness are grounded in social contexts. However, Illich pushes the argument further by addressing the question of the social consequences of the monopolistic control by the medical profession of so many important areas of life. In brief, he proposes that the net effect of the overdependence of a population on the modern system of health care – highly technical, rational, and bureaucratic – for the care, relief, and treatment of the normal and natural pains and sufferings of life is the erosion of individual autonomy for self-care and of community processes of mutual care. Because of their increasing reliance on experts, individuals become less and less competent in taking care of themselves; indeed, efforts to take care of one's self or of others without medical intervention may be treated as an illegal act by the courts.

Illich's recommendation might be read as a paraphrase of the well-known statement about war and generals: Health is too serious an affair to be left to the physicians. Throughout his analysis, he is elaborating the point that the forms and consequences of health-care services, as they are embodied in the institutions and practices of modern scientific medicine, reinforce and support a significant sociopolitical trend in contemporary society: the expansion of corporate, bureaucratic, centralized control over people's lives. In this way, he asserts, medicine serves the interests of powerful controlling groups in the society and undermines the political, civil, and natural human rights of individuals for autonomy and control over their own lives.

It is important to recognize that Illich's critique is directed to the society and to health care as a subsystem within it; he is not accusing physicians as individual practitioners of malpractice. In their practices, physicians and other health professionals reflect general cultural values and orientations; they are agents of society. The dominance of medicine depends on and requires the active participation and collusion in these matters of other members of the society. Further, the preeminence of experts in the management and treatment of normal life problems is not restricted to issues of health and illness. Problems in other significant areas – for example, child care and marital relations – have also been turned over to "experts."

Illich's commentary on the role of medicine is broad-gauged and comprehensive. His view of the "medicalization of life" may be applied to any society. However, it does not include an analysis of differentials within society in the power and dominance of different social groups and classes and, for this reason, it does not direct us to the study of relations between systems of social stratification and differential patterns of health care and their consequences. Investigators whose work is presented in the following sections are specifically concerned with social, economic, and political differentials and with linkages between institutions of health care and particular patterns of social stratification. They view the medical profession as having sociopolitical interests that correspond to its position as a group with high status and dominance and, therefore, with interests that parallel those of other such groups in the society. They focus, accordingly, on the ways in which medical concepts and practices both reflect and serve the interests of the medical profession in maintaining its position of relative dominance and, at the same time, serve the interests of other dominant groups.

Health consequences of social change and economic development

The new critics often reinterpret studies reported by more "mainstream" researchers in the social and behavioral sciences. We have noted repeatedly that in many studies, the initial formulation of problems as well as the conclusions remain within the conceptual boundaries of the biomedical model: Functional connections between health issues and larger social forces are not examined. A critique of these limitations of traditional research is one of the primary tasks the new critics have set for themselves. This task involves a reconceptualization of problems of health and health care so as to demonstrate their relationships to socioeconomic characteristics of the larger society.

A study by Weisbrod et al.[19] and its review by Aronson[20] provide an instructive example of contrasting interpretations. The investigators' formulation of the problem and their interpretation of findings are cast within the traditional framework of social epidemiology; the critic views the study's approach, findings, and interpretation as intimately connected to the economic and political organization of the society.

The research team of health economists defined the problem for study as the determination of the economic and social consequences of the prevalence of schistosomiasis, which they refer to as "the world's reputedly number one public health disease."[21] The disease is caused by parasitic blood flukes, which lodge and propagate in the liver and migrate to a variety of other internal organs; it leads to internal hemorrhages, fever, abdominal pain, diarrhea, and probably decreased resistance to other infections. A critical element in the life cycle of the parasite is that it is carried by and transmitted to humans through an intermediate host, a specific species of snail. The cycle is maintained by disposal and drainage of human wastes into bodies of water that contain the carrier snails and, in turn, the use of infected water for various purposes.

Saint Lucia, the site of the study, is a small Caribbean island off the northeast coast of South America, with an estimated population of about 110,000. Since the mid-1950s its principal economic base has shifted from sugar to banana production. This 1950s shift coincided with a "seemingly explosive rise in prevalence"[22] of schistosomiasis.

Methods of cost–benefit analysis were used by the investigators to assess the economic effects of schistosomiasis and other parasitic diseases. Briefly, birth and death rates, school performance, and labor productivity were compared for populations of people with and without the disease. Findings from their complex and detailed analyses are easily summarized: "Our findings are that, on the whole, infection by schistosomiasis and also by any of the other parasitic diseases studied appears to cause few statistically significant adverse effects on these variables."[23]

One specific set of results may serve to illustrate this general conclusion. Although the investigators reported that there is some effect of the disease on daily productivity levels, they found the overall economic impact to be minimal. Apparently, one important aspect of adjustment to infection is to increase the amount of time worked and thus offset the reduction in productivity potential: ". . . the weekly wages of male workers who have the infection are not lower than those who are not infected, because the infected group is absent less from the job."[24] The authors also point out that ". . . the cost of schistosomiasis infection for males is a reduction, not in market production and earnings, but in leisure."[25] Their analyses of children's academic performance produce similar results; there is no association between infection and academic standing and some evidence, counter to their original hypothesis, that children with schistosomiasis have lower rates of school absenteeism.

Aronson's review reflects the perspective of the new critics. She points out that in Weisbrod et al.'s formulation of the problem, little attention is given to the effects of economic change and development on rates of disease and, further, that the effects of disease that Weisbrod et al. analyzed do not include noneconomic aspects of victims' lives. Within the text of Weisbrod et al.'s report, nonetheless, but presented in the eighth technical appendix and not otherwise referred to in any consequential way, is a separate study of a very different question than those around which the main text is organized. This question is this: Was the change from sugar to banana cultivation responsible for the 1950s increase in the rate of schistosomiasis? The grounds for expecting such a relationship are that large-scale banana production, in contrast to sugar production, requires extensive use of irrigation systems, which are potential breeding grounds for snails. The analyses reported in the appendix (written by the junior author, Helminiak, and based on his dissertation) provide strong support for the hypothesis that rates of schistosomiasis infection are a function of whether individuals work on a large banana estate or live near such workers. Detailed prevalence data show that the probability of infection is related to household distance from the households of the banana workers, the latter having significantly higher prevalence rates than other workers. "This," Aronson states, "indicates that schistosomiasis is an occupational disease of banana plantation workers."[26] She goes on to point out that because "Weisbrod et al. are concerned only that the disease of the St. Lucians does not affect their work; the idea that the St. Lucian's work makes them sick does not fit the framework of their investigation."[27]

Aronson's reanlaysis of Weisbrod et al.'s findings highlights several principal features of the new critical perspective on the health-care system. Rather than restricting her attention to rates of schistosomiasis and their social correlates, she examines the relationship between dominant economic interests and the medical conception of illness and its socially relevant consequences, a relationship that informs both the study itself and policy recommendations for preventive health measures. Because illness does not reduce productivity – affected workers adjust to the disease by working longer hours – the overall economic interests of banana plantation owners are not affected. The reduction in workers' leisure time and the drain on their energy from the disease may, as we suggested earlier, be functional for the status quo distribution of political and economic power. The workers' lack of political power makes it unlikely that measures will be introduced to improve their health. At the same time, because the economic interests of plantation owners are not negatively affected by the disease, they have little reason to introduce changes in the current system of large-plantation cultivation of bananas. Such changes might be viewed by them as counter to their interests, because they would likely involve a shift to small-scale cultivation that does not require the large network of irrigation ditches, a network that is directly implicated in the high prevalence of schistosomiasis. As Aronson's analysis makes evident, not only are population health levels related to social and economic conditions, but the approach to and understanding of disease as well as patterns of health care and prevention are closely linked to the socioeconomic structure of society.

Medicine as profession and social institution

The traditional aims of medicine, the care and healing of the sick, are not merely abstract values. They have concrete consequences in institutions such as medical schools, clinics, laboratories, offices, and hospitals through which medicine takes on its reality as courses of action in a real world. Further, these values are not simply internalized guides to and constraints on the action of physicians as separate individuals; they function as collective norms. In a word, medicine is a social institution with rules governing membership, the rights and privileges of members, and forms of appropriate practice.

Among sociologists, it is a commonplace to note that organizations and institutions designed and developed for certain specific purposes come to serve other aims and imperatives. It has often been observed, for example, in bureaucratic organizations, that maintenance needs may supersede service and productivity needs and that means tend to become ends. It would not be unexpected for us to find similar forces at work in the institutions of medicine.

The claims by physicians that professional control of all aspects of health care, from recruitment and training to the regulation of practice, is necessary for effective and proper treatment have been challenged by many critics. Freidson[28] argues that the demand for monopoly control of the profession by the profession may have less to do with the corpus of specialized and technical knowledge of medicine, which is used to justify this demand, than with efforts to sustain the position of power and status of physicians vis-à-vis other health professionals and their patients.

Among the important rights that a profession claims as both necessary and legitimate is the power to regulate itself, that is, the right to define professional standards of conduct, to evaluate whether or not practitioners act in accordance with these standards, and to apply sanctions if there are violations. Freidson documents the ineffectiveness of self-regulatory processes in medicine. He asserts that the profession appears to be more interested in furthering the interests of its members and in maintaining its autonomy from external control than in enforcing conformity to professional standards. As Freidson puts it, ''. . . expertise is more and more in danger of being used as a mask for privilege and power rather than, as it claims, as a mode of advancing the public interest."[29]

In his analysis, Freidson distinguishes sharply between the "codified" knowledge of medicine, the scientific theories and data about illness and treatment, and the knowledge required for practices that are effective as well as in accord with societal values and norms. For the latter, which is a critical component of a consulting profession like medicine, physicians have no stronger claim to expertise than the members of the community that are served by the profession. However, the historical record suggests that the medical profession has made its claim for autonomy and control in the domain of "applied" knowledge in addition to "pure" knowledge. The consequence has been the dominance of professional values and interests over public values and interests in the development of health policy and health services: ". . . after becoming autonomous the profession has less and less come to reflect what the public asks of it. . . . Social policy is coming to be formulated on the basis of the profession's conception of need and to be embodied in support for the profession's institutions. . . . Professional 'knowledge' cannot therefore properly be a guide for social policy if it is a creation of the profession itself, expressing the commitments and perception of a special occupational class rather than that of the public as a whole."[30]

The general values about health and health care with which Illich is concerned and the specific interests of medicine as a profession examined by Freidson are actualized in the concrete work settings through which health care is organized and delivered to patients. We have already discussed, in an earlier chapter, some consequences of certain organizational variables, such as size, stratification, and personnel turnover in hospitals. In the context of this chapter, it is useful to consider how patient care is affected by the organization of the hospital as a treatment system. As we shall see, how hospitals function tends more to reflect the needs and interests of the health professionals than the needs and interests of patients.

Duff and Hollingshead[31] conducted a study of patient care in a general hospital associated with a medical school; they refer to it as a component in a "modern medical center." A central focus of their work is the analysis of associations between variations of patient care, treatment, and outcome with variations in social attributes of patients, interprofessional and interpersonal relationships within the staff, and modes of "sponsorship" for hospital admission.

They emphasize the important effects on patients of whether they are in ward, semiprivate, or private accommodations. Their status in the hospital in this respect is closely tied to whether or not they are under the care and sponsorship of a private physician or under the charge of the house staff of students and residents, referred to as committee or semicommittee sponsorship. Type of sponsorship and accommodation are closely related to social characteristics of the patients, particularly to their ability to pay for services. "Physician sponsorship in the hospital was related to the patient's ability through knowledge and economic power to draw attention to his problems. . . . nothing affected it more profoundly than the socioeconomic position of the patient." And, their summary comment, based on their observations, indicates the important consequences of type of sponsorship: "From self-interest or interest in others with attributes like their own, physicians appeared to perform more adequately for high-status persons."[32]

Overall, they found patients fearful about their illness, confused and ill informed about their symptoms. Duff and Hollingshead refer to a "framework of evasions" within which care is given. "Patients and physicians commonly had a tacit agreement that the real situation would not be confronted. . . . choices [with regard to diagnosis and treatment] were not clearly reasoned ones but were shaped, in part, by evasion of the truth. . . . On the wards suspicion, distrust, and confusion were extreme and common."[33] Suspicion was the most prominent feature of physician–patient relationships, and the authors argue that distrust was maintained through the ways in which physicians performed.

Duff and Hollingshead point to a number of factors they consider responsible not only for the atmosphere of distrust and suspicion and the lack of adequate communication between patients and physicians, but also for significantly high levels of misdiagnosis and inappropriate management of patients and their illnesses. For example, based on an independent review of patients' records and their own interviews and observations, they report that only 46 percent of patients on the medical service and 75 percent on the surgical service were diagnosed correctly.[34] One important source of these problems was the insulation of physicians from the everyday concerns of their patients. Physicians did not know about their patients' lives, and did not ask about it. This had many consequences, for example, "errors in diagnosis were linked clearly to the patient's and the physician's failure to take into consideration major factors in the patient's history. Inappropriate management of the patient followed."[35]

Within their biomedical conception of illness and treatment, physicians are neither interested in social and psychological components of disease nor are prepared through training or experience to use such information. Duff and Hollingshead note that "scientific" medicine was sometimes used as "insulating" medicine. That is, physicians were fearful of being drawn into the larger real-world problems of patients and their families if they deviated from a physical disease approach; they used the model of scientific medicine to defend against and insulate themselves from these concerns. The various problems build on and reinforce each other so that negative effects are particularly marked for ward patients with committee sponsorship. "When the conditions of poverty, low social status, committee sponsorship, and personal and family turmoil were combined, as they so often were on the wards, the results were spectacularly tragic for the patient and his family."[36]

Duff and Hollingshead are not alone among observers of the medical-care system to remark the insensitivity to patient needs of physicians and other health professionals. However, their interpretation of these findings shares the perspective of the new critics that we have been describing. They view the pattern of insulation from patients' lives and withdrawal into the shell of the medical model as motivated by economic and professional interests. They propose that physicians subordinate patients' problems to their own concerns for protecting and maintaining ongoing physician–patient relationships so as to avoid any loss of status or income that might result from the disruption of these relationships.

The hospital is only one component, though a critical one, of the health-care system. Another important though quite different part of the system is the colleague network, that is, the set of professional relationships among practicing physicians. Coleman, Katz, and Menzel[37] found that a physician's place in a professional network affected the time involved for a physician to introduce a new drug into his or her own practice.

Framing the problem in terms of the rate and pattern of diffusion of an innovation, in this instance the spread of a new drug through a community of practicing physicians, the investigators examined the effects of the degree to which physicians were either integrated into or isolated from professional and social networks. Their results show a marked impact on this specific change in practice, namely, the use of a new drug, of physicians' connection with their professional colleagues. For example, comparison of physicians integrated into both professional and social networks with those relatively isolated from both shows that 90 percent of the former had used the new drug within less than eight months after its introduction whereas 50 percent of the latter had not yet used it ten months after its introduction.

In addition to differentials in rate of use, different diffusion processes are at work for integrated and isolated physicians. Among integrated physicians, the curve of drug use shows a pattern of increasing acceleration over time, a snowball or chain-reaction process. Essentially, the increasing rate of adoption over time reflects the increased proportion of users in each previous time period. For integrated nonusers, there are more and more physicians with whom they associate professionally and socially who can transmit information and advice about the new drug. Because they are integrated into these networks of communication, there is an increased likelihood at each successive time period that they will hear about the new drug. For the nonintegrated physicians, whose initial rate of use does not differ very much from the initial rate of integrated physicians, their rate of adoption does not change over time. Because they are not part of an effective communication network, the likelihood of their hearing about and adopting the new drug is not affected by increases in the number of previous adoptions. Thus, at the end of each successive time period, physicians who are closely connected to their professional and social networks show significantly higher rates of use than isolated physicians, and this differential increases with time.

Although Coleman et al. did not interpret their findings in terms of the critical perspective we are describing, we have used their findings to illustrate a significant effect on treatment practices of an aspect of the social organization of medicine that is rarely examined, namely, the networks of relationships among physicians. From the viewpoint of the new critics, these findings serve to illustrate once again their general point: The treatment that patients receive is influenced more by the ways in which medical-care systems are organized than by the needs of different patient populations.

In this section we have centered attention on professional and institutional variables that affect patient care and treatment. Our aim has been to document, through concrete examples, the argument of the new critics that the ways in which health services are organized and provided are more likely to reflect these factors than be responsive to the needs of patients or satisfy objective criteria for the application of scientific knowledge. More specifically, these systems appear to be designed and to function primarily on behalf of the professional and economic interests of physicians rather than the needs of patients. In the next section, we turn to studies that show how particular forms of medical practice function so as to serve the interests and values of dominant groups in society.

Social functions of medicine

In his introduction to a series of papers representing the new "cultural critique" of medicine, Ehrenreich[38] comments that a central theme in this critique is that physicians do not simply apply technical knowledge but impart social messages. Further, these messages incorporate a specific ideology, which represents the interests of ruling classes and groups in the society. "Above all, both the doctor–patient relationship and the entire structure of medical services are not mere technical relationships, but social relationships which express and reinforce (often in subtle ways) the social relations of the larger society: e.g., class, racial, sexual, and age hierarchy; individual isolation and passivity; and dependency on the social order itself in the resolution of both individual and social problems."[39]

A striking example of this concordance between a dominant social ideology and medical theory and practice is found in the treatment of women and their diseases during the latter part of the nineteenth century. Ehrenreich and English[40] examine the "cult of female invalidism" among the "sick women of the upper classes" during this period and the ways in which physicians reinforced and supported repressive cultural stereotypes about women. They note that "Sickness pervaded upper- and upper-middle-class female culture,"[41] and that it was associated with the prevalent medical view of that time that normal female functions, such as menstruation and pregnancy, were signs of illness. As an aside, we may note that this belief is consistent with the assumption of the biomedical model of illness as deviation from normal biological functioning; in this instance, the definition of normality is clearly dependent on male-dominated cultural values and forms, which viewed female biological processes as deviations.

This medical perspective had consequences not only for medical practice but for the social order as well. "The doctor's view of women as innately sick did not, of course, make them sick, or delicate, or idle. But it did provide a powerful rationale against allowing women to act in any other way."[42] Medical arguments were used as grounds for barring women from medical school and other forms of higher education, from areas of public life, and even from voting. There is a contemporary echo in the scandalous comment a few years ago by the health advisor to an American President that women's "raging hormones" interfered with their ability to serve effectively as public officials.

"Bed rest" was a prominent recommendation for all the "normal illnesses" to which females were prone, such as menstruation, pregnancy, and menopause. The more time spent lying down, the better. One could hardly devise a more effective way of ensuring that women would be passive nonparticipants in economic and political life, and dependent on men. In addition to serving the general interests of men as the dominant group in the society, this approach also served the particular interests of the medical profession. Ehrenreich and English point out that there was much competition between physicians and other "doctors" and within the medical profession itself. For example, there were three times as many doctors engaged in primary patient care per 100,000 population in 1900 as there are today. The "sick" women were a large and easily available pool of patients, and the fact that their illnesses were chronic, indeed inseparable from their biological status as women, ensured a stable and steady income for practitioners.

Finally, this mode of medical practice reduced the risk that women might organize politically and rebel against the pattern of sexist discrimination and oppression. "In fact, the medical attention directed at these women amounted to what may have been a very effective surveillance system. Doctors were in a position to detect the first signs of rebelliousness, and to interpret them as symptoms of a 'disease' that had to be 'cured.'"[43] We shall return later to this function of physicians in the control of deviance.

The work that physicians do as "certifiers" of illness, that is, as social decision makers determining whether or not a person may be legitimately exempted from normal social demands and role requirements, is implicit in Ehrenreich and English's analysis. The idea that illness is a form of deviance that differs in particular ways from other types of deviant behavior, such as delinquency or criminality, is now common among sociologists.[44] The critical significance of medical criteria and of the function of physicians in the determination of competence for social role performance is evident in newspaper headlines. In recent years physicians have been asked to judge whether political leaders were rendered disabled or were recovered sufficiently from an episode of illness to perform effectively and sanely. Ileitis, strokes, heart disease, exhaustion, and alcoholism have fallen within the range of medical determination, and, what is most important, these "political" decisions have been accepted as legitimate and warranted.

Physicians are routinely called upon to make such decisions in a variety of other, more mundane suituations. For example, a recent headline in the *Harvard Gazette,*[45] "Fear of Finals: 'Illness' Up," introduces an account of an increased number of medical excuses from final exams. A faculty study found an "alarming trend" in such legitimized exemptions and concluded that such students gain a competitive advantage by the extra time they have to prepare for exams "by claiming an illness which is not, in fact, serious." In response to this criticism, physicians in the university health service are quoted as recognizing the difficulty in making such judgments "fairly and with certainty." The physicians also suggest that the increase in medical make-up exams may result from an increase in the number of students who are "reluctant to take an exam unless than feel themselves to be in top physical condition." It may be noted that this criterion of "top physical condition" may reflect a radical change in our usual definition of illness, and in commonly accepted grounds for exemption from normal role performance.

In their monograph on the social functions of medicine and the use of illness as a category for deviance, Waitzkin and Waterman[46] examine in some detail the ways in which the certifying function of physicians may serve the ideology and interests of dominant groups in the society. They propose that the ". . . sick role contributes to social stability in a wide variety of institutional settings" by providing "a controllable form of deviance which mitigates potentially disruptive conflicts between personality needs and the social system's role demands. . . . adoption of the sick role relieves strains which otherwise could become a focus of dissatisfaction, conflict, and change. To the extent that it fosters social stability and defuses potential opposition, the sick role's effects tend to be conservative and, perhaps in some cases, counterrevolutionary."[47]

In their view, labeling an individual as sick on the basis of inadequate role performance is a choice that is made in the interest of system stability. Thus, in documenting the effects of medical certification of illness in such organizations as prisons and the army, they suggest that placing an individual in the sick role, rather than labeling him as malingering, delinquent, or insubordinate, serves a number of institutional needs. For example, the overt deviant is temporarily isolated from his unit, thereby protecting group morale and efficiency, and, at the same time, certain "troublesome" members are managed without recourse to explicit disciplinary actions. In addition, the sick role adoptee takes on the normative obligation of this role, which is to cooperate with treatment agents so as to recover from his "illness" and return to his unit as rapidly as possible. This is less likely a course if his deviance had been defined in terms of a motivated violation of rules or orders.

Waitzkin and Waterman also analyze the sociopolitical effects of medical deferment and exemption practices during the Vietnam war. In this highly unpopular war, the function of physicians as certifiers of medical and psychiatric suitability for service was of considerable importance. The total rate of disqualification for all medical reasons rose steadily from 1965 through 1968 from about 23 to 30 percent of all draftees receiving preinduction physical examinations. From the perspective of radical critics who see the profession of medicine as serving the specific interests of dominant social classes, the more significant fact is that rates of disqualification were not equally distributed among different social groups. In general, for example, rates of disqualification for whites were about 10 percent higher than for blacks; further, this white–black differential increased slightly over the period during which there was a general rate increase.

On the other hand, blacks had consistently higher disqualification rates than did whites for mental reasons when these criteria were based on a battery of psychological tests. However, when test standards were lowered in 1965 because of high overall rejection rates, disqualification rates for blacks decreased sharply, by about 25 percent, whereas there was only a slight decline for whites. In other words, the disproportion in disqualification for service on "mental" grounds between blacks and whites was markedly reduced by a shift in standards. This, of course, had the consequence that white disqualification rates for all reasons increased markedly vis-à-vis blacks and that blacks, therefore, had a much higher probability of being inducted into military service. Waitzkin and Waterman also show regional effects that interact with race. For example, the highest rates of disqualification for medical reasons were for whites in the Northeast and on the West Coast and the lowest rates were for blacks in the South.

Waitzkin and Waterman conclude that the medical profession, through its power to disqualify persons for service, facilitated access to the sick role for certain social groups. Specifically, they argue that, by expanding access to the sick role for young white males on the East and West Coasts, medicine functioned to reduce organized opposition to the war both within and outside the armed forces. That is, disqualification from service for medical reasons, by placing persons in the "sick role," which is a relatively controllable and socially acceptable form of deviance, served to draw draft-age men away from alternative forms of deviance that might have been more disruptive to the social system and to the national policy of that period.

The general observation that physicians are certifiers of illness is hardly original or radical. After all, certifying illness is their job. What the new critics offer that is new is a way of interpreting the social meanings and consequences of how this work is done. They begin with a conception of society as a complex social system and of medicine as one subsystem within it, interdependent with and functionally connected to other subsystems. Further, they conceive of society as an area of conflict; power and resources are differentially and unequally distributed, and there is an ongoing struggle between the needs and interests of different social groups and classes. In this struggle, these critics argue that medicine has tended to align itself with the interests of dominant groups, that is, for the maintenance of the status quo and their own relative positions of social, economic, and political power.

These analyses are not concerned with the motivations of individual practitioners. Physicians who prescribed bed rest for the "sick women of the upper classes" may have seen themselves as alleviating the pain and discomfort that women were prone to have; physicians who provided medical grounds for deferment may have themselves been active protestors against the Vietnam war. The new critics view motivational analyses as of limited significance for understanding how medicine functions in the society. These limitations are particularly evident when such analyses are disconnected from analyses of the social functions of medicine, which tends to be the case in studies that uncritically incorporate the biomedical assumption that scientific medicine is objectively neutral with regard to social values and interests.

In this section, we have indicated how the new critics support their position through analyses of the social consequences of medical practice, of the ways in which conceptions of illness and patterns of clinical work function in the control of social deviance.

Discussion

There is a sense in which this chapter might be thought of as a recapitulation of much of what has gone before in our analyses of patients and physicians in social context and the social construction of illness. We have pointed out that more is involved, that the perspective of the new critics can result in a rereading and reinterpretation of traditional social science studies and findings.

There is another view of the progression of analyses through this text, in which the perspectives of the social and behavioral sciences have been applied respectively to patients, physicians, health practices, and finally to the health-care system. Each section, in turn, shifted our focus further and further away from the traditional biomedical model. The analyses became successively more different than those usually found in medicine, and for this reason became successively more difficult to integrate into standard medical ways of thinking about these problems. For example, to repeat an earlier point, epidemiological findings are not too difficult for bioscientists and health professionals to understand and to integrate into their ways of thinking about illness. In a sense, these studies simply introduce an additional set of social variables to be considered along with biological variables; however, the medical definition of illness itself remains unquestioned. Only a bit more stretching of the biomedical model is necessary to incorporate studies of the effects on medical practice of institutional and organizational factors. Here, too, the studies do not raise questions about core definitions and values of medicine; the findings show that organizational variables introduce difficulties and lead to a gap between the ideals and the realities of practice, but definitions of ideal practice are retained.

With the chapters on the social construction of illness, the shift in perspective was more pronounced. Medical practices, such as diagnosis, were seen as interpretive work, as one of the ways through which reality is socially constructed. The logic of the new critics, discussed in this chapter, is an extension of this view. In part it pushes further the limits of the sociological perspective on the construction of illness as a social reality, and in part it represents still another shift. Not only is medicine a social practice, but the new critics argue that it is a practice that has functional significance for the larger society. Not only is clinical diagnosis a way of classifying certain behaviors as symptoms and therefore as a special category of deviance, namely, illness, but diagnosis is a way of controlling deviance in the interest of the larger society. In this view, physicians are not only "actors," they are "agents" of social control.

It is important to make some distinctions so that the argument is not misunderstood. The new critics are not attacking physicians or criticizing efforts to care for and heal the sick. Rather, they are proposing that, in the context of relations between the health-care system and other institutions and specific social interests, these medical acts have collective social consequences. For example, providing medical care involves choices and the choices are related to the social functions of medicine. Thus, that physicians cluster in large metropolitan areas and leave rural areas unserved may be the result of many individual decisions, but the consequence is a pattern of practice that fits with functional requirements of a technical, urbanized population.

In sum, the new critics ask us to look beyond medical boundaries in order to understand fully both the sources and the consequences of particular forms of medicine. They are saying that the full, and perhaps the real, significance of medical work cannot be understood if problems of health and illness are defined within the limited boundaries of medicine itself.

Notes

1. Ehrenreich, B., and Ehrenreich, J. (Eds.). *The American Health Empire: Power, Profits and Politics*. New York: Vintage Books (Health-Pac Book), 1971.

2. Ehrenreich, J. (Ed.). *The Cultural Crisis of Modern Medicine.* New York: Monthly Review Press, 1978.
3. Waitzkin, H., and Waterman, B. *The Exploitation of Illness in Capitalist Society.* Indianapolis, IN: Bobbs-Merrill, 1974.
4. Illich, I. *Medical Nemesis: The Expropriation of Health.* New York: Bantam Books, 1977.
5. Krause, E. A. *Power and Illness: The Political Sociology of Health Care.* New York: Elsevier, 1977.
6. Illich, *Medical Nemesis,* p. xi.
7. Ehrenreich, *The Cultural Crisis of Modern Medicine,* p. 1.
8. Dubos, R. *Mirage of Health.* New York: Anchor Books, 1961.
9. McNeill, W. *Plagues and Peoples.* New York: Doubleday, 1976.
10. McKeown, T., and Lowe, C. R. *An Introduction to Social Medicine.* Philadelphia: F. A. Davis, 1966.
11. Ibid., p. 6.
12. Ibid., p. 13.
13. Ibid., p. 18.
14. Ibid., p. 14.
15. Illich, *Medical Nemesis.*
16. Ibid., p. 12.
17. Ibid., p. 17.
18. Ibid., p. 23.
19. Weisbrod, B. A., Andreano, R. L., Baldwin, R. E., Epstein, E. H., and Kelley, A. C., with Helminiak, T. W. *Disease and Economic Development: The Impact of Parasitic Diseases in St. Lucia.* Madison: University of Wisconsin Press, 1973.
20. Aronson, N. "Review of: B. A. Weisbrod et al., *Disease and Economic Development,*" *Social Science and Medicine,* 1978, *12*(1C):66–8.
21. Weisbrod et al., *Disease and Economic Development,* p. xv.
22. Ibid., p. 188.
23. Ibid., p. 81.
24. Ibid., p. 77.
25. Ibid., p. 75.
26. Aronson, "Review of Weisbrod et al.," p. 68.
27. Ibid., p. 68.
28. Freidson, E. *Profession of Medicine: A Study of the Sociology of Applied Knowledge.* New York: Dodd, Mead, 1970.
29. Ibid., p. 337.
30. Ibid., p. 350.
31. Duff, R. S., and Hollingshead, A. B. *Sickness and Society.* New York: Harper & Row, 1968. Other aspects of this study were discussed earlier in Chapter 5.
32. Ibid., pp. 370–1.
33. Ibid., p. 369.
34. Ibid., p. 165, Table 15.
35. Ibid., p. 178.
36. Ibid., p. 376.
37. Coleman, J. S., Katz, E., and Menzel, H. *Medical Innovation: A Diffusion Study.* Indianapolis, IN: Bobbs-Merrill, 1966.
38. Ehrenreich, *The Cultural Crisis of Modern Medicine.*
39. Ibid., p. 15.
40. Ehrenreich, B., and English, D. "The 'sick' women of the upper classes," ibid. Reprinted from Ehrenreich, B., and English, D. *Complaints and Disorders: The Sexual Politics of Sickness.* Old Westbury, NY: Feminist Press, 1973.

41. Ehrenreich and English, "The 'sick' women of the upper classes," p. 124.
42. Ibid., p. 127.
43. Ibid., pp. 138–9.
44. A prominent source of this conception of illness as one subtype of deviance is the paper by Talcott Parsons, "Definitions of health and illness in the light of American values and social structure," in Jaco, E. G. (Ed.). *Patients, Physicians and Illness*. Glencoe, IL: The Free Press, 1958.
45. "Fear of finals: 'illness' up," *Harvard Gazette*, January 12, 1979. The *Harvard Gazette* is a weekly paper published by the administration that reports university news and activities.
46. Waitzkin and Waterman, *The Exploitation of Illness in Capitalist Society*.
47. Ibid., pp. 37–38.

9   The machine metaphor in medicine

Samuel Osherson and Lorna AmaraSingham

Medicine [has] perhaps more than any other profession, symbolically reflected down the centuries the influence of the civilization of each epoch.[1]

The opening statement by a physician-historian touches on the focus for this chapter: the way medicine is shaped by, and in turn helps to shape, its cultural milieu. To pursue this connection we shall examine modern medicine's conception of the human body. Our specific purpose is to illustrate how cultural understandings become incorporated into medical models to explain the workings and treatment of the body. We hope to show that modern medicine is one part of a whole, part of the society or culture in which it is embedded. We shall discuss some of the origins of, and changes in, the biomedical model, as well as the relationship between medicine and other professions and institutions in Western culture. From this perspective the growth of modern medicine is viewed not as autonomous but as an evolving institution within a changing culture, with its own functions and interests but responsive to, and productive of, the ideas, stresses, and interests of the larger society.

The history of medicine offers much evidence of links between cultural themes and medical conceptions of the body. Egyptian physiology, for example, described the body as a series of conduits for carrying the blood and the humors, and linked the floods and droughts of the sacred Nile with "floods" and "droughts" in the body that were believed to cause illness.[2] A predominant image in Grecian culture was the four-humor theory (blood, black bile, yellow bile, and phlegm) of illness accepted by Hippocratic physicians.[3] In ancient India the conception of the body reflected the strong hierarchical character of the social and political organization of the country. In an ancient Indian medical text, the body is described as a beleaguered fortress inhabited by a king: "The kingdom of Jita [self or soul] is . . . besieged with diseases. But the king has retired to the innermost fortress of the body, having entered the inner citadel of the heart through the gate of the mind. There he approaches Lady Bakkti [loving devotion to god] in the hope that she will appeal to Siva [god] to

218

grant the king the elixir of immortality. . . ."⁴ The text goes on to describe the king's "battle" with disease as he tries to balance the advice given by his various advisors.

A modern example of the parallel between features of the social and natural environment and the metaphors used to describe medical treatment can be found in Ayurvedic medicine, which is an Asian medical system based on homeopathic and humoral theory. Obeyesekere, in a recent article on Ayurvedic medicine in Sri Lanka, has shown that "Ayurvedic conceptions create diseases that could hardly exist in a different system."⁵ "Prameha" diseases, which he describes, are disorders of the urinary and reproductive systems, which constitute a large proportion of the disease treated by Ayurvedic physicians in Sri Lanka. Symptoms of these diseases are vaginal discharge in women and nocturnal emission in men, symptoms the Sinhalese interpret as a result of too much "heating food" or "bad living." The imbalance in the humoral system that is believed to be manifested in these symptoms must be treated, according to Ayurvedic theory, by herbal remedies that reestablish the equilibrium of the body. We can see in this case that values in the society concerning appropriate self-control, classification of foods, and the preservation of bodily and social boundaries all come together to focus on a particular image of the body as vulnerable in a specific and (to our minds) "imaginary" way.

Another conception of the body that is prevalent in many Indo-European and Latin American cultures is based on the hot – cold theory of folk medicine.⁶ In this system it is believed that the body must maintain an equilibrium between "hot" and "cold" states; foods and medicines are classified according to whether they are heating, cooling, or neutral. The body is conceived as a field of interplay between hot and cold forces, with heat arising within and cold attacking from without. Thus there is a correspondence between the body, seen as a confluence of cold and hot, and the outside world, seen as the locus of heating and cooling influences. In this system medical treatment consists of the ingestion of appropriately hot or cold substances, as well as the application of heating or cooling ointments to the body.

It is relatively easy to recognize the connection between cultural images and medical models in other cultures because their very strangeness to us throws such patterns into relief. There have also been several recent attempts to establish this connection in the history of Western culture. Illich and Aries, for example, have traced the history of death in European culture; they have shown how there has been an evolution of the concept of death so that at each point in history people's image of death corresponds with their social situation, their conception of self, and their religious assumptions.[7] In a similar, though more focused work, Foucault has traced the development of recent Western views of the body to the political philosophy of eighteenth-century France.[8] Recently, Miller has presented a historical survey of medical descriptions of the body in which he emphasizes that the mysteries of anatomy have repeatedly been understood in terms of broad cultural preoccupations.[9] Within our own culture, Sontag has traced the different metaphorical conceptions of tuberculosis and cancer predominant in medical and social circles, from the nineteenth century to the 1970s.[10]

We shall explore the connection between social transformations and changes in science and medicine, especially in our ways of comprehending, explaining, and treating the human body. The focus of our analysis is that in the Western medical tradition, the body is seen as analogous to a machine. This perception of the body as a machine has been expressed in an elaborate way by Buckminster Fuller, the scientist and writer, who describes man as:

. . . a self balancing, 27 jointed adapter-base biped, an electrochemical reduction plant, integral with the segregated stowages of special energy extracts in storage batteries, for subsequent actuation of thousands of hydraulic and pneumatic pumps, with motors attached: 62,000 miles of capillaries, millions of warning-signals, railroad, and conveyor systems; crushers and cranes . . . and a universally distributed telephone system needing no service for 70 years if well managed; the whole extraordinary complex mechanism guided with exquisite precision from a turret in which are located telescopic and microscopic self-registering and recording range finders, a spectroscope, et cetera.[11]

In our culture, medicine has made extensive use of this machine model of the human body. Miller shows that the increasing technological sophistication of Western culture helped physicians to comprehend the way our own bodies function. Commenting on the impact on medical thought of such inventions as steam engines and telephones, Miller says: "whatever devices were designed to do, they have incidentally provided conjectural models for explaining the human body."[12] This connection between social interests and medical concerns raises a number of questions: Why, for example, does our culture compare the body to a machine rather than, as in ancient Egyptian societies, to a river, or as in the tradition of China, to the earth, with its balance of two elemental forces – Yin (positive, male, light, and warm) and Yang (negative, female, dark, and cold)? Is there an implicit set of beliefs about the human body contained in such a comparison? And have specific medical practices and treatments developed that reflect this metaphor of the body as a machine? In addressing these questions we shall uncover some of the "silent assumptions" underlying the everyday procedures and practices of medicine.

We begin with the historical and cultural roots of this mechanical way of seeing the body. This is, of course, a complex and detailed topic, which cannot be given the extensive discussion it deserves in a single chapter. However, we have selected for discussion two watershed periods in medical history: European science during the 1700s and the period in America from 1890 to 1914 that culminated with the Flexner report in 1910 and the consequent reorganization of medical education. Events during these two important periods in medical and cultural history illustrate the roots in large cultural preoccupations and social problems of a medical model of the body as a machine. Following discussion of the Flexner report, we shall discuss the history of the medical management of childbirth as a concrete example of the connection between medicine and society. The medical management of death will then serve to illustrate the underlying assumptions of the mechanical model of the body in *current* doctor – patient interaction. Childbirth and death are not illnesses per se, yet they came to be incorporated into medicine. We shall explore the sociocultural reason why this occurred and how treatment changes came about over time.

European science and medicine in the eighteenth century: a mechanical universe

In this section we shall show how events in medicine and science in Europe in the 1700s led to an increase in the psychological distance between doctor and patient and to a mechanical view of the body in medical theory and practice.

The "machine" has been present in Western culture for centuries. The gradual "mechanization of the world picture" of the West and evolution of the "myth of the machine" can be traced back at least to the Middle Ages. As Deutsch point outs:

Actual mechanisms of some complexity – such as mills, clocks, and pumps – became widespread in the Western world during the latter Middle Ages. Their growing familiarity and continuing improvements, the successes in their rational analyses, the mathematical calculation of their behavior and in the discovery of new applications of the principles involved – all these furnished the background for the elaboration and adoption of the classical conceptions of mechanism.[13]

We can best understand this "classical conception of mechanism" by examining the point at which the machine became a dominant model for understanding as a result of the mechanical model of science that came to fruition during the eighteenth century. In the 1700s a positivistic, mechanical science developed that was influenced by and in turn influenced the practice of medicine.[14] This development of a mechanistic science reflected a shift in world outlook in European culture, a shift that had repercussions both in medical theory and in the entire world view of the Western world. We shall first describe some of these medical–scientific changes in the eighteenth century and then relate them to some of the social transformations of the time.

Medicine was integrally involved with the development of this mechanistic science because some of the greatest scientists of the time were doctors, and biology, chemistry, and anatomy were areas of extremely productive inquiry. Starting with Kepler and Galileo's observations of the solar system, the centuries-old dialectic between the Platonic–Pythagorean tradition and Renaissance Naturalism versus the Mechanical or Natural Philosophy began to be resolved in favor of the latter.[15] Renaissance Naturalism, or vitalism, had emphasized the union of spirit and matter in the world; it saw underlying essences reflected in all of nature. These essences were essentially God's handiwork, as all of the universe reflected the order and harmony of God's plan. Natural objects and processes were believed to be the result of a union of spirit and matter, and all events in the natural world were seen as manifestations of the vital spirit inherent in matter. Thus, for example, one belief was that the universe was constructed of a series of crystalline spheres; the elegant geometric principles governing them revealed the harmony of God's plan. In medicine, this view resulted in an emphasis on formal aspects of the body's shape and on a reliance on the principle of analogy in understanding disease: like affecting like. The assumption that nature could be understood through an understanding of God's purposes also discouraged direct experimentation and investigation.

The work of Kepler and Galileo in the early 1600s dealt a powerful blow to Renaissance Naturalism by showing that the universe could be better understood by empirical observation and the application of principles of planetary dynamics and motion than by analysis of vital spirits. Physical causation was shown to underlie planetary motion, and different aspects of physical reality – terrestial motion and celestial motion – were explained in terms of the same mechanical principles. Throughout the 1600s and 1700s this idea – that there are causal mechanisms (different from those perceived by our senses) for all known phenomena – and the gradual appearance of a number of sensory expanding technologies for investigation of the universe (telescope, microscope, etc.) coincided with the decline of explanations based on spirits, essences, and the geometric perfection of God's universe.

Perhaps the most historically influential voice for the ascendant school of mechanical philosophy was that of René Descartes, who provided the philosophic and methodological base for separating the material world from the spiritual world by demonstrating that there is no necessity that the physical world bear any correspondence to the world as our senses depict it. Sensory observations and the inherited theories of Naturalism were illusory, and the only path to truth that of the empirical study of the causal mechanisms underlying observed phenomena. For Descartes, as Westfall comments, "the world is a machine, composed of inert bodies, moved by physical necessity, indifferent to the existence of thinking beings."[16] The corresponding view of science can be summarized as emphasizing the search for invisible (to the senses) causative mechanisms, an analysis of phenomena into their component parts, the use of quantitative methods and physical measurement in research, and an objective stance toward phenomena.

Medicine in the 1700s both reflected and contributed to the development of this view of science, and of man. In particular, studies in anatomy and physiology served to demonstrate the power of empirical investigation and mechanical explanation, often contradicting established wisdom about the body that dated back to Aristotle and Galen. Harvey, for example, was able to use a mechanical model to describe the circulation of the blood, seeing the heart as a pump that moves fluid through a closed circuit of conduits; a system – as Westfall notes – "reminiscent of the waterworks that ran the elaborate fountains admired by the seventeenth-century monarchs." As Harvey writes in his notes: "From the structure of the heart it is clear that the blood is constantly carried through the lungs into the aorta as by two clack [valves] of a water bellows to raise water."[17] Yet Harvey retained the influence of Renaissance Naturalism in seeing the heart as "the beginning of life" and the primary organ of the body. For him, the mechanism of circulation was less important in understanding the body than was the vitalistic idea that the "heart and blood together forming a single functioning unit which is the very seat of life."[18]

Here we find the vitalism of the universal rhythms that govern all life, very different from the mechanical principles of mechanism. It remained for Descartes to utilize Harvey's work on circulation as the basis for a truly mechanistic perception of the body. In his volume, *Treatise on Man*, Descartes describes the body as a machine – a machine that performs all the physiological functions of man:

I want you to consider [he concluded] that *all these functions in this machine* follow naturally from the disposition of its organs alone, just as the movement of a clock or another automat follow from the disposition of its counterweights and wheels; so that to explain its functions it is not necessary to imagine a vegetative or sensitive soul in the machine, or any other principle of movement and life other than its blood and spirits agitated by the fire which burns continually in its heart and which differs in nothing from all the fires in inanimate bodies.[19]

Thus the *idea* of mechanism became important in medicine, as such discoveries showed that some aspects of the body could be understood in mechanical terms.

Prior to 1700 physicians had relied almost entirely on patients' own descriptions of their symptoms and on visual observation. In a recent book Reiser has shown how the development of a number of medical techniques after 1700 made it possible to learn a great deal more about the patient's body. These new techniques contributed to the search for objective markers of disease and contributed to the later conception of disease as a specific and localized entity. Reiser discusses the impact on medicine of such inventions and techniques as objective markers of disease.[20] These inventions were part of a shift in the doctor–patient relationship from a patient-centered focus in which the doctor was dependent on the patient for information to a more technical focus in which concern centered on objective signs of illness and in which illness could be seen for the first time as being localized in the body. The localization of illness changed the status of the patient's body; no longer was it primarily the seat of subjective impressions interpreted by the patient to the doctor, but rather it became the site of specific disease entities to be detected and evaluated by the doctor independently of the patient. As Reiser notes, the physiological actions were translated into "the language of machines" and the perceptions of the doctor into "a fundamentally mechanical view of human beings."[21] The problematic doctor–patient relationship discussed in Chapter 5 is rooted in these changes as both doctors and patients narrowed their focus of inquiry to the patient as object, rather than to the patient as a person.

In these events of the seventeenth and eighteenth centuries we can see the interrelationship of medicine and culture very clearly; indeed, each of the assumptions of the biomedical model of disease discussed in Chapter 1 can be grounded in characteristics of the positivistic mechanical model of science developed during the 1700s. In the evolving emphasis on objective, physical measurement we can see the concern with defining disease as deviation from the normal or average; in the emphasis on underlying causation, not visible to the subjective senses but objectively rooted in the physical world, we find the roots of the search for generic, universal diseases; and the high value placed on the dispassionate, objective investigator empirically observing the basic mechanisms of nature is an important source of the belief in the scientific neutrality of medicine.

To understand more fully these changes in medicine we need to turn to some of the sociocultural transformations that occurred during the eighteenth century. As we noted earlier, Descartes' model of absolute mechanism was never fully accepted in biology and was soon thrown into question by subsequent discoveries. Further, mechanical models had existed for centuries. Yet the mechanistic model of man and the universe had a tremendous influence on seventeenth- and eighteenth-century thought and has continued, as we shall see, to influence the practice of medicine in significant ways. What made this model so attractive at this time? First, this model worked as an explanation for certain phenomena. Just as the technical triumphs of astronomy, biology, and chemistry provided systematic descriptions of aspects of the physical universe, so, too, the body could productively be seen as a mechanism.

In the economic sphere, the mechanical model fit with the rise of industry and the market approach to labor in which, for example, individuals were seen as interchangeable parts of a whole within ''the machine'' of the factory. Even in later developments in the nineteenth and twentieth centuries, advances in technology fit the needs of industry to centralize and control a manageable labor force.[22] Illich also points out that the mechanical interventions facilitated by this model of humanity interlocked in the seventeenth and eighteenth centuries with the rise of a middle class who were able to buy services of all kinds; among those were services to the body.[23] The notion of the body as the possession of a consumer of services who is able to buy ''repairs'' for it became current at the same time that the buying and selling of services for other possessions became a major economic force. Related to this economic context for the development of a mechanical ideology in medicine is the fact that the idea of service began to provide a professional function for the medical practitioner that made him socially equal to the providers of other services. From being a practitioner of the ''black art'' of manipulating a body that could belong only to God, in a few centuries the doctor became respected as the provider of a legitimate service. These activities were consistent with other social definitions of expertise.

Politically, there is a similarity between the political absolutism prevalent in the seventeenth century and the mechanistic world view, particularly as there was an increasing contrast between scientific order and the social disorder of Europe through the seventeenth and eighteenth centuries. Foucault has recently described the rise of what we have been describing as a "mechanical model" of humanity within medicine in terms of its congruence with the increasing role of state constraint and control in the affairs of its citizenry.[24] In this regard, Gould has offered a fascinating analysis of why Darwin's theory of evolution as a slow, gradual process was more appealing than alternative views of evolution as a series of rapid, cataclysmic events despite the absence of empirical support for either view. Gould argues that this attraction reflected fears of revolutionary ideas that were widespread in Europe during the latter half of the nineteenth century.[25]

Finally, from a psychological perspective, a view of the body as being merely a machine allows a certain degree of emotional distance between doctor and patient. The body could be regarded as a separate "thing" outside the patient's self. Surgical intervention in particular seemed to require that the body, at least temporarily, be removed from spiritual or personal meanings. Thus, although physical distance between the doctor and the patient's body decreased after the sixteenth century (as a variety of technological advances allowed exploration and intervention), the psychological distance increased as the patient's body was objectified.

The Flexner report: the professionalization of American medicine at the turn of this century

In this section we shall focus on a key period in the formation of the profession of medicine in America as we know it today: the end of the nineteenth century and the beginning of the twentieth century. During this period a number of social and economic tensions in American society gave rise to the creation of what we know now as professional classes such as physicians and lawyers. The major point we shall make in this section is that the needs of the developing profession of medicine were tied to prevalent ways of solving pressing social problems. Both the development of medicine and the alleviation of stresses were facilitated by the mechanical model of science that we outlined in the previous section.

The years 1890–1914 were a watershed period in the relation of university education to the kind of careers we have come to call "the professions": law, medicine, scholarship, the sciences, and so on. During these years there was a coming together of the educational establishment, industry, and the professions. Two themes characterize this reorganization of a number of disciplines: (1) the nature of entrance requirements, competency standards, and the types of knowledge and skills that comprised a number of different professions became increasingly defined; and (2) these definitions of discrete bodies of knowledge were based, in varying ways characteristic of the specific discipline, on mechanical models of science that came to characterize humanity and nature.

The major impetus for this reorganization within medicine was the Flexner report on medical education, completed in 1910 by Abraham Flexner for the Carnegie Foundation for the Advancement of Teaching.[26] The Flexner report was a seminal document in medical education, leading to changes in the number and nature of medical schools, their curricula, and the research and clinical roles of American physicians. This report, funded by a prestigious private foundation, explored the nature of medical education and offered a number of recommendations regarding the structure, curriculum, and composition of medical schools. It had a profound impact on the subsequent structure of medical education in America, and thereby on the nature of the medical profession itself. Major effects of the report were to define the domain of knowledge that characterized medicine, to establish the requirements for certifying doctors, and to locate medical education firmly within the major universities. As one observer has noted:

The Flexner Report was to have many influences on medical education. Its major effects were (1) to encourage the adoption of a four-year medical school curriculum; (2) to introduce laboratory teaching exercises and to improve the quality of instruction through a full-time faculty; (3) to expand clinical teaching through the introduction of the clinical clerkship; (4) to bring the medical schools into the framework of the universities; and (5) to incorporate research into the teaching program – a different pattern from the separation of research programs into institutes, common in many other countries.[27]

In examining the Flexner report, there are two points to keep in mind: (1) The Flexner report institutionalized within medicine a view of medicine based on a positivistic science that included a mechanical construction of the human body, and (2) the report was part of a larger reorganization and definition at the time within American society of what have come to be called "the professions." The reorganization of medicine and other professions reflected an attempt at the solution of a number of social stresses and problems during the period 1890–1914.

A mechanical view of the body in the Flexner report is found in its very strong emphasis on (1) *the parts-of-a-whole curriculum*; (2) *a reductionist approach* to the human body; (3) *the central role of instrumentation* in diagnosis and therapy, and subspecialization of the physician; and (4) an emphasis on *efficiency and standardization,* with relative inattention to the social context of treatment.

Flexner often uses mechanical paradigms to refer to and conceptualize the human body, seeing medicine exclusively as a biological science. At one point he refers to the body "as an infinitely complex machine" and comments: "Medicine is part and parcel of modern science. The human body belongs to the animal world. It is put together of tissues and organs, in their structure, origin and development not essentially unlike what the biologist is otherwise familiar with; it grows, reproduces itself, decays according to general laws."[28]

Flexner's reliance on a mechanical science and a paradigm of the body as a machine had particular consequences for the way in which the body came to be understood and treated within the new profession of medicine. Berliner discusses the impact of the Flexner report on medicine's way of seeing the body: Wholistic medicine declined, and certain kinds of knowledge about illness and patients were excluded from the doctor's domain:[29]

In medicine, the effects were felt most clearly in the comprehension of the body, in the way research was structured, and in the basis of therapy and diagnostics.
Conceptually, the image of the human body as a single, integrated organism – with effects on one part of the body having effects upon the rest of the body – was finally eliminated from the mainstream of medical thought. While whole-body medicine had been challenged at least since the beginning of the seventeenth century, it had always occupied a significant place in medical thought. With the new paradigm of scientific medicine, the body began to be conceptualized in terms of systems unrelated to other systems of the body. And although specialization had been present in the context of whole-body medicine, specialization under scientific medicine began to emphasize individual systems or organs to the exclusion of the totality of the body. The most explicit dimension of the decline of wholistic medicine is manifested in the rise of the mind-body duality and the subsequent distinction between mental disease and physical [somatic] disease. . . . Diagnostics and therapy were also affected by the new paradigm. In terms of both diagnostics and therapy, the body was considered to be the analogue to the machine, thus allowing for an instrumentalist approach to the body. Individual parts could be examined and treated without the rest of the body being affected. . . .[30]

The emphasis on a machine metaphor for structuring knowledge was not confined to medicine. The same kind of reorganization and definition that was occurring in medicine was also occurring elsewhere in the society. The favored model for redefining the content and structure of postgraduate education in America during the "reformist era" of the early 1900s was that of the professional engineer.[31] The dominant reformers and social theorists of the early 1900s – the same people who helped to shape medical education – relied heavily on a machine model of humanity and society.[32] The undercurrent of mechanical metaphors in the writings of various industrial leaders, intellectuals, and educators can be seen both in their view of *people as machines* and of *society as a gigantic machine,* with individual professions as parts of a well-functioning whole. Noble quotes several scientific educators:

"Man-stuff," in the view of Elmo Lewis, was the "most important thing" with which the companies had to deal; it was the substance "out of which they make their business." E. A. Deeds of the National Cash Register company agreed; "I am most interested," he said, "in increasing the efficiency of the human machine." In addition to technical proficiency, these educators all stressed the need for training for management. "Electrical engineers," Arthur Williams observed, "are from the practical standpoint. . . men without a peer in running machines, in running plants, but not men trained, necessarily, in running human machines."[33]

Noble comments: "The corporations were turning their energies toward the production of men and commodities. Their approach to education was perhaps most clearly offered by C. D. Braclett of National Cash Register in his description of that company's agents in training school: 'Product: men and cash registers.' "[34] Similarly, Gilbert quotes Van Wyck Brooks' view of society as typical of the "biological metaphor" so dominant in reformist thought and the planning ideology of the time: "Society is a colossal machine of which we are all parts and . . . men in the most exact sense are members one of another."[35]

Two questions stand out. First: Why did the reorganization of medicine and other professions occur during this progressive or reform era of 1890–1914; Why especially was it characterized by concern with certification and delineation of discrete bodies of knowledge to define the professions? Second: Why was this reorganization in medicine based so strongly on scientific positivism and a mechanical model of the body? To answer these questions we need to examine what was going on in the society as a whole. In doing so, we find this reorganization process part of an attempt to solve certain social problems, with the machine model particularly important to this effort.

During the period 1890–1914, there was a major shift in America from a largely rural, farm economy to an industrial economic base, with resulting social dislocations. A large labor pool was moving from the farms into the cities. There was a disintegration of traditional, hierarchical means of social control and organization. The traditional family and community role in socialization was being eroded in a newly urban society. In addition there was a need for a technical class to utilize the developing new technologies that fueled American industrial expansion as the nineteenth-century revolution in scientific knowledge in this country expanded and altered the nature of what earlier had been craft industries and guilds. Corporate capitalism became the directing force of American technology, with a concomitant need for the standardization and control of labor.[36]

Important, too, was the increasing number of immigrants allowed into the country in the early 1900s as part of a cheap labor pool who were not easily integrated into the social fabric.

The Flexner report and changes in the definition of medicine reflected, and reinforced, attempts to resolve these strains in American society at the time.

The creation of professional classes (doctors, lawyers, et al.) was one solution. The competency requirements, certification, and discrete bodies of knowledge defined by the professional bodies institutionalized and provided a means of upward mobility and status to the emergent middle class created by the industrial upheavals of the time.[37] The definition of professional status provided a vertical, upward future path for those who earlier had viewed the future horizontally as a continuation of the laborers', farmers', or artisans' lives as these had always been known.

The increasing professionalism of the time emphasized as well standardization, social planning, and control. This emphasis reflected, and represented, an attempt to solve the problem engendered by the breakdown of traditional, hierarchical, and community-based sources of social organization and control. Given the migration of rural labor off the farm and the influx of large numbers of immigrants, concern with rational planning and control reflected the need to assimilate what might have been disruptive groups within society. This can be seen in the efforts at this time to rationalize social "chaos" through city planning, public education, penology, and so on.

At the systemwide level in medicine we find increasing concern with standardization and control (e.g., public health programs). Flexner, for example, stressed the expanding role of medicine in managing social, not just individual, health problems. Interest in social status, regulation, and control was not limited to medicine, however, similar themes characterized changes in many areas of American life at the time. Kunitz describes the similarities in development of a number of professions during this reformist or "progressive era" in America:[38]

Social control and efficiency became dominant themes in the writings of the reformers of the Progressive Era. . . . As social problems had proliferated, new mechanisms were required, new institutions and occupations had to be created. Thus it was that during this period we see the efflorescence of a variety of social movements, all concerned with some aspect of social control and regulation; and thus it was that many of the workers in these movements ultimately began to claim professional status on the basis of their special knowledge of some social problem.

For all these new professions, new schools were needed.[39] Medicine, like the other emerging professions, became increasingly preoccupied with standardization, regulation, and control. The machine model and, more generally, mechanistic models of science, converged with these pre-occupations at a time when social forces militated toward professionalization. Machine models of the body and mechanistic notions of science are particularly amenable to the development of technological rather than social solutions to problems; such paradigms allow and justify careful planning and control; and precisely because of the parts-of-a-whole, reductionistic nature of mechanical paradigms, they provide discrete, testable, certifiable bodies of knowledge that can be defined as the purview of one professional class.

The delimitation of medicine as a profession reinforced the attempt of emerging corporate capitalism to transform social problems into technological ones. Here we see why the large chemical, mining, and industrial companies worked so closely during this period with the educational establishment to create a research and teaching superstructure that would define, certify, and advance the emerging professions, including medicine, on a positivistic–scientific basis. This model of the professions saw human–social problems of health as being rooted in economic dislocations and inequities in income as well as pathologic effects of the workplace and industrial means of production as translatable into technological problems solvable by nonpolitical means. Discussing the machine model in medicine, Berliner comments:

The machine model allows for the use of statistical assumptions about the body – in particular the assumption of a mode of central tendency [normality] which allows diseases to be treated as universal entities rather than as individual afflictions different for everyone. While diagnosis and therapy are based upon collective assumptions employing the use of the normal distribution, the patient is thought of almost as an abstraction apart from the collectivity, with the social context of the problem not being accounted for on an individual basis. Illness is treated as a natural process and, as such, the possibility of social causality becomes alien to diagnosis and therapy. Medicine becomes individualistic not only in that it treats the individual patient, but also in that it excludes the social aspects of the patient's life. . . .[40]

Berliner goes on to point out that this narrow view of disease had the ultimate effect of making individuals responsible for their own health, thus taking the responsibility away from social conditions:

The concept of the bacteriological causation of disease brought with it the notion that all the ills of society were caused by an as yet undiscovered microbe along with the promise, that, in time, with sufficient resources trained on the objective of finding the microbe, all social problems could be solved with a vaccine. Thus Frederick T. Gates, an aide to John D. Rockefeller, and the guiding light behind the creation of the Rockefeller Institute, could say: "Disease is the supreme ill of human life and it is the main source of almost all other human ills, poverty, crime, ignorance, vice, inefficiency, hereditary taint and many other evils." The fact that it was capitalists who were endowing research institutes and medical schools tended to focus curative and preventive research on the individual rather than the collectivity. This had the effect of making the individual responsible for his or her own health, and, in effect, of taking this responsibility away from society.[41]

Thus we find that a machine model of the body is central to the way the profession of medicine entered the twentieth century. The Flexner report redefined the nature of medicine as a profession and institutionalized a machine model of the body in medical education and practice. Such a machine model was consistent with the social alterations of American society. In medicine – as in other professions – such alterations were reflected in reforms and innovations by educators, industrialists, and doctors who were redefining the nature of medicine at the turn of the century. Medical curricula and practice were shaped around what was easily standardized and defined in technological models. To work appropriately and to claim expertise in the late nineteenth and early twentieth centuries was to work with standardized objects defined in isolation from their social context. The body became such a standardized object, and the medical curriculum organized around standardizable skills.

In this section we have linked the central involvement of a mechanical model of the body in the definition of medicine as "a profession," to professional and social needs, as we have tried to illustrate the interpenetration of medicine and the social strains of an emerging industrial–capitalist society at the time of the Flexner report in 1910. In the next section we shall focus on the place of medicine in social life. To examine the relation of the machine model in medicine to cultural changes in American society, we shall focus on two specific domains of medical practice: childbirth and death.

Childbirth: the cultural role of the machine model in medicine

In this section we shall examine the history of childbirth practices in America as an example of the way in which developing medical knowledge interacted with social and cultural changes to produce specific medical practices. Childbirth is a good example because it is so deeply embedded in the everyday life of the community and because it has been integrated into American medicine in a way that is unique among Western nations. Thus the history of childbirth practices illustrates both the interaction of social and medical models over time and the way in which techniques that appear, from a historical point of view, to be logical outcomes of biomedical theory and experience alone are rooted in a specific history.[42] This section follows very closely Wertz and Wertz' book, *Lying In: A Natural History of Childbirth in America,* a fascinating discussion that includes much more than can be presented here; the historical references that follow are from Wertz and Wertz unless otherwise noted.[43]

In the seventeenth and eighteenth centuries the French, following Descartes and the other mechanistic philosophers already discussed, began to see birth as a mechanical rather than a spiritual process. A number of French birth manuals of the time present birth from an objective, nonmagical perspective, and describe mechanical intervention as the only solution to difficult birth. As Wertz and Wertz point out: "It was common practice at the time to sever the sacred and the natural and to posit mechanical models for natural processes. But the mechanical model of birth was fortuitously accurate and adequate to describe many of the normal and abnormal events of birth."[44] The theoretical understanding thus gained, however, had little practical application, for the French did not have the mechanical or surgical techniques that would allow for safe intervention in the actual birth process.

At this same period in England, a number of practical procedures were developed for intervening in birth. English barber–surgeons and male midwives had used hooks, knives, and loops to aid in difficult deliveries, usually to save the life of the mother at the expense of the child. In the early seventeenth century, Peter Chamberlain invented the forceps, which could free the child without killing it. Once use of the forceps became widely known, it initiated an era of division between male midwives, who practiced mechanical intervention in birth, and female midwives, who generally did not. In England, male midwives competed with and sometimes superseded female midwives, although female midwives continued to practice and still do so today. In America, however, the old tradition of female midwifery brought by the colonists was challenged, beginning around 1810, by male midwives who had at their disposal techniques for intervening in birth that were unavailable or unacceptable to the more traditional female midwives. Although women continued to have a choice of birth attendants throughout the nineteenth century, male midwives, who began to call themselves obstetricians at midcentury, became increasingly popular. Throughout the nineteenth century, birth continued to occur in the home, but gradually the doctor became the major attendant, with perhaps a paid nurse. During this period, intervention in birth became increasingly common; however, until 1910, when medicine became more organized, the obstetrician was largely self-taught.

Wertz and Wertz relate the rise of male midwives to several social factors.[45] They make the point that, with the beginning of the Industrial Revolution, men were defined as particularly suited to the mastery of machines. Thus, it was felt in the early nineteenth century that only men could use mechanical means to intervene in birth. At the same time, women were increasingly defined as passive beings. In the nineteenth century, upper-class women in particular came to be viewed as weak and vulnerable. As Ehrenreich and English point out, upper-class women were encouraged to depend on their doctors, who focused attention largely on the vulnerability of the reproductive organs.[46] In fact, the whole reproductive function was seen as pathological and dangerous, with certain inherent problems – an indication of not only physical but also moral and spiritual weakness. For women to become dependent on doctors, however, the problem of female modesty had to be resolved. Wertz and Wertz produce many intriguing examples to show that during the nineteenth century women and their doctors gradually developed a set of rituals and attitudes to distance the doctor from his patient's sexuality. For instance, doctors were expected to examine women, deliver babies, and perform various medical procedures entirely through the sense of touch, without ever looking at the woman's body. The doctor–patient relationship then took its form, not from the relations between men and women, but from submissive or dependent relationships that were already available as models. The result of these and other changes during the nineteenth century was that by the early twentieth century male attendance at and intervention in birth had become accepted practice.

Although the mechanical model of birth was applied rather haphazardly in the nineteenth century, in the twentieth century the same changes in American medicine that we have discussed in relation to the Flexner report had a profound and unifying influence on obstetrics. With the reorganization of medicine that began around 1910, doctors began to practice in hospitals and to receive the clinical training for which hospitalized patients were necessary. At the same time several developments in obstetrical knowledge and in women's attitudes combined to make hospital delivery attractive to both doctors and patients. Perhaps most important was the increasing use of general anesthesia, particularly scopolamine, in childbirth.

Chloroform had been used for home deliveries in the nineteenth century, but its use was unsystematic and, in fact, doctors were often reluctant to employ it. One reason was that pain in birth was considered women's rightful lot; it was symbolic at once of exalted femininity and self-sacrifice and of vulnerability and inferiority. Doctors and the general public in the nineteenth century believed that pain was necessary for proper bonding with the infant; further, some doctors were afraid that women would behave in an unseemly manner if chloroform loosened inhibitions during birth. Thus, women's pain in general and pain in birth in particular had moral meanings in the nineteenth century, which prevented widespread use of anesthesia.

In the early twentieth century women campaigned for greater use of anesthesia, and after scopolamine was introduced hailed it as a liberating discovery of modern medicine. For the middle- and upper-middle-class woman, birth in the hospital with "twilight sleep" became highly desirable; to be relieved of pain in childbirth was equated with freedom from the bondage to physical necessity that had characterized women's lives. As Wertz and Wertz put it: "Many women sought a painless birth as a sign of their own release from feminine roles which made them weak and dependent."[47] By the 1920s one-half of all births occurred in hospitals.

Hospital procedure was shaped partly by the use of general anesthesia, which made the woman's body inert and separated her consciousness from it. Perhaps more important, hospitals in the early twentieth century were involved in a sometimes losing battle with puerperal fever. Usually transmitted by the hands of the attendant, the incidence of puerperal fever had increased significantly in the nineteenth century as a result of increased intervention in birth by physicians. Once infection was recognized as the cause, hospitals seemed a safer place for birth; hospitals themselves undertook rigorous procedures to try to eliminate infection. Women entering hospitals were washed, given enemas and douches, prevented from moving around, and delivered in sterile delivery rooms. Many of the procedures still in use today were developed to deal with infection. Perhaps the most important result of this emphasis was that all birthing women were treated in the same way, and each was treated *as if* she might become infected. As Wertz and Wertz say:

Doctors not only had to control more carefully the processes and contexts of birth care, they also had to bring preventive treatment to each pregnant and parturient woman, however healthy, because each woman was susceptible to infection from the . . . medical environment. Doctors had to regard each woman as diseased.[48]

By the late 1930s, birth had been "streamlined" into a process that was controlled entirely by the doctors and by the demands of hospital procedures. Labor was speeded or slowed with medication, anesthetics and analgesics were routine, women were delivered in the lithotomy position with arms strapped down; the episiotomy had become routine, and forceps deliveries reached 50 percent or more of all deliveries. Wertz and

Wertz say that "during the 1940s, 1950s, and 1960s birth was the process-ing of a machine by machines and skilled technicians."[49]

Wertz and Wertz point out that this mechanization of birth was attrac-tive to women who wanted a painless delivery and "guaranteed results." Also:

Women seem to have taken . . . a kind of aesthetic delight in the efficiencies of the hospital, in its paring away of the economic, social and psychological aspect of birth in order to focus only on the pelvis as a machine that needed preventive maintenance and, sometimes, repair. The reduction of concern to mechanics may have pleased women who for long had been burdened with social and moral ex-pectations about births.[50]

The removal of birth from the moral sphere, in which pain, and success or failure, were indications both of moral status and of individual character, gave women a chance to view their bodies more as objects – as Wertz and Wertz say, to *have* rather than *be* a body.

In an article on the "cultural warping of childbirth," Haire points out that few nations share the "American tendency to warp the birth experi-ence, distorting it into a pathological event. . . ."[51] She presents a long list of modern hospital practices, such as separation of the birthing woman from her family, confinement of the laboring woman to bed, rou-tine fetal monitoring, the lithotomy position and the routine episiotomy, which are much less common in countries that have a lower incidence of infant mortality than our own.[52] Wertz and Wertz show that these prac-tices have emerged from a history in which efficiency, control of birth by male attendants, intervention in birth, and separation of the woman from her family and from her own body were socially and culturally acceptable. What Berliner calls "the body conceptualized in terms of systems unre-lated to other systems" came to be seen mechanically both as a kind of "machine" and as susceptible to impersonal and instrumental manipula-tion.[53]

In the 1950s women began to question this mechanization and streamlin-ing of birth; "natural" childbirth began as a coherent philosophy. From the point of view of the mechanization of childbirth, perhaps the most interesting thing about the natural birth movement has been the way it has (1) remained within the hospital and medical context and (2) provided images of birth that fall somewhere between the mechanical and the nine-teenth-century views of birth. Natural birth advocates emphasize that the woman should be awake during birth; however, many of the hospital pro-cedures that had become routine remained unchanged by this innovation. Childbirth classes prepared women to accept the hospital environment and to work within it in experiencing the birth process. At the same time hospitals gradually made modifications that provided a less institutional experience, while retaining power over the major procedures used.

Mid-twentieth-century women had gained a sense of control over their bodies while at the same time relinquishing actual control of birth to doctors. In natural childbirth, the image of "control" became central in a new way; women could control their bodies *during* birth by learning specific scientific techniques. Thus control shifted from the doctor to the laboring woman; the body, however, was viewed in a similar way by both – it was a mechanism in need of external, formal controls. The shame felt by the nineteenth-century woman about having to display her body at all was shifted to a sense of shame about "going out of control" during labor and failing to join forces efficiently with the doctor in managing the birth. "Production" metaphors abound in descriptions of natural childbirth, with the birth viewed most often as a "job well done" that has "produced" a child whose separation from the mother is the high point of an orderly and predictable process.

In this example of the history of childbirth we can see that images of the body are shared in varying degrees by members of a culture. The mechanical view of the body that became dominant in the nineteenth century was meaningful both for doctors, to whom it provided the possibility of effective action and intervention, and for women, to whom it meant a lessening of the moral stigma often attached to bodily functions. This shared perspective made possible radical changes in the management of birth, changes that culminated in birth defined almost entirely in terms of efficiency and impersonality.[54] We have focused on the social details of this period to illustrate the foundation of medical practice in social life. As social preoccupations about women's bodies and roles changed, so, too, did the role of the medical practitioner during childbirth.

In the next section, we shall draw on current medical practice to illustrate more fully how the interaction between physician and patient expresses a mechanical view of the body.

The medical management of death: the machine metaphor in doctor–patient interaction

To this point in the chapter, we have traced historical, economic, and sociocultural reasons why a mechanical model came to constrain ways of seeing and constructing the body in modern medicine. We focused on two watershed periods in Western medical history and discussed the history of childbirth in some detail.

Chapter 5 reviewed problems of distortion and miscommunication in doctor–patient interaction. In that chapter, the focus was on the roots of such problems in medical education and the structure of medical institutions. In this chapter, our attention to historical and economic forces allows an additional perspective on problems of doctor–patient interaction, one that emphasizes the role of a machine metaphor. These alternative explanations do not contradict, but rather supplement, each other.

In this section we shall discuss the management of death as an exemplar of the influence of the mechanical metaphor on contemporary medical treatment. We need first to examine more closely the attributes of a machine organized into a model of the human body. For heuristic purposes we can conceive of three dimensions of a machine metaphor:

1. Machines are reducible to their component parts. They are capable of being understood entirely by analysis into their discrete subsystems or component parts. The whole is *not* more than the sum of its parts.

2. Machines are without emotion. As expressions of the interaction of observable, objective physical forces, machines do not feel. Machines can be understood entirely from the outside, without reference to inner states (affect, mood, etc.).

3. Machines are instrumental (means, not ends in themselves) and non-purposive, and as such are not guided by considerations of value. A machine technology is one that emphasizes efficiency and utility over (or in the absence of) purpose. Machines are neutral in relation to ends; machines "do," and their value resides in the uses to which they are put by their operator.

How might this larger cultural model be expressed in medicine? When the body is being compared to a machine, do these three dimensions help us understand some of the attributes being applied to the body? Here is one possible description of a machine metaphor of the human body in terms of the three dimensions discussed:

1. A mind–body split. Because the body can be reduced to component parts, there is no more to the "whole" and we can exclude considerations of "spirit" and psyche. This is the central point of Descartes' distinction between the human body and mind: reason or thought was a separate faculty independent of the machinelike body. This position was reinforced by the decline of the "vitalist" argument of the nineteenth century, in which little evidence was found to support the view of a "life force" characterizing the human organism. In modern times we see this tendency to exclude considerations of spirit from those of the body in the distinction between psychological and physical experience. The belief here would be that (psychosomatic medicine to the contrary) psyche and soma are easily separable, and that in dealing with the latter we need not deal with the former.

2. An exclusion of emotion. Machines, as merely the expression of the interaction of observable physical forces, do not feel. Similarly, the human body as "a device for converting one form of energy into the one best suited to do the work at hand"[55] or "a physiochemical machine"[56] can be seen as without affect. Emotion is not a part of mechanical systems composed of objectively observable, physical causes.

3. Inattention to considerations of value. Efficiency (what "can" be done, how quickly, cleanly) is to be emphasized over considerations of meaning and purpose (what "should" be, which of several choices has salient meaning for the person).

To summarize, we can say that the dimensions of the metaphor of "the body as machine" are the body as (1) spirit-free, (2) affect-free, and (3) value-free.

The question now becomes: How is this model of the body expressed in individual cases, on the level of specific doctors and patients? What is the impact of this model in treatment and practice? Because people cannot report directly their "silent assumptions" derived from the machine metaphor, we are drawing on two experiences documented by a great deal of "public," published material open to scrutiny. The management of death, the second of these, like childbirth, the first, offers a special advantage as a case example: Medical practices are in the process of evolution as our society attempts to redefine conceptions of both birth and death. In change, the underlying assumptions organizing medical treatment and procedures are more apparent than they are in the static treatment of illnesses and application of procedures not so much open to recent questions. Note, too, that we have picked *extreme examples* from observational studies to illustrate our point.

Over the past five centuries there have been profound changes in Western attitudes toward death.[57] Through the Middle Ages, death was seen as a nonmedical affair, with little attention paid to the body and far more to the individual experience of the dying person. Aires quotes *Don Quixote* to indicate the attentiveness of the doctor to "the soul's health," or what we might call psychological issues attendant to the end of life:

A physician was sent for, who, after feeling his pulse took a rather gloomy view of the case, and told him that he should provide for his soul's health, as that of his body was in a dangerous condition.[58]

Aires also notes the intensely *personal* nature of death in earlier historical periods:

In the late Middle Ages . . . and the Renaissance, a man insisted upon participating in his own death because he saw in it an exceptional moment – a moment which gave his own individuality its definitive form . . .[59]

After the Renaissance, however, the personal, individual experience of death gave way – as Illich shows – to a conception of death as a natural phenomenon, susceptible to the intervention and control that characterized humanity's evolving relation to the natural world.[60] As the mechanistic world view of the West developed through the late Middle Ages and Renaissance, the machine metaphor allowed resolution of a problem in people's relation to death: How was one to understand and depersonalize the fact of death? In regard to the management of death, then, the machine metaphor of the body filled a vacuum in the post-Renaissance understanding of the world. The transformation of death from a psychological–religious event into a mechanical problem of bodily function allowed its depersonalization and removed it from the arena of separate individual experience, blameable on personal failure or supernatural causation. As Illich comments, "the new image of death helped to reduce the human body to an object."[61] In this postmedieval project of conquering death, medicine played a major role: Attention was directed to the body and – as with so many aspects of nature – it became a machine, susceptible to repair and intervention.

This shift in attention from the death of the person to the death of the body and the transformation of the human body into "an object" has continued in modern medical approaches to the management of death. Before exploring the operation of a machine metaphor in this area, let us draw on a number of observational studies to describe traditional medical management of the dying.

Glaser and Strauss discuss "closed awareness" situations in some hospitals where staff collude in hiding awareness of dying from the patient. The patient's mind – kept separate, then, from the event being experienced – is supposed to be directed to "safe topics." Glaser and Strauss quote the following conversation:

FIRST NURSE: A stern face, you don't have to communicate very much verbally, you put things short and formal. . . . Yes, very much the nurse.
SECOND NURSE: Be tender but don't. . . .

FIRST NURSE: Sort of distant, sort of sweet.
SECOND NURSE: Talk about everything but the conditions of the patient.
FIRST NURSE: And if you do communicate with them, when you are not too much
the nurse, you could talk about all kinds of other things; you know,
carefully circling the question of death.[62]

In addition to this deemphasis of the patient's awareness, we often find
the attention of medical people to procedures and machinery in the management of death. There is as well the emphasis on mechanical functions
in treatment of dying patients. Thus, during "death watch," Sudnow has
noted that nurses' "major items of interest became [the patient's] number
of . . . heartbeats and the changing condition of his eyes."[63] Sudnow also
describes the "attention to parts" and the emphasis on "getting practice"
in the emergency ward. The former behavior refers to the attention of
specialists in specific anatomical areas to the posted lists of terminally ill
patients, in the hope of obtaining such organs through donation after
death. The concern with "getting practice" refers to performing difficult
treatments or mock surgical procedures on patients DOA (dead on arrival) so as to learn a technique better.

Finally, Glaser and Strauss describe what they found to be a consistent
emphasis by hospital personnel on "an acceptable style of dying."[64] This
style emphasized control and avoided outbursts of emotion, despair, or
noise. Composure, cheerfulness, and cooperation are the major components of the "acceptable" style most emphasized. Other behavior is seen
as inappropriate:

Miss Jones mentioned that Mr. James was giving a great deal of trouble today.
They had been trying everything on him, and nothing worked. He was refusing all
kinds of things, such as medication, pills, and food, and having trouble getting him
to take his temperature. They had tried to be persuasive and now there was a
nurse who was trying just the opposite. Miss Jones giggled and said it wasn't
getting her anywhere either. . . . To this the other nurse said, "Tough customer,
isn't he?" She looked stolid and said, "He just wants to be ornery." Then added,
"He's been ornery all day."
. . . Miss Smith came into the nursing station saying, "I'm sick of insight."
According to her, this woman patient gets scared and there's nothing you can do,
and then she gets more scared. . . . At the staff meeting, Miss Smith said that this
lady gags more and belches, and the nurse finally decided there was no physical
reason for this. The nurse put on a big dramatic act as she said this because she
was in a big stew about it. She had spoken to the patient and told her it was just
doing her harm and would hurt her more. Later I heard this lady belching pretty
loudly, and the nurses just looked at each other.[65]

To summarize, we can in general describe modern medical management of death in terms of the "closed awareness" of the patient, an atten-

tion to mechanical functions on the part of the doctor, and an emphasis on an "acceptable" style of dying. How do these dimensions of the medical management of death reflect a machine metaphor of the body? Let us consider each of our three dimensions of this metaphor, as discussed above: the body as spirit-free, value-free, and affect-free.

1. The mind–body split. The essence of a "closed-awareness" situation in the management of death is that the patient's attention is directed away from what is happening to his or her body. The body is perceived in a machine metaphor as separate from psychological considerations ("spirit"), and thus death is approached as primarily a physical event, with specific attention to issues of bodily mechanism. Consideration of the person's attitude toward death or the problem of coming to terms with death are excluded. This can be seen in Glaser and Strauss' report of one doctor's manner of handling reports of carcinomas to his patients: The "doctor walks into the patient's room, faces him, says 'It's malignant,' walks out."[66] In general we can ask whether instead of attention to "the soul's health," or providing care that allows for integration of the patient's experience, the emphasis today is on body mechanism and technological intervention in the process. And Cassell claims that in our society, "death is a technical matter, a failure of technology in rescuing the body from a threat to its functioning and integrity."[67] A resulting problem is a *fragmentation of experience,* in which the individual's awareness is split off, and attention is directed away from what is happening to his or her body.

2. The body as value-free. We noted the emphasis on mechanical function and machinery in the management of death. We can see this as related to the emphasis on efficiency and utility in the machine metaphor of the body. Thus the ability exists – through a variety of mechanical and chemical interventions – to extend the functioning of the human body. But have considerations of what medicine can do in extending bodily functions obscured issues of individual choice, value, and meaning (what *is* as compared to what *should* be done)? Cassell has noted that exclusion of value considerations in the machine metaphor leads to technological, legal, and administrative solutions (when to "pull the plug") to what are essentially questions of personal or social value and choice. This can be seen in the discomfort evinced when patients assert their individuality in the dying process or in their "right to die." A recent newspaper account reveals some of this sense of shock at a patient choosing *not* to further bodily function beyond what to him seems reasonable:

The advent of improved kidney dialysis techniques for the treatment of acute renal failure has offered us probably the most clear-cut examples of patients themselves choosing to die. After noting that *"only about three or four patients* of the 1400 that we have treated in this facility have withdrawn from therapy," one leading renal expert consented to tell the story of one such person. "There was an elderly lawyer from in town who decided that coming here to be treated three times a week was arduous, who had difficulties with the treatments, such as vomiting, lack of sleep, and constant pain." This man decided that it was not worth it at age 72 to extend his life. So he simply said, "I will not have you touch me again." It was his own decision, and his family agreed with it. *We made a very vigorous attempt to talk him out of it,* but he withdrew shortly thereafter. Within a week he was dead.

"Pain is not a predominant aspect of the life on dialysis," he continued. "The problems are emotional and social, and a commitment to be dependent on a machine" [italics added].[68]

The emphasis on the "commitment to be dependent on a machine" leads to a second aspect of the depersonalization process: The attention to bodily mechanics easily results in an *abstraction of the individual* to a general category of mechanical function: "heart failure," "stroke," and so on. The attention of nurses to mechanical functions during "death watch," discussed earlier, is an example of such abstraction of the patient. The predominance of mechanical function in this approach to the human body can also be seen in the treatment of individuals in which such function is gone. Sudnow defines "social death" as that period before biological death when hospital staff and others relate to the patient as if he or she were indeed dead. That the comatose individual, for example, is seen as "almost dead" is not surprising. It is the content of the social behavior toward the individual that is of note. Sudnow and Glaser and Strauss point to the *nonperson* status suddenly attached to the individual: The person loses his or her social prerogatives and is no longer attended to in the same manner by the physician – "physicians lose their interest in the patient."[69] The "sense of person" can easily fail when the mechanical function of the body breaks down. "Nonperson status" reveals the problem of depersonalization of the patient. So do the "attention to parts" at social death and emphasis on "getting practice" described by Sudnow.[70]

Depersonalization can also be seen in the *predominance of institutional values* in dying. As the salience of mechanical and chemical intervention increases, control of the process of dying passes, subtly, from the patient to the physician: Because prolonging the mechanical operation of the body is the major consideration, the technical expertise of the doctor – seen especially in the specialized vocabulary of medicine – separates him or her from the patient and gives the doctor a special power. This subtle shift in agency characterizes the whole process of dying. For example, the move from home to hospital as the context of dying means that the event is no longer a private, individual affair, but rather a public, homogenized one, dominated, as Cassell points out, by "symbols of interpersonal sameness." Thus has Kastenbaum described the impact of institutional dynamics on the death of geriatric patients: "[They] often behave as though . . . attempting to make their demise as acceptable and unthreatening as possible [for the staff]."[71] Glaser and Strauss offer many examples of the impact of these institutional values in teaching the patient "how to die."

3. The body as affect-free. Here the content of the "acceptable style of dying" is of special interest. The emphasis is on unemotional, controlled, and standardized behavior. We can see the impact of the "affect-free" dimension of the metaphor in the *elimination of affectively rooted ritual* from the process. In part, this elimination dovetails with the depersonalization of the patient in that personally meaningful opportunities for the experience of dying are not made available. Gorer years ago pointed to the absence of culturally sanctioned grief or mourning and the difficulty this absence presents to individuals in trying to cope with death, either their own or that of others.[72]

Summary and conclusions

The primary message of this chapter is that to understand medicine truly we must look beyond it. Looking beyond it entails stating the ways in which medicine is responsive to, and productive of, forces in its larger sociocultural setting. We should note that in so doing we are engaging in a dialectic: Medicine not only responds to influences from the society in which it exists, but also generates changes within the society. We have tried to illustrate this mode of analysis by presenting the history of one image of the body; this mechanical image provides a focus for our examination of historical connections between the development of medicine and changes and strains in society itself.

Many discussions of the history of medicine center either on the history of ideas or on the history of people and events; they view medicine either as the evolution and advance of important concepts and theories or as the product of key discoveries by researchers. Both these approaches tend to stay *within* medicine; in them its development is isolated from significant social forces outside the profession. Their implication is that the way medicine developed is the only way in which it could have developed, and

– "should" replacing "could" – that medicine has been a constant advance of "better" theory and practice.

Our focus, in contrast, has been primarily on the social, political, and economical changes and strains that have shaped the medical profession. This focus is consistent with the perspective of such recent observers of medicine as Foucault and Illich, as well as other writers. The implication of this chapter is that the way in which medicine has developed is only one of many alternative ways in which it could have developed, and that medicine's growth reflects not the evolution of "pure" concepts, ideas, and procedures, but rather the interplay of many different social forces and pressures.

Images of the body change over time. We have traced one particular image, a model of the body as a machine. However, there are complementary and competing images. A "war" metaphor can, for instance, be invoked when the body is "fighting" an illness. Sontag has recently offered a rich description of the different kinds of metaphors applied to illness.[73] It may be that the machine metaphor, which we have singled out, is appropriate for certain aspects of medicine (e.g., heart surgery, kidney dialysis, birth and death, where the body is producing or "running down"), but less appropriate for others: the treatment of illnesses such as infections or cancer.

As we have seen in this chapter, medicine is constantly changing. The predominance of the machine metaphor has set up a counterforce within medicine. For example, in the domains of birth and death the machine model may be undergoing alteration – as evidenced by the increase in home births and living wills and hospices for the dying.[74] Considerable work has been done recently on ethical issues in medicine, particularly in relation to the problems of the dying and patients' responsibility for decisions in the course of treatment.[75] So, too, has there been an effort to integrate patients' feelings and concerns into medicine, as exemplified by the work of Kubler-Ross.[76] Whether these innovations, designed to remove some of the mechanical, context-stripping features from a person's experience of childbirth and death, mean new ways of looking at the body, health, and illness is still unclear. To understand and decide such a question, however, requires elucidating the relationship of these new concerns in medicine to the larger socioeconomic and political forces currently at work in our society.

Notes

1. Martí-Ibañez, F. *Ariel: Essays on the Arts and the History and Philosophy of Medicine.* New York: MD Publications, 1962, p. 42.

246   The machine metaphor in medicine

2. Ibid. See also Marti-Ibañez, F. *A Prelude to Medical History*. New York: MD Publications, 1961. For a more detailed discussion of Egyptian medicine, see Sigerist, H. E. *A History of Medicine*, Vol. 1, *Primitive and Archaic Medicine*. New York: Oxford University Press, 1951.
3. Sigerist, H. E. *A History of Medicine*, Vol. 2, *Greek, Hindu and Persian Medicine*. New York: Oxford University Press, 1961.
4. Zimmer, H. *Hindu Medicine*. Baltimore, MD: Johns Hopkins University Press, 1948. Quoted in Needleman, J. "The two sciences of medicine," *Parabola*, August 1978, *111*(3):38.
5. Obeyesekere, G. "The impact of Ayurvedic ideas on the culture and the individual in Sri Lanka," in Leslie, C. (Ed.). *Asian Medical Systems*. Berkeley: University of California Press, 1976. See also Obeyesekere's "The theory and practice of psychological medicine in the Ayurvedic tradition," *Culture, Medicine and Psychiatry*, 1977, *1*:155–81.
6. Harwood, A. "The hot–cold theory of disease: implications for treatment of Puerto Rican patients," *Journal of the American Medical Association*, 1971, *216*:1153. See also Currier, R. L. "The hot–cold syndrome and symbolic balance in Mexican and Spanish-American folk medicine," *Ethnology*, 1966, *5*:251–63.
7. Aries, P. *Western Attitudes Toward Death: From the Middle Ages to the Present*. Baltimore, MD: Johns Hopkins University Press, 1974. And Illich, I. *Medical Nemesis: The Expropriation of Health*. New York: Bantam Books, 1977. In Illich, see especially chap. 5.
8. Foucault, M. *The Birth of the Clinic: An Archeology of Medical Perception*. New York: Pantheon Books, 1973.
9. Miller, J. *The Body in Question*. New York: Random House, 1978. For a more general discussion in cultural interpretations of the body, see Benthall, J., and Polhemus, T. (Eds.). *The Body as a Medium of Expression*. New York: Dutton, 1975.
10. Sontag, S. *Illness as Metaphor*. New York: Farrar, Strauss and Giroux, 1977.
11. Quoted in Mumford, L. "The myth of the machine," in *The Pentagon of Power*, Vol. 2. New York: Harcourt, Brace, Jovanovich, 1964.
12. Miller, *The Body in Question*, p. 182.
13. Deutsch, K. W. "Mechanism, teleology and mind," *Philosophy and Phenomenological Review*, December 1951, *12*(2):185–223. For a more extensive discussion of the concept of mechanism through Western history, see also Gimpel, J. *The Medieval Machine: The Industrial Revolution of the Middle Ages*. New York: Holt, Rinehart and Winston, 1976. And Loeb, J. *The Mechanistic Conception of Life*. Cambridge, MA: Belknap Press, 1964.
14. Westfall, R. S. *The Construction of Modern Science: Mechanisms and Mechanics*. Cambridge: Cambridge University Press, 1977. See also the discussion by Mumford, "The myth of the machine."
15. Westfall, *The Construction of Modern Science*, pp. 1–2, and chap. 2.
16. Ibid., p. 33.
17. Quoted in ibid., p. 90.
18. Ibid., p. 91.
19. Quoted in ibid., p. 93, italics added.
20. Reiser, S. J. *Medicine and the Reign of Technology*. Cambridge: Cambridge University Press, 1978.
21. Ibid., p. 229.
22. Braverman, H. *Labor and Monopoly Capital: The Degradation of Work in the Twentieth Century*. New York: Monthly Review Press, 1974.
23. Illich, *Medical Nemesis*, chap. 5.
24. This is a theme Foucault has pursued in several different studies. See Foucault, *The*

Birth of the Clinic, and Foucault, M. *Discipline and Punish: The Birth of the Prison.* New York: Pantheon Books, 1977.
25. Gould, R. J. "Evolution's erratic pace," *Natural History,* May 1977, *86*(5):12–16.
26. Flexner, A. *Medical Education in the United States and Canada.* New York: Carnegie Foundation for the Advancement of Teaching, Bulletin No. 4, 1910.
27. Richmond, J. *Currents in American Medicine: A Developmental View of Medical Care and Education.* Cambridge, MA: Harvard University Press, 1969, p. 3. For other discussions of the origins and impact of the Flexner report, see Miller, H. "Fifty years after Flexner," *Lancet,* 1966, *II*:647–54; Kunitz, S. J. "Professionalism and social control in the progressive era: the case of the Flexner report," *Social Problems,* 1974, *22*:16–27; and Berliner, H. S. "A larger perspective on the Flexner report," *International Journal of Health Services,* 1975, *5*(4):573–92.
28. Flexner, *Medical Education,* pp. 53 and 63.
29. Berliner also shows how a mechanical metaphor served to exclude detailed attention in medicine to social causality of disease, a theme discussed in the first chapter of this book. Berliner comments: "The accumulation of knowledge in medicine [i.e., research] was also drastically influenced by the new paradigm. By definition, scientific medicine rejected the idea of social causality of disease or illness since the social basis of humanity was placed outside the realm of what was considered scientific. Research was structured in such a way as to reinforce this exclusion of social causality. The predominant focus of medical research became pathology and pathological anatomy. Therapeutics, hygiene, and symptomatology, all mainstays of wholistic medicine, were largely ignored. Physiology, which in previous times had meant the relationship of man to nature (from the Greek "physus"), now meant only the study of the workings of man." See Berliner, "A larger perspective on the Flexner report," pp. 576–7.
30. Ibid.
31. Noble, D. *America by Design: Science, Technology, and the Rise of Corporate Capitalism.* New York: Alfred A. Knopf, 1977.
32. Gilbert, J. *Designing the Industrial State: The Intellectual Pursuit of Collectivism in America, 1880–1940.* Chicago: Quandrangle Books, 1972.
33. Noble, *America by Design,* p. 179.
34. Ibid., pp. 179–80.
35. Gilbert, *Designing the Industrial State,* p. 55.
36. Noble, in particular, makes this point clearly. See Noble, *America by Design.*
37. For a discussion of the rise of professions in America during the period 1890–1914, see Bledstein, B. J. *The Culture of Professionalism: The Middle Class and the Development of Higher Education in America.* New York: W. W. Norton, 1976.
38. Kunitz provides some examples of changes parallel to the Flexner report during this Progressive Era in America:
"It was at this time that birth control, efficiency engineering, conservation in the use of natural resources, mental hygiene, good government, Prohibition, anti-trust legislation, pure food and drug laws, the Harrison Narcotics Act, juvenile court reform, and many other reforms emerged.
"The result was the development of new consulting professions. The Johns Hopkins economist, Richard T. Ely, claimed that government was a profession, not a business. Indeed, city planners and city managers, along with bureaus of municipal research, emerged at this time. Civil service reforms were enacted to make government service more professional. Forestry and social work emerged as occupations claiming professional status. Management experts of all sorts developed from the occupation of mechanical engineer. Teaching began to seek professional status. Even business became a profession instead of just business. . . . Government agencies required 'scientific facts'

as the basis for solving their particular problems, so numerous research agencies and bureaus were formed in various levels of government and staffed by professional experts."

See Kunitz, "Professionalism and social control," p. 18.

39. Ibid., p. 18.
40. Berliner, "A larger perspective on the Flexner report," pp. 576–7.
41. Ibid.
42. Childbirth is also an interesting example because it shows how birth, which is seen in many cultures as a natural process rather than a disease, has been gradually made to fit into the biomedical model of specific pathology. Wertz and Wertz quote one doctor saying, in 1920, that "[labor] is a decidedly pathological process." Wertz, R., and Wertz, D. *Lying In: A Natural History of Childbirth in America*. New York: Schocken Books, 1979, p. 142.
43. Wertz and Wertz present an unusual case history of medical practice in which they show how the development of medical theory and practice is rooted in cultural and social history.
44. Ibid., p. 33.
45. Ibid., pp. 29–76.
46. Ehrenreich, B., and English, D. *Complaints and Disorders: The Sexual Politics of Sickness*. Old Westbury, NY: Feminist Press, 1973.
47. Wertz and Wertz, *Lying In,* p. 115.
48. Ibid., p. 128.
49. Ibid., p. 165.
50. Ibid., p. 159.
51. Haire, D. "The cultural warping of childbirth," Ehrenreich, J. (Ed.). *The Cultural Crisis of Modern Medicine,* New York: Monthly Review Press, 1978, p. 187.
52. It is Haire's contention that our infant mortality rate is partly the result of the way childbirth is managed, particularly the use of anesthetics during labor and delivery. See Haire, "The cultural warping of childbirth."
53. Berliner, "A larger perspective on the Flexner report," p. 576.
54. At present, there is more variation and difference of opinion about the management of birth than there has been in the recent past. One alternative is increasingly family-centered, even home-centered births, with far less intervention than has been the norm in America. The other alternative seems to be increasingly large and centralized maternity hospitals with an even greater routinization and emphasis on efficiency. It is probably because this is a period when the prevailing way of looking at the body in childbirth is being called into question that it is relatively easy to see this as a historical and cultural phenomenon. We shall turn at the end of this chapter to the question of whether there are other, competing metaphors of the body.
55. Clark-Kennedy, A. E. *Medicine,* Vol. 1, *The Patient and His Disease.* Baltimore, MD: Williams & Wilkins, 1947.
56. Goffman, E. "The medical model and mental hospitalization: some notes on the vicissitudes of the tinkering trades," in *Asylums: Essays on the Social Situation of Mental Patients and Other Inmates.* New York: Doubleday Anchor, 1961, p. 340.
57. Aries, *Western Attitudes Toward Death.* See also Steinfels, P., and Veatch, R. (Eds.). *Death Inside Out.* New York: Harper & Row, 1974.
58. Aries, *Western Attitudes Toward Death,* p. 10.
59. Ibid., p. 11.
60. Illich, *Medical Nemesis,* chap. 5.
61. Ibid., p. 184.
62. Glaser, B. G., and Strauss, A. L. *Awareness of Dying.* Chicago: Aldine, 1965, p. 56.

63. Sudnow, D. *Passing On: The Social Organization of Dying.* Englewood Cliffs, NJ: Prentice-Hall, 1967, p. 84.
64. Glaser and Strauss, *Awareness of Dying,* pp. 89–93.
65. Ibid., pp. 87–8.
66. Ibid., p. 125. In chap. 5 of their book, Glaser and Strauss present a discussion of a variety of styles of disclosing to patients that their illness is probably terminal.
67. Cassell, E. J. "Dying in a technological society," in Steinfels and Veatch, *Death Inside Out,* pp. 43–4.
68. *The Real Paper,* May 2, 1976.
69. Glaser and Strauss, *Awareness of Dying,* p. 108; and Sudnow, *Passing On,* p. 81.
70. Sudnow, *Passing On,* pp. 107–8.
71. Kastenbaum, R. "The interpersonal context of death in a geriatric institution," abstract of paper presented at the 17th Annual Scientific Meeting, Gerontological Society, Minneapolis, MN, October 29–31, 1964. Quoted in Glaser and Strauss, *Awareness of Dying,* p. 65n.
72. Gorer, G. *Death, Grief and Mourning in Contemporary Britain.* London: Cresset Press, 1965.
73. Sontag, *Illness as Metaphor,* pp. 64–71.
74. Neitsky, N. "Dying in a system of 'good care,' case report and analysis," pp. 318–24; Woodsor, R. "Hospice care in terminal illness," pp. 325–39; and, Goodman, E. "The Shanti project: a hopeful scenario for the dying," pp. 340–2; in Garfield, C. (Ed.). *Stress and Survival.* Saint Louis, MO: C. V. Mosby, 1979.
75. See, for example, Fox, R., and Swazey, J. *The Courage to Fail: A Social View of Organ Transplants and Dialysis,* 2nd ed. Chicago: University of Chicago Press, 1979.
76. Kubler-Ross, E. *On Death and Dying.* New York: Macmillan, 1969.

10   In conclusion: a new perspective
on health and medicine

Elliot G. Mishler

This text might appropriately be viewed as a set of variations on a single theme, namely, the proposition that illness is a social fact. In the preceding chapters we have explored and developed the implications of this proposition for our understanding of a number of significant problems in health care. Because our intent was to introduce a new perspective, based on the social and behavioral sciences as an alternative to the biomedical model, we focused on the effects of sociocultural, institutional, and historical factors on forms of illness and modes of clinical practice. We want our work to be useful to students, practitioners, and research scientists and have attempted to provide a guide to relevant theory and research and to raise questions and encourage critical reflection about current assumptions and practices in health care.

The text records our efforts, and we shall not attempt here to summarize detailed analyses presented in previous chapters. Rather, these last comments highlight some recurrent themes and touch briefly on considerations that influenced our approach.

In undertaking this work, we appreciated the persistent and well-known difficulty of explaining social science approaches and findings to health professionals, and, beyond that, the further difficulties of applying them to ways of thinking and practice. We have repeatedly noted the dominance of the biomedical model. It is so pervasive that it appears to be the "normal," natural, and perhaps only way to think about health and illness. In the context of this strong tradition, the alternative perspective we have proposed may appear strange. It generates different types of questions and provides interpretations that draw on concepts and mechanisms that are not part of the biological sciences.

We believe that the communication problem is a real one, and we have no easy solution to propose. We have tried to deal with it by carefully sifting the empirical studies and by organizing and presenting them in a particular form. To clarify the issues involved, we put considerable emphasis on the features and functions of social contexts, gave explicit recognition to different approaches within the social and behavioral sciences, and attended carefully to details of methods and concepts entailed by these different approaches.

The term "context" is ubiquitous in the text and central to our several analyses. We eschewed a specific definition and allowed it to take on a broad and all-inclusive range of reference through diverse examples. All features of social life – social norms, cultural values, shared codes of meaning and rules of conduct, institutional structures and processes, forms of economic and political organization – are encompassed in our conception of social context. The reason for its dominant role in our presentation stems directly from our critique of the biomedical model. We have argued that reliance on the biomedical model has led to a decontextualization of, and thus an overly narrow technical approach to, the problems of health, illness, and patient care. It seems to us that the result of this reliance has been serious limitation, of both theory and practice. Further, we believe that the social and behavioral sciences have a unique contribution to make in exactly the areas of theory and practice where the biological sciences are weakest. By putting patients, clinical practices, and health-care institutions in their social contexts, the social and behavioral sciences permit a fuller and more comprehensive understanding of and approach to health and illness.

Our broad definition of context has played a central role in our analyses, and also allowed us to cover a variety of *different* approaches and studies. We have drawn upon work in various social and behavioral science disciplines – most prominently, anthropology, social psychology, and sociology – but have not focused on disciplinary concerns or attended to disciplinary boundaries. Instead, we have distinguished among the types of questions asked in different investigations – questions about the social contexts of patients, of physicians, and of health-care systems. We wished, in this way, to convey a sense of the complexity and differentiation of work on health-related topics by investigators from a variety of backgrounds who share an interest in social contexts.

Our distinction of types of questions serves a more specific function. We have pointed out that studies of the social contexts of patients have significantly different implications than, for example, studies of the social organization of clinical practice or of the social functions of the health-care system. Essentially, variations in the focus of inquiry and in the specific questions asked are associated with differences in the degree to which studies depart from assumptions of the biomedical model. This association has been noted often, and the text moved progressively, from studies the design of which retained essential features of the biomedical model in the sense that they relied on clinical definitions and clinical criteria, to studies that proposed alternative definitions of health and illness. We believe that an understanding of this continuum is particularly important for a proper understanding of the diverse findings we have sought to interpret, and for their integration into medical theory and practice.

Related to our concern for the reader's appreciation of different approaches and their implications is our emphasis on the details of studies, on their particular concepts, theories, and methods. We are aware that it may be easier to grasp a summary statement, such as that schizophrenia is related to social class, than to understand the significance of specific technical differences among studies of this relationship. Nonetheless, we think that such a statement is insufficient, even if true. The relationship between social class and mental illness is complex, and there are several different approaches to its investigation as well as competing models of explanation. The broad generalization is not adequate as a guide to theory or practice. In some respects, the generalization may detract from the usefulness of findings. The clinical relevance of work in the social and behavioral sciences depends on the specification of particular mechanisms in much the same way as does that of work in the biological sciences. A generalization that does not entail specific consequences need not be taken seriously. Too often, health-relevant findings from the social sciences are presented and learned in the form of simple generalizations, and remain undigested ideas, protected from critical examination and from confrontation with clinical realities. To have real impact, work in the social and behavioral sciences must be understood in its particulars, and we have tried to provide some foundation for such understanding.

Finally, it is important to take note of two ideas that have surfaced occasionally in the text but have remained largely implicit. The first is that medicine is a social or moral practice; the second is that issues of power are pervasive. These ideas bear on each other because of the status and authority of the medical profession and the particular form taken by modern medicine.

It is usual to contrast two alternative views of medicine, as an art or a science. We think it more important to recognize that medicine is a social practice, a moral practice in terms of its functions and consequences. We mean this in the double sense that medicine is socially framed and organized and that it is socially consequential. We have shown how medical practice is influenced by such factors as the dominant social ideology, for example, in the treatment of women in the nineteenth century, and by the social class position of patients, as in how treatment is provided in a modern hospital. We have provided evidence to support our view that medicine is responsive to and reflects sociocultural values and norms as well as dominant economic and political interests. We have urged the adequacy of this view over a view of medicine as guided primarily by norms of technical–scientific rationality, oriented toward standards of objectivity.

Medicine is also a technical practice, but we do not believe that technical practice should be treated, as it often is, as its sole definitive characteristic. In this regard, we have been particularly concerned with the effects of the dominant technical–scientific framework for medicine, in which social context is first removed from the model of disease and treatment and the resulting abstraction is then reapplied to problems that are inherently grounded in social contexts. A more adequate approach to health care requires an expanded scientific world view that includes an understanding of the various social contexts we have discussed.

All of these issues take on increased importance because of the power of the medical profession and the ways in which it exercises its power in health care. These ways are evident wherever we look – in the assymetries of power between physicians and patients, in the high status and economic position of physicians, in the hierarchical organization of hospitals and other health-care institutions, in the ways that medicine functions to serve the interests of dominant economic and political interest groups. A shift from a biomedical to a social perspective will not change the realities of power, and indeed, it can be argued persuasively, that such a shift in perspective may itself depend on shifts in the present balance of power.

We have been concerned primarily with discussing conceptual models of health and illness rather than objective conditions and structures of economic and political power. Nonetheless, we have tried to show that the models we choose have consequences in the real world. The biomedical model is not merely a way of thinking; because it is so basic to clinical practice, its effects are seen in real events and actions. For this reason, we do not consider our approach as competing with that of those who focus mainly on the economics and politics of medicine and health care. Rather, we view both types of analysis as supplementing each other.

Writing this book has been an important learning experience for us. The effort has given us a fuller and more complex understanding of issues related to health and illness than we had when we began and has pressed us toward clarifying our own position. We hope that readers will benefit in similar ways and that our work will serve as a basis for further inquiries into critical questions about theory and practice in health care.

Bibliography and citation index

Abrams, R. "The patient with cancer – his changing pattern of communication," *New England Journal of Medicine*, 1966, *274:* 317–22. P. 137.

Ambuel, L., Cebulla, J., Watt, N., and Crowne, D. "Doctor–mother communications, a study of information communicated during clinic visits for acute illness," Columbus: Ohio State University, unpublished, 1964. P. 136.

American Leprosy Missions. *Annual Report,* 1977. Pp. 186, 193.
Bulletin, Fall 1978. Pp. 184, 186, 193.

Angell, R. *The Family Encounters the Depression.* New York: Scribner & Sons, 1936. P. 75.

Antonovsky, A. "Conceptual and methodological problems in the study of resistance resources and stressful life events," in Dohrenwend, B. P., and Dohrenwend, B. S. (Eds.). *Stressful Life Events: Their Nature and Effects.* New York: John Wiley & Sons, 1974. P. 76.

Aries, P. *Western Attitudes Toward Death: From the Middle Ages to the Present.* Baltimore, MD: Johns Hopkins University Press, 1974. Pp. 239, 240, 246, 248.

Aronson, N. "Review of: B. A. Weisbrod et al., *Disease and Economic Development,*" *Social Science and Medicine,* 1978, *12*(1C): 66–8. Pp. 202, 203, 204, 216.

Artiss, K., and Levine, A. "Doctor–patient relations in severe illness," *New England Journal of Medicine,* 1973, *288:* 1210–14. P. 137.

Bakke, E. *Citizens Without Work.* New Haven, CN: Yale University Press, 1940. P. 75.

Balint, M. *The Doctor, His Patient and the Illness.* New York: International University Press, 1957. Pp. 8, 23, 104, 136, 139.

Becker, H. S. *The Outsiders.* Glencoe, IL: The Free Press, 1963. P. 166.

Becker, H., Geer, B., Hughes, E., and Strauss, A. *Boys in White: Student Culture in Medical School.* Chicago: University of Chicago Press, 1961. Pp. 122, 139.

Beeson, P. "Review of: R. Duff and A. B. Hollingshead, *Sickness and Society,*" *Yale Journal of Biology and Medicine,* 1968, *41:* 226–41. P. 140.

Belknap, I. *Human Problems of a State Mental Hospital.* New York: McGraw-Hill Book Company, 1956. P. 103.

Ben-Sira, A. "The function of the professional's affective behavior in client satisfaction: a revised theory," *Journal of Health and Social Behavior, 1976, 17:* 3–11. Pp. 120, 138.

Benthall, J., and Polhemus, T. (Eds.). *The Body as a Medium of Expression.* New York: Dutton, 1975. P. 246.

Bergen, B. "Psychosomatic disease and the role of the physician: a social view," in Lipowski, S. J., Lipsitt, D. R., and Whybrow, P. C. (Eds.). *Psychosomatic Medicine*. New York: Oxford University Press, 1977. Pp. 136, 138.

Berger, P. L., and Luckmann, T. *The Social Construction of Reality*. New York: Doubleday Anchor Books, 1967. Pp. 141, 166.

Berki, S. E., and Heston, A. W. "Introduction to: The Nation's Health: Some Issues," *The Annals of the American Academy of Political and Social Science*, January 1972, *399:* IX– XIV. P. 101.

Berliner, H. S. "A larger perspective on the Flexner report," *International Journal of Health Services*, 1975, *5*(4): 573– 92. Pp. 227, 228, 231, 236, 247, 248.

Bernstein, B. *Class, Codes and Control, Vol. 2, Applied Studies Towards a Sociology of Language*. London: Routledge and Kegan Paul, 1973. P. 137.

Blackwell, B. "Drug therapy: patient compliance," *New England Journal of Medicine*, 1973, *289:* 249– 52. P. 138.

Blaxter, M. "Diagnosis as category and process: the case of alcoholism," *Social Science and Medicine*, 1978, *12:* 9– 17. Pp. 152, 153, 166, 167.

Bledstein, B. J. *The Culture of Professionalism: The Middle Class and the Development of Higher Education in America*. New York: W. W. Norton, 1976. P. 247.

Bloom, S. W., and Wilson, R. N. "Patient– practitioner relationships," in Freeman, H., Levine, S., and Reeder, L. (Eds.). *Handbook of Medical Sociology*. Englewood Cliffs, NJ: Prentice-Hall, 1972. P. 139.

Bloombaum, M., and Gugelyk, T. "Voluntary confinement among lepers," *Journal of Health and Social Behavior*, 1970, *11:* 16– 20. Pp. 193, 194.

Bosk, C. L. *Forgive and Remember*. Chicago: University of Chicago Press, 1979. P. 101.

Braverman, H. *Labor and Monopoly Capital: The Degradation of Work in the Twentieth Century*. New York: Monthly Review Press, 1974. P. 246.

Brenner, M. H. *Mental Illness and the Economy*. Cambridge, MA: Harvard University Press, 1973. Pp. 57, 58, 75.

Estimating the Social Costs of National Economic Policy: Implications for Mental and Physical Health, and Criminal Aggression. Prepared for the Joint Economic Committee of Congress, Washington, DC: U.S. Government Printing Office, 1976. Pp. 61, 75.

Bronfenbrenner, U. "Toward an experimental ecology of human development," *American Psychologist*, 1977, *32*(7): 513– 31. P. 101.

Brown, G., and Birley, J. "Crises and life changes and the onset of schizophrenia," *Journal of Health and Social Behavior*, 1968, *9:* 203– 14. P. 76.

Byrne, P. S., and Long, B. E. *Doctors Talking to Patients*. London: Her Majesty's Stationary Office, 1976. Pp. 8, 23, 112, 113, 127, 137, 139, 140.

Cannon, W. *Bodily Changes in Pain, Hunger, Fear and Rage*. Boston: Charles T. Branford Co., 1953. Pp. 64, 76.

Caplan, G. *Principles of Preventive Psychiatry*. New York: Basic Books, 1970. P. 75.

Cartwright, A. *Human Relations and Hospital Care*. London: Routledge and Kegan Paul, 1964. Pp. 106, 136.

Patients and Their Doctors. London: Routledge and Kegan Paul, 1967. Pp. 106, 136.

Cassell, E. J., "Dying in a technolgical society," in Steinfels, P., and Veatch, R. (Eds.). *Death Inside Out.* New York: Harper & Row, 1974. Pp. 242, 249.

Catalano, R., and Dooley, D. "Economic predictors of depressed mood and stressful life events," *Journal of Health and Social Behavior.* 1977, *18:* 292–307. P. 75.

Caudill, W. *The Psychiatric Hospital as a Small Society.* Cambridge, MA: Harvard University Press, 1958. P. 103.

Center for Epidemiologic Studies, National Institute of Mental Health. *Bibliography: Epidemiology of Mental Disorders, 1966–68.* Washington, DC: U.S. Government Printing Office, 1970 (NCMHI Publication No. 5030); and 1969–70. Washington, DC: U.S. Government Printing Office, 1973 (DHEW Publication No. HSM: 73-9043). Pp. 28, 51.

Charney, E., Bynum, R., Eldredge, G., Frank, D., MacWhinney, J., McNabb, N., Scheiner, A., Sumpter, E., and Iker, H. "How well do patients take oral penicillin? A collaborative study in private practice," *Pediatrics,* 1967, *40:* 188–95. Pp. 117, 138.

Clark-Kennedy, A. E. *Medicine,* Vol. 1, *The Patient and His Disease.* Baltimore, MD: Williams & Wilkins, 1947. P. 248.

Clendening, L. (Ed.). *Source Book of Medical History.* New York: Dover Publications, 1960. P. 166.

Coates, D., Moyer, S., and Wellman, B. "Yorklea study: symptoms, problems and life events," *Canadian Journal of Public Health,* 1969, *60:* 471–81. Pp. 67, 77.

Cobb, S., and Kasl, S. *Termination: The Consequence of Job Loss.* Cincinnati, OH: OHEW (NIOSH) Publication No. 77-224, 1977. Pp. 68, 77.

Cochrane, A. L. *Effectiveness and Efficiency: Random Reflections on Health Services.* England: Nuffield Provincial Hospitals Trust, 1972. P. 167.

Coe, R. M. *Sociology of Medicine.* New York: McGraw-Hill Book Company, 1970. P. 102.

Cohen, H. "The evolution of the concept of disease." In Lush, B. (Ed.). *Concepts of Medicine.* New York: Pergamon Press, 1961. Pp. 3, 22.

Coleman, J. S., Katz, E., and Menzel, H. *Medical Innovation: A Diffusion Study.* Indianapolis, IN: Bobbs-Merrill, 1966. Pp. 208, 209, 216.

Cooper, B., and Morgan, H. G. *Epidemiological Psychiatry.* Springfield, IL: C. C. Thomas, 1973. P. 51.

Conrad, P. "The discovery of hyperkinesis: notes on the medicalization of deviant behavior," *Social Problems,* 1975, *23*(1): 12–21. Pp. 153, 154, 155, 156, 167, 168.

   Identifying Hyperactive Children: The Medicalization of Deviant Behavior. Lexington, MA: D. C. Heath, 1978. Pp. 153, 156, 167, 168.

Cousins, N. "Anatomy of an illness (as perceived by the patient)," *New England Journal of Medicine,* 1976, *295:* 1458–83. P. 140.

Currier, R. L. "The hot–cold syndrome and symbolic balance in Mexican and Spanish-American folk medicine," *Ethnology,* 1966, *5:* 251–63. P. 246.

Curtis, G. "Physiology of stress," in Ferman, L., and Gordus, J. (Eds.). *The Consequences of Work Transition: Resource Papers in Mental Health and the Economy.* Kalamazoo, MI: UpJohn Institute, 1980. P. 76.

Daniels, M. J. "Affect and its control in the medical intern," *American Journal of Sociology*, 1960, *66:*259–67. P. 139.

Davis, M. S. "Variation in patient's compliance with doctor's advice: empirical analysis of patterns of communication," *American Journal of Public Health*, 1968, *58:*274–88. Pp. 115, 138.

Dayton, N. A. *New Facts on Mental Disorders.* Springfield, IL: Charles C. Thomas, 1940. P. 75.

Deutsch, K. W. "Mechanism, teleology and mind," *Philosophy and Phenomenological Review*, December 1951, *12*(2):185–223. Pp. 221, 246.

Dingwall, R., Heath, C., Reid, M., and Stacey, M. (Eds.). *Health Care and Health Knowledge.* New York: Prodist, 1977. P. 167.

Dohrenwend, B. P. "Social status and psychological disorder: an issue of substance and an issue of method," *American Sociological Review*, 1966, *31*(1):14–34. Pp. 40, 41, 52.

Dohrenwend, B. P., and Dohrenwend, B. S. (Eds.). *Stressful Life Events: Their Nature and Effects.* New York: John Wiley & Sons, 1974. P. 76.

Dohrenwend, B. S. "Life events as stressors: a methodological inquiry," *Journal of Health and Social Behavior*, 1973, *14:*167–75. P. 77.

Dubos, R. *Mirage of Health.* New York: Anchor Books, 1961. Pp. 6, 7, 22, 23, 51, 101, 199, 216.

Dubos, R. J. "Infection into disease," in Ingle, D. J. (Ed.). *Life and Disease.* New York: Basic Books, 1963. Pp. 7, 23.

Duff, R., and Hollingshead, A. B. *Sickness and Society.* New York: Harper & Row, 1968. Pp. 108, 131, 133, 137, 140, 206, 207, 208, 216.

Dunbar, J., and Stunkard, A. "Adherence to diet and drug regimen," in Levy, R., Rifkind, B., Dennis, B., and Ernst, N. (Eds.). *Nutrition, Lipids, and Coronary Heart Disease.* New York: Raven Press, 1979. Pp. 115, 138.

Dunham, H. W. *Community and Schizophrenia: An Epidemiological Analysis.* Detroit, MI: Wayne State University Press, 1965. Pp. 32, 42, 51, 52.

Dunham, H. W., and Weinberg, S. K. *Culture of the State Mental Hospital.* Detroit, MI: Wayne State University Press, 1960. P. 103.

Durkheim, E. *Suicide: A Study in Sociology.* New York: The Free Press, 1951. Pp. 61, 75.

Editorial, *The Medical Journal of Australia*, 1977, *2*(11):345–7. P. 193.

Ehrenreich, B., and Ehrenreich, J. (Eds.). *The American Health Empire: Power, Profits and Politics.* New York: Vintage Books (Health-Pac Book), 1971. P. 215.

Ehrenreich, B., and English, D. *Complaints and Disorders: The Sexual Politics of Sickness.* Old Westbury, NY: Feminist Press, 1973. Pp. 210, 216, 217, 234, 248. "The 'sick' women of the upper classes," in Ehrenreich, J. (Ed.). *The Cultural Crisis of Modern Medicine.* New York: Monthly Review Press, 1978. Pp. 210, 216, 217.

Ehrenreich, J. (Ed.). *The Cultural Crisis of Modern Medicine.* New York: Monthly Review Press, 1978. Pp. 195, 210, 216, 248.

Eisenberg, L. "Delineation of clinical conditions: conceptual models of 'physical' and 'mental' disorders," in *Research and Medical Practice: Their Interaction,*

CIBA Foundation Symposium 44 (New Series). North-Holland: Elsevier/ Excerpta Medica, 1976. Pp. 142, 166.

"Psychiatry and society: a sociobiologic synthesis," *New England Journal of Medicine,* April 21, 1977, *296*(16):903–910. Pp. 13, 23.

Ekman, P., and Friesen, W. "Nonverbal behavior and psychotherapy research," in Shlien, J., Hunt, H., Matarazzo, J., and Savage, C. (Eds.). *Research in Psychotherapy, Vol. 3.* Washington, DC: American Psychological Association, 1968. P. 139.

"Nonverbal language and clues to deception," *Psychiatry,* 1969, *32*:88–106. P. 139.

Engel, G. L. *Psychological Development in Health and Disease.* Philadelphia: W. B. Saunders, 1962. Pp. 7, 11, 23.

"A unified concept of health and disease," in Ingle, D. J. (Ed.). *Life and Disease.* New York: Basic Books, 1963. Pp. 3, 22, 23.

"Are medical schools neglecting clinical skills," *Journal of the American Medical Association,* 1976, *236*:861–3. P. 139.

"The need for a new medical model: a challenge for biomedicine," *Science,* April 8, 1977, *196*:129–36. Pp. 2, 6, 22.

Engelhardt, H. T. Jr. and Spicker, S. F. (Eds.). *Evaluation and Explanation in the Biomedical Sciences.* Dortrecht, Holland: D. Reidel Publishing Co., 1974. P. 22.

Engle, R. L. "Medical diagnosis: present, past, and future. II. Philosophical foundations and historical development of our concepts of health, disease, and diagnosis," *Archives of Internal Medicine,* 1963, *112*:520–43. P. 166.

Engle, R. L., and Davis, B. J. "Medical diagnosis: present, past and future. I. Present concepts of the meaning and limitations of medical diagnosis," *Archives of Internal Medicine,* 1963, *112*:512–19. Pp. 144, 145, 166.

Epstein, S. S. *The Politics of Cancer.* Totowa, NJ: Sierra Club Books, 1978. P. 23.

Fabrega, H., Jr. "The need for an ethnomedical science," *Science,* September 19, 1975, *189*:969–75. Pp. 10, 17, 23.

"Toward a theory of human disease," *Journal of Nervous and Mental Disease,* 1976, *162*(5):299–312. Pp. 23, 146, 167.

Fabrega, H., Jr., and Manning, P. K. "Disease, illness, and deviant careers," in Scott, R. A., and Douglas, J. D. (Eds.). *Theoretical Perspectives on Deviance.* New York: Basic Books, 1972. P. 166.

Faris, R. E. L., and Dunham, H. W. *Mental Disorders in Urban Areas.* Chicago: University of Chicago Press, 1939 (Phoenix Paperback Edition, 1965). Pp. 28, 29, 30, 31, 32, 51, 63, 75.

"Fear of finals: 'illness up'." *Howard Gazette,* January 12, 1979. Pp. 211, 217.

Feighner, J. P., Robins, E., Guze, S. B., Woodruff, R. A., Winokur, G., and Munoz, R. "Diagnostic criteria for use in psychiatric research," *Archives of General Psychiatry,* 1972, *26*:57–63. P. 167.

Feinstein, A. R. *Clinical Judgement.* Baltimore, MD: Williams & Wilkins, 1967. Pp. 144, 166.

Feldman, R. A. "Leprosy surveillance in the USA: 1949–1970," *International Journal of Leprosy,* 1968, *37*:458–60. P. 192.

Ferman, L., and Gordus, J. (Eds.). *The Consequences of Work Transition: Resource Papers in Mental Health and the Economy*. Kalamazoo, MI: UpJohn Institute, 1980. P. 76.

Fiore, N. "Fighting cancer: one patient's perspective," *New England Journal of Medicine*, 1979, *300:*284–9. Pp. 126, 140.

Flexner, A. *Medical Education in the United States and Canada*. New York: Carnegie Foundation for the Advancement of Teaching, Bulletin No. 4, 1910. Pp. 227, 228, 247.

Fontana, A., Marcus, J., Nobel, B., and Rakusin, J. "Prehospitalization coping styles of psychiatric patients: the goal directedness of life events," *Journal of Nervous and Mental Disease*, 1972, *155:*311–21. P. 77.

Foucault, M. *The Birth of the Clinic: An Archeology of Medical Perception*. New York: Pantheon Books, 1973. Pp. 220, 226, 246, 247.

Discipline and Punish: The Birth of the Prison. New York: Pantheon Books, 1977. P. 246.

Fox, R. "Training for uncertainty," in Merton, R. K., Reader, G., and Kendall, P. L. (Eds.). *The Student Physician*. Cambridge, MA: Harvard University Press, 1957. Pp. 123, 124, 139, 167.

Fox, R., and Swazey, J. *The Courage to Fail: A Social View of Organ Transplants and Dialysis*, 2nd ed. Chicago: University of Chicago Press, 1979. P. 249.

Francis, V., Korsch, B. M., and Morris, M. J. "Gaps in doctor–patient communication," *New England Journal of Medicine*, 1969, *280:*535–40. Pp. 106, 107, 136.

Freeman, B., Negrete, V., Davis, M., and Korsch, B. "Gaps in doctor–patient communication: doctor–patient interaction analysis," *Pediatric Research*, 1970, *5:*298–311. Pp. 106, 107, 137.

Freeman, H. Levine, S., and Reeder, L. (Eds.). *Handbook of Medical Sociology*. Englewood Cliffs, NJ: Prentice-Hall, 1972. P. 139.

Friedman, H. S. "Nonverbal communication between patients and medical practitioners," *Journal of Social Issues*, 1979, *35:*89–99. Pp. 138, 139.

Friedson, E. "Dilemmas in the doctor–patient relationship," in Rose, A. (Ed.). *Human Behavior and Social Process*. Boston: Houghton-Mifflin, 1962. Pp. 134, 135, 140.

(Ed.). *The Hospital in Modern Society*. New York: Free Press of Glencoe, 1963. P. 102.

Profession of Medicine: A Study of the Sociology of Applied Knowledge. New York: Dodd, Mead, 1970. Pp. 17, 23, 80, 101, 102, 135, 140, 205, 206, 216.

Garbarino, J. "A preliminary study of some ecological correlates of child abuse: the impact of socioeconomic stress on mothers," *Child Development*, 1976, *47:*178–85. P. 75.

Garfield, C. (Ed.). *Stress and Survival*. Saint Louis, MO: C. V. Mosby, 1979. P. 249.

Garmezy, N. "Children at risk: the search for the antecedents of schizophrenia. Part I. Conceptual models and research methods," *Schizophrenia Bulletin*, Spring 1974, No. 8:14–92. P. 53.

"Children at risk: the search for the antecedents of schizophrenia. Part II: Ongo-

ing research programs, issues, and intervention," *Schizophrenia Bulletin,*
Summer 1974, No. 9:55–125. P. 53.

Gersten, J., Langner, T., Eisenberg, J., and Orzeck, L. "Child behavior and life
events: undesirable change or change per se?" in Dohrenwend, B. P., and
Dohrenwend, B. S. (Eds.). *Stressful Life Events: Their Nature and Effects.*
New York: John Wiley & Sons, 1974. P. 77.

Gersten, J., Langner, T., Eisenberg, J., and Simcha-Fagan, O. "An evaluation of
the etiologic role of stressful life changes in psychological disorders," *Journal
of Health and Social Behavior,* 1977, *18:*228–44. P. 77.

Geil, R., and van Luijk, J. N. "Leprosy in Ethiopian society," *International Journal of Leprosy,* 1970, *38:*187–98. Pp. 192, 193.

Gilbert, J. *Designing the Industrial State: The Intellectual Pursuit of Collectivism
in America, 1880–1940.* Chicago: Quadrangle Books, 1972. Pp. 228, 247.

Gillam, R. F., and Banshy, A. "Diagnosis and management of patient noncompliance," *Journal of the American Medical Association,* 1974,
*288:*1563–7. P. 138.

Gimpel, J. *The Medieval Machine: The Industrial Revolution of the Middle Ages.*
New York: Holt, Rinehart and Winston, 1976. P. 246.

Glaser, B. G., and Strauss, A. L. *Awareness of Dying.* Chicago: Aldine, 1965. Pp.
108, 137, 240, 241, 242, 248, 249.

Glick, L. B. "Medicine as an ethnographic category: the Gimi of the New Guinea
Highlands," *Ethnology,* 1967, *6*(1):31–56. P. 23.

Goffman, E. *Asylums: Essays on the Social Situation of Mental Patients and Other
Inmates.* New York: Doubleday Anchor, 1961. Pp. 94, 103, 248.

Golden, J. S., and Johnston, G. D. "Problems of distortion in doctor–patient
communications," *Psychiatry in Medicine,* 1970, *1:*127–49. Pp. 111, 130, 137,
139, 140.

Goldfarb, W. *Childhood Schizophrenia.* Cambridge, MA: Harvard University
Press, 1961. P. 53.

Goldstein, M. J., and Rodnick, E. H. "The family's contribution to the etiology of
schizophrenia: current status," *Schizophrenia Bulletin,* Fall 1975, No.
14:48–63. P. 53.

Goodman, E. "The Shanti project: a hopeful scenario for the dying," in Garfield, C.
(Ed.). *Stress and Survival.* Saint Louis, MO: C. V. Mosby, 1979. P. 249.

Gore, S. "The effect of social support in moderating the health consequences of
unemployment," *Journal of Health and Social Behavior,* 1978, *19:*157–65. P.
77.

Gorer, G. *Death, Grief and Mourning in Contemporary Britain.* London: Cresset
Press, 1965. Pp. 244, 249.

Goss, M. E. W. "Patterns of bureaucracy among hospital staff physicians," in
Friedson, E. (Ed.). *The Hospital in Modern Society.* New York: Free Press of
Glencoe, 1963. P. 102.

Gould, R. J. "Evolution's erratic pace," *Natural History,* May, 1977, *86*(5):12–16.
Pp. 226, 247.

Gove, W. R. (Ed.). *The Labeling of Deviance.* New York: John Wiley & Sons,
1975. P. 166.

Greenblatt, M., Levinson, D. J., and Williams, R. H. (Eds.). *The Patient and the Mental Hospital*. Glencoe, IL: The Free Press, 1957. Pp. 103, 139.

Greenblatt, M., York, R. H., and Brown, E. L. *From Custodial to Therapeutic Patient Care in Mental Hospitals*. New York: Russell Sage Foundation, 1955. P. 103.

Groves, J. E. "Taking care of the hateful patient," *New England Journal of Medicine*, 1978, *298*:883–7. Pp. 120, 138.

Gussow, Z., and Tracy, G. "Status, ideology, and adaptation to stigmatized illness: a study of leprosy," *Human Organization*, 1968, *27*:316–25. P. 193.

"Stigma and the leprosy phenomenon: the social history of a disease in the nineteenth and twentieth centuries," *Bulletin of the History of Medicine*, 1970, *44*:424–49. P. 192.

"The use of archival materials in the analysis and interpretation of field data: a case study in the institutionalization of the myth of leprosy as 'leper,'" *American Anthropologist*, 1971, *73*:695–709. Pp. 177, 192, 193.

Haan, N. "Psychological meanings of unfavorable medical forecasts," in Stone, G., Cohen, F., and Adler, N. (Eds.). *Health Psychology*. San Francisco: Jossey-Bass, 1979. P. 137.

Haire, D. "The cultural warping of childbirth," in Ehrenreich, J. (Ed.). *The Cultural Crisis of Modern Medicine*. New York: Monthly Review Press, 1978. Pp. 236, 248.

Hansen: Research Notes, 1975, *6*(1–2):202. P. 187, 193.

Harwood, A. "The hot–cold theory of disease: implications for treatment of Puerto Rican patients," *Journal of the American Medical Association*, 1971, *216*:1153. P. 246.

Hassleblad, O. W. "Leprosy . . . present-day understanding," American Leprosy Mission, n.d. P. 193.

Hayes-Bautista, D. E. "Modifying the treatment: patient compliance, patient control and medical care," *Social Science and Medicine*, 1976, *10*:233–8. P. 101.

Hayes-Bautista, D., and Harveston, D. "Holistic health care," *Social Policy*, April 1977:7–13. P. 140.

Heffner, L. T. "A study of Hansen's disease in Ceylon," *Southern Medical Journal*, 1969, *62*:977–85. P. 192.

Hertroijs, A. R. "A study of some factors affecting the attendance of patients in a leprosy control scheme," *International Journal of Leprosy*, 1974, *42*:419–27. P. 192.

Hinde, R. A. (Ed.). *Nonverbal Communication*. Cambridge: Cambridge University Press, 1972. P. 138.

Hinshelwood, R. D., and Manning, N. (Eds.). *Therapeutic Communities: Reflections and Progress*. London: Routledge and Kegan Paul, 1979. P. 103.

Hollingshead, A. B., and Redlich, F. C. *Social Class and Mental Illness*. New York: John Wiley & Sons, 1958. Pp. 37, 38, 39, 40, 52, 85, 102.

Holmes, R., and Masuda, M. "Life change and illness susceptibility," in Dohrenwend, B. P., and Dohrenwend, B. S. (Eds.). *Stressful Life Events: Their Nature and Effects*. New York: John Wiley & Sons, 1974. P. 76.

Holmes, T., and Rahe, R. "The social readjustment rating scale," *Journal of Psychosomatic Research,* 1967, *11:*213–18. P. 76.

Howard, L. "Workplace and residence communities of Indian factory and non-factory workers." Paper presented at the Annual Meeting of the American Sociological Association, Chicago, September 1977. P. 77.

Hughes, C. C., Tremblay, M., Rapport, R. N., and Leighton, A. H. *People of Cove and Woodlet.* New York: Basic Books, 1960. P. 52.

Hulka, B., Cassel, J., Kupper, L., and Purdette, J. "Communication, compliance and concordance between physicians and patients with prescribed medication," *American Journal of Public Health,* 1976, *66:*847–53. Pp. 117, 138.

Illich, I. *Medical Nemesis.* New York: Bantam Books, 1977. Pp. 164, 168, 195, 196, 200, 216, 219, 220, 225, 240, 246, 248.

Ingle, D. J. (Ed.). *Life and Disease.* New York: Basic Books, 1963. Pp. 22, 23.

Israel, L. *Conquering Cancer.* New York: Random House, 1978. Pp. 18, 19, 23.

Jaco, E. G. (Ed.). *Patients, Physicians and Illness.* Glencoe, IL: The Free Press, 1958. P. 217.

Jacob, T. "Family interaction in disturbed and normal families: a methodological and substantive review," *Psychological Bulletin,* 1975, *82*(1):33–65. Pp. 47, 48, 53.

Jacobs, M., Spilken, A., Norman, M., and Anderson, L. "Life stress and respiratory illness," *Psychosomatic Medicine,* 1970, *32:*233–42. P. 76.

Jahoda, M., Lazarsfeld, P., and Zeisel, H. *Marienthal, The Sociography of an Unemployed Community.* Chicago: Aldine, Atherton, 1971. P. 75.

Jaques, E. *Equitable Payment.* New York: John Wiley & Sons, 1961. P. 76.

Johnson, T. J. *Professions and Power.* London: Macmillan, 1972. P. 23.

Jones, E. "Social class and psychotherapy: a critical review of research," *Psychiatry,* 1974, *37:*307–20. Pp. 108, 137.

Jones, M. *The Therapeutic Community.* New York: Basic Books, 1953. Pp. 95, 103.

Jones, M., and Rapport, R. "The absorption of new doctors into a therapeutic community," in Greenblatt, M., Levinson, D., and Williams, R. (Eds.). *The Patient and the Mental Hospital.* Glencoe, IL: The Free Press, 1957. P. 139.

Kahne, M. "Suicide in mental hospitals: a study of the effects of personnel and patient turnover," *Journal of Health and Social Behavior,* 1968, *9*(3):255–66. Pp. 93, 94, 101.

Kapoor, J. N. "Lepers in the city of Lucknow," *Indian Journal of Social Work,* 1961, *22:*239–46. P. 192.

Kasl, S., Gore, S., and Cobb, S. "The experience of losing a job: reported changes in health, symptoms, and illness behavior," *Psychosomatic Medicine,* 1975, *37:*106–22. Pp. 68, 77.

Kastenbaum, R. "The interpersonal context of death in a geriatric institution." Abstract of paper presented at the 17th Annual Scientific Meeting, Gerontological Society, Minneapolis, MN, October 29–31, 1964. P. 249.

Katz, M. N., Cole, J. O., and Barton, W. E. (Eds.). *The Role and Methodology of Classification in Psychiatry and Psychopathology.* Washington, DC: U.S. Government Printing Office, 1968 (PHS Publ. No. 1584). Pp. 166, 167.

Kleinman, A., Eisenberg, L., and Good, B. "Culture, illness, and care: clinical lessons from anthropologic and cross-cultural research," *Annals of Internal Medicine*, 1978, *88*(2):251-8. P. 166.

Knapp, M. *Nonverbal Communication in Human Interaction*. New York: Holt, Rinehart, 1972. P. 138.

Kohn, M. L. "The interaction of social class and other factors in the etiology of schizophrenia," *American Journal of Psychiatry*, 1976, *133*(2):177-80. Pp. 40, 41, 52.

Kohn, M. *Class and Conformity*, 2nd ed. Chicago: University of Chicago Press, 1977. P. 137.

Komarovsky, M. *The Unemployed Man and His Family*. New York: Dryden Press, 1940. Pp. 69, 77.

Komora, P. O., and Clark, M. A. "Mental disease in the crisis," *Mental Hygiene*, April 1935, *19*:289-301. Pp. 56, 74.

Koos, E. L. *The Health of Regionville*. New York: Columbia University Press, 1954. P. 102.

Koran, L. M. "The reliability of clinical methods, data and judgements: I," *New England Journal of Medicine*, 1975, *293*(13):642-6. Pp. 167, 168.

"The reliability of clinical methods, data and judgements: II," *New England Journal of Medicine*, 1975, *293*(14):695-701. Pp. 146, 167, 168.

Korsch, B. M., Gozzi, E., and Francis, V. "Gaps in doctor-patient communication: doctor-patient interaction and patient satisfaction," *Pediatrics*, 1968, *42*:855-71. Pp. 106, 107, 136.

Korsch, B., and Negrete, V. F., "Doctor-patient communication," *Scientific American*, 1972, *227*:66-74. Pp. 101, 106, 107, 108, 116, 130, 136, 138, 140.

Kramer, E. "Judgement of personal characteristics and emotions from nonverbal properties of speech," *Psychological Bulletin*, 1963, *60*:408-20. P. 138.

Kramer, M. "A discussion of the concepts of incidence and prevalence as related to epidemiologic studies of mental disorder," *American Journal of Public Health*, 1957, *47*:826-40. P. 52.

"Classification of mental disorders for epidemiologic and medical care purposes: current status, problems, and needs," in Katz, M. M., Cole, J. O., and Barton, W. E. (Eds.). *The Role and Methodology of Classification in Psychiatry and Psychopathology*. Washington, DC: U.S. Government Printing Office, 1968 (PHS Publ. No. 1584). Pp. 147, 167.

Krause, E. A. *Power and Illness: The Political Sociology of Health Care*. New York: Elsevier, 1977. P. 216.

Kubler-Ross, E. *On Death and Dying*. New York: Macmillan, 1969. Pp. 245, 249.

Kunitz, S. J. "Equilibrium theory in social psychiatry: the work of the Leightons," *Psychiatry*, 1970, *33*(3):312-28. Pp. 36, 52.

"Professionalism and social control in the progressive era: the case of the Flexner report," *Social Problems*, 1974, *22*:16-27. Pp. 227, 230, 247, 248.

Laver, R. "The social readjustment scale and anxiety: a cross-cultural study," *Journal of Psychosomatic Research*, 1973, *17*:171-4. P. 76.

Lazarre, A., Eisenthal, S., and Wasserman, L. "The customer approach to patienthood: attending to patients' requests in a walk-in clinic," *Archives of General Psychiatry*, 1975, *32*:553-8. Pp. 128, 140.

Lazarre, A., Eisenthal, S., Wasserman, L. and Havford, T. C. "Patient requests in a walk-in clinic," *Comprehensive Psychiatry*, 1975, *16:*466–77. Pp. 128, 140.

Lazarus, R. *Psychological Stress and the Coping Process*. New York: McGraw-Hill Book Company, 1966. P. 76.

Lechat, M. "Sulfone resistance and leprosy control," *International Journal of Leprosy*, 1978, *46:* 64–7. P. 194.

Lee, E. S. "Socio-economic and migration differentials in mental disease, New York State, 1949–51," *Milbank Memorial Fund Quarterly*, 1963, *XLI* (3):249–68. Pp. 31, 51.

Leighton, A. H. *My Name is Legion*. New York: Basic Books, 1959. P. 52.

Leighton, A. H., Clausen, J. N., and Wilson, R. N. (Eds.). *Explorations in Social Psychiatry*. London: Tavistock Publications, 1957. P. 22.

Leighton, D. C., Harding, J. S., Macklin, D. B., Macmillan, A. M., and Leighton, A. H. *The Character of Danger: Psychiatric Symptoms in Selected Communities*. New York: Basic Books, 1963. Pp. 34, 35, 51, 52.

Leslie, C. (Ed.). *Asian Medical Systems*. Berkeley: University of California Press, 1976. P. 246.

Levin, H. "Work, the staff of life." Paper presented at the Annual Convention of the American Psychological Association, Chicago, September 1975. P. 76.

Levine, S., and Kozloff, M. A. "The sick role: assessment and overview," *Annual Review of Sociology*, 1978, *4:*317–43. P. 139.

Levine, S., and Scotch, N. (Eds.). *Social Stress*. Chicago: Aldine Press, 1970. P. 76.

Levy, R., Rifkind, B., Dennis, B., and Ernst, N. (Eds.). *Nutritions, Lipids, and Coronary Heart Disease*. New York: Raven Press, 1979. P. 138.

Liebow, E. *Tally's Corner: A Study of Negro Street Corner Men*. Boston: Little, Brown, 1967. Pp. 71, 77.

Lief, H. I. (Ed.). *The Psychological Basis of Medical Practice*. New York: Harper and Row, 1963. P. 139.

Lief, H. I., and Fox, R. C. "Training for 'detached concern' in medical students," in Lief, H. I. (Ed.). *The Psychological Basis of Medical Practice*. New York: Harper & Row, 1963. Pp. 122, 139.

Liem, R. "Economic change and individual psychological functioning," Final Report, Research Grant No. R03MH27443, Center for Metropolitan Studies, National Institute of Mental Health, September 1977, app. A. P. 75.

Lindemann, E. "Symptomatology and management of acute grief," *American Journal of Psychiatry*, 1944, *101:*141–8. P. 75.

Lipkin, M. "On lying to patients," *Newsweek,* June 4, 1979, p. 13. P. 137.

Lipowksi, S. J., Lipsitt, D. R., and Whybrow, P. C. (Eds.). *Psychosomatic Medicine*. New York: Oxford University Press, 1977. P. 136.

Loeb, J. *The Mechanistic Conception of Life*. Cambridge, MA: Belknap Press, 1964. P. 246.

Lush, B. (Ed.). *Concepts of Medicine*. New York: Pergamon Press, 1961. P. 2.

MacMahon, B., Pugh, T. F., and Ipsen, J. *Epidemiologic Methods*. Boston: Little, Brown, 1960. P. 51.

Mahl, G., and Schulze, G. "Psychological research in the extralinguistic area," in Sebeok, T. A., Hagnes, A. S., and Bateson, M. C. (Eds.). *Approaches to Semiotics*. London: Mouton, 1964. Pp. 138, 139.

Malzberg, B. *Social and Biological Aspects of Mental Disease.* New York: State Hospital Press, 1940. P. 75.

March, J. G. (Ed.). *Handbook of Organizations.* Chicago: Rand McNally, 1965. P. 102.

Martí-Ibañez, F. *A Prelude to Medical History.* New York: MD Publications, 1961. P. 246.

Ariel: Essays on the Arts and the History and Philosophy of Medicine. New York: MD Publications, 1962. P. 245.

McIntosh, J. "Processes of communication, information seeking and control associated with cancer," *Social Science and Medicine,* 1974, *8:*157–87. Pp. 108, 137, 140.

McKeown, T., and Lowe, C. R. *An Introduction to Social Medicine.* Philadelphia: F. A. Davis, 1966. Pp. 51, 101, 199, 200, 216.

McLaughlin, M., and Sum, A. "Interrelationships between unemployment and poverty in Massachusetts," Massachusetts Department of Manpower Development, n.d. P. 78.

McNeill, W. *Plagues and Peoples.* New York: Doubleday, 1976. Pp. 25, 26, 51, 101, 199, 216.

Mechanic, D. *Medical Sociology.* New York: The Free Press, 1968. P. 101.

Mercer, J. R. *Labeling the Mentally Retarded.* Berkeley: University of California Press, 1973. Pp. 156, 157, 158, 159, 160, 164, 168, 197.

Merton, R. K., Reader, G., and Kendall, P. L. (Eds.). *The Student Physician.* Cambridge, MA: Harvard University Press, 1957. Pp. 139, 167.

Meyer, A. "The life chart and the obligation of specifying positive data in psychopathological diagnosis," in Winters, E. E. (Ed.). *The Collected Papers of Adolph Meyer, Vol. III, Medical Teaching.* Baltimore, MD: The Johns Hopkins Press, 1951. Pp. 65, 76.

Meyer, R. W. "Report of the Agent, Board of Health at the Leper Settlement, Molokai, Hawaii," in *Appendix to the Report on Leprosy of the President of the Board of Health to the Legislative Assembly.* Honolulu, Hawaii, 1886. P. 192.

Miller, H. "Fifty years after Flexner," *Lancet,* 1966, *II:*647–54. P. 247.

Miller, J. *The Body in Question.* New York: Random House, 1978. Pp. 220, 246.

Miller, S. M., and Mishler, E. G. "Social class, mental illness, and American psychiatry: an expository review," *Milbank Memorial Fund Quarterly,* 1959, *37*(2):174–99. P. 52.

Millman, M. *The Unkindest Cut.* New York: Morrow, 1977. Pp. 128, 129, 130, 131, 137, 140.

Milmoe, S., Rosenthal, R., Blane, H. T., Chafetz, M. E., and Wolf, I. "The doctor's voice: postdictor of successful referral of alchoholic patients," *Journal of Abnormal Psychology,* 1967, *72:*78–84. Pp. 118, 138.

Mishler, E. G. "Meaning in context: is there any other kind?," *Harvard Educational Review,* 1979, *49*(1):1–19. P. 22.

Mishler, E. G., and Scotch, N. A. "Sociocultural factors in the epidemiology of schizophrenia," *Psychiatry,* 1963, *26:*315–53. Pp. 38, 40, 52.

Mishler, E. G., and Tropp, A. "Status and interaction in a psychiatric hospital," *Human Relations,* 1956, *IX:*187–205. P. 102.

Mishler, E. G., and Waxler, N. E. "Decision processes in psychiatric hospitalization: patients referred, accepted and admitted to a psychiatric hospital," *American Sociological Review,* 1963, *28:*576–87. Pp. 102, 168.

"Family interaction patterns and schizoprenia: a review of current theories," *Merrill-Palmer Quarterly,* 1965, *11:*269–315; also in Wechsler, H., Solomon, L., and Kramer, B. M. (Eds.). *Social Psychology and Mental Health.* New York: Holt, Rinehart & Winston, 1970. P. 52.

"Family interaction and schizophrenia: alternative frameworks of interpretation," in Rosenthal, D., and Kety, S. S. (Eds.). *The Transmission of Schizophrenia.* New York: Pergamon Press, 1968. Pp. 46, 47, 53.

(Eds.). *Family Processes and Schizophrenia: Theory and Selected Experimental Studies.* New York: Science House, 1968. P. 52.

Interaction in Families. New York: John Wiley & Sons, 1968. Pp. 44, 46, 47, 53.

Mitroff, I. I. *The Subjective Side of Science.* New York: American Elsevier, 1974. P. 23.

Moos, R. A. *Evaluating Treatment Environments.* New York: John Wiley & Sons, 1974. Pp. 88, 102.

Morse, N., and Weiss, R. "The function and meaning of work and the job," *American Sociological Review,* 1955, *20:*191–8. P. 76.

Mortson, M. "Compliance with medical requirements: a review of literature," *Nursing Research,* 1970, *19:*312–23. P. 138.

Mosher, L. R., and Feinsilver, D. *Special Report: Schizophrenia.* Washington, DC: U.S. Public Health Service Publication No. (HSM) 72-9007, 1971. P. 53.

Mouritz, A. "Report of the Superintendent of the Molokai Leprosy Hospital," in *Appendix to the Report on Leprosy of the President of the Board of Health to the Legislative Assembly.* Honolulu, Hawaii, 1886. P. 192.

Mumford, E. *Interns: From Students to Physicians.* Cambridge, MA: Harvard University Press, 1970. Pp. 124, 137, 139.

Mumford, L. "The myth of the machine," in *The Pentagon of Power,* Vol. 2. New York: Harcourt, Brace, Jovanovich, 1964. P. 246.

Murphy, J. M. "Psychiatric labeling in cross-cultural perspective," *Science,* March 12, 1976, *191:*1019–28. Pp. 13, 23.

Myers, J. K., and Bean, L. L. *A Decade Later: A Follow-Up of Social Class and Mental Illness.* New York: John Wiley & Sons, 1968. P. 102.

Myers, J., Lindenthal, J., and Pepper, M. "Social class, life events, and psychiatric symptoms: a longitudinal study," in Dohrenwend, B. P., and Dohrenwend, B. S. (Eds.). *Stressful Life Events: Their Nature and Effects.* New York: John Wiley & Sons, 1974. P. 77.

"Life events, social integration, and psychiatric symptomatology," *Journal of Health and Social Behavior,* 1975, *16:*121–7. P. 77.

Myers, J. K., and Schaffer, L. "Social stratification and psychiatric practice: a study of an out-patient clinic," *American Sociological Review,* 1954, *19*(3):307–10. Pp. 85, 102.

National Center for Health Statistics. "Medical care, health status, and family income: United States," *Series 10, No. 9.* Washington, DC: U.S. Government Printing Office, May 1964, pp. 24–5. Pp. 85, 101.

Needleman, J. "The two sciences of medicine," *Parabola*, August 1978, *111*(3):38. P. 246.

Neitsky, N. "Dying in a system of 'good care,' case report and analysis," in Garfield, C. (Ed.). *Stress and Survival*. Saint Louis, MO: C. V. Mosby, 1979. P. 249.

Noble, D. *America by Design: Science, Technology, and the Rise of Corporate Capitalism*. New York: Alfred A. Knopf, 1977. Pp. 228, 229, 247.

Obeyesekere, G. "The impact of Ayurvedic ideas on the culture and the individual in Sri Lanka," in Leslie, C. (Ed.). *Asian Medical Systems*. Berkeley: University of California Press, 1976. Pp. 219, 246.

Obeyesekere, G. "The theory and practice of psychological medicine in the Ayurvedic tradition," *Culture, Medicine and Psychiatry*, 1977, *1*:155–81. P. 246.

Oken, D. "What to tell cancer patients: a study of medical attitudes," *Journal of the American Medical Association*, 1961, *175*:1120–8. P. 137.

Oppenheimer, R. H. "Significance of symptoms in medical teaching," *Southern Medical Journal*, 1930, *233*:58. P. 139.

Park, R. E., and Burgess, E. W. *The City*. Chicago: University of Chicago Press, 1925. Pp. 29, 51.

Parsons, T. *The Social System*. Glencoe, IL: The Free Press, 1951. Pp. 101, 125, 126, 139.

"Definitions of health and illness in the light of American values and social structure," in Jaco, E. G. (Ed.). *Patients, Physicians and Illness*. Glencoe, IL: The Free Press, 1958. P. 217.

"The sick role and the role of the physician reconsidered," *Milbank Memorial Fund Quarterly*, 1975, *53*:257–78. Pp. 125, 126, 133, 134, 135, 139, 140.

Paykel, E., Myers, J., Dienelt, M., Klerman, J., Lindenthal, J., and Pepper, M. "Life events and depression: a controlled study," *Archives of General Psychiatry*, 1969, *21*:253–60. P. 76.

Pearse, I. H., and Crocker, L. H. *The Peckham Experiment*. London: Allen & Unwin, 1943. P. 102.

Pellegrino, E. "Medicine and philosophy: some notes on the flirtation of Minerva and Aesculapius," Annual Oration of the Society for Health and Human Values. Washington, DC, November 8, 1973. P. 22.

Perrow, C. "Hospitals: technology, structure and goals," in March, J. G. (Ed.). *Handbook of Organizations*. Chicago: Rand McNally, 1965. P. 102.

Pierce, A. "The economic cycle and the social suicide rate," *American Sociological Review*, 1967, *32*:457–62. P. 75.

Plaja, A., and Cohen, S. "Communication between physicians and patients in out-patient clinics: social and cultural factors," *Milbank Memorial Fund Quarterly*, 1968, *46*:161–213. Pp. 109, 137.

Posner, T. "Magical elements in orthodox medicine," in Dingwall, R., Heath, C., Reid, M., and Stacey, M. (Eds.). *Health Care and Health Knowledge*. New York: Prodist, 1977. Pp. 150, 151, 167, 168.

Powell, D., and Driscoll, P. "Middle class professionals face unemployment," *Society*, 1973, *10*:18–26. P. 76.

Pugh, T. F., and MacMahon, B. *Epidemiologic Findings in United States Hospital Data*. Boston: Little, Brown, 1962. P. 75.

Racy, J. "Death in an Arab culture," *Annals of the New York Academy of Science,* 1964, 871 – 9. P. 137.

Rahe, R., and Paasikivi, J. "Psychosocial factors and myocardial infarction: II, An outpatient study in Sweden," *Journal of Psychosomatic Research,* 1971, *15:*33 – 9. P. 76.

Raimbault, G., Cachin, O., Limal, J., Eliacheff, C., and Rapoport, R. "Aspects of communication between patients and doctors: an analysis of the discourse in medical interviews," *Pediatrics,* 1975, *55:*401 – 5. Pp. 118, 138.

Rapoport, R. N. *Community as Doctor.* London: Tavistock, 1960. Pp. 93, 103.

Ravenscroft, K., "Multiple Integrated Group (MIG) theory: a model for milieu rhythms and cycles," Unpublished, April 1970. Pp. 93, 103.

"Milieu process during the residency turnover: the human cost of psychiatric education," *American Journal of Psychiatry,* 1975, *132*(5):506 – 12. P. 103.

Reader, L. G. "The patient-client as a consumer: some observations on the changing professional client relationship," *Journal of Health and Social Behavior,* 1972, *13:*406 – 12. Pp. 128, 140.

The Real Paper, May 2, 1976. P. 249.

Redlich, F. C. "The concept of health in psychiatry," in Leighton, A. H., Clausen, J. N., and Wilson, R. N. (Eds.). *Explorations in Social Psychiatry.* London: Tavistock Publication, 1957. Pp. 3, 22.

"Discussion of papers on ecology and epidemiology of mental illness," in *Symposium on Preventive and Social Psychiatry.* Walter Reed Army Institute of Research. Washington, DC: U.S. Government Printing Office, 1958. Pp. 39, 52.

Reeder, G., Pratt, L., and Mudd, M. "What patients expect from their doctors," *Modern Hospital,* 1957, *89:*88. P. 136.

Reise, W. *The Conception of Disease.* New York: Philosophical Library, 1953. P. 22.

Reiser, S.J. *Medicine and the Reign of Technology.* Cambridge: Cambridge University Press, 1978. Pp. 79, 101, 123, 139, 224, 246.

"The medical student and the machine," *Harvard Medical Alumni Bulletin,* September – October 1978, *53*(1):14 – 16.

Reitz, H. J. *Behavior in Organizations.* Homewood, IL: R. D. Irwin, 1977. P. 103.

Relman, A. S. "Holistic medicine," *New England Journal of Medicine,* 1979, *300:*312 – 13. P. 140.

Richmond, J. *Currents in American Medicine: A Developmental View of Medical Care and Education.* Cambridge, MA: Harvard University Press, 1969. P. 247.

Rose, A. (Ed.). *Human Behavior and Social Process.* Boston: Houghton-Mifflin, 1962. P. 140.

Rosenthal, D., and Kety, S. S. (Eds.). *The Transmission of Schizophrenia.* New York: Pergamon Press, 1968. P. 53.

Ross, J. A. "Social class and medical care," *Journal of Health and Human Behavior,* 1962, *4:*35 – 40. P. 102.

Ross, W. F. "Questions people ask about leprosy," *American Leprosy Missions,* (n.d.) Pp. 188, 193.

Roth, J. *Timetables.* Indianapolis, IN: Bobbs-Merrill, 1963. P. 137.

Ryle, J. "The meaning of normal," in Lush, B. (Ed.). *Concepts of Medicine*. New York: Pergamon Press, 1961. Pp. 5, 6, 22.

Ryrie, G. A. "The psychology of leprosy," *Leprosy Review*, 1951, *22:* 1, 13– 24. P. 192.

Schlien, J., Hunt, H., Matarazzo, J., and Savage, C. (Eds.). *Research in Psychotherapy, Vol. 3*. Washington, DC: American Psychological Association, 1968. P. 139.

Schur, E. M. *Labeling Deviant Behavior*. New York: Harper & Row, 1971. Pp. 166, 192.

Schwartz, M. S., Schwartz, C. G., Field, M. G., Mishler, E. G., Olshansky, S., Pitts, J. R., Rapoport, R., and Vaughan, W. T., Sr. *Social Approaches to Mental Patient Care*. New York: Columbia University Press, 1964. P. 103.

Sclar, E., and Hoffman, V. *Planning Mental Health Services for a Declining Economy*. Final Report to the National Center for Health Services Research, Waltham, MA: Brandeis University, 1978. P. 75.

Scott, R. A. *The Making of Blind Men*. New York: Russell Sage, 1969. Pp. 23, 160, 161, 162, 163, 164, 168, 186, 190, 191, 193, 194.

Scott, R. A., and Douglas, J. D. (Eds.). *Theoretical Perspectives on Deviance*. New York: Basic Books, 1972. P. 166.

Sebeok, T. A., Hagnes, A. S., and Bateson, M. C. (Eds.). *Approaches to Semiotics*. London: Mouton, 1964. P. 138.

Seeman, M., and Evans, J. W. "Stratification and hospital care: I. The performance of the medical intern," *American Sociological Review*, 1961, *26*(1):67– 80. Pp. 90, 91, 102.

"Stratification and hospital care: II. The objective criteria of performance," *American Sociological Review*, 1961, *26*(2):193– 204. Pp. 91, 102.

Selye, H. *The Stress of Life*. New York: McGraw-Hill Book Company, 1956. Pp. 64. 76.

"Set apart," London: The Leprosy Mission, 1978. Pp. 184, 193.

Shem, S. *House of God*. New York: Marek, 1978. Pp. 137, 139.

Shiloh, A. "A case study of disease and culture in action: leprosy among the Hausa of northern Nigeria," *Human Organization*, 1965, *24:* 140– 7. Pp. 192, 193.

Shlien, J., Hunt, H., Matarazzo, J., and Savage, C. (Eds.). *Research in Psychotherapy, Vol. 3*. Washington, DC: American Psychological Association, 1968. P. 139.

Shuy, R. "Problems of communication in the cross-cultural medical interview," *Working Papers: Sociolinguistics #19*. Washington, DC, mimeo, 1974. Pp. 110, 137, 139, 140.

Sigerist, H. E. *A History of Medicine, Vol. 1, Primitive and Archaic Medicine*. New York: Oxford University Press, 1951. P. 246.

A History of Medicine, Vol. 2, Greek, Hindu and Persian Medicine. New York: Oxford University Press, 1961. P. 246.

Sontag, S. *Illness as Metaphor*. New York: Farrar, Straus and Giroux, 1977. Pp. 245, 246, 249.

Spitzer, S. P., and Denzin, N. K. (Eds.). *The Mental Patient: Studies in the Sociology of Deviance*. New York: McGraw-Hill Book Company, 1968. P. 168.

Stanton, A. H., and Schwartz, M. S. *The Mental Hospital.* New York: Basic Books, 1954. P. 103.

The Star, 1976, *35*(3):4. Pp. 187, 193.

Steinfels, P., and Veatch, R. *Death Inside Out.* New York: Harper & Row, 1974. Pp. 248, 249.

Stimson, G. V. "Obeying doctor's orders: a view from the other side," *Social Science and Medicine,* 1974, *8:*97–104. P. 101.

Stone, G., Cohen, F., and Adler, N. (Eds.). *Health Psychology.* San Francisco: Jossey-Bass, 1917. P. 137.

Strauss, A., Schatzman, L., Ehrlich, D., Bucher, R., and Sabshin, M. "The hospital and its negotiated order," in Friedson, E. (Ed.). *The Hospital in Modern Society.* New York: Free Press of Glencoe, 1963. P. 102.

Sudnow, D. *Passing On: The Social Organization of Dying.* Englewood Cliffs, NJ: Prentice-Hall, 1967. Pp. 137, 241, 243, 249.

Szasz, T., and Hollander, M. "A contribution to the philosophy of medicine: the basic models of the doctor–patient relationship," *Archives of Internal Medicine,* 1956, *97:*585–92. Pp. 126, 127, 140.

Tausky, C. "Meaning of work among blue collar men." Paper presented at the Annual Meeting of the American Sociological Association, San Francisco, 1968. P. 76.

Temkin, O. "The history of classification in the medical sciences," in Katz, M. M., Cole, J. O., and Barton, W. E. (Eds.). *The Role and Methodology of Classification in Psychiatry and Psychopathology.* Washington, DC: U.S. Government Printing Office, 1968 (Publ. No. 1584). Pp. 154, 166, 167.

Theorell, T. "Life events before and after the onset of a premature myocardial infarction," in Dohrenwend, B. P., and Dohrenwend, B. S. (Eds.). *Stressful Life Events: Their Nature and Effects.* New York: John Wiley & Sons, 1974. P. 76.

Theorell, T., Lind, G., and Floderus, B. "The relationship of disturbing life changes and emotions to the early development of myocardial infarctions and other serious illness," *International Journal of Epidemiology,* 1975, *4:*281–93. P. 77.

Turner, R. J. "Social mobility and schizophrenia," *Journal of Health and Social Behavior,* 1968, *9:*194–203. Pp. 41, 52.

"The epidemiological study of schizophrenia: a current appraisal," *Journal of Health and Social Behavior,* 1972, *18:*360–9. Pp. 40, 52.

Turner, R. J., and Wagenfeld, M. O. "Occupational mobility and schizophrenia: an assessment of the social causation and social selection hypotheses," *American Sociological Review,* 1967, *32*(1):104–13. Pp. 41, 52.

Ullman, L. P. *Institution and Outcome: A Comparative Study of Psychiatric Hospitals.* New York: Pergamon Press, 1967. Pp. 88, 102.

U.S. Bureau of the Census. *Statistical Abstract of the United States: 1971.* Washington, DC: U.S. Government Printing Office, 1971. P. 51.

van Etten, G. M., and Anten, J. C. "Evaluation of health education in a Tanzanian leprosy scheme," *International Journal of Leprosy,* 1972, *40:*402–9. Pp. 192, 193.

Bibliography and citation index 271

Vida, F., Korsch, B., and Morris, M. J. "Gaps in doctor–patient communication," *New England Journal of Medicine,* 1969, *280*(10):535–40. P. 101.
Waitzkin, H., and Stoeckle, J. D. "Information control and the micropolitics of health care: summary of ongoing research project," *Social Science and Medicine,* 1976, *10:*263–76. Pp. 136, 140.
Waitzkin, H., Stoeckle, J. D., Beller, E., and Mons, C. "The informative process in medical care: a preliminary report with implications for instructional communication," *Instructional Science,* 1978, *7:*385–419. P. 136.
Waitzkin, H., and Waterman, B. *The Exploitation of Illness in Capitalist Society.* Indianapolis, IN: Bobbs-Merrill, 1974. Pp. 23, 195, 212, 216, 217.
Waxler, N. E. "Culture and mental illness," *Journal of Nervous and Mental Disease,* 1974, *159*(6):379–95. Pp. 12, 23.
"Parent and child effects on cognitive performance: an experimental approach to the etiological and responsive theories of schizophrenia," *Family Process,* 1974, *13*(1):1–22. Pp. 47, 53.
"Is mental illness cured in traditional societies? A theoretical analysis," *Culture, Medicine and Psychiatry,* 1977, *1:*233–53. Pp. 16, 23.
"The social career of lepers in Sri Lanka." Unpublished study, 1977. P. 192.
Waxler, N. E., and Mishler, E. G. "Hospitalization of psychiatric patients: physician-contered and family-centered influence patterns," *Journal of Health and Human Behavior,* 1963, *4:*250–7. P. 102.
Webster's New International Dictionary of the English Language, 2nd ed., Unabridged. Springfield, MA: G. & C. Merriam, 1956. P. 22.
Wechsler, H., Solomon, L., and Kramer, B. M. (Eds.). *Social Psychology and Mental Health.* New York: Holt, Rinehart & Winston, 1970. P. 52.
Weisbrod, B. A., Andreano, R. L., Baldwin, R. E., Epstein, E. H., and Kelley, A. C., with Helminiak, T. W. *Disease and Economic Development: The Impact of Parasitic Diseases in St. Lucia.* Madison: University of Wisconsin Press, 1973. Pp. 202, 203, 216.
Wertz, R., and Wertz, D. *Lying In: A Natural History of Childbirth in America.* New York: Schocken Books, 1979. Pp. 233, 234, 235, 236, 248.
Westfall, R. S. *The Construction of Modern Science: Mechanisms and Mechanics.* Cambridge: Cambridge University Press, 1977. Pp. 222, 223, 246.
White, E. L. "A graphic representation on age and income differentials in selected aspects of morbidity, disability, and utilization of health services," *Inquiry,* 1968, *5:*18–30. P. 102.
Wing, J. K., and Brown, G. W. *Institutionalism and Schizophrenia.* Cambridge: Cambridge University Press, 1970. Pp. 23, 96, 97, 103.
Winters, E. E. (Ed.). *The Collected Papers of Adolph Meyer, Vol. III, Medical Teaching.* Baltimore, MD: The Johns Hopkins Press, 1951. P. 76.
Woodsor, R. "Hospice care in terminal illness," in Garfield, C. (Ed.). *Stress and Survival.* Saint Louis, MO: C. V. Mosby, 1979. P. 249.
Work in America: Report of a Special Task Force to the Secretary of Health, Education and Welfare. Cambridge, MA: The MIT Press, 1976. P. 76.
World Health Organization. *Report of the International Pilot Study of Schizophrenia, Vol. 1.* Geneva: World Health Organization, 1973. Pp. 13, 23.

World Health Organization Expert Committee on Leprosy. *World Health Organization Technical Report Services,* No. 459. Geneva: World Health Organization, 1970. Pp. 172, 192.

Worthy, J. C. "Organizational structure and employee morale," *American Sociological Review,* 1950, *15*(2):169–79. Pp. 87, 102.

Wyler, A., Masuda, M., and Holmes, R. "The seriousness of illness rating scale: reproducibility," *Journal of Psychosomatic Research,* 1970, *14:*59–64. P. 76.

Zabarenko, R. N., and Zabarenko, L. M. *The Doctor Tree.* Pittsburgh, PA: Pittsburgh University Press, 1978. Pp. 124, 139.

Zimmer, H. *Hindu Medicine.* Baltimore, MD: Johns Hopkins University Press, 1948. P. 246.

Zola, I. K. "Culture and symptoms: an analysis of patients' presenting complaints," *American Sociological Review,* 1966, *31:*615–30. P. 102.

Subject index

alcoholism, study of diagnosis, 152– 3
American Leprosy Mission, 184, 186, 188
  Bulletin of, 186, 188
anomie, sociological theory of, 94
artificial families, experimental paradigm, 47
Asclepius, cult of, 24

biomedical definition of illness, 43, 45– 6, 48, 50, 114
biomedical model:
  alternative frameworks to, 198
  assumptions and critique, 1– 22, 25, 49– 50, 79, 86, 99, 196– 8, 251: disease as deviation from biological norm, 3– 6, 197, 224; doctrine of specific etiology, 6– 9, 97, 100; generic diseases, 9– 15, 197, 224– 5; scientific neutrality of medicine, 15– 19, 196, 225
  dominance in medicine, 1, 4, 18– 19, 25, 50, 250
  epidemiology and assumptions of, 40, 43
  limitations, 2, 8– 9, 12, 26: equates illness with symptoms, 14; strips away social contexts, 2, 19– 20, 25
  medicine as applied technology, 79
biomedical tradition in psychiatry, 42
blind persons, labeling of, 160– 2, 190– 1
blindness, medical-legal definition of, 160, 190

Carville, see U. S. Public Health Service Hospital
certifiers of illness, physicians as, 211– 13
childbirth, history of practices of, 233– 7
  mechanical model of, 233– 4, 236
committee sponsorship, see hospital admissions
community integration-disintegration, epidemiological study of, 34– 6
  concepts and measures, 36
  and psychiatric disorders, 34
concentric zones, model of city as set of, 29
constructivism, see illness, social construction
continuous treatment rates, 38– 9

cost-benefit analysis, 203
crisis in health care, 101
crisis intervention, 60
custodial care, 85
custodial institutions, 95

death, views of, 237– 44
  as fragmentation of experience, 244
  as mechanical problem of body functions, 240
  Western attitudes, 239
diabetes, treatment of as belief system, 149– 51
  see also illness, social construction
diagnosis in medicine, 112, 118, 144– 9, 152– 3, 156
  assumption of equivalence of biological signs and specific diseases, 145
  clarity of, 108
  instrumental function of, 152– 3
  as interpretive practice, 142, 156
  physician statement of, 107
  reliability of, 146– 7, 149, 153
  as social process, 143, 146
  view of as technical problem, 156
diagnosis, social, 152
disease, see illness
diseases:
  nomenclature of, 146
  taxonomy of, 9, 13
dual system of health care, 83– 7, 98
dying patients, witholding information from, 108

ecological approach to study of mental disorders, 28– 9
ecological correlations, 59
economic change, effects on rate of:
  child abuse, 60
  mental illness, 62
  physical illness, 61
  suicide, 60
economic change and illness, direction of causality, 61– 2

273